Beginning
film studies

Andrew Dix

Manchester University Press
Manchester and New York
distributed exclusively in the USA by Palgrave

Published by Manchester University Press
Oxford Road, Manchester M13 9NR, UK
and Room 400, 175 Fifth Avenue, New York, NY 10010, USA
www.manchesteruniversitypress.co.uk

Distributed exclusively in the USA by
Palgrave, 175 Fifth Avenue, New York,
NY 10010, USA

Distributed exclusively in Canada by
UBC Press, University of British Columbia, 2029 West Mall,
Vancouver, BC, Canada V6T 1Z2

British Library Cataloguing-in-Publication Data
A catalogue record for this book is available from the British Library

Library of Congress Cataloging-in-Publication Data applied for

ISBN   978 0 7190 7254 3 *hardback*
ISBN   978 0 7190 7255 0 *paperback*

First published 2008

17 16 15 14 13 12 11 10 09 08   10 9 8 7 6 5 4 3 2 1

Typeset in Ehrhardt
by Action Publishing Technology Ltd, Gloucester
Printed in Great Britain
by Antony Rowe Ltd, Chippenham, Wiltshire

For my parents

Contents

List of figures

Figures 1, 2, 4, 5, 7, 9, 10, 11, 14, 15 and 16 have been supplied by the British Film Institute. Figures 3, 6, 8, 12, 13, 17, 18, 19, 20, 21, 22 and 23 have been supplied by the Ronald Grant Archive.

Acknowledgements

This book would not have been written without the friendship, support and advice of some very good colleagues at Loughborough University: in particular Brian Jarvis, John Schad and Jonathan Taylor.

I wish to thank the staff of Derby's Metro Cinema – especially Sally Griffith – for their great help with regard to a section of Chapter 10; at a hectically busy time when their institution was not only moving buildings but being reconstituted as part of a new local arts organisation, they welcomed my interest and generously supplied me with information. Thanks also to Russell Wilson for taking the photograph of the Metro that appears in the book; to Salinder Nijran for discussions and loans of Bollywood films; and to Bill Kennedy, Cynthia Kennedy, Mandi Ridding, Abi Smith, Andy Smith, Gill Smith and James Smith for their support. For help in sourcing the book's illustrations I am grateful to Mark Balsam, executive producer of John Sayles's *Matewan*, and to the staffs of BFI Stills (especially Nina Harding) and the Ronald Grant Archive (especially Martin Humphries).

At Manchester University Press, many thanks are due to the readers who carefully reviewed both proposal and completed manuscript, and to Matthew Frost for his warm commitment towards the book from the start and his advice during its writing.

Throughout this project, Karen Kennedy has been a source of much love and support; she also submitted selflessly to watching with me all the Johnny Depp films discussed in Chapter 7.

A debt going all the way back to the beginning is owed to the book's dedicatees, my parents.

Introduction: what is film studies?

From magic lanterns to videogames

'Then came the film', writes the German cultural theorist Walter Benjamin, evoking the arrival of a powerful new art form at the end of the nineteenth century. For Benjamin, cinema's innovatory techniques such as slow motion and the close-up explode what he calls our 'prison-world', disclosing a hitherto unsuspected complexity and dynamism ('The Work of Art in the Age of Mechanical Reproduction', *Illuminations* (New York: Schocken Books, 1968), p. 236). By this account film not only liberates but is a medium that can be differentiated clearly from previous modes of visual culture. Some other scholars, in contrast, describe the late-Victorian emergence of film less as revolutionary event than as the combination and modification of numerous technologies already in existence. Film's early intertwining with other optical forms provides a starting point for this book. In recalling this media overlap, however, we do not simply indulge historical curiosity but witness something that eerily foretells our contemporary visual culture.

What sort of story should film studies tell about the emergence of its object of inquiry? Although film's founding moment is often taken to be the Lumière Brothers' first public demonstration of their cinematograph in Paris over Christmas 1895, this is too straightforward a birth narrative. Instead, genealogists of cinema frequently construct much longer timelines. For the early twentieth-century French director Abel Gance, film actually descends from ancient visual forms like Egyptian hieroglyphics. While Laurent Mannoni does not look back quite so far, his magisterial study, *The Great Art of Light and Shadow* (2000) proposes that the history of film begins with scholars' optical experiments during the thirteenth century. Mannoni's book details a host of pre-cinematic technologies of image capture and projection. The best-known of these is the magic lantern, a device which peaked in popularity in the nineteenth century and mesmerised spectators by employing a system of lenses and a light source in order to project vivid images upon a wall, curtain or even primitive screen. Many other optical machines, however, also contained in miniature aspects of the cinematic experience. Note the Phenakistoscope, first demonstrated in 1833 and consisting of a cardboard disc decorated with pictures which was whirled in front of a mirror so as to give a sense of uninterrupted image flow. Or take the slightly later Zoetrope, memorialised in the name of American director Francis Ford Coppola's production company and consisting of a drum rotated at sufficiently high speed for the pictures painted on its interior surface to generate the illusion of continuous sequence. If Heath Robinson devices of this kind are part of the story of film's emergence, so too are numerous other visual apparatuses popular in the Victorian period and before, including waxworks, dioramas, panoramic paintings and, of course, photography.

Tom Gunning suggests that this early slippage between film and other visual media is now happening again. Much of the twentieth century witnessed attempts by film criticism and, later, by a more academicised film studies to establish securely what Gunning calls their 'analytical object'. The initial validation of film's artistic value in the teeth of resistance by anti-modern forces was followed by such efforts of disciplinary consolidation as assembling a canon of primary works for discussion and agreeing upon a technical language for the analysis of film practices. Recent developments in visual culture, however, put in question once more this aspiration to intellectual autonomy. As Gunning argues, film is in the process of being 'dispersed into a number of new image technologies. The last modern art seems to be dissolving into a postmodern haze' ('"Animated Pictures": Tales of Cinema's Forgotten Future, After

100 Years of Films', *Reinventing Film Studies*, eds Christine Gledhill and Linda Williams (London: Arnold, 2000), p. 317). A moment's reflection on the irrepressible visuality of everyday life now – at least in technologically privileged societies – seems to bear this out. As well as moving outwards from the cinema into many other exhibition sites, feature films confront a host of rival forms of the spectacular, including videogames, internet sites, webcam footage, television shows and electronic and printed advertisements. 'The cinematic society', to use Norman Denzin's phrase, appears to be splintering, putting in doubt not only the cultural prestige of film as a medium but also the conceptual integrity of film studies itself.

The discussion so far may look self-defeating, even suicidal, occurring as it does at the start of a book that aims to introduce film studies. Yet this is far from the case: the point is simply to acknowledge that now, just as elsewhere in its history, film studies confronts objects of inquiry which are messy rather than pristine, mutable rather than fixed. Gunning is unmoved by suggestions that film's 'contemporary crisis threatens an established sacral identity'; instead, he says, 'there is no single identity to guard' (p. 327). Tasked with interpreting multiple histories and geographies of image production, distribution and exhibition, film studies itself is better evoked as plural, contentious, always in flux, rather than sacral or monolithic in character. To say this, however, is not to indicate the discipline's impossibility but rather to register its intellectual excitement and its ongoing life.

About this book

This volume aims to introduce key questions, concepts and methodologies in film studies. Specifically, it seeks to provide readers with

- a knowledge of conceptual shifts in twentieth-century film studies;
- a vocabulary for the analysis of film form and style;
- a sense of the ideological dimensions of film;
- an awareness of key 'post-textual' or 'extra-textual' domains of film studies;

- a prospectus of possible directions for film studies in the twenty-first century.

Some detail here about each of these subject areas may be helpful. Running throughout the book is the conviction that film studies is less a single set of orthodoxies for its participants to master and repeat than a field of diverse activities to engage in and extend. At times, it is true, particular critical and theoretical positions have come close to supplying the discipline with a kind of received wisdom. The strongest candidates are the director-centred *auteur theory* that emerged from France in the late 1950s and early 1960s, and the composite of Marxist, psychoanalytic and feminist approaches that started to cohere a decade later. Even during the pre-eminence of each of these doctrines, however, dissenting voices could still be heard, hinting at other valuable ways in which to do film studies. The book will assess the benefits of both these 'strong' conceptual frameworks – and others – while welcoming the fact of their relaxation to the point whereby film studies at present is welcoming to a wide range of research projects.

The organisation of chapters can be regarded as a set of concentric circles, at the centre of the smallest of which is found the film text itself. Chapters 1–3 assume that knowledge of film's stylistic options as they emerged over the course of the twentieth century is indispensable for any study of the medium (whatever the eventual direction of research); these sections aim to give the reader a language in which to describe and evaluate matters of mise-en-scène, editing and soundtrack. From early, pre-disciplinary days, when writing on cinema was sometimes done by people with training as art critics, film studies has understandably been interested in developing protocols for detailed assessment of the texture of films themselves. Such narrowing of focus is not without risks. Charles Acland wittily suggests that 'the problem with film studies has been *film*, that is, the use of a medium in order to designate the boundaries of a discipline' (*Screen Traffic: Movies, Multiplexes, and Global Culture* (Durham, NC and London: Duke University Press, 2003), p. 46). At times, Acland's withdrawal of interest from the particularities of film texts is so complete that he resembles a literature professor who has stopped reading books in order to discuss the economics of publishing instead. Nevertheless, his critique of an 'artifactual approach to film' (p. 52) is bracing, and helps to guard against the kind of formalism that reads a film minutely but has little sense of the institutional contexts of production and consumption in which it is embedded.

If the book's first three chapters focus closely on cinematic stylistics, Chapters 4–8 move outwards, while continuing to promote a detailed engagement with the film text itself. They are concerned respectively with film narrative, film authorship, film genre, film stars and the ideologies – class, gender, sexual and racial – of film representation. In each of these sections, the text is less a discrete, impermeable thing than a prism reflective of a host of real-world concerns, from genre's importance in film industry economics to mutations of film authorship in the digital era, and from questions of social power raised by film narrative to cinema's role in the stereotyping of non-white or non-straight identities.

Chapters 9 and 10, however, decentre the film text more thoroughly, along the lines proposed by Acland and some other contemporary writers. For these scholars, the discipline has now mined the last seams of a textual approach and can renew itself only by other kinds of research. This desire to turn away from 'readings' and do something totally different is not unique to contemporary film studies. Franco Moretti – whose work on genre figures in Chapter 6 – urges a similar change of direction for his own field of literary study. Instead of concerning itself with 'individual works' or 'separate bits of knowledge about individual cases', Moretti says that literary criticism should acknowledge that its proper object of inquiry is 'a collective system, that should be grasped as such, as a whole' (*Graphs, Maps, Trees: Abstract Models for a Literary Theory* (London and New York: Verso, 2005), pp. 1, 4). In film studies, 'systemic' work of this sort aims to provide ever more detailed accounts of production, distribution and consumption. 'Post-textual' research might focus, say, on the mechanisms by which 'global Hollywood' extends the commercial reach of its products, or on the politics of watching films in multiplexes. Chapters 9 and 10 welcome these expanded topic areas, while arguing that the best work in film studies will combine such savvy about broad institutional forces with sensitivity to how they play themselves out in the detail of specific films.

Though this book cannot pretend to 20/20 foresight, it does touch on emerging subject areas for film studies. Besides intensifying a general interest in geographies of making and watching films, the discipline might in future have more to say about such topics as the relations between cinematic and sporting (and other) stardoms, or the challenge posed to the authority of film narratives by fan fiction disseminated through internet channels. The Conclusion considers the impact of the 'digital revolution' upon some of film studies' established paradigms and vocabularies. Digitisation may prove, in the future, to have more drastic effects still upon the direction of the discipline. Take, for example, the ever-increasing home consumption of feature films. Film studies' developing interest in this phenomenon looks like a holding position, one which concedes the importance of a reception site other than the cinema, but asserts the continuing centrality of the film text (albeit in modified forms like the DVD). Ultimately, however, this stance may prove unsustainable: films might lose their privilege in a home-consumed visual array also featuring videogames, internet diversions and so on. In these circumstances film studies could be reconfigured as part of a more comprehensive *screen studies*, or as an element in a still more expansive *cultural studies*, alongside literary and fine arts programmes (their own traditional primary materials also much modified).

Two other points should be made. Firstly, some readers new to the subject may be anxious that film's sensuous, immersive pleasures will be lost as a result of cultivating an analytic habit. What happens to the ecstasy of floating in an image or dreaming of a star when we watch films in an austerely critical and theoretical spirit? One (weak) answer is that a film's absorptive powers while it unfolds continue to be such as to deflect – at least until later – overly earnest interrogation. However, a stronger response is to emphasise the pleasures of film criticism and theory themselves – gratifications different from, but at least equal to, a condition of naïve capture by the spectacle. As well as introducing a number of critical models, the book frequently includes *Stop and think* sections encouraging reflection upon the explanatory power and the appeal of these. At times this critical language – drawn from mise-en-scène categories, narrative theory, genre theory, psycho-analysis and so on – may seem unappetisingly abstract. It certainly does to the great Spanish director Luis Buñuel. With his Surrealist sensibility, Buñuel was no manufacturer of briskly commonsense cinema; nevertheless, he tells the story of encountering 'a young man in a suit and tie' at a film studies centre in Mexico City. 'When I asked him what he taught, he replied "The Semiology of the Clonic Image"'; Buñuel adds: 'I could have murdered him on the spot' (*My Last Breath* (London: Flamingo, 1985), p. 222). While absorbing the lesson here about a self-regarding jargon, we should not rush to abandon abstract discourse. Peter Wollen puts the case forcefully for film studies' sometimes difficult language: 'clearly any kind of serious critical work must involve a distance, a gap between the film and the criticism, the text and the meta-text. It is as though meteorologists were reproached for getting away from the "lived experience" of walking in the rain or sunbathing' (*Signs and Meaning in the Cinema*, 4th ed. (London: BFI 1998), p. 115).

Secondly, a word on the book's choice of films to support its arguments. Although many of these are drawn from the Anglo-American cinema with which most readers will be especially familiar, this is by no means exclusively the case. While lacunae remain – African filmmaking both north and south of the Sahara, say – the book is committed to a wide geographical remit. Films are cited therefore from nations ranging from Spain to South Korea and from Iran to Chile. Such territorial expansiveness coincides with the emergence in Anglophone cultures of 'world cinema' as a critical and commercial category; and the pitfalls as well as promises of this development are considered in Chapter 9. Chronologically, too, the book often wanders beyond the recent and contemporary, alluding to such earlier filmmaking as the first single-shot documentaries, the radical Soviet experiments of the 1920s and Hollywood film noir of the Second World War and its aftermath. The German film theorist Siegfried Kracauer offers a mainly defensive reason for his similar choice not to use all-new examples: 'What is the talk of the town today will have sunk into oblivion tomorrow; the cinema voraciously devours its own children' (*Theory of Film: The Redemption of Physical Reality* (New York: Oxford University Press, 1960), p. viii). However, this book's frequent recourse to non-contemporary cinema has the much stronger motivations of sketching some of the mutations in film history and of alerting readers to films they may find absorbing.

Note on the text

Dates of all films mentioned for the first time are given in parentheses; where a film appears without a date, this is supplied earlier in the book. Full publication details for each secondary source are included in the text in parentheses; where these seem to be lacking, it is because that book or article is catalogued in the chapter's 'Selected reading'. Finally, every effort has been made to check the accessibility of useful websites listed throughout the text; although the internet is a highly fluid resource, all URLs are correct at the time of publication.

1

Seeing film: mise-en-scène analysis

In starting to think about film's material specificity, it might seem odd to take instruction from another scholarly discipline. Yet we can learn from the American New Critics – a dominant force in literary study before the Second World War – when they identify a sin called 'heresy of paraphrase'. They have in mind readings of a text which attempt prematurely to say *what* it means and show, by contrast, little interest in or even knowledge of *how* it means. The paraphrasing heretic is liable to summarise what a Shakespeare sonnet expresses about true love, but stay mute about how the poem's thematic implications only emerge through its detailed transactions of versification, syntax and metaphor. The result is a disembodied kind of literary criticism, curiously obtuse about the textures of its own object of study.

Much of the discourse on film with which we are most familiar is weakened by similar insensitivity towards the particularities of its primary material. The reader of most newspaper film reviews, or watcher of popular TV programmes on cinema, encounters, precisely, heresies of paraphrase. Such work summarises a film's narrative contents, but tends not to comment on its material qualities: its modes of cinematography, say, or its key editing choices or its distinctively fashioned soundtrack. Yet to be concerned with such issues of cinematic form is not indulgent or somehow minor in relation to more ambitious projects we should have as film scholars. On the contrary, any attempt to place a given film in larger cultural or ideological contexts is itself inadequate if it does not include some reckoning with the work's distinctive form. The formal strategies of a film text are not neutral or background facts but meaning-generating processes. Another insight originating in literary criticism is again equally persuasive for film studies: 'the meaning of art is completely inseparable from all the details of its material body' (P. N. Medvedev/M. M. Bakhtin, *The Formal Method in Literary Scholarship* (Baltimore and London: Johns Hopkins University Press, 1978), p. 12).

Film's 'material body' is the subject of this book's first three chapters. Before turning to editing and soundtrack, we begin with an account of film's visual phenomena, grouped together under the French term, *mise-en-scène*.

Defining mise-en-scène

'What is mise-en-scène?' asks Jacques Rivette, a key member of the *Nouvelle vague* ('New Wave'), the group of filmmaker-critics which energised French cinema in the late 1950s and 1960s. 'My apologies for asking such a hazardous question with neither preparation nor preamble, particularly when I have no intention of answering it. Only, should this question not always inform our deliberations?' (Jim Hillier (ed.), *Cahiers du cinéma*, Vol. 1 (London: Routledge and Kegan Paul, 1985), p. 134). While Rivette's skirting away here from an emphatic definition of mise-en-scène is alarming, he valuably insists upon the fundamental importance for film studies of engagement with matters of visual style. What is it that we see and give significance to as we watch films?

Consider the start of *American Beauty* (1999), as a fade-in takes the viewer from a black screen disclosing nothing to a scene abundant in visual information. When the sequence opens, we see a young woman lying on a bed. Even as this figure stays silent, the spectator begins interpretive work, making provisional assessments of the significance of her location, and of her body position and clothing. We might also register the harsh lighting scheme, linking this detail tentatively to the woman's lack of flattering make-up and glamorous clothing as evidence of her distance from stereotypical feminine image. For the moment, we may be content to gather and process these particular visual contents of the scene, contents that can be arranged under the subheadings of setting,

props, costume and lighting. To these should be added the category of acting, even while the woman lies still. However, our eye may
be more mobile and inquisitive still, registering not merely the
figure on the bed but also the distinctive ways in which shots of
her are composed. What are the implications of the camera's proximity to her, admitting no other human presence into the visual
field? And what seems indicated by the texture of the image itself,
shot on grainy video rather than customary 35mm film?

In carrying out interpretive work of this kind on a film's visual
specificities, the spectator is performing mise-en-scène analysis.
As Rivette notes, however, the term 'mise-en-scène' is
'hazardous', open to several competing definitions. It translates
from the French as 'staging' or 'putting into the scene', and thus
has its provenance in theatre rather than cinema. The theatrical
bias of the term can be traced even in the most recent edition of
the *Oxford English Dictionary*, which includes citations relating to
the staging of plays from 1833 to 1983, but gives no acknowledge-
ment of the fact it has also migrated into cinematic usage. But this
imprint of the theatre is also apparent within film studies itself,
where some writers – including David Bordwell and Kristin
Thompson in their highly influential, much-reissued *Film Art: An
Introduction* – have chosen to define filmic mise-en-scène exclusively by what it has in common with theatrical staging: setting,
props, costume, lighting and acting. If we stop our account of the
start of *American Beauty* after discussing such visible signs as the
harsh lighting and the woman's body position, we are doing mise-
en-scène work of this circumscribed, theatrically derived kind.
But if the spectator goes on to assess other information offered to
the eye – the camera's framing of the woman or the video footage's
imperfect quality – then he or she is pursuing instead that expanded, more satisfactory approach to mise-en-scène which considers
not merely the elements cinema shares with theatre but also visual
properties that are distinctive to film as a medium: those phenomena summarised by John Gibbs as 'framing, camera movement,
the particular lens employed and other photographic decisions'
(*Mise-en-scène*, p. 5).

This chapter adopts the broader of these two understandings of
mise-en-scène. After considering the elements that film carries

across from theatrical staging, it discusses key aspects of cinematography. Even such an inclusive definition of filmic
mise-en-scène is itself in some respects narrow and arbitrary.
Jean-Luc Godard, another major figure in the *Nouvelle vague*,
writes with reference to a particular editing practice that 'montage
is above all an integral part of mise-en-scène' (Jean Narboni and
Tom Milne (eds), *Godard on Godard* (London: Secker and
Warburg, 1972), p. 39). Bernard F. Dick, in a much-used textbook
in film studies, suggests somewhat eccentrically that sound, too,
should be accounted an element of mise-en-scène (*Anatomy of
Film*, 4th ed. (Boston: Bedford/St. Martin's, 2002), p. 19). While
sound's vital contribution to the sum of a film's meanings is undeniable – in the scene from *American Beauty*, another character's
voice from off-camera complicates the sense of the woman's alien-
ation that may be visually implied – the proposition made by Dick
is one, for the moment, to resist in the interests of isolating the
peculiarly visual components of film. Similarly, while Godard
shows a proper distaste for any approach to cinema that under-
plays the effect of combining shots, the mise-en-scène analysis
elaborated in this chapter still finds it valuable to identify and categorise visual elements that may be discerned even in a single shot
and to reserve until later any treatment of editing.

Pro-filmic elements of mise-en-scène

'Pro-filmic' names those contents of a film's visual field that are
considered to exist prior to and independent of the camera's activity: precisely the attributes of setting, props, costume, lighting and
acting which cinema shares with forms of staged spectacle such as
theatre, opera and dance. The artificiality of isolating these
elements from cinematography is immediately apparent: Anthony
Hopkins's lip-smacking expression as Hannibal Lecter in *The
Silence of the Lambs* (1991) – an example of performance, therefore
pro-filmic – would not communicate so vividly were it not registered on the screen in close-up (an example of cinematography).
Nevertheless, with the proviso that ultimately they will be reinte-
grated with cinematography itself, we begin here by separately
considering film's pro-filmic materials.

Setting

Cinematic settings vary in scale from the interplanetary distances of sci-fi to the coffin that The Bride briefly occupies in Quentin Tarantino's *Kill Bill: Vol. 2* (2004). In opulence they stretch from the Roman palaces of epics to the hellish lavatory that Renton visits in *Trainspotting* (1996). Settings also range along a spectrum from obvious artifice to apparent realism: contrast the Yellow Brick Road in *The Wizard of Oz* (1939) with teeming city streets that have been exploited throughout the history of filmmaking (from brief 'actuality' films made in France by the Lumière Brothers during the 1890s, through Italian neo-realism of the 1940s and early 1950s, to such recent instances of Latin American cinema as *Amores perros* (2000) and *Cidade de Deus / City of God* (2002)).

Whether expansive or narrow, magnificent or squalid, artificial or naturalistic, film settings require our close attention. They are not merely inert containers of or backdrops to action but themselves charged with significance. At the most basic level, locations serve in narrative cinema to reinforce the plausibility of particular kinds of story. An American urban crime drama might seem sterile and unconvincing without locales such as the crowded street, the neighbourhood diner, the smoke-filled bar; similarly, a work such as Coppola's *Bram Stoker's Dracula* (1992) seeks to guarantee the integrity of its much more fantastical story world by the details of gloomy precipices, brooding castles and London by gaslight. As these examples suggest, setting also functions as a clue to a given film's generic status. Chapter 6 will return to the question of setting's role in genre classification; for the moment, we just note how particular spaces have become associated with certain film genres rather than with others. When Sergio Leone's *For A Few Dollars More* (1965) opens with an extreme long shot of rocky desert terrain, the spectator can make a reasonable, if still tentative assumption that the film is a western (albeit one that proves to have a playful relationship to the western's conventions as codified by Hollywood). The fact that in this scene we also observe a lone horseman, looking insignificant against sand and sky, alerts us to another basic function of setting: its revelatory quality with respect to character. As well as serving in quite obvious ways to specify the geographical coordinates, socio-economic status and occupation of film protagonists, settings may also work more subtly to symbolise their psychological conditions. Such symbolic use of space is especially vivid in German Expressionist cinema, which flourished after the First World War. To take just one example: when the vampiric protagonist in F. W. Murnau's *Nosferatu* (1922) is seen in one shot standing behind the latticed window of an apartment block, we learn not just matter-of-factly about his living arrangements but, more profoundly, something about his sense of incarceration and estrangement within conformist Weimar society. While heightened investment in symbolic spaces is a signature of this particular cinematic tradition, such moments should encourage us to be sensitive to expressionistic uses of setting elsewhere in film.

Props

Setting's functions of substantiating narrative, signalling genre and revealing character are also performed by props: objects of whatever dimensions that appear on screen. Like particular landscapes, certain props are correlated with some genres more than with others (again a topic for development in Chapter 6). If we see a parachute it is a fair guess we are not watching a western (unless of a surreal sort); if a cigarette flares atmospherically into life in close-up, the film noir devotee is liable to experience a greater thrill of recognition than the fan of epic.

Props – or, speaking less technically, *things* – have also been at the centre of long-running theoretical debates over film's realism or otherwise as a medium. For key studies in a broadly realist tradition, including André Bazin's *What is Cinema?* and Siegfried Kracauer's *Theory of Film*, cinema shares with photography a vocation to reveal with heightened vividness the material world that we inhabit. From this perspective, the chief value of showing a prop such as a cigarette or parachute is to disclose it in all its detailed particularity (which, to be sure, may exceed the evidence of our customary sight because of the camera's capacity for close-up). Yet for writers from other critical positions, cinema actually frees objects like these from their material detail and instead endows them with other, non-realist meanings. Luis Buñuel regrets the fact that for Italian neo-realists – favourite filmmakers, incidentally, of Bazin and Kracauer – 'a glass is a glass and nothing more' (Paul Hammond (ed.), *The Shadow and Its Shadow: Surrealist Writings on the Cinema*, 2nd ed. (Edinburgh: Polygon, 1991), p. 121). In his 1918 essay 'On Décor', the French Surrealist author Louis Aragon positively thrives upon the elusive and multiple significances of film props: 'on the screen objects that were a few moments ago sticks of furniture or books of cloakroom tickets are transformed to the point where they take on menacing or enigmatic meanings' (*The Shadow and Its Shadow*, p. 57).

In thinking about the use of props in film, there is no need to be committed exclusively to either of these opposing positions. Depending on context, exactly the same object on screen may be a thing valued for its concrete particularities, or its narrative suggestiveness, or its symbolic density. 'Sometimes', as Freud may have said, 'a cigar is just a cigar'; at other times, though, it may be more or other than this (a phallic symbol, most obviously). A television set that figures in one film as a relatively unobtrusive piece of furniture becomes in *The Truman Show* (1998) an index of a society of surveillance and manipulation. Like settings, props also perform an informational role with respect to character. Sometimes this function will be restricted to confirming socio-economic and occupational status (a reporter's notebook, a businessman's briefcase); elsewhere, however, props can take on expressionistic power. When Travis Bickle drops an Alka-Seltzer into water in *Taxi Driver* (1976), the fizzing tablet seems not just one small part of his material world but indicative of his synaptic disturbance to the point of explosion (this effect enhanced by close-up and non-naturalistic sound).

Costume

Like props and setting, costume, which also includes make-up and hairstyle, has a wide range of possible significances. Studies such as Roland Barthes's *The Fashion System* (1967) have long accustomed us to reading costume also as a structured set of signs replete with connotations. Particular items and combinations of clothing index national identity, class allegiance, sub-group affiliation, gender position, emotional and psychological status, and so on. In addition, they too may encourage the spectator to make assumptions about a film's genre. If we see figures wearing space-suits, we might reasonably conclude that we have missed the martial arts movie. Similarly, the fact that Bickle in *Taxi Driver* transgresses norms of costuming – wearing military fatigues unobtrusive in a war film but incongruous in a contemporary New York setting – supplies a visual clue to the character's Vietnam background and resultant sociopathy.

The work on costume that develops from Barthes and others aims to treat every piece of clothing as a signifier from which, in quite orderly fashion, particular 'signifieds' or meanings may be read off. To be adequate to the task of analysing film costume, however, such a semiotic approach needs to be coordinated with more historically and geographically responsive studies. For example, the top hat that signifies a boss's arrogance and a struc-ture of class exploitation in *Stachka/Strike* (1924) – a Soviet film discussed in Chapter 2 – communicates dandyish lightness and charisma when worn by Fred Astaire in 1930s American musicals (Figure 1). In both these instances, costume combines harmo-niously with other pro-filmic elements – first the boss's corpulence and huge cigar, second Astaire's lithe body shape – so as to reinforce already established meanings. However, there are cases where costume is excessive in style or colour and thereby clashes with, rather than simply confirming, other parts of a film's visual scheme. Jane Gaines argues that certain 1950s US melodra-mas exhibit such overdevelopment of what she calls 'the vestural code' (from *vesture* or 'garment'). Rather like Buñuel and Aragon speaking about props, Gaines welcomes this heightened visibility of clothing in film, its freeing-up from a relatively mundane func-tion of supporting the realism of character and story. In the 1950s examples, extravagant clothing of this kind hints at desires or neuroses not otherwise expressible. For Alfred Hitchcock, by contrast, such costumes are 'eye-catchers' that dangerously distract the spectator from the key tasks of following narrative and characterisation (Jane Gaines, 'Costume and Narrative: How Dress Tells the Woman's Story', *Fabrications: Costume and the Female Body*, pp. 203–11).

Figure 1 Fred Astaire in *Top Hat* (US, 1935).

Lighting

Hitchcock is anxious here about one of the pro-filmic elements becoming autonomous and drawing excessive attention to itself. Concern is sometimes expressed about similarly blatant promotion of lighting. One technical manual intended for new entrants to the film industry states that 'most skilled lighting is self-effacing. The more subtle the treatment, the more natural or "obvious" it appears to be' (Gerald Millerson, *Lighting for Television and Film*, 3rd ed. (Oxford: Focal Press, 1991), p. 236). From this industry perspective, ideal film lighting is invisible, a key contrib-

utor to the fashioning of cinematic illusions that absorb the spectator to the point where she responds to them almost as natural
phenomena and fails to recognise their artifice. However, we
cannot afford to be such critically unaware viewers. Without
repressing the pleasure yielded by our vivid sensory engagement
with everything on screen, we should aim also to be knowledgeable
about the manifold practices by which this pleasure is produced.
These practices include well-established lighting conventions.

This is not the place to describe in detail the various combinations of key lighting, fill lighting, backlighting, sidelighting,
underlighting and top lighting used to achieve different qualities
of light and shadow in films (including in outdoor scenes, where
natural illumination from sun and sky may be artificially augmented or varied). Anyone seeking specialised technical knowledge can
readily find it in manuals such as Millerson's. But it is important
to note the distinction that has been made between two basic lighting schemas in film: *high-key* and *low-key* (the latter sometimes
called *chiaroscuro*, a term first applied to Italian Renaissance paintings that included major areas of darkness). High-key describes an
even diffusion of lighting across a shot, resulting in low contrast
between brighter and darker areas and quite full detailing of any
portions that are still shaded; under a regime of low-key lighting,
on the other hand, there is much higher contrast between bright
and dark, with less penetrable areas of shadow. If these two lighting types are treated in semiotic fashion as signifiers, then
particular meanings might be attached to each of them. Whereas a
high-key lighting design tends to evoke a sense of clarity and optimism, low-key lighting, by contrast, may induce feelings of moral
ambiguity, anxiety, even terror. Yet, as with the assessment of
particular props or costumes, a broad hypothesis of this kind
needs to be tested in detailed work on how exactly lighting functions in specific cases. High-key lighting might disperse such
brightness across a scene that it becomes monotonous, producing
a feeling not so much of well-being as of nausea (again *The Truman
Show* comes to mind). Low-key lighting can be similarly nuanced
or multiple in its effects. Certainly it evokes foreboding where it is
deployed, again in signature fashion, in German Expressionist
cinema and then in one of Expressionism's stylistic descendants,

the Hollywood film noir of the 1940s and early 1950s. Even in a noirish work like *The Big Sleep* (1946), however, strongly contrasted light and shade communicate mystery and romantic charisma as much as they do existential crisis. And when contemporary noir continues to utilise this low-key lighting pattern, the spectator, far from being thrown into anxiety, may experience a pleasurable nostalgia (consider the nostalgic value of chiaroscuro in *L.A. Confidential* (1997) and *Sin City* (2005)).

Acting

Lighting is crucially articulated with the final pro-filmic component: *acting* or *performance* (the repertoire of on-screen facial expression, gesture, positioning, movement and speech). After all, an actor's facial arrangement that is perfectly adequate for romance in conditions of abundant, soft-fill lighting becomes more suited to horror film if underlit instead. There have been surprisingly few attempts to discuss acting in cinema (other than those that collapse it into the phenomenon of 'the star' discussed in Chapter 7). Some of the most striking, if still fragmentary statements on this topic set film performance against theatre acting and see it as humanly impoverished by comparison. In his groundbreaking essay, 'The Work of Art in the Age of Mechanical Reproduction' (1935–39), Walter Benjamin evokes the film actor as an almost ghostly figure, surviving minimally in the two-dimensional screen image but deprived of that vivid bodily presence – or 'aura' in Benjamin's language – which the theatre actor has in front of an audience. It is then little compensation that the film industry responds to this 'shrivelling of the aura with an artificial build-up of the "personality" outside the studio' (*Illuminations* (New York: Schocken Books, 1968), p. 230). Under some influence by Benjamin, Kracauer also evokes an existential crisis for the film performer, referring to the 'decomposition of the actor's wholeness', both by different focal lengths that break up the body and by the discontinuous way during shooting in which an actor plays his or her role (*Theory of Film: The Redemption of Physical Reality* (New York: Oxford University Press, 1960), p. 97).

However, there are dangers in judging film acting by criteria used in the assessment of theatrical performance. Here a remark by the American actor Fredric March, who worked on both stage and screen from the 1930s, may be helpful. Interrupted by his film director during the shooting of one scene, March apologised: 'Sorry, I did it again. I keep forgetting – this is a movie and I mustn't act' (Kracauer, *Theory of Film*, p. 94). Of course this may just be evidence of a persistent hierarchy of cultural forms: from early in the twentieth century, in the United States and elsewhere, actors noted for careers in theatre have often been defensive or mocking about accepting work in the supposedly lesser domain of film. Nevertheless, March's comment also hints that film acting has conventions which may overlap only partially with those of theatrical performance. In the film version of *Hamlet* (1948), for example, Laurence Olivier takes advantage of the close-up and draws on a different set of gestures, as well as altered voice modulation, than when he was trying in the theatre to communicate to the dress circle. Variously magnified, distanced or distorted by the camera's positioning, and further modified during editing, the performance of film actors signifies not less than – but differently from – that of their theatre counterparts.

The assessment of film acting also requires sensitivity to historically and geographically variant performance styles. When a woman in silent film indicates anguish by wringing her hands and violently throwing her head back, a contemporary temptation might be to identify overstated, even 'bad' acting (an 'Oscar Clip' of the sort identified in *Wayne's World* (1992)). But it is vital to go beyond an evaluative language and to recognise how such movements form part of a well-established performance style of the period that was still strongly influenced by theatre (especially melodrama). Film acting in later periods – including our own – is equally codified, even if its relative restraint in deploying both body and voice may make it more difficult to recognise its conventions. Most recent performance in English-speaking cinema is broadly *naturalistic*, aiming to align itself not with the artifice of some theatre but with observed human behaviour; yet actors in this tradition, from Marlon Brando in *On the Waterfront* (1954) to Imelda Staunton in *Vera Drake* (2004), draw upon a systematic repertoire of expressions, gestures, movements and intonations in order to achieve the effect which we are now habituated to think of as 'truth to life'.

Acting in a non-naturalistic mode has not entirely disappeared even from Anglo-American cinema. Think, say, of Jack Nicholson's work in *The Shining* (1980). What disconcerts some critics about this performance is that it seems histrionic, excessive, a violation of verisimilitude (not least by comparison with some of Nicholson's own earlier roles). But rather than judging his acting as a failure of plausibility, a more interesting task is to consider how this particular performance style interacts – either harmoniously or clashingly – with other elements of mise-en-scène in the film (the acting style of Shelley Duvall, or the choice of setting and props, or director Stanley Kubrick's cinematographic decisions). Does Nicholson's collection of heightened gestures and facial tics undermine a prevailing naturalistic effect, or, rather, does it advance tendencies already in the film towards Gothic excess? While many general accounts of mise-en-scène assume that its various elements always cooperate to produce a fully coherent, homogeneous work, it is important to recognise that, sometimes, these may also cut across each other and so disrupt the smooth, continuous surface of a film.

STOP and THINK

- Choose a sequence some two or three minutes long from any narrative film. Be as exhaustive as possible in listing the extract's significant pro-filmic features (leaving to one side for the moment its cinematographic aspects). Be unafraid to be inventive, even provocative in interpreting the meanings of these pro-filmic items. Although Jonathan Culler may overstate the case by saying that 'interpretation is interesting only when it is extreme' (Umberto Eco et al., *Interpretation and Overinterpretation* (Cambridge: Cambridge University Press, 1992), p. 110), 'over-reading' is certainly to be preferred to 'under-reading' – in film studies as in Culler's own discipline of literary criticism.
- Chapter 7 will discuss the 'commutation test', a valuable exercise that considers how the meaning of a particular film would be modified if a different star played a particu-

lar role. In a similar vein, replace each pro-filmic item in your selected film sequence with an equivalent (for example, substituting a windowless basement for an apartment with an ocean view, a four-poster bed for a futon or a baseball cap for a trilby). How do these modifications affect previous assumptions about character, narrative, genre classification, realism, ideology and so on?

- Mise-en-scène analysis often mimics literary critical modes such as American New Criticism in assuming harmony and continuity among all stylistic elements. Assess whether the pro-filmic components of your sequence are organically interrelated in this way, thereby affirming the coherence of the film world. Or do pro-filmic elements jar against each other? Instabilities of this sort might sometimes be ascribed to the continuity person's doziness (Roman gladiators wearing watches; jet vapour trails hanging in the sky above nineteenth-century cowboys); consider, however, the possibility of more profound motivations and consequences of any disarray among pro-filmic features.

Cinematography

Even if she grants relatively little significance to them, the spectator has little choice but to notice and, perhaps still in an unconscious fashion, to inventory pro–filmic contents. Unless we are watching through our fingers or from behind a cloth – cinemagoing habits developed by the Surrealist filmmaker and photographer Man Ray – our eyes cannot avoid falling upon all these components of a film's visual field. However, spectators vary considerably in the extent to which they also notice the numerous cinematographic processes that endow props, costumes and so on – infinite in their possible implications prior to the camera's activity – with certain meanings rather than others.

Becoming aware of the camera's material presence in this way may initially be alien or disquieting. In mainstream cinema, evidence of the means of film production itself is generally withheld from the spectator (other than in inadvertent sightings of a microphone boom or camera operator's shadow). A particular moment in Mel Brooks's Hitchcock spoof *High Anxiety* (1977) – when the camera tracking towards a window, in thriller fashion, goes too far and crashes through the glass – derives its comic effect precisely from making visible technical operations that are unadvertised and, as it were, 'naturalised' in mainstream film. The demystification of cinematic process this affords may still be forgotten the next time we encounter a thriller's tracking shots (given the power of such techniques to enthral). Yet the aim of the current section is to preserve the self-conscious, *High Anxiety* moment – though not in killjoy style – and to offer a basic apparatus for recognising and evaluating cinematographic strategies.

'Cinematography' describes the host of decisions taken during the recording and processing of the film image. Some of these technical options are relatively distinct from those bound up with the functioning of the camera itself. Filmmakers may, to begin with, choose between different types of film stock that produce particular gradations of contrast between the darkest and lightest portions of the image. The director and cinematographer of *Three Kings* (1999) chose a stock more customarily used in still cameras so as to yield bizarre, highly saturated colours for the episode of their protagonists' journey through alien Iraqi desert. However, another section of the film – where a visual approximation of war documentary footage was wanted – instances the many post-recording laboratory manipulations that are also available, as it was created by 'bleach bypass', the omission of bleach during developing so as to give a silver effect to the image.

Without discounting the creative importance of such decisions taken either side of shooting, we concentrate here upon some major properties and tactics of the film camera itself.

Distance
Allowing for alternatives such as wildlife documentary or abstract film, most cinema is human-centred; and it is unsurprising therefore that distances between camera and subject are frequently expressed in terms of the relative smallness or largeness of the human figure as it appears on screen. The most distant perspective – more common in westerns, say, than in romantic comedy – is provided by the *extreme long shot*, in which the figure is barely

visible in an overpowering setting (hence the industry's alternative term, 'the geography shot'). Background is still dominant in the *long shot* also, although by now the figure has been brought sufficiently close to allow the spectator to make quite confident judgments about its identity. From this point on, shots do not show the entire human body, but cut it instead into successively smaller portions: the *medium long shot* generally frames the subject from below the knee upwards; the *medium shot* from the waist up; the *medium close-up* from roughly chest height; while the *close-up* isolates the head and perhaps neck. Finally, the camera is nearest in the *extreme close-up*, which is most frequently used to break up the unity of the face by showing only particular features such as the eyes or mouth.

This terminology may be subject to historical adjustment. David Bordwell argues that the close-up – a term entering English around 1912 – originally referred to a shot which still included a significant quantity of background, rather than, as now, one tending to show the human face in isolation (*On the History of Film Style* (Cambridge, MA and London: Harvard University Press, 1997), pp. 122–4). For Bordwell, this is not semantic quibbling, since grasping the precise definition of shot-types in given periods allows the scholar to make more informed assessments of the development of film style. It is also crucial that we reach specific and nuanced – rather than absolute – judgements about the significance of shot distances. Here brief discussion of a single example – the extreme close-up – may be helpful.

One practical guide to cinematography asserts that this shot 'lacks dignity': since it 'makes nearly any subject sinister, aggressive and nasty', it should not be used in narrative cinema but restricted instead to such specialised forms as medical documentary (Roy Thompson, *The Grammar of the Shot* (Oxford: Focal Press, 1998), p. 84). Leaving aside the question of whether it should always be film's aspiration to confer 'dignity' upon its subjects – what about satirical or polemical cinema? – Thompson also narrows unduly the semantic possibilities of the extreme close-up. A shot showing the eyes may communicate grief or love or religious fervour as easily as it does brutishness. Even where the extreme close-up is used with respect to more morally questionable figures, effects can vary. When the film noir *Force of Evil* (1948) cuts from a close-up of a telephone known now to be bugged by the police to an extreme close-up of the protagonist's eyes, the result is a more striking representation of panic than would be afforded by a more discreet camera distance. Yet when eyes appear in extreme close-up in the climactic gunfight of Leone's 'spaghetti' western, *The Good, the Bad and the Ugly* (1966), the strategy is no longer principally informative about character – though it does disclose the relative poise of the three protagonists – but, rather, stylistically playful, even exuberant, exemplifying the director's reworking of this genre's familiar scenic choreography.

Height, angle and level
The first of these categories refers to the degree of elevation in the camera's positioning. As with disparate meanings of the same shot distance, variable effects can be generated by a seemingly identical choice of camera height: consider how placing the camera distinctively low procures identification with insects in the grass at the start of David Lynch's *Blue Velvet* (1986) and a sense of anti-suburban critique in Tim Burton's *Edward Scissorhands* (1990), where a bleakly coloured carpet appears to stretch to infinity.

With respect to camera angle, three basic options are available: *high angle*, *straight-on angle* and *low angle*. If the straight-on angle appears to be fairly neutral and devoid of emphasis, the other two permutations have often been correlated with specific meanings: broadly speaking, the high angle shot is taken to diminish the power of its subject, and the low angle shot, conversely, to enhance it. Yet, as in the case of camera distances, such claims about the fixed significance of different angles are highly suspect. Again, our reading of particular film sequences needs to be contextually sensitive: after all, even if filmed from below, shots of a baby held up in the air by its parent scarcely impress as an image of power. Barthes argues similarly that 'the analogical relationship between "high angle shot" and "domination" strikes us as naïve' (Jim Hillier (ed.), *Cahiers du cinéma*, Vol. 2 (London: Routledge and Kegan Paul, 1986), p. 279). Evidence for the greater semantic range of the high angle shot can be found in the credits sequence of the original *Shaft* (1971). As the camera zooms in from high above on its African American protagonist crossing a busy Manhattan street, he might be expected to seem vulnerable, a mere ant in the metropolis; however, this use of high angle allows us better to recognise the cool with which he weaves through the traffic – an early judgement about his character that is quickly confirmed as the film cuts to a straight-on, much closer shot of him giving an irate white motorist the finger.

The spectator tends to become aware of level in cinematic framing only when there is significant variation from the norm. Although the frame is almost always balanced, filmmakers can alter it from the horizontal so as to produce a *canted shot* (sometimes referred to as an 'oblique shot' or 'Dutch angle'). A signature use of such technique occurs in *The Third Man* (1949), where an American's disorientation in post-war Vienna is visually reinforced by canted shots that increase in their obliquity according to stages in his predicament (Figure 2). However, the device survives into current cinema, not least for its usefulness in indicat-

Figure 2 Canted camera angle in *The Third Man* (UK, 1949).

ing a world out of joint. In *The Constant Gardener* (2005), the lopsidedness of the frame first fulfils a low-grade function of denoting the viewpoint from an overturned truck in the African bush, but then hints at unholy political and commercial forces behind the truck's destruction.

Masking

While the canted shot has the effect of rotating the customary film image on its axis, other techniques go further and offer alternatives to the image's rectangular format itself. In masked shots, variously shaped attachments to the camera block out some of the incoming light, leaving portions of the frame black. This device is most frequently used to mimic the perspective given by other optical devices such as a telescope or microscope: think only of the countless war films that cut from a shot of one army's general to an extreme long shot – masked in the shape of binocular lenses – of the opposing forces. Another variation in masking is the *iris shot*, whereby the usual rectangular image either contracts towards or opens out from a small circular point on the screen (respectively 'irising-out' and 'irising-in'). Given the relative obsolescence of the iris compared with its heyday in silent cinema and immediately afterwards, its occurrence in contemporary film tends to have nostalgic or historical or playful connotations (consider Michael Winterbottom's frequent, witty irising in *A Cock and Bull Story* (2005)).

Movement

None of the many cinematographic options covered so far implies or requires that the camera actually has to *move* during filming. Yet cinema is a dynamic art not only because images passing at sufficient speed through a projector generate the sense of continuous movement but because the apparatus involved in recording them is itself frequently mobile. An accurate account of the camera's movement, however, should distinguish between practices involving shifts in its entire body and those where there is only modification of some more peripheral part of equipment. Into this latter category should be placed, first of all, such strategies as the *pan* and the *tilt shot* (respectively horizontal and vertical rotation

of the frame along a fixed axis, achieved not by relocating the
camera itself but by activation of a pivoting device attached to it).
It is striking that some textbooks in professional cinematography
argue against the use – or, at least, overuse – of pans and tilts. To
Bruce Mamer, the pan is actually 'unnatural' since its systematic
lateral movement falsifies the rapid, impressionistic, often
reversible scanning of the visual field which we perform when
looking to the side in life itself (*Film Production Technique*, 3rd ed.
(Belmont, CA: Wadsworth, 2003), p. 26). As well as being *normative* in its implication – seeking to instil certain preferred
techniques as the essence of cinema and to discount others – this
argument ties film aesthetics too closely to the biology of the
human eye. Such biologically based reasoning has also been used
against another common way of achieving mobility without repositioning the camera itself: namely the *zoom* (in which utilising a
lens of variable focal length produces the sense of progressively
moving towards or back from a subject – respectively 'zooming-in'
and 'zooming-out' – even while the camera body remains station-
ary). For Roy Thompson, wedded to a realist approach that would
effectively outlaw much distinctive filmmaking, the zoom is alien
because it is 'a highly artificial way of recording a picture' (*The
Grammar of the Shot*, p. 54).

Categorically distinct from pans, tilts and zooms are those
techniques that do involve relocation of the camera itself. A basic
distinction may be made here between horizontal and vertical
types of camera mobility. Camera movements along the ground
are most commonly called *tracking* or *dolly shots* (depending on
whether the camera proceeds on specially laid tracks or on a
wheeled apparatus called a 'dolly'). The tracking shot can be
varied in both momentum and direction so as to generate diverse
effects: a prowling forward motion is apt for enhancing the
suspense of a thriller but less usual in a costume drama, where
the camera might instead trace elaborate circular patterns while
recording a formal dance. Movements above ground level – with
the camera rising or descending on a mechanically operated
mount of variable length – are known as *crane shots*. While horizontal and vertical kinds of mobility are more usually kept
separate, they may sometimes be strikingly combined. Here a

particularly bravura example is the three-minute opening shot of Orson Welles's *Touch of Evil* (1958). After beginning at ground level, in a Mexican border town, the camera cranes upwards and also moves laterally for a rooftop perspective before descending and resuming a tracking motion along several streets. The same unbroken shot is elaborated so as to incorporate most conceivable directions of movement (up, down, left, right, forwards, backwards), as well as variable forms of motion (rapid tracking, stately aerial sweeps, occasional pauses) and degrees of distance (from the extreme close view of a bomb to extreme long views of buildings). Besides advertising itself as a grand stylistic flourish, the shot also fluidly draws together individuals and interests whose labyrinthine relationship will gradually be disclosed in the film.

When a cut finally occurs in *Touch of Evil*, it signals a switch of cinematographic style. The elegant swoops and sashays of the camera give way, for a while, to a jerky filming motion as people are shown running towards the scene of an explosion. This hectic, staccato effect is achieved by use of *handheld* equipment – quite innovatory at the time of Welles's work but widespread, even institutionalised since in genres from war film to documentary, and indeed in any cinematic context where the sense of ragged movement is required. One highly significant piece of portable apparatus is the *Steadicam*, invented in the early 1970s by the American cinematographer Garrett Brown. This consists in a stabilising mount for the camera that is attached to the operator, thus enabling the handheld camera's intimacy and territorial range but without reproducing its unsteady movements. Chapter 2 – with reference to Aleksandr Sokurov's film *Russian Ark* (2002) – will note how the Steadicam has extended possibilities not only in mise-en-scène but also in editing.

Focus

All of those camera movements just described potentially have an effect upon one further dimension of the film image: its quality of focus. Here the filmmaker's specific selection among lenses that range from wide-angle through medium focal lengths to the tele-photo will also be significant. The possible results include *shallow focus*, where the foreground of the frame is sharply outlined in contrast to fuzzier rear portions; *racking focus*, where focal sharpness is redistributed in the course of the shot from foreground to background or vice versa; and *deep focus*, where all of the planes within an image are sharp. As with all other cinematographic options, these are more than merely technical matters. Deep focus – classically achieved in such films as Welles's *Citizen Kane* (1941) and William Wyler's *The Best Years of Our Lives* (1946) – has, in fact, figured as a topic of ideological and philosophical, as well as narrowly aesthetic, importance for film studies. Bazin argues in *What is Cinema?* that because it mimics our natural habits of vision, and unifies rather than hierarchises elements within the frame, deep focus is the most humanly enriching of film modes. He writes elsewhere that 'every technique relates to a metaphysic' (*Cahiers du cinéma*, Vol. 1, p. 78); the philosophical significance of deep focus – which shows with clarity multiple events occurring simultaneously on different planes of the image – consists for Bazin in its implying the unbrokenness of space and time. Yet it has been a key argument of this chapter that it is dangerous to derive any such fixed meaning from a particular technical choice. If the use of deep focus indeed seems in some films to have the harmonious, humane connotations Bazin suggests, this may still be challenged in others by, say, clashing pro-filmic elements or by a canted camera angle. As with all other aspects of mise-en-scène, more locally sensitive interpretation is necessary to assess the value of deep focus in a given work.

STOP and THINK

- Return to the film sequence that you surveyed earlier for pro-filmic elements and concentrate now upon giving a detailed account of its cinematography. List each shot – that is to say, each segment of continuous filming between cuts or some other break – and analyse it according to the headings set out above. Depending on the primary material you are working with, some cinematographic categories will be more activated than others: for example, if you are considering Julie Andrews's mountaintop singing at the start of *The Sound of Music* (1964), you may be stuck for comment on shallow focus and handheld camerawork but will have much to say about extreme long shots and high angles. What meanings are produced, singly and collectively, by aspects of cinematography in the sequence? Is there coherence – or perhaps dissonance – among the techniques used?

- Narrowing your focus still further, select just a few shots from the sequence. In each of these shots, alter at least one cinematographic variable. As an example, the extreme long shot of Julie Andrews singing with her arms outstretched might remain but be masked now by binocular lenses or occur with the camera lowered in height from aerial to edelweiss level. How do the shot adjustments that you make transform the meaning of your sequence?

- As a more general exercise, select one or two of the key cinematographic practices outlined above – the pan, say, or the close-up or the canted shot – and review their use in films with which you are familiar. Evaluate one of this chapter's arguments by assessing whether such techniques tend to be relatively uniform in their meanings or whether their connotations may actually be less stable and more context-specific.

Colour and its meanings

When the Russian writer Maxim Gorky saw an early programme of Lumière films in 1896, cinema struck him not so much as generating positive new experiences for the senses as causing two sorts of sensory deficit. Chapter 3 will return to Gorky's remarks on the soundlessness of film compared with everyday hubbub; here, however, we draw attention to his observations on film's uncanny lack of colour: 'Everything there – the earth, the trees, the people, the water and the air – is dipped in monotonous grey. Grey rays of the sun across the grey sky, grey eyes in grey faces, and the leaves of the trees are ashen grey' (Jay Leyda, *Kino: A History of the Russian and Soviet Film* (London: Allen and Unwin, 1960), p. 407).

Gorky is writing during that earliest cinematic period in which only monochrome images – their monochrome also quite undifferentiated tonally – were possible. A little later, the handpainting of some film frames would begin, followed firstly by artificial colouring of sequences through stencilling, toning and tinting, then by capturing of the entire spectrum on film's photographic medium itself, most famously in the Technicolor process. Yet it is striking that Gorky immediately gives the chromatic question – the meanings and implications of colour – a central place which it has occupied only intermittently in later film commentary. Film studies, in fact, has been marked by that 'neglect of colour' or 'apparent renunciation of colour' which John Gage argues has also weakened the discipline of art history in the West (*Colour and Culture* (London: Thames and Hudson, 1993), p. 7). There have been only a few moments when colour in cinema has become intellectually paramount. Its growing availability to Hollywood before the Second World War, for example, occasioned a sharp polemic between those welcoming it just as they had sound as an enhancement of cinema's capacity to document the world fully, and those anti-realist opponents like the German-born theorist Rudolf Arnheim who deplored it – in places including his 1935 essay, 'Remarks on Colour Film' – as a threat to the distinctive principles of cinematic composition which had developed during the monochrome era. Subsequent waves of film study, however, have tended either to treat colour cursorily or to omit it altogether. The topic's marginal contemporary status is indicated by the fact that it occupies only a few pages even in such encyclopaedic accounts of mise-en-scène as Bordwell and Thompson's *Film Art* and Corrigan and White's *The Film Experience*.

Bordwell and Thompson initially place colour within the pro-filmic elements of mise-en-scène as a subclass of 'setting'. Certainly this makes some sense: colour is already potent in cinematic locations from green Vietnamese rainforests to white hospital wards. It is also to be found elsewhere in the pro-filmic range, especially as a key element in costume. However, besides dwelling, as it were, on the surface of objects viewed by the camera – in the blue of the sea or the red of a cardinal's robes – colour is also liable to be augmented, altered, even invented at the cinematographic level. As in the case of *Three Kings*, filmmakers may begin by choosing a stock that produces unexpected colour relations. During filming itself they might select from a number of filter media that drain or even exclude certain colours while promoting others (Steven Soderbergh's *Traffic* (2000) systematically uses filtering to achieve three distinct looks of bleached-out yellow, steely blue and vibrant primaries that mark off its various narrative strands). Colour may also be chemically modified even after filming via manipulations of the developing process. All of these adjustments to colour are feasible even without taking into account the creative possibilities that have been opened up by digital technology.

However it is achieved, colour performs a number of functions in film. As well as serving as a marker of historical and geographical authentication (the black of Victorian England), and even of genre classification (few dull browns in 1950s American musicals and few pinks in Ken Loach's fierce political dramas), it may, as with *Traffic*, figure at least partly as a means of narrative organisation. A comparable example is the Chinese martial arts film, *Ying xiong/Hero* (2002), which has a tripartite colour scheme – in which red and gold, blue, then white and pale green prevail. Unlike in Soderbergh's film, however, these colour motifs are distributed not spatially but temporally, with one replacing the other to mark our passage to another interpretation of events that are in dispute. The fact that *Hero* concludes in white perhaps gives this final version a truth claim stronger than the others.

This particular example also alerts us more generally to colour's symbolic and thematic potentials. Consider briefly the work of one of contemporary Hollywood's more distinctive colourists, Tim Burton. In *Edward Scissorhands* the primary colours used for the suburb's houses would normally communicate optimism and well-being; yet a slight excess in their brightness, coupled with the fact that no darker or mixed hues are visible anywhere, alerts the spectator to a critique of suburban blandness and conformity. By contrast, the black in clothing worn by Johnny Depp as Edward carries connotations here of attractively Gothic, romantic, even punk sensibility (as well as hinting at a racial otherness barely countenanced in the all-white suburb). While preserving such a

broadly thematic approach to colouring, however, Burton modifies
the value of particular hues in the animated *Tim Burton's Corpse
Bride* (2005). Vivid primary colours signify positively now,
suggesting the vibrancy of the underworld as against the oppressive world above ground that subsists in a grey as monotonous and
desolate as that observed by Gorky.

Such variation in just one director's work indicates that the
spectator needs to be sensitive to the different contexts of colour.
Film studies, like art theory, demands alertness to the many possible forms of what Gage calls 'colour-thinking' (*Colour and Culture*,
p. 8). The filmmaker, painter and gardener Derek Jarman, for
instance, evokes a potential chaos of colour meanings when he
refers to 'the bordello of the spectrum': one person's 'green of
birth' might be another's 'colour of pus' (*Chroma: A Book of
Colour – June '93* (London: Vintage, 1995), pp. 52, 70). While
Jarman is undoubtedly correct about people's differing colour
sensibilities, there is a risk of breaking apart the study of film spectatorship into a mere inventory of subjective impressions. Rather
than arresting discussion at the level of individual idiosyncrasies,
it may be profitable instead to note how colour also has powerful
cultural determinants. Chromatic effects in film have a history: the
Technicolor portions of *The Wizard of Oz* (1939) carried a more
utopian charge in Depression-era America than they can do in the
colour-saturated consumer economy of the United States today.
Chromatic effects also have a geography: the Soviet film director
and theorist S. M. Eisenstein – a key protagonist of Chapter 2 –
notes that 'different countries have different notions of colour. For
example, white here is not associated with grief, whereas for the
Chinese it is the colour of mourning' (*Selected Works*, Vol. 3
(London: BFI, 1996), p. 323) (note, in passing, how Eisenstein's
example may have implications for the reading of white in *Hero*).
Finally, we should also acknowledge what Gage terms 'the gendering of colour' (*Colour and Culture*, p. 208). Without adopting a
crudely classificatory cast of mind – looking for 'masculine' earth
tones, 'feminine' lilacs and so on – there may still be the opportunity in specific film contexts to explore the relations between
colour coding and sexual politics.

Analysing mise-en-scène: *In the Mood for Love*

The Hong Kong film *Fa yeung nin wa* (2000), known in English as *In the Mood for Love*, turns significantly upon the interpretation of visual evidence. As Mrs Chan, the female protagonist played by Maggie Cheung, says: 'You notice things if you pay attention.' What she – and Chow, her male counterpart, played by Tony Leung – notice first of all are small details of dress and accessories that indicate their respective spouses are having an affair. Later, Chow and Mrs Chan read minute changes in the body postures and facial expressions of each other for clues about the nature and possible outcome of their own mutual feelings. Such heightened activity of the eye is duplicated at the level of the film's own spectatorship, with viewers continually required to reflect upon the meanings of both pro-filmic and cinematographic choices. Discussion of a single shot from *In the Mood for Love* – taken from almost exactly one hour in and lasting thirty seconds – is thus suited to show the strengths of mise-en-scène analysis (as well as demonstrating its limitations).

In the context of such a stylistically lavish film, the shot chosen is relatively modest. Unlike a number of celebrated sequences – the slow-motion choreography of the protagonists entering a noodle bar, or the temporal tour de force of a restaurant scene that costume changes indicate is actually stitched together from many different occasions – it is not obviously virtuosic. During the shot, Mrs Chan merely stands by an open window, looking out as she drinks from a glass. Yet if we draw upon the approach to film's visual elements that has been elaborated in this chapter, even a seemingly mundane sequence such as this becomes highly articulate.

The shot does not initially disclose an unobstructed view of Mrs Chan. Instead, as the camera begins tilting upwards to reveal more of her head and body, it passes an unfocused black volume that is presumably the top of a wall beyond the window. As well as adding to the sense of Mrs Chan's imprisoned situation, this indistinct shape at first obscuring her is significant for how its strong horizontality evokes the edge of a strip of film. This may alert us, then, to the work's playful, self-conscious aspects, the way in which it presents the lives of the two protagonists through the filter of various movie scenarios. However, as the camera continues to move upwards and Mrs Chan is seen with clarity, more familiar psychological and social concerns become paramount. For the rest of the sequence, she is shown in medium shot, positioned in the frame just slightly left of centre. She thus commands spectator interest, without obliterating the detail of her surroundings as would be achieved by use of close-up. Indeed, it is thematically suggestive that details of her environment are apparent. In the left foreground, part of the window frame juts into the shot at a diagonal: while it is both open and painted in a pastel yellow – thus hinting at some optimism regarding Mrs Chan's situation – the window nevertheless figures as a means of confinement that she cannot burst beyond. It thereby extends a series of symbolic spaces in the film that include narrow corridors, cramped stairways and – even when there are brief forays into the exterior world – claustrophobic street corners. The shot further indicates a sense of stuffy domestic enclosure by subtly juxtaposing real and merely pictorial plant life. While fertile green leaves of a bush growing outside are prominent in the scene – occupying a position in the right foreground – their closeness to the camera leaves them blurred and at a focal disadvantage when compared with the sharply seen floral motifs on both the curtains and the back of a chair in the room behind Mrs Chan. Although we see only a small portion of these furnishings, their decorative heaviness speaks eloquently of a traditional social environment – the conservative Shanghainese community in exile in Hong Kong – that seems suffocating.

The plant motif is extended to the protagonist's costume, as she is wearing a mainly white dress on which are printed green leaves and, centrally, the vivid trumpet of a daffodil (Figure 3). The flower's complete openness in this design evokes not only Mrs Chan's yearning towards the world that lies beyond all the confining frames but perhaps a more specifically sexual desire. In terms of Gaines's 'vestural code', however, the positive sign of this flower clashes with the implications of the formal, extremely high neck of Mrs Chan's dress – a costumed kind of incarceration similar to the business suits and ties which Chow, her putative lover, is almost invariably shown wearing.

Figure 3 Mrs Chan (Maggie Cheung), wearing the daffodil dress in a
scene with Chow (Tony Leung) from *Fa yeung nin wa / In the Mood for
Love* (Hong Kong/France, 2000).

Setting, props and costume are thus not unitary in their meanings in this shot but, rather, mixed and conflicting. The tension between contradictory impulses – conservative and progressive, confining and liberatory – is evident not only within single elements of mise-en-scène in this way but also in the ensemble of relationships among them. The fairly high-key lighting of the shot, for example – certainly the flattering lighting that falls upon Mrs Chan – might be taken in formulaic fashion to communicate an essential optimism; yet it would be facile to isolate this one stylistic component from the others. Such a cheerful approach to lighting and its connotations neglects the contrary evidence already accumulated from other pro-filmic elements, as well as from cinematographic features such as depth of focus and camera positioning. It also, even more culpably, overlooks the significance of Cheung's movements here as Mrs Chan. While she drinks from the glass, she looks seemingly with longing towards an unseen world beyond or beneath the camera. Yet at the end of the sequence, she turns her back and retreats into the claustrophobic domestic space – a reticent-seeming 'dorsality', to use Bordwell's term (*On the History of Film Style*, p. 216), which contrasts with the confident frontal positioning and advance of many protagonists in cinema. All of Mrs Chan's gestures, moreover, are presented not in real time but in slow motion, stating even more powerfully her suffocation and desire for an alternative.

Wong Kar-wai, the director of *In the Mood for Love*, has spoken in interviews of wanting to evoke a 'non-verbal' mode of experience. Analysis of the kind attempted above should indicate how in his film even the smallest items of the visual field – a chair covering, a few leaves, the turning of a character's back – are suggestive. Such a mise-en-scène approach is of course extendable to all works, including those that appear not to foreground 'non-verbal' elements as strikingly as Wong's. Yet even as we proselytise for this heightened sensitivity to any film's visual repertoire, we should also be cautious. Mise-en-scène interpretation can be overdeveloped until it becomes an end in itself, producing a rather static, pictorial attitude towards cinema. It risks abstracting the work the film spectator does with the eye from other possible programmes of inquiry. In the particular case of *In the Mood for Love*, the film student might, say, take a genre-based approach that explores its connections to melodrama (including Chinese examples and the 1950s American work of Douglas Sirk); or a geographically and historically oriented approach that assesses its representation of this period in Hong Kong's past; or a postcolonial angle that reviews the positioning of the film – and Wong's work generally – in the category of 'world cinema'. Mise-en-scène factors remain important to a varying extent in all these – and other – analyses, but without any longer being isolated or fetishised.

What is also omitted in mise-en-scène study is attention to those other items in film's specific formal inventory that will be the concern of the next two chapters: editing and sound. Although no dialogue is spoken in the sequence from *In the Mood for Love*, it includes another 'non-verbal' element besides the various components of mise-en-scène: a piece of music for stringed instruments, dominated by a melancholy violin. During the film this acts as a leitmotiv, repeated across scenes of the tentative connection of the two protagonists. An adequate reading of the selected shot entails, not least, consideration of the interplay between visual elements and this key auditory feature. Such fuller interpretation will also reintroduce the question of editing. Although there are many ways in which this shot is profoundly significant in itself, meaning also accumulates in its relationships with those that come before and after. When Mrs Chan turns her back, for example, the film cuts to another sequence in slow motion, showing Chow as he moves away from colleagues in his newspaper office and comes forward to gaze through a window. While the cut certainly implies a division between him and Mrs Chan at this stage, the editing also collaborates with mise-en-scène to moderate any sense of fracture. Scenes that centre upon the two protagonists are tightly juxtaposed here and produce a kind of visual 'rhyme' in which each figure stands yearningly at a window. There is auditory connection too, with the violin theme carrying across the two shots. As we watch the sequence showing Chow, then, we implicitly revisit and reinterpret the previous shot of Mrs Chan alone.

Selected reading

General

Bordwell, David and Kristin Thompson, *Film Art: An Introduction*, 8th ed. (Boston: McGraw-Hill, 2007).

Standard work: lucid, compendious and sumptuously illustrated. At times, risks sealing off stylistic topics from film studies' ideological and cultural interests.

Corrigan, Timothy and Patricia White, *The Film Experience: An Introduction* (Boston: Bedford/St. Martin's, 2004).

Covers a slightly broader range of film topics than Bordwell and Thompson, but still treats mise-en-scène in detail and with plentiful visual illustration.

Gibbs, John, *Mise-en-scène: Film Style and Interpretation* (London: Wallflower, 2002).

Brief, accessible guide which, unusually but enlighteningly, gives much space to recounting fierce debates in 1950s and 1960s journals over the place of mise-en-scène in film studies.

Acting

Naremore, James, *Acting in the Cinema* (Berkeley, Los Angeles and London: University of California Press, 1988).

One of the most important of surprisingly few studies that discuss film acting as distinct from – or, at least, only partially absorbed by – the star phenomenon.

Pudovkin, Vsevolod, *Selected Essays*, ed. Richard Taylor (London: Seagull, 2006).

Valuable reissue of theoretical writings by this early Soviet director, including his groundbreaking reflections upon film acting (as well as other topics including sound, the significance of the screenplay and the role of the director).

Wojcik, Pamela Robertson (ed.), *Movie Acting: The Film Reader* (New York and London: Routledge, 2004).

Generous and timely sampling of materials on theories and practices of screen acting, drawn from many critical approaches.

Cinematography

Hummel, Rob, *American Cinematographer Manual*, 8th ed. (Hollywood: A S C Holding Corp, 2002).

Probably the best claimant to the status of the film industry's bible (at least within the United States). At over 900 pages, supplies technical knowledge in a quantity even more suited to the aspiring film worker than the film interpreter.

Colour

Dalle Vacche, Angela and Brian Price (eds), *Color: The Film Reader* (Abingdon and New York: Routledge, 2006).

Much-needed collection of essays on this oddly neglected topic: contributions range from theoretical speculations to specific case studies and also include reflections by filmmakers such as Eisenstein, Oshima and Rohmer.

Costume

Bruzzi, Stella, *Undressing Cinema: Clothing and Identity in the Movies* (London and New York: Routledge, 1997).

Valuable study exploring the plural meanings of clothing in cinematic genres from costume dramas to gangster films. Sections dedicated to male clothing augment the female-centred work in Gaines and Herzog.

Bruzzi, Stella and Pamela Church Gibson (eds), *Fashion Cultures: Theories, Explorations and Analysis* (London and New York: Routledge, 2000).

Substantial, lively collection that ranges beyond cinema's particular fashion cultures, but includes stimulating work on the costuming of Cary Grant, Grace Kelly and Gwyneth Paltrow, and on clothing practices in several national cinemas.

Gaines, Jane and Charlotte Herzog (eds), *Fabrications: Costume and the Female Body* (London and New York: Routledge, 1991).

Pioneering, if uneven collection. See especially Gaines's essay on women's costume and film narrative, and Gaylyn Studlar's psychoanalytic study of the dress of Marlene Dietrich.

Street, Sarah, *Costume and Cinema: Dress Codes in Popular Film* (London: Wallflower, 2001).

A good place from which to begin study of this element of mise-en-scène.

Lighting

Malkiewicz, Kris, *Film Lighting: Talks with Hollywood's Cinematographers and Gaffers* (New York: Prentice Hall, 1992).

Informative on film industry practices but alert also to the aesthetic and symbolic implications of lighting.

Setting

Affron, Charles and Mirella Jona Affron, *Sets in Motion: Art Direction and Film Narrative* (New Brunswick, NJ: Rutgers University Press, 1995).

Explores the significance of décor in a wide range of films, including *2001: A Space Odyssey* and *The Towering Inferno*.

Ramírez, Juan Antonio, *Architecture for the Screen: A Critical Study of Set Design in Hollywood's Golden Age* (Jefferson, NC: McFarland, 2004).

Written by an art historian, and surveying the processes and aesthetics of highly divergent set designs in Hollywood from its earliest film industry until the 1950s.

Useful websites

www.filmsite.org.

Intellectually variable but including among its resources an excellent, extensive and well-illustrated glossary of mise-en-scène terms.

2

Film editing: theories and histories

The Last Tycoon (1976), adapted for the screen by Harold Pinter from F. Scott Fitzgerald's novel, offers a waspish insight into the film editor's traditional status. While Fitzgerald already subjects to corrosive critique the Hollywood movie world in which his book is set, Pinter adds a plot twist of his own that is revealing about the industry's unequal distribution of power and privilege. As the lights come up after a screening in the studio's projection room, it is discovered that the chief editor, or 'cutter', has died of a heart attack without once drawing attention to his plight. He did not want, an assistant speculates, to disturb the omnipotent studio head, also present at the screening.

This individual cutter's fate is irresistible as an allegory of the frequent invisibility of the editor – and of editing practice generally – in our thinking about film. Such human and conceptual neglect has a long history. In the heyday of the Hollywood studio system, editors were frequently perceived more as technicians or assemblers than as figures engaged in creative construction. Historically, their status has also been damaged by a certain gendering of professional roles within film production. In mainstream American cinema, it is noticeable that, while openings as directors or screenwriters have often failed to materialise for women, opportunities have existed for them to develop careers as editors. Although the tradition of women directors in the United States is patchy, a female editorial lineage extends from Dorothy Spencer and Margaret Booth in mid-century to still-active figures like Anne V. Coates, Thelma Schoonmaker and Susan E. Morse.

Women's entry into editing, according to Walter Murch, was eased by the profession's association with such stereotypically feminised forms of labour as sewing and librarianship. In his dialogues on film editing with Murch, Michael Ondaatje adds that there may still be a gendered opposition of 'masculine' film director/cinematographer and 'feminine' editor: 'the man is the hunter-gatherer, coming back with stuff for her to cook!' (*The Conversations: Walter Murch and the Art of Editing Film*, pp. 25–6). This sexist hierarchy may also be observed in film contexts other than Hollywood. In his film *Man with a Movie Camera* (1929), the pioneering Soviet director Dziga Vertov restores the editor to visibility by including shots of a woman seated at a table inspecting, cutting and splicing footage. Yet while this editorial work is shown miraculously animating what seem merely photographs, it still lacks glamour when set alongside the heroism of the film's male cinematographer, who risks incineration in a metal smelting works or suspends himself perilously above a dam in order to obtain the images.

This chapter, however, is not intended primarily as an exposé of the film editor's subjection to class and gender inequalities (important though those topics are). Instead, more broadly, it aims to address Ondaatje's objection that editing is often 'unimagined' or 'overlooked' in film criticism (*The Conversations*, p. xi). We will thus explore the nature, history and implications of diverse editing regimes. Film editing will be presented as not merely supplementary to or confirmatory of the real work that has already been done in production itself but, rather, active, interventionist and creative. Here the chapter follows the lead of the French director Robert Bresson, who describes the careful articulation of pictures and sounds that occurs during the editorial stage as a film's third 'birth', generating something qualitatively different from the work's two earlier embodiments in the scriptwriting and shooting phases. Or, as Eric Rohmer puts it: 'In an extreme case, I could absent myself from the shooting, but I'd have to be there at the editing' (Jim Hillier (ed.), *Cahiers du cinéma*, Vol. 2 (London: Routledge and Kegan Paul, 1986), p. 89).

Beyond the shot

Periodically, attempts have been made in film studies to view cinema quite abstractly as a signifying system based on identifiable rules of articulation. The Soviet filmmaker S. M. Eisenstein experiments in analysing cinematic sequences according to principles of musical notation (an analogy that also interests Murch in *The Conversations*). Later theorists – most ambitiously Christian Metz in texts including *Essais sur la signification du cinéma* (1968; translated in 1974 as *Film Language*) – are motivated more by the post-war linguistic turn in the human sciences and therefore seek to establish a 'grammar' of film comparable to accounts of the functioning of language itself. Whether influenced by musicology, linguistics or by other conceptual models, all such systematic approaches to film face the problem of deciding upon film's minimal unit, its most basic element of signification. What, in this medium, is structurally comparable to the note in music or the morpheme and phoneme in language?

The most frequently proposed candidate for this fundamental unit is *the shot*: that is to say, an unbroken sequence of film recorded by one camera. While generally put into combination with many others in the finished work, shots seem already bearers of meaning in themselves, beguilingly like the words that constitute a sentence. The shot is of course highly variable in length: given film's normal running speed of twenty-four frames per second, it may occupy any number of frames from one to many thousands. At the extreme of miniaturisation, Robert Breer's experimental short animation work, *Fist Fight* (1964) comprises shots lasting only one frame, as if seeking an even tinier basis for film's syntax. However, examples of the opposing impulse – elastically extending the shot, seeking in figurative terms to endow a word with the force and completeness of a sentence – are more common in film history. Recall, from Chapter 1, the prolonged opening shot of *Touch of Evil*. A more ambitious development still of the minimal unit of the shot happens in Hitchcock's thriller, *Rope* (1948). Although the fact that each reel of film allows only nine or ten minutes of footage prevents the director from realising the work in one shot, he nevertheless finds a way of stressing this most basic compositional level rather than larger combinatory patterns. The film finally consists of ten shots, yet minimises signs of editing by ending most of these with a freeze frame on a particular object and beginning the next with the reloaded camera in the same position.

A highly elastic stretching of the shot occurs in *Russian Ark* (2002), directed by Aleksandr Sokurov. In interview, Sokurov speaks of wanting 'to make a film in one breath'. During the film's running length of ninety minutes, a specially adapted Steadicam using digital videotape rather than 35mm film moves without interruption through the ballrooms, galleries, lobbies and back-stairs of St. Petersburg's Winter Palace. This spatial fluidity is matched historically, as scenes from different stages of Russia's past occur in the various rooms. The decision to avoid cutting is not taken merely in a spirit of technical adventurism. On the contrary, the continuity of the shot is thematically motivated by a sense of the palace's unbroken significance in Russian history. The eras of Peter the Great and Catherine the Great, say, are so compa-rable in their strengthening of Tsarist power that they lend themselves to unification by the camera's breathlessly sustained movement rather than to separation by cuts or any other transi-tional device.

It would be inaccurate to regard *Russian Ark* as entirely free from imperatives of editing. While the pictures are captured in one unbroken motion, the film's soundtrack was recorded discon-tinuously during post-production. At the level of image, too, editorial interventions are still discernible, albeit faintly. There can be no escaping what Murch describes as the film editor's obliga-tion 'to carry, like a sacred vessel, the focus of attention of the audience and move it in interesting ways around the surface of the screen' (*The Conversations*, p. 277). Rather than redirecting spec-tator attention by overt transitions, *Russian Ark* achieves this by a kind of *in-camera editing*: moving into and out of close-up within the same camera deployment, or passing from one location to another. In addition, like those very brief single-shot 'actualities' of trains or crowds or other kinds of movement with which cine-matic history begins in the late nineteenth century, the film is already – if minimally – edited in the very choice of actions on which it opens and closes.

Nevertheless, *Russian Ark* does evoke a form of cinema in which the shot prevails at the expense of editing patterns. Despite the logic behind its unbroken composition, it may be vulnerable to the polemic which Eisenstein directed in 1926 against the Hungarian film theorist, Béla Bálazs. Within Bálazs's thesis that film's distinctiveness lies in the 'poetic' or 'figurative' quality of the photographically derived shot, Eisenstein detects an unusual version of bourgeois individualism, or what he calls 'starism': manifested not by any flesh-and-blood figure involved in film production but by the single shot itself, separated now from others. The result is the strange situation of '*The shot itself as "star"*'. Such absolutising of the shot to the detriment of editorial combinations is anathema to Eisenstein, who asserts in the same article that '*The expressive effect of cinema is the result of juxtapositions*' (*Selected Works*, Vol. 1, pp. 79, 80). Where Bálazs's key piece of cinematic apparatus is the camera that generates evocative photographic images in the first place, Eisenstein gives equal weight to the scissors that cuts them up (his article, indeed, is called 'Béla Forgets the Scissors').

Reserving for the moment a detailed discussion of Eisenstein's favoured mode of editorial juxtaposition, we may note the general importance of his claim that film's identity as a medium inheres in editing. It is not necessary to sign up to his ideological programme for cinema in order to be persuaded by his assertion that the single shot is less the commanding structure conceived by Bálazs than 'a detached house, as it were, in "Montage Street"' (*Selected Works*, Vol. 2, p. 11). Aiming to go 'beyond the shot' – as the title of another article, published in 1929, phrases it – Eisenstein powerfully reimagines the minimal unit of cinematic composition, which is understood now as an articulated series of images rather than any image in solitude. Here he not only offers a new conceptual basis for film studies but, incidentally, provides a retrospective rationalisation of early exhibition practices. As Charles Musser and others have argued, those late nineteenth- and early twentieth-century proprietors of fairground booths and vaudeville theatres who placed a number of single-shot films in a particular running order during their programmes were actually the first editors, instinctively grasping the effects of juxtaposition.

An equally provocative dethroning of the single shot was carried out by Eisenstein's collaborator in early Soviet cinema, Lev Kuleshov. Witnesses to the experiments Kuleshov conducted in his Moscow film workshop vary considerably in their recollection of details, but they all testify to a sense of revelation about the power of editing. According to the most authoritative report, Kuleshov took fairly neutral close-ups of the actor Ivan Mosjukhin from an existing film and cut them together with, successively, single shots of a bowl of soup on a table, a woman's body lying in a coffin and a little girl playing with a toy bear. Although Mosjukhin's facial expression was constant in the three sequences, spectators record-ed admiration for his chameleon-like ability to evoke hunger or grief or fatherly love. Limited perhaps in their individual eloquence, shots of an actor's face and a bowl of soup accrued significance in their interrelation. Unpersuaded, Don Fairservice objects that there would have been spatial and logical incongruities between Mosjukhin's material and the new footage, and that the actor's expression must already have been animated enough to allow spectators to infer particular emotional states (*Film Editing: History, Theory and Practice*, pp. 180–3). But even allowing for such empirical uncertainties, Kuleshov's experiment retains its power to unsettle the shot's central place in film study. Meaning is revealed as no longer the possession of the shot viewed in isolation but as flickering instead across a series of shots (recall from Chapter 1 how one admittedly suggestive shot from *In the Mood for Love* is augmented and modified by juxtaposition with the next).

Robert Stam has shown the affinity that the cinematic insights of Eisenstein, Kuleshov and others have with some advanced thinking about language. To argue that the shot in film only signi-fies by virtue of its articulation with others is comparable to the Swiss linguist Ferdinand de Saussure's claim – published only slightly earlier, during the First World War – that any sound-image in language is not itself positively replete with meaning but only becomes meaningful by virtue of its structured position within a multiplicity of other sound-images. As Stam summarises: 'The shot gained meaning, in other words, only relationally, as part of a larger system. In film as in language, to paraphrase Saussure, "there are only differences"' (*Film Theory: An*

Introduction (Oxford: Blackwell, 2000), p. 38). Just as in the linguistic system the word *bat* signifies not in and of itself but because of its difference from adjacent words such as *bag* and *cat*, so in the cinematic system the shot signifies because of its difference from all those that might have been chosen instead and those that come before or after in sequence. While a crucial insight, however, this remains somewhat abstract and generalising. What is important is not merely to acknowledge the integration of one shot with others in 'a larger system', but to recognise and assess the precise forms of such articulation. Rather than a singular editing pattern in film, there are competing modes, all with their distinct histories, protocols and – perhaps – ideological ramifications.

Principles and practices of continuity editing

As a term denoting a particular kind of editing, 'continuity' appears quite late in film history. Citations given in the *Oxford English Dictionary* for the word used in its cinematic context suggest that, initially, it functioned as a simple synonym for a screenplay. One reference from 1926 states that it is 'the correct name for the working script'; another, fourteen years later, records that Scott Fitzgerald has written 'a really brilliant continuity'. The earliest allusion traced by the *OED* to 'continuity' as a distinctive form of editing associated with smoothness and coherence dates from 1940. There is a certain lexicographical lag here behind the facts of actually existing film production. Many writers – perhaps most fully, David Bordwell, Janet Staiger and Kristin Thompson in *The Classical Hollywood Cinema* (1985) – have shown that, in mainstream American cinema at least, the principles of what would be called continuity editing were largely codified and institutionalised by the end of the First World War.

Nevertheless, even this earlier dating of the pre-eminence of continuity editing leaves unclaimed some twenty or so years of film history after the Lumière Brothers' first public display of their *Cinématographe* in 1895. Given that the overwhelming mass of spectators is now most familiar with films based broadly upon continuity principles, such a reminder of other possibilities is salutary in showing this editorial tradition's provisional, historically situated status. While continuity editing has come to dominate film production, it has done so for a complex of economic, industrial and ideological reasons – principally its usefulness in structuring the products of a lucrative narrative cinema – and not because it is intrinsically superior to other editorial modes or is somehow encrypted in film's DNA. Other practices predated continuity editing or have developed alongside it in various if sometimes scattered or subterranean contexts. The course of film editing is best understood not by any linear or teleological model but, rather, as a story of historical and geographical variations, and the perhaps temporary success of one specific mutation.

Positioning continuity editing, then, as just one option in a larger set of possibilities, we may now attempt to describe its principles and key features. With regard to this particular editorial system, however, such analysis seems paradoxical, even violent. Unlike other forms of editing to be discussed later which flamboyantly announce themselves, the continuity mode aims generally at self-effacement to the point of invisibility. Tom Rolf, whose editing credits range from *Taxi Driver* to *Black Rain* (1989), speaks for many practitioners within this tradition when he says that 'the unseen cut is the way it should be. You don't want to remind people they're looking at a movie' (Gabriella Oldham, *First Cut: Conversations with Film Editors*, p. 128).

Rolf's language is not merely normative – proposing a particular kind of editorial move as the common sense of cinema – but innocent of any historical perspective. After all, the cut is itself a highly artificial device that happens to have been familiarised, even 'naturalised' by the spectator's long habituation to films employing it. While unobserved by us now, perhaps, cinematic cutting from one scene to another in this fashion was noticed by early audiences to the point, potentially, of disorientation. Equally, not all of the transitions between shots within this editing mode are quite as discreet as Rolf suggests. Earlier continuity cinema, in particular, makes use of a number of bridging devices besides the cut itself. These include the *dissolve* (or *lap-dissolve*), in which the incoming image appears superimposed on the outgoing one and gradually replaces it; the *wipe*, whereby a line travelling either horizontally or vertically across the screen pushes away one image to clear a space for the next; and the *fade*, a slower manoeuvre during which the screen either becomes progressively darker so that an image disappears (*fade-out*) or progressively lighter so that a new image emerges (*fade-in*). Such devices enable a range of expressive effects. A dissolve between shots may evoke a briefer time lapse than a fade or suggest a closer merging of two characters or spaces than would a cut from one to the other. As the American filmmaker John Sayles says, in justifying his frequent turn away from cutting in *Lone Star* (1996): 'A cut is very much a tear. You use a cut to say there's a separation between this thing and that thing' (Sayles and Gavin Smith, *Sayles on Sayles* (London: Faber and Faber, 1998), p. 230).

But although the dissolve, the wipe and the fade were eventually routinised in such cinemas as the classical Hollywood system to the point where they did not distract or unsettle the spectator, they are liable to seem too conspicuously artificial for current needs. With many exceptions, of course, these transitional devices tend now to occur where a nostalgic or parodic or artfully self-aware effect is required. The dominant form of punctuation between shots in modern continuity editing is thus the *straight cut*, where one image instantaneously replaces another but without causing the viewer significant spatial or temporal disorientation. Patterned relationships of various kinds between the first shot and the next serve to make even such a rapid transition comprehensible. As well as consistencies of character or location across the cut, there might be significant visual harmonies or antitheses. In a lakeside scene in Ang Lee's *Brokeback Mountain* (2005), a shot showing one of the male lovers positioned towards the right edge of the frame is balanced by the next shot of his partner in the frame's left half, demonstrating the emotional gap between the two men while affirming the continuity of time and space. Besides matching graphically in such a way, continuity editing may also *match on action*. Here a cut is made between two phases of a sustained event. From ground level, a person is shown starting to climb a flight of stairs; the next shot may be a high-angle view of her nearing the top, which avoids the potential longueur of seeing every step negotiated but has sufficient continuity of action to render unproblematic the time and space that have been edited

out. Matching of this sort need not be quite so dull. Near the end
of Hitchcock's *North by Northwest* (1959), Cary Grant reaches
down to rescue Eva Marie Saint from falling off one of the presi-
dential faces on Mount Rushmore; after a cut, his hand is still
extended, only now in order to pull her up to his bunk in a train's
sleeping compartment. While this advertises the transition
between shots far more flamboyantly than most matches on action,
the continuity of gesture – Grant's outstretched arm – still serves
to dispel any anxieties we might have about elisions of time and
space between the couple endangered in the mountains and now
amorous on a train.

As these examples of continuity conventions suggest, this form
of editing is designed to anchor the spectator securely in the filmic
world. Besides perfecting methods of fluent transition from one
shot to the next, it has developed elaborate protocols for the representation of cinematic space. One of the key strategies here is
analytical editing (or *découpage*, from the French for 'cutting up').
Whereas early in cinematic history action was often staged relatively far from a fixed camera position, analytical editing within
this broad continuity tradition aims to procure a sense of spatial
fluidity. Commonly, a rhythm develops whereby an initial long, or
establishing, shot of a particular location – a building, say, or landscape – gives way to a series of closer shots of the protagonists or
other centres of attention placed within it. As well as commanding
the space synoptically, the camera thus seems highly mobile across
its details. Note, however, that in the interests of maintaining a
quite rigid spatial logic its freedom of movement is liable to be
more curtailed than this suggests. Continuity editing favours *the
180° rule*, according to which a horizontal *axis of action* is considered to divide the screen into two semi-circles. This imaginary line
is drawn by joining together the foci of interest within a shot (a
simple example would be the line between two lovers running
towards each other). Continuity rules then dictate that, broadly
speaking, any cut to a new shot of these subjects should respect the
axis of action, rather than transgress it by originating from a
camera position on the other side of the line. Such an editing
convention aims to secure coherent spatial relations: for instance,
if one of the two lovers runs across the screen from right to left,

cutting next to a shot of her taken from the other side of the axis would reorient her as going from left to right and suggest, unhelpfully, that she has had a rethink about the relationship.

Despite its apparent mathematical rigour, the 180° rule is not fixed or binding. For a start, the axis of action may shift during a scene (as when the camera follows a character's movement to a point from which a new line can be established). Second, even filmmakers working broadly within the continuity tradition might seek on occasion to complicate spatial relations by including at least some *cross-line edits*. Nevertheless, the convention usually holds and serves to reassure the spectator of the stability of her viewing position. The rule's authority is especially evident in a familiar pattern of edits used during dialogue scenes: the sequence of *shot/reverse-shot*, whereby first one character, then the next, is seen from a position close to the other's perspective. If the two lovers above re-establish contact and begin to talk, continuity editing is likely to alternate shots of them from camera angles that do not violate an imaginary line drawn initially between their bodies (at least, not until they move and so legitimise a reoriented axis of action).

Continuity editing also seeks to stabilise filmic space by the practice of *eyeline matching*. Here a shot of someone looking towards something off-screen is followed by a shot which shows that object of interest. The film's world thereby seems made complete, with any uncertainty about what is not immediately visible resolved (though a horror movie may find it useful to delay eyeline matching to the character's source of panic). As further proof of the artifice of continuity editing – its relative lack of basis in human physiology itself – note that eyeline matches need not correspond in every respect with the onlooker's perspective: a cut to a previously off-screen building that a character is looking towards may show the building magnified to a size not optically justified by the character's location. Even less grounded in the properties of the human eye are those daring eyeline matches pioneered by such figures in early cinema history as D. W. Griffith. In Griffith's *Intolerance* (1916), a guilt-stricken woman looks off-screen; rather than cutting to a view of something in her vicinity, however, the next shot is of a far-off prison cell and the innocent man whom she has helped incarcerate. But, while this transition is for psychological rather than narrowly optical reasons, the fact that it is to a recognisable figure means that it still serves the eyeline match's customary functions of tidily connecting spaces and advancing narrative.

This particular example of eyeline matching is also a case of *cross-cutting*, that editorial procedure which intercuts two or more sequences of action that are occurring simultaneously but in different locations. Early cinema struggled to find a grammar to indicate simultaneous occurrence, and sometimes resorted to showing consecutively incidents that narrative context indicates happened at the same time. Griffith, on the other hand, is noted for what he called his 'switchbacks', cutting repeatedly between someone in peril and others racing to his or her rescue (one such switchback occurs at the climax of *Intolerance*, alternating between the falsely incriminated man approaching the scaffold and the party hurrying to confirm his innocence). Crucially, however, this breaking-up of the unity of place is still tolerable within the parameters of continuity editing. Cross-cutting in the kind of narrative cinema with which we are most familiar tends to occur between characters or locations whose relationship is already clear (or will shortly be so). By indicating simultaneity, cross-cutting also functions to stabilise rather than problematise a film's representation of time. It should thus be distinguished from *parallel editing*, in which alternating sequences of action do not share a temporal framework but, rather, belong to distinct periods whose narrative or symbolic connections the spectator is required to explore. For a sustained example of parallel editing, see Alain Resnais's *Hiroshima mon amour* (1959), which cuts between events in wartime France and post-war Japan.

STOP and THINK

• Using a short sequence from a mainstream film, make explicit what often goes unnoticed by analysing its continuity editing. How many shots are there? What is their average duration? Is the duration of shot fairly constant or subject to variation? What types of transition are employed between shots – straight cuts, dissolves, fade-outs, fade-ins and so on – and what are the consequences of these editing choices? Consider possible alterations to the bridge between any two shots in your sequence: how would meaning be modified if, say, a wipe was substituted for a straight cut?

- Observe how editing choices serve here to organise space. Is space articulated in accordance with the familiar continuity pattern of *découpage*, whereby an initial long shot of a scene is dissected into closer views? Is there also fidelity to such conventions as the 180° rule, shot/reverse-shot routines and eyeline matches? Or perhaps the sequence resists some or all of these manoeuvres, possibly violating the 180° rule by cross-line edits, or preferring to *découpage* a variant practice such as deep-focus editing? Whatever the editorial practices employed, assess whether they reinforce a sense of stable, coherent space or, rather, induce spatial disorientation in the spectator.

- Consider, too, how editing decisions in this sequence contribute to the representation of time. Does the editing evoke a generally coherent linearity? Is there evidence of cross-cutting, which multiplies the number of actions on-screen yet maintains temporal clarity by indicating their simultaneity? Or is there any hint of a problematising of time? As with your judgements on the sequence's spatial mapping, consider the implications of its temporal schema upon meaning production and spectator response.

Continuity editing and its discontents

With its emphasis upon fluency, clarity and coherence, continuity editing is ideally suited for the needs of that narrative cinema which began to develop, in the United States and elsewhere, early in the twentieth century. The techniques that have been outlined above serve in a given work to maintain the momentum of story-telling and to minimise spatial and temporal anomalies in the filmic world. The spectator enjoys seeming command of an intelligible cinematic space and is carried seamlessly from shot to shot by a now largely invisible system of cuts. As a result, she may be considered entirely absorbed by – or 'stitched into' – the film's spectacle (an effect known ominously in film studies as *suture*, after the term for medical stitching). But while this psychological binding of the viewer is clearly vital to narrative cinema's profitability, it is also the focus of critique by figures ranging from Soviet montage theorists to writers associated in the 1970s and 1980s with the radical British journal *Screen*. Continuity editing is strongly resisted from within these and other traditions for its perceived work of ideological conservatism.

We will defer until later in the book a fuller engagement with critiques of the ideology of mainstream cinema. This body of criticism, however, has been valuable in bringing the devices of continuity editing into visibility and showing their potential absorptive power with respect to the spectator. Nevertheless, to argue that the continuity system is always and everywhere complicit with a reactionary political position is open to counterarguments. For a start, the thesis erases variable, potentially complicating textual factors such as the genre to which a film belongs. Does a 1980 horror film have exactly the same ideological status as a 1950 musical simply by virtue of a common editorial pattern? The critique of continuity editing also tends to rely conceptually upon an essentialised, somewhat abstract film spectator, who is, in effect, immobilised by the kinds of device discussed above. The danger is that this overlooks the multiple contexts and modes of film spectatorship that actually exist and that often include the possibility of more dynamic interactions with filmic spectacle than is evoked by the suture model.

Negative accounts of continuity editing are also liable to homogenise it as a system, neglecting its internal variations and lines of experiment. David Bordwell has argued that developments in contemporary mainstream cinema merit a new term, 'intensified continuity' (a thesis first proposed in his article of the same title in *Film Quarterly*, Spring 2002). Bordwell has particularly in mind the increasingly rapid cutting of films now: in comparison with the stately few hundred shots typical of an average-length feature either side of the Second World War, a contemporary example might include a giddying 3,000 or more. Just as Bordwell seeks in his earlier work with Staiger and Thompson on classical Hollywood cinema to co-opt non-continuity practices into a hegemonic continuity system, here, too, he might be expanding unduly the scope of continuity. Even dizzyingly rapid cuts, apparently, do not destabilise its characteristic sense of coherent space and time to the point where a new conceptual framework is called for. Yet whether or not one shares Bordwell's views on the near-infinite adaptability of the continuity system, his thesis still allows for the possibility of its historical variation in a way that the thoroughgoing critiques do not.

At the other extreme to fast-paced cutting, *deep-focus editing* offers further evidence of continuity's capacity for internal modification. Films made according to this tendency eschew the familiar patterns of *découpage* – cutting from long shot into closer views of a scene – and instead show action occurring on the various planes of an image that is kept uniformly in focus. Rather than directed towards key events or motifs by analytical editing, the spectator herself is assigned responsibility for scanning the image for centres of significance. William Wyler, the mid-century American director regularly cited as an exponent of deep-focus, suggests that this particular mode of editorial intervention – or, perhaps, *non*-intervention – 'lets the spectator look from one to the other character, do his own cutting' ('No Magic Wand', *Screen Writer*, February 1947). Such activation of the spectator is stressed, too, by André Bazin, named in Chapter 1 as deep-focus editing's chief philosophical proponent. Bazin's essay, 'The Evolution of the Language of Cinema' – a composite of three shorter articles published in 1952–55 – makes the still bolder claims that, unlike editing systems based upon frequent cutting, deep-focus respects the integrity of the spatiotemporal continuum and echoes our distinctively human experiencing of the world (*What is Cinema?*, Vol. 1 (Berkeley, Los Angeles and London: University of California Press, 2005), pp. 23–40).

There is no need here to expand Chapter 1's doubts regarding Bazin's claims for deep-focus editing. Certainly, he risks universalising his sensitive response to a particular group of films into untenable claims about the essence of cinema itself. More to the point is whether, with its strictly limited cutting, deep-focus can be regarded as a variant of continuity editing at all or whether it is an entirely distinct practice. Bazin's choice of metaphors in his essay suggests a process of adaptation rather than categorical shift. Besides the evolutionary figure in his title, he compares the effect of deep-focus's innovations upon existing continuity practice to the deepening and widening of a river after a major geological event (p. 31). While we should be cautious about the application of the language of natural change to a cultural process like film history, Bazin's argument is still useful in allowing us, again, to recognise irregularities and alternatives within continuity editing. For all the counter-directions which deep-focus allows, however, narrative films such as Wyler's *The Best Years of Our Lives* are still bound to the continuity system by smooth transitions between scenes and orderly configuration of time and space. Typically, in these works, deep-focus sequences are also not absolute but combine with instances of analytical cutting.

Montage(s)

Montage is one of the most plural and unstable terms in film studies. Historically, it has slid back and forth between the particular and the universal, naming both highly specific editing options and the very process of film editing itself. For some users it is a word of flavourless technical description; for others, a term of provocation and controversy, marking intense struggles over the aesthetic and ideological potentialities of cinema. Here we briefly discuss some of the geographically and historically dispersed usages of the term, before turning to the version of montage that emerged in early Soviet cinema.

In French, the word 'montage' refers in very broad fashion to processes of assembly or organisation. Cinematic editing has no exclusive rights upon the term and is positioned as one more technical operation alongside such activities as electrical wiring. By contrast, 'montage' in everyday English usage often signifies not so much the entire feat of putting film images together as, rather, a specific editorial practice that developed for evoking economically the passage of time. Montage of this sort in older Hollywood cinema often condenses days, even years by a series of spinning newspaper headlines or the picturesque twirling of pages from a calendar. While the modern American editor Evan Lottman rejects this stylistic flourish as 'kind of old-fashioned and corny' (Gabriella Oldham, *First Cut*, p. 223), cinema still abbreviates time through montages comprising images of action in rapid succession, connected sonically by voiceover or music. Montage of this updated kind can serve serious purpose – as when lyrically conveying the spread of radical labour activism in John Sayles's *Matewan* (1987), a film discussed later – yet risks its own clichés. The contemporary 'dating' montage, for example, is dismantled by the police spoof, *The Naked Gun* (1988), where two lovers engage in a single day in ludicrously multiple activities from rodeo riding to cinemagoing.

Both flamboyant and temperate instances of this specialised montage-type have the effect of accelerating film narrative. The desire to advance cinematic storytelling also figured in those intense debates over the nature and power of montage which took place in the post-Revolutionary Soviet Union. Where Kuleshov refers enthusiastically to 'American montage', however, he signifies something other than the limited stylistic effects just discussed. He understands by the term a dynamic breaking-up of time and space by shot combination that promises to liberate film from more static, theatre-based forms of presentation. For Kuleshov, montage in this expanded sense is 'the essence of cinema'. Writing in 1918, he proposes the analogies that 'Montage is to cinema what colour composition is to painting or a harmonic sequence of sounds is to music' (Richard Taylor and Ian Christie (eds), *The Film Factory: Russian and Soviet Cinema in Documents, 1896–1939* (London: Routledge, 1994), pp. 46, 73).

But while Kuleshov inaugurated Soviet montage polemics, he was to be overpowered intellectually by his comrade, Eisenstein. By 1929, he was, in Eisenstein's damning assessment, 'the theoretically quite outmoded Lev Kuleshov' (*Selected Works*, Vol. 1, p. 163). Eisenstein concedes that both Kuleshov and his own occasional collaborator Vsevolod Pudovkin understand that cinema's distinctiveness lies not in the discrete image – otherwise it would only be a sub-species of photography – but in the articulation of multiple shots. Where they err, however, is in misconceiving the relationship between images. Eisenstein's satirical brio leads him to assert that, in the benighted film theory of Kuleshov and Pudovkin, one shot is seen as harmoniously connected to the next like links in a chain or bricks laid against each other (pp. 143–4). For Eisenstein, this merely serial accumulation of shots reduces cinema to a practice of efficient storytelling; it also distorts the true nature of film editing, since 'montage is conflict' (p. 144).

To read Eisenstein is an exhilarating intellectual and rhetorical adventure. However, a sober-minded search for his considered, summational views on montage is less satisfying. Although, in Jacques Aumont's phrase, 'Eisenstein equals montage' (*Montage Eisenstein* (Bloomington: Indiana University Press and London: BFI, 1987), p. 145), his montage-thought is less an elegantly fash-ioned object than a hectic lifelong process, full of conceptual leaps and contradictions. The reader must track modulations in ideas across his voluminous texts, besides correlating these with editing practice in the films he directed from the 1920s onwards. At his most expansive, the polymathic Eisenstein comes close to dissolv-ing montage as an object of cinema-specific inquiry, viewing it instead as a compositional principle visible in all aesthetic endeav-ours. The 'montage family tree' (*Selected Works*, Vol. 3, p. 216) that he constructs is less a tidily pollarded specimen than a crazily branched thing which extends to Greek architecture, Indian sculpture and Japanese poetry – also to Dickens, whose multi-centred narratives and scene dissection are taken to comprise an uncannily early 'cinema'. At his most miniaturising, however, Eisenstein is dissatisfied with waiting for the juxtaposition of one shot with another before montage occurs and boldly conceives of a kind of *intra*-shot montage as well: the single image no longer harmoniously disposes its elements but is itself riven by graphic or volumetric or kinetic clashes.

There are dangers, then, in attempting to distil a systematic Eisensteinian theory of montage from his multifarious writings on film. Nevertheless, we can identify key aspects of that particular, heightened form of shot combination which he terms 'intellectual montage'. Eisenstein argues that each new cinematic shot must represent not a mere quantitative addition to the one that comes before but a qualitative leap. Images should not smoothly succeed one another – for purposes only of narrative fluency – but be conflictively juxtaposed. Yet such juxtaposition will differ from the provocative combination of random images – prompted by unconscious association – that is especially identified with Surrealist filmmaking. In Eisenstein's stern words, 'the montage phrase' must comprise 'not just any two fragments and not in random proportions. But precisely and solely those which, when combined, will evoke the image, concept or idea that I shall determine in advance and that I wish to make' (*Selected Works*, Vol. 1, p. 267). Only a systematic, self-conscious arrangement of images will do, since 'the collision of marmalade and ground shinbone will not produce an explosion' (pp. 268, 287).

Note Eisenstein's incendiary metaphor here for filmmaking. If continuity editing has been taken by its critics to embed the spectator comfortably in the film text, such spectatorial inertia could not be further from Eisenstein's models of audience response to montage. The cinemagoer will, on the contrary, be assaulted and scourged: a correctly composed film 'ploughs' the spectator's sensibility, 'cuts through' to the skull and represents a 'fist' delivering a black eye. In a more scientific variant of this language of forceful reshaping, Eisenstein also draws on the contemporaneous researches of the physiologist Pavlov and describes reconditioning the spectator's reflexes through carefully considered juxtapositions on screen. Although these metaphors of physical brutalisation seem to imply a filmmaking practice chiefly intended to galvanise the spectator's body, Eisenstein speaks of a specifically *intellectual* montage. Images are combined in order to disrupt habitual patterns of thought in the viewer and yield a higher level of theoretical reflection.

Like any theory, Eisenstein's reflections on film emerge not from a pure realm of ideas but from specific historical conjunctures. His ideas took shape in the aftermath of the Russian Revolution, a period of intense agitation and experiment aimed at establishing a society transformed in its modes of art and thought as well as in its productive base. At times his concept of filmic juxtaposition seems *dialectical*, thus linking it to Marxist thought: its form and intended effect derive from the schema of thesis,

62	Beginning film studies

antithesis and synthesis, in which a clash of opposite terms is subsequently resolved or unified. To concretise this, take one of Eisenstein's famous montage phrases in *Oktaybr/October* (1927). The film narrates events in the Soviet Union in 1917, from the time of Aleksandr Kerensky's Provisional Government until the October triumph of the Bolsheviks led by Lenin. Oddly, a shot of Kerensky relishing his quasi-Tsarist power in the Winter Palace cuts not to a scene of obvious narrative connection but to a mechanical peacock spreading its feathers (Figure 4). Yet if these two seemingly discrete shots are conceptualised as thesis and antithesis, they can be seen to ignite a moment of intellectual synthesis: suddenly, there is recognition of Kerensky's preening, counter-revolutionary tendencies that might not be conveyed by actor performance alone. Thus the Soviet spectator is mobilised to repudiate the incomplete version of change represented by the Provisional Government and to embrace Bolshevik radicalism instead.

There is a long history of dissent within film studies to this type

Figure 4 Mechanical peacock in one of Eisenstein's montage phrases from *Oktaybr/October* (Soviet Union, 1927).

of montage. Critical voices including Bálazs, Bazin and Kracauer – as well as the later Soviet filmmaker, Andrei Tarkovsky, given in his own work to a lyrical, extended compositional mode rather than to rapid Eisensteinian juxtapositions – deplore what they see as montage's simple-mindedness. Bálazs describes Eisenstein as fatally drawn towards 'film-hieroglyphics', an imagistic mode that yields blatant, easily decipherable meanings. For Kracauer, who values above all else in cinema the medium's capacity for photographic revelation of the world, the problem with Eisenstein's montages is that 'They stand for something outside them; any peacock would do, indeed.' More impoverished even than hieroglyphs, they are 'rebuses which, once solved, lose all their magic' (*Theory of Film: The Redemption of Physical Reality* (New York: Oxford University Press, 1960), p. 208). Yet despite some perceptiveness, these and similar critiques dwindle in their power when we recognise that they are based not upon unimpeachable, absolute grounds of judgement but, more vulnerably, on alternative models of cinema that may themselves be resisted. To reject Eisenstein's montage because of its comprehensible meanings risks overvaluing ambiguity as an aesthetic criterion. Such a view also takes no account of the fact that his films emerged at a time still of political uncertainty in the Soviet Union and were primarily designed not to cultivate nuance but to reinforce revolutionary consciousness in their audiences. Likewise, Kracauer's complaint regarding the scene from *October* that 'any peacock would do' seems almost what philosophers call a category mistake. This sequence is, after all, more intent on satirising counter-revolutionary traitors than observing ornithological particularities.

More damaging to Eisenstein is the argument that there is no *necessary* correlation between montage as he theorises it and a radical politics. While his own films derive politically oppositional effects from the montage phrase, this combinatory form may in itself be neutral, capable of being filled by shots of quite different ideological valency. That this could be the case is glimpsed in Eisenstein's own polymathic forays into aesthetic fields besides cinema. If montage, as a form predicated upon conflictive juxtaposition, is observed everywhere from primitive sculpture to nineteenth-century American poetry, then it seems open to appropriation for diverse cultural and ideological purposes rather than inevitably aligned with the cause of revolution. Stam makes a similar point when he notes the danger of contemporary commercial exploitation of a schema such as Eisenstein's: 'shorn of its dialectical basis ... Eisensteinian "associationist" montage could easily be transformed into the commodified ideograms of advertising, where the whole is more than the sum of its parts: Catherine Deneuve plus Chanel No. 5 signifies charm, glamour, and erotic appeal' (*Film Theory*, p. 41). As with mise-en-scène features discussed in Chapter 1, the effects of particular editing practices cannot be confidently tabulated in advance of their use in a given context.

Meanings of the jump cut

The ideological promiscuity of techniques in editing may be further illustrated by a brief case study of *the jump cut*. Unlike the effect of smooth progression achieved by straight cutting, the jump cut, unsurprisingly, produces a jerky or staccato transition from one shot to the next. It should be distinguished from two sorts of editorial juxtaposition – Soviet montage and the rapid cutting of 'intensified continuity'– with which it otherwise shares some disorienting potential. Rather, the jump cut registers as an uncanny jolt in a film's advance, drawing the spectator's attention to disturbing elisions of time and space. A film might cut abruptly from one location to the next without any attempt to employ those matches of eyeline or action or graphic property that are central to the continuity mode. Or, within a single scene, it may violate another mathematically derived tenet of continuity: *the 30° rule*. This convention decrees that, where a new shot has the same subject as the preceding one, the cut between them should justify its existence by producing a change of angle of not less than 30°. Without such a geometric variation, the new shot risks looking superfluous or awkward, a glitch in the editorial machinery.

Given that the term was adopted in 1974 as the title of an important, left-leaning journal in film studies, we might assume that 'jump cut' invariably carries progressive credentials. The history of its uses, however, discloses a plurality of motivations and effects. It first appears because of technological limitations rather than any radical agenda. When early makers of 'actualities' shot an event from a fixed camera position, their only way of including just the most salient moments on the relatively short reel of film was to stop the camera at some point and then restart it, the identical angle of the second shot resulting in a jump cut. Other filmmakers saw creative possibilities in this otherwise utilitarian elision of time. The French pioneer Georges Méliès recognised that a jump cut could generate magical or comic effects if the appearance of a subject filmed from a single vantage point was altered between shots. While it anticipates radical practice by demonstrating the artifice – rather than 'naturalness' – of film composition, this manoeuvre is nevertheless playful rather than politically earnest.

Modern use of the jump cut is more associated with ideologically purposeful filmmaking, in particular, perhaps, the work of Jean-Luc Godard. Beginning with his first full-length film, *A bout de souffle / Breathless* (1959) and continuing through films of the 1960s and beyond, Godard utilises the jump cut as a disruptive device. At times the technique still operates within largely familiar cinematic composition: in *Breathless*, successive shots from the same angle of the female protagonist in a speeding car condense time and space without questioning filmic illusion entirely. Later in Godard's work, however, in more troubling fashion, the jump cut frequently occurs between entire sequences and so heightens a sense of their disconnection. Yet note that it is still only one item in his array of devices for systematically dismantling continuity cinema. His films also distort soundtrack, or use intertitles that signal – sometimes sardonically – a pedagogic intent, or include characters aware, in Brechtian fashion, of their own constructed status. Godard attempts thereby a genuinely radical cinematic practice, one which asserts traditional film narrative's complicity with the structures of power and seeks new forms that will answer to the radical political movements of the 1960s in France and beyond.

Nevertheless, there can be no guarantee that the jump cut, in and of itself, transmits political radicalism. Deprived of its place in a larger revisionary apparatus, it may still serve less challenging purposes. Consider the jump cuts used during the Normandy landing sequence of Spielberg's *Saving Private Ryan* (1998). Certainly, use here of the technique corrects dainty representations of war familiar from earlier cinema. Because they intensify a sense of war's visceral aspects, however, Spielberg's jump cuts actually share continuity editing's aim of suturing the spectator more tightly into the spectacle (rather than, as with Godard's practice, provoking questions about the cinematic illusion itself). The jump cut may thus become part of narrative cinema's extended formal repertoire, instead of always signifying oppositional intent. If further evidence were needed of its liability to mainstream appropriation, recall a Stella Artois advertisement, *Le Sacrifice* (2005) that was constructed to look like a rediscovered Surrealist film. Images were cut together in staccato fashion, their non-logical transitions mimicking early avant-garde cinema. Yet the whole exercise was a nakedly commodified one, intended simply to boost lager sales. As with Stam's observations earlier on the potentially banal fate of those montage phrases that advanced Bolshevik revolution, here, too, in advertising's turn to the jump cut, we see a formerly oppositional tactic seized by the very capitalism it was once deployed against.

STOP and THINK

• This chapter has suggested it might not be possible to align particular editing practices with fixed ideological meanings. Test this thesis with examples from different film traditions. Consider initially whether it is possible to reach a decision on the politics of continuity editing. As noted above, radical critiques of continuity indict it for its manufacture of the passive spectator who is tied into cinematic illusion and carried from shot to shot as smoothly as the film itself advancing over its sprockets. Would you agree with this assessment of spectator quiescence? Or does this theory strike you as too dogmatic and despairing a calculation of the effects of continuity editing?

• By way of contrast, explore the politics of anti-continuity cinema: examples might include Eisenstein's intellectual montages in *Strike, October* or *Battleship Potemkin* (1925) or Godard's use of the jump cut in his 1960s work. Assess the effect upon the spectator of these editing practices. Consider whether they carry an oppositional charge that may still be activated by filmmakers, or whether there is a danger of their routinisation now as part of the mainstream cinematic repertoire.

Analysing editing: *Strike* and *Matewan*

Eisenstein's *Stachka/Strike* (1924) and Sayles's *Matewan* are linked by subject matter. Set respectively in a Russian factory town before the Revolution and the West Virginia coalfields in 1920, they both narrate the course of labour struggle from initial optimism to ultimate, bloody defeat. In other ways, however, these are radically distinct works. They are marked, to begin with, by very different circumstances of production. While *Strike* is Eisenstein's first feature, it is less an individual experimentalist's vision than part of collectively organised cinematic output in the early Soviet Union. The film was envisaged not as a self-contained project but as one component of *Towards the Dictatorship*, an officially designed yet ultimately uncompleted seven-film sequence narrating the origins and course of the Russian Revolution. *Matewan*, by contrast, lacks such powerful backing and is the fifth feature of an American director and screenwriter who works independently of the mainstream. It rests upon 'this pastiche of money' (*Sayles on Sayles*, p. 121), with some funding provided by a small production company, some by investors and the rest by Sayles himself from pieces of Hollywood hackwork. Besides this asymmetry in cultural status, the two films also differ markedly in their formal paradigms: *Strike* is the first practical exercise in Eisensteinian montage, while *Matewan* observes a modified version of continuity editing.

Their shared story material, however, offers a good opportunity to reconsider the politics of variant editing practices. Since both films plainly have the intention of showing labour activism in a sympathetic light, setting them against each other raises the question of whether different spectator responses may be generated by differences in editing itself. Compared with *Strike*, *Matewan* is, in its director's own words, 'very dissolve-y and slow' (*Sayles on Sayles*, p. 188). At least until the climax, it tends to resist contemporary continuity editing's preference for the straight cut and to rely instead upon dissolves and slow fades. Rather than being rudely pushed aside by the next shot, images overlap or succeed each other lyrically. This editing mode inhibits any suggestion of trauma or crisis (Sayles has written about how important a cyclical sense of time is to this corner of the US). Signs of social change within the narrative itself – as the miners struggle for union recognition – thus risk obliteration by editorial emphasis instead upon recurrence and harmony.

By contrast, cuts come thick and fast in *Strike*, helping to evoke a dynamic, conflictive political situation. Where Eisenstein does use a dissolve, it carries a polemical force, rather than the lyricism achieved by Sayles. Early on, the faces of three agents-provocateurs employed by the factory manager dissolve into the features of, respectively, a monkey, an owl and a bulldog (there was to be a frog, too, but Eisenstein rejected as lacking the necessary bulbous ugliness the specimens his crew obtained from a freezing lake). In these dissolve sequences, Eisenstein constructs a rudimentary montage phrase. The juxtaposition of seemingly unrelated shots – humans followed by animals – precipitates the spectator's understanding of the 'bestial' nature of the managerial class in pre-Soviet Russia. Such moments compose a cinematic hieroglyph or rebus of the kind disliked by Bálazs and Kracauer. So, too, does the most vivid of *Strike*'s montages, which occurs very near the end. Scenes of the strikers and their families brutally cut down by mounted troops are intercut with shots – originating from outside the film's narrative – of a bull being slaughtered for meat (Figure 5). Eisenstein writes that whereas footage of an abattoir used elsewhere by Vertov is of merely documentary interest, his own incorporation of such scenes is '*gorily effective*' (*Selected Works*, Vol. 1, p. 63). The montage forces an equation between two forms of slaughter – not to advance vegetarian sentiment, of course, but to consolidate rage against owners who are prepared to

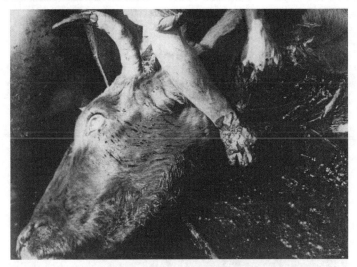

Figure 5 Slaughtered bull in *Stachka / Strike* (Soviet Union, 1924).

regard their own workforce as so many carcasses for disposal.

There is no such enraging conclusion to *Matewan*. While the film's habitually slow rhythm is varied near the end by an increased pace of cutting, this is not in order to produce a searing sense of contradiction between classes. Indeed, the director describes trying to edit the final shoot-out sequence so as 'to really make it flow' (*Sayles on Sayles*, p. 136) (Figure 6). Fluidity, of course, is precisely what Eisenstein does *not* want at the conclusive point of his own film; instead, he seeks an editing style which promotes the jarring and discontinuous. Sayles's alternative emphasis upon flowing rhythms does not exactly function to reunite boss and worker, but it perhaps minimises any sense of fracture and evokes a continuous, eternal time within which political differences are absorbed as transient. Lacking Eisenstein's immediate polemical context for his work, Sayles disavows satirical or agitating montages and aims instead to register human complexities (albeit still within the framework of sympathy for the striking miners).

However, we should pause before reaching the simple conclusion that it is entirely because of montage that *Strike* serves

Figure 6 The fluidly edited gunfight at the end of *Matewan* (US, 1987).

revolutionary praxis and, conversely, that the tendency of *Matewan* towards political quiescence is attributable to its continuity-based system of editing. Rather than abstracting editing strategies in this way, it is important also to consider the impact upon the ideological status of the two films of historically and culturally variable conditions of spectatorship. Here we follow the lead of Eisenstein himself, where he recognises that, without appropriately receptive audiences, even the most daring montage phrases may be empty or inert. While his film theory generally implies a somewhat decontextualised spectator who always responds in the intended way, he acknowledges that viewers of the climactic montage in *Strike* are liable to react variably. A 'worker audience' in the Soviet Union, for example, might not be shocked by the juxtaposition of human and bovine casualties, because of its own proximity to urban abattoirs; a 'peasant', used to slaughtering his or her own beasts, is even less likely to be stirred (*Selected Works*, Vol. 1, pp. 65–6). This montage, then, risks remaining purely virtual, in need of activation by some other audience that will make the necessary metaphoric leap between shots of a bull and of striking workers and invoke the idea of a 'human slaughter-house' that requires redemption by a new political settlement.

Even the programmatic forms of Soviet montage are thus incomplete without the spectator's appropriately channelled inter-pretive activity. The political potency of *Strike* is traceable not only to Eisenstein's editorial brilliance but to the fact that the film originally appeared in a time of political ferment, to audiences already ideologically primed for rousing narratives of oppressive bosses and martyred labourers. *Matewan*, on the other hand, emerged in a context much less conducive to agitative viewing. Its release in the late 1980s coincided with the corporate splurges of Reaganomics, when American labour – indeed, the cause of the US left generally – was in a state of crisis. The film's own editing decisions – evoking continuity and organicism rather than fracture – may already reflect and reinforce that mood of political retrenchment. At the same time, however, *Matewan*'s lack of revo-lutionary impetus cannot be ascribed purely to its editorial manoeuvres. After all, it is possible to imagine other spectatorial conditions – times of increased labour militancy, say – in which even the film's dissolves and fades will not prevent its narrative of heartless mine owners and their hired thugs from having a radical-ising effect.

Selected reading

Besides the specialist titles below, see also the books by Bordwell/Thompson and Corrigan/White cited in Chapter 1.

Crittenden, Roger, *Fine Cuts: The Art of European Film Editing* (Oxford and Burlington, MA: Focal Press, 2006).

Valuable counterpart to Oldham's volume, comprising interviews with European editors active from the *Nouvelle vague* to more recent films by Catherine Breillat, Patrice Chéreau and Lars von Trier.

Eisenstein, S. M., *Selected Works*, Vols. 1–3, ed. Richard Taylor (London: BFI, 1988–96).

Indispensable, expertly annotated edition of writings by cinema's foremost philosopher-practitioner. With prodigious energy and huge erudition, Eisenstein theorises all aspects of film, but constantly returns to the key topic of montage. Though Vol. 2 is subtitled 'Towards a Theory of Montage', Vols. 1 and 3 include more concentrated statements of Eisenstein's montage-thought.

Fairservice, Don, *Film Editing: History, Theory and Practice* (Manchester: Manchester University Press, 2001).

Theoretically underdeveloped in places but accessible, well-researched and wide-ranging in its choice of examples of significant editing practice.

Morrey, Douglas, *Jean-Luc Godard* (Manchester: Manchester University Press, 2005).

Lucid review of Godard's career, placing his experiments in the disjunctive editing of film in broader cinematic, cultural and political contexts.

Nesbet, Anne, *Savage Junctures: Sergei Eisenstein and the Shape of Thinking* (London and New York: I. B. Tauris, 2003).

Useful companion to Eisenstein's own writings, providing a timely reassessment of the totality of his cinematic thought and practice. Includes detailed analysis of *Strike*.

Oldham, Gabriella, *First Cut: Conversations with Film Editors* (Berkeley, Los Angeles and London: University of California Press, 1992).

Homelier and less intellectually rigorous than the dialogues of Ondaatje and Murch but valuable for first-hand assessments of shifts in editing practice in American cinema, including documentary filmmaking, since 1940.

Ondaatje, Michael, *The Conversations: Walter Murch and the Art of Editing Film* (New York: Knopf, 2002).

Wonderfully eloquent, learned and suggestive dialogues. Drawing upon his work on such films as *The Godfather*, *Apocalypse Now* and *The English Patient*, Murch explores the aesthetic complexities of picture and sound editing.

Orpen, Valerie, *Film Editing: The Art of the Expressive* (London: Wallflower, 2002).

A convenient place to start; without Fairservice's historical range and detail but clear, concise and including case studies of editing patterns in such films as Hitchcock's *Rear Window* and Scorsese's *Raging Bull*.

Reisz, Karel and Gavin Millar, *The Technique of Film Editing*, 2nd ed. (London and New York: Focal Press, 1968).

Long superseded by other books as a compilation of editing practices, yet still of historical interest. While Reisz's original text, written in 1953, follows the prescriptions of Anglo-American continuity editing, Millar's 1968 additions are shaped instead by enthusiasm for European editing experiments.

Sayles, John, *Thinking in Pictures: The Making of the Movie 'Matewan'* (Cambridge, MA: Da Capo Press, 2003).

Detailed, illuminating account of the film's genesis and production – and editing. Also includes the screenplay.

Useful websites

www.hatii.arts.gla.ac.uk/MultimediaStudentProjects/98-99/9505060m/html.

Friendly, yet erudite site on Eisenstein's struggles to develop a cinematically and politically effective form of montage.

3

Hearing film: analysing soundtrack

For the pianist and conductor Daniel Barenboim, hearing is 'the neglected sense'. He says in the 2006 BBC Reith Lectures that 'we not only neglect the ear, but we often repress it'. Barenboim has musical contexts in mind, citing the decay caused to previously acute modes of listening by the permeation of Muzak into public spaces and the reduction of symphonies to advertising jingles. Nevertheless, his thesis of an inequality of the senses may be extended to film studies itself. Historically, the ear in this discipline has been subordinated to the prestige of the eye. From the scientific to the popular, the medium's very names inscribe the pre-eminence of the visual: the term *film* itself draws attention not to a mixed-media experience but to the material on which a photographic record of events is left; while, at the colloquial level, *pictures* could hardly be more 'ocularcentric'. This original naming has cast a long shadow over subsequent approaches to film. Claudia Gorbman is typical of many scholars of cinematic sound in referring to the discipline's tendency towards 'visual chauvinism' (*Unheard Melodies: Narrative Film Music*, p. 2). Even Michel Chion – the French composer and theorist who has perhaps done more than any other writer to restore and conceptualise the neglected acoustic dimension of film – says gloomily that 'The sound-camel continues to pass through the eye of the visual needle' (*Audio-Vision: Sound on Screen*, p. 143).

This trumping of the ear by the eye reverses what we know about the relative development of the two senses. While the infant in the womb keeps its eyelids closed until approximately twenty-six weeks old, it is already immersed in a soundscape as complex as one of David Lynch's, with ears sufficiently developed from eighteen weeks onwards to register its mother's voice, her intestinal resonances and the gurgling of her blood vessels. If not quite the originary sense – the infant's responsiveness to touch, for example, begins at eight weeks – sound still has a suggestive temporal priority over vision. Later, we will see several theorists of film music alluding to these experiences in the womb. Yet film studies more broadly should acknowledge what human biology tells us about hearing's fundamental role in the making of meaning. From the beginning, after all, cinema has palpably been a mixed sensory form, acoustic as well as visual; indeed, Chion proposes that we no longer speak of a film's 'viewer' but refer instead to an 'audio-spectator' engaged in 'audio-viewing'. Less explicitly, Christian Metz also contests the hegemony of the eye within the discipline when he enumerates the five 'tracks', or 'matters of expression', that signify in cinema. There is here an auditory majority: only two of the tracks are visual phenomena (the photographic image itself; writing that appears on screen); the remaining three – dialogue, music and sound effects – are provinces of the ear.

In *Audio-Vision* Chion offers the aphorism – seemingly a crisis for the text in which it appears – that 'there is no soundtrack' (p. 39). He means there can be no discrete laying-out of soundtrack components, since each sound's 'horizontal' relation to the next is complicated or overridden by its 'vertical' articulation with the image that accompanies it. But while taking Chion's point, this chapter, like that on mise-en-scène, still assumes the usefulness of temporarily isolating a key element of cinematic form. Later we will consider some terminology for analysis of a film's acoustic composition. First, however, we discuss important stages in the history of cinematic sound, beginning with the paradoxical noisiness of silent film.

Deafening silents

Chapter 1 cited Maxim Gorky's anxiety, while watching a programme of films by the Lumières in 1896, that all the colours in the world had leached away. But if Gorky found the cinematic spectacle 'dipped in monotonous grey', it struck him with no less force as ominously silent. Carriages could clearly be seen on screen rolling along a Paris street, yet

> no rumble of the wheels is heard, no sound of footsteps or of speech. Nothing. Not a single note of the intricate symphony that always accompanies the movements of people. Noiselessly, the ashen-grey foliage of the trees sways in the wind, and the grey silhouettes of the people, as though condemned to eternal silence and cruelly punished by being deprived of all the colours of life, glide noiselessly along the grey ground. (Jay Leyda, *Kino: A History of the Russian and Soviet Film* (London: Allen and Unwin, 1960), p. 407)

Spooked by this new medium, Gorky writes that it presents 'not motion, but its soundless spectre'. His spectral metaphor – registering the uncanny combination of movement and silence – has been taken up by several later writers on cinema. Kracauer describes how the images of silent film 'affect us as a ghost-like replica of the world we live in – the limbo through which the deaf are moving' (*Theory of Film: The Redemption of Physical Reality* (New York: Oxford University Press, 1960), p. 135). Such noiseless motion violates the true evocation of the world that he prizes, and he therefore welcomes the addition of sound to the medium as a defence against any ghostly, estranging effects. For Theodor Adorno and Hanns Eisler, meanwhile, it is not so much sound in general as music in particular that functions to protect the spectator of early film from 'the unpleasantness involved in seeing effigies of living, acting, and even speaking persons, who were at the same time silent' (*Composing for the Films*, p. 75).

While all these expressions of anxiety are powerful, they nevertheless overstate the silence of 'silent' film. The screen watched by Gorky might itself have been mute, but the luxurious theatre-cum-brothel in which the exhibition took place was not; indeed, he is rescued from the fearful silence by ambient noises: 'suddenly, alongside of you, a gay chatter and a provoking laughter of a woman is heard . . . and you remember that you are at Aumont's' (p. 408). Gorky may also be repressing other, less glamorous acoustic phenomena. His account of the mechanical processes of film exhibition is confined to saying that 'something clicks', and he leaves unmentioned the whirring of the projector itself (a machine that prior to soundproof projection booths was noisily – sometimes catastrophically, given the combustibility of early nitrate film – housed in the auditorium). To itemise incidental laughs and clicks in this way may seem trifling and far removed from the project of analysing the composition of soundtrack; yet it accords with a recent turn within the discipline towards registering the materiality of the film experience itself, including acoustic stimuli whatever their sources.

But even if we discount Gorky's laughing woman as irrelevant to serious considerations of film sound, it is crucial to recognise the multiple ways in which early cinema was an audiovisual medium. While several decades would pass before the material integration of vision and sound – an optical soundtrack was first placed on the edge of the filmstrip itself around 1930 – exhibitors from the very beginnings of cinema devised a wide range of acoustic accompaniments for the image. Some of the most exciting work in recent film studies has been in documenting and theorising this variegated soundscape. Scholars such as Rick Altman and James Lastra have urged that silent cinema be seen as a truly performative medium, one which offered not so much on-screen spectacle in isolation as an interaction between spectacle and sound-generating activities in the auditorium. Most frequently, silent films were accompanied by live musical performance: depending on the venue, music might be supplied by a solitary pianist or organist, or by a larger ensemble, even a full-scale orchestra. But there were many sounds other than music in the acoustic environment of early film. Images were sometimes interpreted by a lecturer stationed near the screen (a function that generally disappeared as narrative cues were integrated into films themselves, but that survived in places, as in Japan where lecturers, or *benshi*, were culturally important until the 1930s). On other occasions, performers might provide a range of sound effects – from the feeble to the breathtaking – to synchronise with on-screen actions. More ambitiously still, the silent film itself would sometimes be only one component of an elaborate multi-media event, playing alongside actors engaged in live theatre.

Within these diverse exhibition practices, the relations of image and sound were fluid rather than stable and hierarchical. For every spectator drawn to the nickelodeon or, a little later, to the newly built cinemas by film's visual magic, there was another who attended chiefly because of the virtuoso playing of a favourite pianist. Lastra also refers to the early practice of 'funning' a film, whereby the authority, even coerciveness of the image was subverted by parodic musical accompaniment from the auditorium (*Sound Technology and the American Cinema: Perception, Representation, Modernity*, p. 112). Another early mode of cinema exhibition – the 'illustrated song' – even hints at a new power relationship in which sound may be privileged and the image seem secondary or belated. As first a soloist and then the entire audience sang a romantic ballad or comic song, a series of slides would appear on screen, as if conjured up by sound itself. Although the illustrated song belongs to silent cinema's earliest period, its inverting of the hierarchy of image and sound can be traced in later film also (as well as in specialised visual forms such as MTV). Sequences in Leone's *Once Upon a Time in the West* (1968), say, may be regarded as 'illustrations' of Ennio Morricone's music, which had already been composed before shooting began.

Sound and fury

The coming of synchronised sound in the late 1920s was of more than merely technological significance. In adding to the quantity of cinema's formal options, sound also became a privileged site for arguments about the nature of film itself. As the complexity of soundtracks accompanying the image increased – from the Vitaphone discs attempting rudimentary and partial synchronisation that were supplied for *Don Juan* (1926) and *The Jazz Singer* (1927) to the fuller acoustic track imprinted on the filmstrip – voices could be heard pronouncing that this development was the death of cinema or, on the contrary, its liberation. Rudolf Arnheim, whose despondency regarding the arrival of colour was mentioned in Chapter 1, was just as melancholy about the sound era. Writing in 1928, he concedes that it might benefit cinema 'in the areas of instruction and journalism' but adds that it threatens the integrity of silent film art that had been carefully elaborated over three decades (*Film Essays and Criticism* (Madison: University of Wisconsin Press, 1997), p. 30). In another essay written a few years into the regime of sound film, Arnheim acknowledged there had been interesting experiments of asynchronism between acoustic and image tracks; however, he found most works to be dully or redundantly matching picture and sound in a way that betrayed cinema's artistic vocation. Yet where Arnheim deplored the violence that sound did to the aesthetics of silent film, Salvador Dalí welcomed it. For Dalí cinema had become increasingly formalist and abstract, and the addition of soundtrack functioned as a corrective: 'Sound cinema brings with it a marvellous impurity ... the reestablishment of certain notions of the concrete' (Paul Hammond (ed.), *The Shadow and Its Shadow: Surrealist Writings on the Cinema*, 2nd ed. (Edinburgh: Polygon, 1991), p. 72).

Such debates over film sound were cast, at times, in almost theological language. While Arnheim does not explicitly draw upon biblical rhetoric in his pessimistic account of a fall into sound, the French Surrealist Marcel Mariën is perhaps evoking cinema's long Good Friday when he describes weeping over 'the tomb of silent pictures' (*The Shadow and Its Shadow*, p. 151). From the other side of the argument, André Bazin mobilised the trope of resurrection when he wrote that, because of the increase it allows in the medium's realist power, 'sound has given proof that it came not to destroy but to fulfil the Old Testament of the cinema' (*What is Cinema?*, Vol. 1 (Berkeley, Los Angeles and London: University of California Press, 2005), p. 23).

In thinking about the relation of sound film to silent, two things seem advisable. First, as noted above, it is crucial to inventory silent film's multiple sounds and so to recognise that it was already an experience not solely governed by the image. Second, we should be cautious about the extremes of rhetoric deployed by both sides in this debate. After all, there is no 'essence' of cinema to be either betrayed or realised by the coming of sound; instead, more modestly, there is a range of film practices, not assessable by appeal to some ideal cinematic form. Such caution against narratives variously of regression or fulfilment is important, given the temptation they continue to exert for some commentators on film sound. Invited to call the Dolby era the 'second coming of sound', the contemporary Hollywood sound editor Bruce Stambler replies that he would rather describe the present as 'the coming of sound, period! ... because we didn't really have sound. We pretty much had dialogue and had a centre speaker [behind the cinema screen] and that was it' (Gianluca Sergi, *The Dolby Era: Film Sound in Contemporary Hollywood*, p. 134). For a film professional, the era of Vitaphone discs must indeed seem impoverished compared with the present regime of digital sound manipulation and speakers positioned all around the cinema delivering an acoustic experience Chion terms the 'superfield'. However, it is possible to register technological changes of this sort – and to explore the undoubted shifts which they engineer in our responses to film – without thereby constructing a story of cinema's redemption (or of its death).

Terminologies of sound analysis

Rick Altman wishes to take into account all of the auditory materials produced by the film experience. Analysis should focus not only upon those textual elements of dialogue, music and effects contained within the soundtrack of a given work but on their interplay with *contextual* soundtracks also: 'the kids in the front rows, the air conditioner hum, the lobby cash register, the competing sound track in the adjacent multiplex theater, passing traffic' ('General Introduction: Cinema as Event', *Sound Theory/Sound Practice*, p. 6). This list can be infinitely extended: the rustling of popcorn, the 'ringing' of mobile phones or murmurs of conversation when audio-viewing a film at home. This broader interpretation of 'soundtrack' has greatly enriched our knowledge of diverse cultures of film reception. Exemplary in this regard is Annette Kuhn's *An Everyday Magic: Cinema and Cultural Memory* (New York and London: I. B. Tauris, 2002), which recalls the auditory chaos of pre-war cinema matinees in Britain as children would crack open monkey nuts and stamp clog-covered feet on bare wooden boards. Besides movingly retrieving the detail of lives often ignored by scholarship, Kuhn's account also remodels cinemagoing so that it is perceived less as passive textual reception and more as an interactive process that involves, among other things, the making of noise.

Nevertheless, there are risks in a sociological approach to the sounds of film. To begin with, the listing of noises generated by any film experience may produce information of such detail, eclecticism and even triviality as to resist theorisation. A proper interest in ambient sound may be taken so far that it threatens to overpower or displace the films themselves. Research into the acoustics of draining milkshakes in the American multiplex, say, might carry as much conceptual weight as a study of the carefully calibrated soundtracks of those Robert Altman films which the drinkers are watching. Kuhn, to be sure, avoids this pitfall, since her book juxtaposes the active audience with the textual force itself of such works as early horror films and Astaire/Rogers musicals. However, it is because of these dangers that the remainder of this section seeks to restore the text itself to centre-stage and, at least provisionally, to detach the film soundtrack from more incidental noises that accrue around it.

Yet establishing a universally shared terminology for the analysis of soundtrack has proved difficult. There is agreement at least that it comprises four basic elements: *speech (including voiceover besides dialogue)*, *music*, *sound effects* and *silence*. These elements will be disposed in various combinations and rhythms, and may be subject to hierarchical ordering. Conventionally, within narrative cinema, the highest premium has been put upon the intelligibility of dialogue: hence the potential disorientation of films like Altman's *McCabe and Mrs Miller* (1971) and *Nashville* (1975), with their overlapping and fading voices. Walter Murch notes how Hollywood's practice in this regard tends to occlude other acoustic materials in which he is interested: 'Dialogue is the moon, and stars are the sound effects' (Michael Ondaatje, *The Conversations: Walter Murch and the Art of Editing Film* (New York: Knopf, 2002), p. 175). Murch does not mention music, the subject of this chapter's next section. Nor does he say anything here about silence, the fourth possible component of soundtrack. Paradoxically, according to Robert Bresson, silence as a strategic choice of the filmmaker began with the sound era; where it occurred in pre-talkies cinema, it might have been only an accidental outcome, as when the pianist paused for breath.

Beyond this initial categorising of sound groups, however, rival terminologies multiply. As an aspect of film form, sound proves more elusive than image. There is, to begin with, no exact auditory equivalent of the image's minimal unit, the shot. On the visual track a long shot might cut to a medium shot, then to a close-up; but can a comparably straightforward account be given of the acoustic sequencing here? In addition, whereas image analysis focuses only upon the space of the screen, discussions of film sound – at least in the stereo era – must be alert to its dispersal, the sense it may be all around us and occupying significant off-screen places. Even when critics pinpoint particular sounds, they differ on how to describe their quality. Bordwell and Thompson's preferred terms – *volume, pitch, timbre* – are not unhelpful but have been criticised for drawing too heavily upon musical precedents. The same dissension occurs with regard to attempts to describe the overall effects of a soundtrack: Bordwell and Thompson suggest in *Film Art* that it has attributes of *rhythm, fidelity, space* and *time*, whereas Sergi's own quadripartite model in *The Dolby Era* favours *orchestration, contrast, focus* and *definition*.

Different vocabularies have emerged, also, for the fundamental relationship between what is audible on the soundtrack and what is visible on screen. Influentially, Reisz and Millar's *The Technique of Film Editing*, 2nd ed. (London and New York: Focal Press, 1968) proposed that, in this respect, film sounds be divided into two broad types, *actual* and *commentative*. Actual sounds are those that can be ascribed to a visible or implied on-screen source, as when a character variously speaks or plays her guitar or produces noise by starting the car engine. Commentative sounds, on the other hand, name those acoustic phenomena which have no point of origin on screen, such as voiceover and musical score. While Reisz and Millar's attempt at a basic typology of film sounds has survived into work by later scholars, their favoured terms have been challenged because of their potential for confusion (an 'actual' sound could prove to be an engineer's ingenious construction; it may also have the commentative sound's characteristic revelatory function, as when the character's choice of guitar piece says something about her state of mind). Instead of 'actual' and 'commentative', most critics now prefer the more technical terms *diegetic* and *non-diegetic*, respectively (*diegesis*, from the Greek for 'narration' or 'recital', referring in this context to the narrative world of a film).

'Diegetic' and 'non-diegetic' mark out two indispensable categories into one or other of which film sounds may be assigned. We should acknowledge, however, that critical work on soundtrack has also been interested in those difficult or ambiguous cases on the diegetic/non-diegetic borderline. In *Audio-Vision* Chion suggests numerous terms for a more refined cataloguing of film sound. Even Bordwell and Thompson's primer adds the sub-category of *internal diegetic sound* – renaming Metz's *semi-diegetic sound* – to describe acoustic materials from the narrative space but not quite of it, such as a character's inner soliloquy when she is visible on screen. These more precise specifications are only the discipline's attempt to catch up with filmmakers themselves. The many film sounds that trouble the relatively coarse division of 'diegetic' and 'non-diegetic' range from paranoia-inducing industrial hums in David Lynch's work to unlocalisable voices in Tarkovsky that hint at religious transcendence. More playfully, soundtracks of comic films also transgress the boundary between narrative and extra-narrative spaces. Recent proof that the spirit of Mel Brooks and early Woody Allen is alive comes in *Wallace & Gromit in The Curse of the Were-Rabbit* (2005), when a blood-curdling announcement about the predator's power is followed by a series of crashing organ chords. Instead of this music remaining securely in the non-diegetic zone of added score – where its instrumentation, volume and pitch would respect signatures of the horror genre – the next shot proves it to be diegetic noise produced by an enthusiastic organist in the corner.

Regardless of whether film sounds are characterised as diegetic, non-diegetic or something in-between, they relate in a number of different ways to the images they accompany. Although the industry suggestively refers to the final unifying of vision and sound during post-production as 'the married print', the harmonious matching this evokes is only one permutation: tensions, separations, even divorces between these two tracks are also feasible. In *Theory of Film* Kracauer proposes that the terms *parallelism* and *counterpoint* be used to describe two basic alternatives of agreement and discord between sound and vision. Despite its broad usefulness, however, 'parallelism' still seems impoverished with respect to sound's wide-ranging effects of clarifying, interpreting and heightening the contents of the image. 'Counterpoint' is problematical, too, even as it productively hints at possible antagonisms between the two tracks. To begin with, Chion has shown that the musical analogy intended by Kracauer is inexact: if counterpoint in music is the extended playing against each other of two or more voices or instruments, film's more momentary mismatching of image and sound is better described as *dissonant harmony* (*Audio-Vision*, p. 37). There is also a danger of hierarchism since, with its refined musical provenance, 'counterpoint' seems to promise something aesthetically superior to the less ambitious-sounding 'parallelism'. Indeed, avant-garde currents fastened upon counterpointed sound as a potential means of salvaging cinema from the excessive realism they feared would result from the new audio-technology. Eisenstein, Pudovkin and Alexandrov made this case in the Soviet Union in their 'Statement on Sound' (1928); while the French Surrealist Georges Hugnet proposed in 1929 that all cinematic sounds should be 'mistranslations', with a kiss accompanied by the rolling of a drum and a seduction by a banging door. But like the jump cut considered in Chapter 2, acoustic counterpoint carries no guaranteed meaning and is available for light-hearted as well as transgressive usages. Here a moment from *Singin' in the Rain* (1952) comes to mind. As Gene Kelly's voiceover recalls his vaudeville past before he broke into films, the final claim that his performances always had 'dignity' plays across images of embarrassing costumes and unfortunate pratfalls.

All soundtracks are of course constructions, even fictions. Although the relation between sound and picture is often conventionalised to the point where such invention is unnoticed, it is in an important sense arbitrary. As the third of four-and-a-half fallacies that he suggests still undermine study of cinema's auditory dimension, Altman cites 'the reproductive fallacy': 'Recordings do not reproduce sound, they represent sound' (*Sound Theory / Sound Practice*, p. 40). The most apparently 'faithful' on-location recording is not a slice of raw acoustic life but already mediated by numerous decisions such as microphone placement. Elsewhere, during post-production, dialogue might be rerecorded, location sounds transformed and extra auditory effects acquired from sound libraries or digital archives. Far from bringing a deadening weight of realism and authenticity to cinema, sound often proves mutable and playful. Noises that seem unproblematically attached to objects on screen may turn out to be acoustic artifice. Bruce Stambler recalls trying to render a lion's roar for African scenes in *The Ghost and the Darkness* (1996). Since the lion's own efforts were considered insufficiently leonine, the effect used in the end was a composite of a bear, a tiger and a drag-racing car (*The Dolby Era*, p. 129). One sound can also, in promiscuous fashion, attach itself to more than one on-screen image: Chion notes that the sound of a watermelon smashing in a comedy might be equally suited to accompany a 'head blown to smithereens in a war film' (*Audio-Vision*, p. 23).

Music for films

Edward Bast, a serious young composer in William Gaddis's novel *J R* (1975), finds himself undertaking some commercial projects in order to keep body and soul together. He is dismayed, however, when one film producer requires from him 'some nothing music', which, so as to leave intact the sovereignty of dialogue on the soundtrack, 'couldn't have any real form, anything distinctive about it any sound anything that would distract'. This fictional character's horror at such a peculiar (non-)commission has a precedent in the responses of various concert hall composers who have been asked to write music for films. Most forcefully, Stravinsky declared in 1941 that 'I cannot accept it as music'. Unlike the complete and organic form of the symphony, opera or concerto, even the fullest film score is discontinuous, emerging in fragments and bursts and seemingly never able to achieve autonomy as aesthetic statement because of its binding to the image on screen.

At its simplest, musical fidelity to visual material takes the form known as *mickey-mousing*. Initially associated as its name suggests with animations – the violin's pizzicato as Jerry tiptoes towards the sleeping Tom – this consists in attempting to find a musical approximation of on-screen movements. The unfortunate Bast in *J R* suffers here, too, as he is asked to provide 'zebra music' to accompany shots of their stampeding in a wildlife documentary. But if mickey-mousing is the score at its least ambitious, some critics argue that film music even of a less literal-minded sort similarly tends towards banality. According to Adorno and Eisler, the characteristic Hollywood score 'converts a kiss into a magazine cover, an outburst of unmitigated pain into a melodrama, a scene from nature into an oleograph' (*Composing for the Films*, p. 32). Film music in this view is not simply reproductive – providing an equivalent of image contents in another artistic language – but also reductive, stereotyping what is on screen and inciting a spurious emotionalism in the audience. Music is thus central to the standardisation and commodification Adorno and Eisler see at the heart of classic Hollywood cinema. While they write in very specific circumstances – as German Marxists exiled in capitalist America just after the Second World War – their critique may also be suggestive with regard to later film. What is achieved by John Barry's prairie music in *Dances With Wolves* (1990), say, if not the conversion of 'a scene from nature' into a decorative object, 'an oleograph' indeed?

If cultural conventions inhibit the protean potential of all sounds, and anchor them to particular sorts of cinematic image, this tendency is especially apparent in the case of film music. Shots denotative of specific times, places, racial and ethnic groups and so on often have, almost as a second skin, a familiar type of musical accompaniment. No approach of Native Americans in the classic western was complete without scoring by the beating of tom-toms. Even today such musical reductionism and stereotyping persists in cinema. Scenes of rural Ireland, for example, may still come sonically replete with bodhran, fiddle and uillean pipes. At one level, scores of this kind play a relatively harmless role of narrative cueing: the bodhran may tell us economically that an as yet unidentified geography is Irish rather than Welsh, or it might be a musical signature – a leitmotiv – associated with a given character and signalling that she is about to re-enter the story-space. More damagingly, however, this type of film music risks that flattening-out of complexities to which Adorno and Eisler refer. Choosing, in the Irish instance, a traditional musical arrangement rather than a soundtrack amenable to the full range and modernity of music in Ireland threatens to turn the image of the nation on screen into a sentimental postcard.

The gravitational pull that film images exert upon certain kinds of music means that Quincy Jones is indulging in daydream when he says: 'I've always wanted to see a juxtaposition of a Victorian setting with modern soul music. It would really crack me up to find, in the middle of [a] scene out of Dickens, James Brown screaming away as the town crier' (Gorbman, *Unheard Melodies*, p. 83). It was never likely that Elizabethan lute music would accompany *Gladiator* (2000), or that Elizabeth Bennet and Mr Darcy in the newest *Pride & Prejudice* (2005) would kiss to a hip hop accompaniment. Yet the problem with these imaginary soundtracks is precisely not one of historical inauthenticity. For it is not as if *Gladiator* and *Pride & Prejudice* seek to recreate the musical forms and instrumentations of ancient Rome and early nineteenth-century England respectively: lute-fingering and hip hop sampling would actually be no more alien as musical expressions to the period settings of these films than are the orchestral modes finally used. But the tradition of scoring established in the classic Hollywood era means that the romantic symphonic-style score has been 'naturalised', as it were, and is not heard as asynchronous with respect to a film's historical context in the way that Lizzie Bennet's hip hop would be. Conventions restricting what music may accompany an image are still powerful, despite examples of counterpointing that range from Brian Eno's electronic score for Jarman's *Sebastiane* (1976), set in an outpost of the Roman Empire in 300 AD, to the delirious (mis)matching of contemporary pop song and late nineteenth-century Paris that occurs in *Moulin Rouge!* (2001).

These experiments in disparity between image and music have the effect of making us aware of the strangeness, in general, of film's musical accompaniment. Given that dominant cinema's project has been to naturalise the storytelling situation, to remove all evidence of production itself from films, the use of something as obviously artificial and constructed as a musical soundtrack would seem counter-intuitive. As Gorbman asks: '*why music* ... why is it permitted into the narrative regime of the sound film at all?' (*Unheard Melodies*, p. 4). The answers that she and other scholars give to this question vary. In terms of cultural history, cinema may be following expressive modes like Greek tragedy, Victorian melodrama and Wagnerian opera that also combined narrative and spectacle with music; indeed, the composer Arnold Schoenberg and painter Wasily Kandinsky believed that, because of its technological force, film could become the supreme audiovisual medium. Another suggestion is that music provides continuity across a series of disparate shots and thereby serves to distract from the artifice of the editing process. Considered from this perspective, film music does not expose the cinematic illusion, as might have been presumed, but actually reinforces it.

There is another cluster of possible reasons for film music's existence which Gorbman terms *psychological/anthropological*. Earlier we quoted Adorno and Eisler's argument that, in silent cinema, music served to re-humanise disturbing scenes of figures moving without sound. Gorbman herself suggests that film music – particularly the classic Hollywood score – procures for the audio-viewer the kind of gratification associated with psychological infancy. It offers a 'bath or gel of affect' into which the audience sinks; it 'relaxes the censor, drawing the spectator further into the fantasy–illusion suggested by filmic narration'; it resembles 'the hypnotist's voice' in both its lulling, melodic quality and its invitation to submit to a process of regression (*Unheard Melodies*, pp. 5–6). Not just any regression either, but, extremely, immersion once more in the primal space of the womb: Gorbman proposes that film music allows re-entry into what the French psychoanalyst Guy Rosolato terms the 'sonorous envelope', that all-around ambience of pulsations, bubblings and faraway voices in which the infant is enfolded while still within its mother's body.

Gorbman powerfully evokes the backwardness of much of our cinemagoing, the way in which the score might be a sonic counterpart to the darkness of the auditorium in recalling uterine space. However, this psychoanalytic construction of the audio-viewer may be at the cost of understating her cultural and social positioning. Film music, after all, is replete with socialised meanings as well as – or instead of – holding out possibilities of a primal return. The audio-spectator hearing Indian tom-toms in a western is not necessarily induced into blissful regression but may be led towards real-world reflections on the past and present of Native Americans. Nevertheless, such theoretical repression of the social dimensions of music continues to have some effect in this field. Kevin Donnelly's *The Spectre of Sound* (2005), for instance, seems initially antithetical to Gorbman by arguing that music in cinema, far from representing a return to infantile pleasure, resembles instead a demonic visitation. Yet this major shift in tone masks what is a similarly unworldly thesis.

If the film score offers, in Gorbman's terms, a gel of affect, it is spread unevenly and intermittently. Even the fullest scores give way for long periods to the other elements of soundtrack, rendering music less likely to immerse the audio-viewer in some primal sonic state. But while a case might still be made for Gorbman's thesis with respect to the extended, single-authored scores of classic Hollywood, it is ill-suited for analysing the music in much recent film. Musical soundtracks conceived as heterogeneous, discontinuous sampling of already existing materials are now an important alternative to – or adjunct of – the commissioned work of a composer. Stanley Kubrick is a key figure here, setting a precedent for others' work besides his own by rejecting the commissioned score for *2001: A Space Odyssey* (1968) and substituting selections from classical composers including Johann Strauss, Richard Strauss and Ligeti. But where Kubrick seems interested in the counterpoint of music and image – what happens to our viewing of a spacecraft when it is accompanied by a Viennese waltz? – other, later filmmakers appear absorbed by possibilities of sampling to the point where music's dynamic with images or its role in advancing narrative becomes less important and it almost stands alone as a source of pleasure. We can loosely measure this change by juxtaposing Kubrick's earnest practice with the use of music in Tarantino. The soundtracks for the two *Kill Bill* films (2003–4) are a musical hyper-market, showcasing earlier movie music by Bernard Herrmann and Ennio Morricone, songs by Nancy Sinatra and Johnny Cash, Japanese and Latino fragments, the theme tune from the US TV series *Ironside*, and much more. While not indiscriminately chosen, these eclectic musics may detach themselves from the films' visual field and become rapidly changing objects of sensation in their own right (a delight then extended by purchase of the musical soundtrack).

Tarantino may be quite thoroughgoing in his hiving-off of musical pleasure but he is far from unique: think of other recent works like *Trainspotting* (1996), *About a Boy* (2002) and the two *Bridget Jones* films (2001–4) that exist almost as powerfully in the spin-off CD music compilation as in the on-screen images. There is nothing new about such slippage between cinematic and musical industries: this synergy was clear as early as the silent era, when audiences would buy sheet music of songs or instru-mental pieces they had heard accompanying a film. Nevertheless, some film music now appears semi-autonomous, only temporar-ily and imperfectly anchored to the film image before it finds its true place in the home stereo system. The logical next step would be full autonomy itself – 'soundtracks without films' (as Donnelly terms them). Here, as in many other musical ventures, Brian Eno is ahead of the game. His *Music for Films* album (1978) includes tracks with such cinematically suggestive titles as 'Events in Dense Fog', 'Patrolling Wire Borders' and 'Final Sunset' – film music freed from subordination to vision and, finally, in a kind of answer to Stravinsky, realising itself as artis-tic expression.

STOP and THINK

- As in Chapters 1 and 2, begin by taking a manageably short segment of any film. Explore, this time, its acoustic proper-ties, shaking off what remains of the ear's 'indolence, dreaminess, and dullness' (Adorno and Eisler, *Composing for the Films*, p. 23). Consider initially how the sequence distributes – and perhaps hierarchises – the four acoustic elements of speech (dialogue and/or voiceover), effects, music and silence. Arrange this soundtrack also into diegetic and non-diegetic phenomena, assessing their respective power.

- To explore further sound's role in the production of meaning, play the game that Chion calls *masking* (*Audio-Vision*, pp. 187–8). This involves running your chosen sequence several times but in different ways: first with both image and sound intact, then with sound muted, and then, most counter-intuitively, with the image concealed and your attention only upon sound. What happens to the image and its meanings when sound is withdrawn? What do you learn about film sound by listening to it in its pure state, momentarily freed from its Siamese twinning with the image? Does such heightened acoustic sensitivity survive once sound and vision are reunited in a final viewing of the sequence?

- As a second exercise, Chion proposes a *forced marriage* of sound and vision (*Audio-Vision*, pp. 188–9). Of course *any* matching of these two tracks involves a degree of coercion; even apparently spontaneous sounds such as the bark that accompanies the on-screen dog are subject to technical interventions that range from microphone positioning on location to the bark's reworking or even fabrication during post-production. However, Chion has in mind a specific activity to sharpen awareness of the interaction between image track on the one hand and added musical score on the other. Following his suggestion, choose a film sequence that is accompanied by non-diegetic music. With a wide selection of musical alternatives to hand, substitute each of these in turn for the original score. You could replace Celine Dion singing 'The Heart Will Go On' at the lachrymose conclusion of *Titanic* (1997) with a Chopin piano prelude or a traditional military march or Kylie Minogue's 'Can't Get You Out of My Head'. Assess what happens to the image and also to each piece of music during these juxtapositions. What general conclusions might be drawn about the functions and powers of film music?

- These exercises require a listening environment that, if not hermetically sealed, is protected from many incidental noises. Writers including Altman and Sergi, however, resist as artificial any such approach that detaches film sound-track from the ambient sounds that occur in all actual audio-viewing situations (from crowded multiplex to family living-room). Are they right to argue that analysis of the composed soundtrack should be embedded in this larger acoustic attention?

Analysing soundtrack: *Le Mépris*

The French director Jean-Luc Godard is noted above all for his interrogation of the image. Beginning in the late 1950s, his work in cinema and television has persistently explored questions of vision, such as the status of a film star's photograph (1972's *Letter to Jane*) or the permeation even into film itself of the look of advertising (as in *Deux ou trois choses que je sais d'elle* in 1967). While critics have properly emphasised this concern with the politics of the visual, however, they have sometimes downplayed Godard's long-standing interest in ideologies of sound also. Such dual concerns are embodied in the very name of one of the production companies he formed: *Sonimage*, nicely conjoining the French terms for sound and picture.

Despite favouring post-production dubbing over sound record-ed on location until *Une Femme est une femme* (1961), Godard's approach to soundtrack at the start of his career stressed an ideal of fidelity. Along with *Nouvelle vague* collaborators, he wished for a cinema that would not only reconfigure the image but 'return to greater authenticity in dialogue and soundtrack' (Jean Narboni and Tom Milne (eds), *Godard on Godard* (London: Secker and Warburg, 1972), p. 185). In remarks about his own early films he repeats this concern for the careful correlation of sound and vision. With regard to scenes of war in *Les Carabiniers* (1963), he expresses a commitment to acoustic verisimilitude that would put to shame even the most pedantic military specialist: 'Each aircraft is accompanied by the sound of its own engine, and we never had a Heinkel roar for a Spitfire, nor a Beretta rattle when what you see is a Thompson sub-machine gun' (p. 198). The ethos of authenticity is apparent as well in the soundtrack of another early work, *Le Mépris / Contempt* (1963), subject of this brief case study. But if sports cars roar convincingly in this film, the soundtrack is also marked by infidelities and experiments that look ahead to Godard's radical later practice.

Sprinkled with the stardust of Brigitte Bardot's presence at the height of her Mediterranean fame and glossy in its images of Rome and Capri, *Le Mépris* is an unusual film in the Godard canon. The film narrates the degenerating marriage of a writer Paul Javal and his wife and former secretary Camille. Their personal crisis occurs during – and is suggestively aligned with – the fraught making of a movie, as the distinguished German director Fritz Lang and Jerry Prokosch, a crass American producer, struggle over how to adapt Homer's *Odyssey* for the screen. For Prokosch, the world, including old Greek epics, is entirely transformable by his own fantasies and desires. Yet, as well as encountering dissent from the dignified, austere Lang at the level of dialogue itself, the kind of crudely wish-fulfilling imagination Prokosch stands for is resisted more implicitly elsewhere in the soundtrack. The harshly loud smashing of a plate, for example, evokes the weight and density of the material world. Waves crash noisily on the Capri shore, drowning out the human presences of Prokosch and Camille high in a villa above. Most shatteringly, powers of fantasy yield to the sound of a car crash near the end.

These particular aspects of the film's soundtrack observe *Nouvelle vague* tenets of worldliness and realism. So, too, does Godard's respect for the different acoustic signatures of variant spaces: voices are frail and tinny in the high-ceilinged villa on Capri but less distanced in the Javals' smaller apartment in Rome. Elsewhere, however, *Le Mépris* departs from a plain acoustic philosophy and demonstrates an overt concern, in Rick Altman's terms, to represent rather than reproduce sounds. After one quarrel with Camille, Paul returns to work at his typewriter;

however, the seemingly straightforward diegetic noise as keys are clattered intensifies to the point where it resembles a machine-gun, thus implicitly prolonging tensions between the couple that had seemed settled. In another scene, an aspiring actress sings on stage while the Javals, Lang and Prokosch talk amongst themselves in the auditorium. Several times, however, the diegetic sound that she visibly continues to make is – fantastically – erased from the soundtrack, ensuring a monopoly on the audio-viewer's attention of the protagonists' voices as their conjoined aesthetic and person-al disputes increase in intensity.

Yet, just as, across his career, Godard's editing practice habitu-ally avoids routines like that of shot/reverse-shot by which a mastery of space is achieved, so too his characteristic approach to dialogue evokes contestation and rupture rather than authority. Dialogue in *Le Mépris* is rudely challenged by other sounds, both diegetic and non-diegetic. Further diegetic sounds besides those of the waves accumulate around and above voices, dispersing narrative cinema's customary focus upon intelligible conversation between a set of protagonists. Late in the film, a dialogue between Prokosch and Camille at a filling-station is partially muffled by metallic clanks. Since the two figures are standing to the rear and these other noises emanate from the foreground of the image, this downplaying of voice is, in a simple sense, faithful to spatial logic; yet Godard's tactic here is significant ideologically as well as a feat of acoustic fidelity. Voice in *Le Mépris* may also be displaced or at least diminished in force by non-diegetic components of the soundtrack. In one of the Capri sequences, for example, Prokosch's autocratic speech competes unequally with Georges Delerue's plangent musical theme which increases in volume until it becomes the dominant sound while the producer visibly contin-ues to talk. Dialogue may even be stripped of its usual power where it is still clearly intelligible. Colin MacCabe describes *Le Mépris* as 'one of the few real examples of European cinema: four of the great European languages – English, French, German and Italian – circulate freely' (*Godard: A Portrait of the Artist at 70* (London: Bloomsbury, 2003), p. 160). But if the film's multilin-gualism anticipates the 'transnational' cinema discussed later in this book, it also provokes a crisis of dialogue. The long pauses for translation as German is converted into English, or French into Italian, disrupt mainstream cinema's ideal of continual advance; at other times – as when 'Monsieur Lang' is rendered as 'Mr Lang' – the translations seem redundant to the point of comedy. Multilingualism thus functions as Chion suggests it might in *Audio-Vision* – as one of several available strategies for destroying centres of authoritative speech.

Within the marriage of Paul and Camille, verbal authority initially seems vested in the male figure; as a writer he embodies a mastery of words compared with Camille's – the former secretary's – passive reception and transcription of them. Yet as their relationship crumbles, power and articulacy are, at least to an extent, redistributed between the couple. This shift is strikingly registered at the level of soundtrack. When Paul taps a bronze statue several times in their apartment, he says that 'she sounds different in different places'. This might stand as a testimonial to Camille also. Although the image track would seem to confine her to sensuous glamour because of the connotations of Bardot, she is released into other identities in the film's sonic space (Figure 7). For example, she swears, the harshly enunciated words seeming in counterpoint with her languorous body image. She also offers an intellectually acute commentary on the break-up of the relationship with Paul. Significantly this reflection occurs as voiceover. Generally in cinema the voiceover is marked out as masculine territory, further extending patriarchal power that may already be evident at the levels of image and narrative. But Camille has several voiceovers and these, at times, float free of her body image, recalling Kaja Silverman's argument in *The Acoustic Mirror* (Bloomington: Indiana University Press, 1988) that asynchronisation between women's bodies and their voices may serve to trouble traditional masculine authority. This seems especially plausible very late on in *Le Mépris*: as Paul studies Camille's letter of farewell to him, her voiceover reads out the words, yet her body is entirely absent from the screen.

However, the extent of Camille's liberation should not be overstated. To begin with, the acoustic space of the voiceover is not only hers but accessible to Paul also. And the film goes on to narrate not her escape into a new life beyond the stagnant

Figure 7 The female voice: Brigitte Bardot in *Le Mépris* (France/Italy, 1963).

marriage but her death. Just like the indications of her freedom, this punitive conclusion registers first at the level of sound: the audio-viewer hears the crashing of the car in which she is travelling with Prokosch before seeing the wreckage on screen. This is not quite the film's own ending, however. One further scene shows the crew on the Homer project preparing to shoot Ulysses' homecoming. Initially, as Paul and Lang talk on screen, the sequence appears to restore a masculine vocal authority that had earlier been disrupted by Camille's speech. Yet they end their conversation and pass out of the frame, allowing the camera to focus upon the sea, which is blank right to the horizon. Then the film's suggestive last word is pronounced by a crew member from off-screen: 'Silence!' In the most trivial sense this is merely a request not to spoil location recording by extraneous noises. But, beyond this, it resonates ominously (especially as the pronouncing of the word is conjoined with such a featureless final image). Every film's soundtrack, of course, has to give up its earlier liveliness to conclude in a moment of silence, a minor death; yet the explicit marking of this silence at the end of *Le Mépris* evokes a particular desolation.

As the word 'Fin' (The End) appears on screen, sound very briefly revives, with a few notes of Delerue's score. His music mainly for strings is frequent in the film, and interacts both harmoniously and contrapuntally with those other acoustic elements described above (as well as with the contents of the image track). Since the music is associated with both Paul and Camille, it suggests their unity, counteracting the sense of tension and dislocation between them evoked by their separate voiceovers. Here we might draw a comparison with the unifying potential of music in *In the Mood for Love*, discussed in Chapter 1: even as separate shots there of Chow and Mrs Chan denote their unbridgeable distance, the continuity of the violin theme playing across both images hints at the possibility still of union. Such an optimistic reading, however, has to be qualified by the elegiac contents of the music itself. This is the case, too, with Delerue's score for *Le Mépris*. Although it suggests an emotionally resonant, even transcendent space for Paul and Camille beyond the mundane circumstances of their quarrelling, the sombre strings also hint at its unattainability, its impossibility other than in death itself. Martin Scorsese intends precisely these connotations of tragic non-fulfilment when he uses Delerue's theme in the conclusion of *Casino* (1995).

Selected reading

As well as the specialist titles below, see also Bordwell/Thompson and Corrigan/White (Chapter 1), and Ondaatje (Chapter 2).

Abel, Richard and Rick Altman (eds), *The Sounds of Early Cinema* (Bloomington: Indiana University Press, 2001).
   Groundbreaking collection of essays that anticipates Altman's still more compendious research in *Silent Film Sound*.
Adorno, Theodor and Hanns Eisler, *Composing for the Films* (London: The Athlone Press, 1994).
   Collaborative work by a major Marxist cultural critic and a politically engaged film composer. First published in 1947 but still fascinating as

it moves between a scourging critique of film music and a tentative programme for its renewal.

Altman, Rick, *Silent Film Sound* (New York: Columbia University Press, 2004).

The definitive work on the variegated soundscapes of silent cinema: prodigiously researched, accessibly written and handsomely illustrated.

Altman, Rick (ed.), *Sound Theory / Sound Practice* (New York: Routledge, 1992).

Important contribution to sound's emerging status within film studies. Essays range across topics from women's voices in Third World cinema to the religiously suggestive sound practices of Tarkovsky.

Brown, Royal S., *Overtones and Undertones: Reading Film Music* (Berkeley, Los Angeles and London: University of California Press, 1994).

Sometimes strained in its theoretical claims, and maddening in its prose, yet informed by sustained reflection and by greater musical erudition than most other studies. More enthusiastic about film music than Flinn and Gorbman.

Buhler, James, Caryl Flinn and David Neumeyer (eds), *Music and Cinema* (Hanover, NH: Wesleyan University Press, 2000).

A packed and stimulating collection of essays, exploring the articulations of image and music in a wide range of cinematic contexts from classical Hollywood to recent German production.

Chion, Michel, *Audio-Vision: Sound on Screen* (New York: Columbia University Press, 1994).

The most sustained and stimulating attempt yet to raise conceptualisation of film sound to the level of studies of the image. Occasionally disconcerting in terminology – *acousmatic*, *emanation speech*, *synchresis* – but indispensable.

Donnelly, K. J., *The Spectre of Sound: Music in Film and Television* (London: BFI, 2005).

Suggestive, if overstated argument that music signifies a ghostly, paranormal, even demonic presence on the film soundtrack.

Donnelly, K. J. (ed.), *Film Music: Critical Approaches* (Edinburgh: Edinburgh University Press, 2001).

Less compendious than the Buhler, Flinn and Neumeyer collection but valuably including essays on the methodology of analysing film music (besides specific studies of music in *Citizen Kane*, *Performance* and Tarantino).

Flinn, Caryl, *Strains of Utopia: Gender, Nostalgia, and Hollywood Film Music* (Princeton, NJ: Princeton University Press, 1992).

Drifts at times from the specificities of film music – indeed, from the topic of music itself – but offers a sophisticated approach, informed by psychoanalysis, feminism and Marxism, to the classical Hollywood score.

Gorbman, Claudia, *Unheard Melodies: Narrative Film Music* (Bloomington and Indianapolis: Indiana University Press and London: BFI, 1987).

Key text in the consolidation of film music as an object for semiotic, narratological and psychoanalytic investigation. As well as general reflections, includes case studies of classic French and Hollywood films.

Kassabian, Anahid, *Hearing Film: Tracking Identifications in Contemporary Hollywood Film Music* (London and New York: Routledge, 2001).

Valuably updates Flinn and Gorbman, discussing in lively, accessible fashion the gender and racial politics of post-classical musical scoring (films include *Dangerous Liaisons*, *Thelma and Louise* and *The Hunt for Red October*).

Lastra, James, *Sound Technology and the American Cinema: Perception, Representation, Modernity* (New York: Columbia University Press, 2000).

Conceptually and empirically very rich, this book explores the industrial, aesthetic, ideological, even philosophical antagonisms within US cinema's conversion to sound.

Sergi, Gianluca, *The Dolby Era: Film Sound in Contemporary Hollywood* (Manchester: Manchester University Press, 2004).

Valuable study of the artistic, technological and economic complexities of sound construction in current American cinema. Also includes interviews with innovators and practitioners of film sound such as Ray Dolby.

Useful websites

www.filmsound.org.

Wonderful resource, assembled with a rare mixture of passion and scholarliness: offers a rich archive of materials on the history, theory, practice and terminology of film soundtrack.

www.digitalhistory.uh.edu/historyonline/sound.cfm.

Brief sampling of materials on the introduction of synchronised sound; notable for Aldous Huxley's vicious reflections, in 1930, on what he calls the 'most frightful creation-saving device for the production of standardized amusement'.

www.filmmusicsociety.org.

Lacking the critical edge of filmsound.org, but still a well-maintained resource, featuring such things as plentiful film composer biographies.

4
Film and narrative

'N, there's no doubt about it, has to be for Narrative', says Peter Wollen in 'An Alphabet of Cinema' (*Paris Hollywood: Writings on Film* (London: Verso, 2002), p. 12). Wollen tells a miniature narrative of his own, proposing that the history of cinema from its beginnings be understood as 'the history of the development of a "film language" that would facilitate storytelling'. This seemingly linear progress, however, is not without major reversals and digressions. Tom Gunning famously describes much film production and exhibition at the start of the twentieth century as a 'cinema of attractions', which supplied its audiences with sporadic visual and aural pleasures not restricted by the needs of narrative construction. Even as late as the 1920s, faced by then with an advanced storytelling apparatus in America and elsewhere, significant figures resisted the notion of film as a medium predestined towards narrative. This anti-narrative expression was especially fierce in French avant-garde circles. In 1921 the director and theorist Jean Epstein went so far as to call narrative in film 'a lie'; six years later, Germaine Dulac accused fellow filmmakers who neglected the particular qualities of the image in order to tell stories instead of 'a criminal error' (Siegfried Kracauer, *Theory of Film* (New York: Oxford University Press, 1960), pp. 178–9). The strange spectatorial habit of some French Surrealists at the time – moving rapidly from cinema to cinema, watching only a fragment of film in each – speaks of a suspicion of narrative, the desire to configure cinema as a source of local, discontinuous sensations rather than a mere machine for storytelling.

In its sheer idiosyncrasy, Surrealist cinema-hopping already testifies to narrative's dominance and to the inventive strategies required to outwit or challenge this. More substantial resistance from the same period is evident in Luis Buñuel and Salvador Dalí's two films, *Un chien andalou* (1928) and *L'âge d'or* (1930). Here images are juxtaposed in such a way as to disrupt spatiotemporal continuity and undo the unity of character; the image tracks in each case are thus irreducible to customary narrative order (though they evoke alternative logics, notably Freud's account of dreamwork). The Surrealism of Buñuel and Dalí can be joined to all those other avant-garde and experimental traditions in cinema that seek to explore the medium's imagistic, graphic or material properties rather than its facility for storytelling. All these ventures, however, may look marginal or aberrant, given the twentieth century's massive institutionalisation and globalisation of narrative film. This privileging of narrative form extends into the discipline of film studies as well. Symptomatically, when Kristin Thompson discusses non- or even anti-narrative elements in Eisenstein, she refers to them as 'excess', in other words as surplus to the prior and pre-eminent work of storytelling (see *Eisenstein's 'Ivan the Terrible': A Neo-Formalist Analysis* (Princeton: Princeton University Press, 1992)).

Contemporary film may appear in some ways to be renewing the non-narrative 'cinema of attractions'. In big-budget Hollywood production especially, computer-generated special effects, kinetic action sequences and intensified soundtracks seem to free themselves from a subordinate, strictly storytelling function and become autonomous pleasures. Yet one of Thompson's more recent books rightly acknowledges 'the immense demand for narrative material by modern media systems' (*Storytelling in Film and Television* (Cambridge, MA and London: Harvard University Press, 2003), p. 83). Stories are required to feed expanding television and internet appetites besides those of the film industry itself. Far from dwindling in power, narrative is still central to the economics and aesthetics of cinema and, consequently, to any critical discussion of the medium. Yet to recognise, categorise and evaluate the protocols of the stories in which we are often blissfully immersed is no easy thing. In film as in other media, narrative does not generally draw attention to its own operations; it is, as Roland Barthes says, 'simply there, like life itself' (*Image – Music – Text* (New York: Hill and Wang, 1977), p. 79). Analysing something as deeply embedded as this requires a theoretical vocabulary that can seem alien at times or obtusely inattentive to the sheer pleasure that is taken in cinematic narrative. Nevertheless, such terminology is helpful in developing our critical self-consciousness as viewers and in enabling us to perceive, if not necessarily resist, the designs which film's stories have upon us.

Russian Formalists at the cinema

Flourishing in the Soviet Union in the 1920s, until falling foul of Stalinist orthodoxy, the critics known as the Russian Formalists were relatively unconcerned with the contents of artistic works. Instead, as their name indicates, they were preoccupied with uncovering the formal or structuring principles of aesthetic production, including the workings of narrative. Most of their critical output focused upon literature. Nevertheless, resisting the type of intellectual specialisation that would take hold later in the century, several key literary scholars in the movement also took a keen interest in cinema, their enthusiasm galvanised by the wave of innovative filmmaking in the Soviet Union by Eisenstein, Vertov, Kuleshov and others. In one of the earliest phases of film theory, articles on the nature and meaning of the medium poured forth, with such ambitious titles as Viktor Shklovsky's 'The Semantics of Cinema' (1925) and Boris Eichenbaum's 'Problems of Film Stylistics' (1927). Like his fellow Formalist Yury Tynianov, Shklovsky also attempted to concretise his reflections upon cinema by writing screenplays.

This section, however, is concerned with the implications for film studies of a Formalist who was less obviously engaged by the medium. Far from affiliating himself with such a modern artistic practice, Vladimir Propp actually took as his object of study the archaic form of the Russian fairytale. His pioneering *Morphology of the Folktale* (1928) identifies the 'two-fold' nature of the traditional tales he analysed. On the one hand is their 'amazing multiformity, picturesqueness, and colour', all of the surface details that vividly differentiate one story from another. But on the other is the 'no less striking uniformity', the sense of 'repetition' from one story to the next (*Morphology of the Folktale*, 2nd ed. (Austin: University of Texas Press, 1968), pp. 20–1). Indeed, once the underlying structural principles of the fairytale have been discovered, variations among particular examples of the genre become conceptually insignificant.

Propp's analysis of this story structure has a rather forbidding arithmetical exactitude. The prototypical tale is subdivided into thirty-one *functions*, a function being defined as a major narrative event placed in a linear sequence that begins with the crisis-inducing 'One of the members of a family absents himself from home' and culminates happily in 'The hero is married and ascends the throne'. These functions are performed by seven key dramatis personae or, in Propp's non-humanistic terminology, *spheres of action*: the villain, the donor, the helper, the princess (and her father), the dispatcher, the hero and the false hero. Few potential adapters of this model to film will want to emulate such precise mathematics (though Peter Wollen, writing on Hitchcock's *North by Northwest*, has a determined go). Given its literary provenance, the very applicability of Propp's schema to the materially different medium of cinema has also been questioned, most trenchantly by David   Bordwell   in   his   article   'ApProppriations   and ImProprieties: Problems in the Morphology of Film Narrative' (*Cinema Journal* 27, 3 (Spring 1988): 5–20).

Flexibly deployed, however, Propp's narratology has many uses in the analysis of filmic storytelling. Its example encourages us to suspend the myriad local differences of the films we watch and inquire instead into the possibility of group resemblances between these works. Most obviously, it enables the identification of recurrent narrative patterns and character-types within a given genre. In setting, tone and the presentation of their respective stars, *Pretty Woman* (1990) and *Bridget Jones's Diary* (2001) are highly diverse films; a Proppian analysis of these two romantic comedies, however, may disclose the working of what he calls a 'law of transference', whereby 'components of one tale can, without any alteration whatsoever, be transferred to another' (*Morphology*, p. 7). More ambitiously, Propp's schema can allow us to identify a commonality of narrative-type *across* as well as within genres. For all their lurid differences, John Ford's western *The Searchers* (1956) and Scorsese's neo-noir *Taxi Driver* share a sequence of functions and a common set of spheres of action (or character-types). This sort of attention to deep narrative structure lends itself to other uses as well, such as investigating possible continuities across the body of work of a given director. Is *Taxi Driver* telling essentially the same story as a seemingly different later Scorsese film like *The Aviator* (2004)?

Propp's narratology is too rigid to take account of cultural changes and the effects these have upon the structure of the fairytale. We might then legitimately wonder about its sensitivity with respect to film narratives, produced in very different circumstances from those of traditional Russian literature. Yet even if the princesses Propp speaks of are now in short supply, there are still equivalent female quest objects in cinematic storytelling: the kidnapped Debbie in *The Searchers*, say, or the young prostitute Iris in *Taxi Driver* (Figure 8). Similarly, the villain in film may look different but in his or her actions could be structurally analogous to the fairytale figure described by Propp. Even where the sequence of functions set out in *Morphology of the Folktale* is blocked or radically modified by film narratives, such negative information can be illuminating. In both *The Searchers* and *Taxi Driver*, the hero does not exactly 'ascend the throne' at the end: Ford's protagonist, played by John Wayne, is famously framed in the doorway of a homestead, looking out towards the desert rather than inwards to the scene of family reunion; while Scorsese's Travis Bickle (Robert De Niro) is also an isolate figure, though enjoying a dubious celebrity for his vigilantism. Yet these shifts towards social disintegration, even anomie, are more vividly disclosed by placing the narratives of the two films against Propp's schema, applying as it does to a mode of storytelling in feudal times that aimed to reinforce hierarchy, communal bonds, the cohesive rites of marriage and coronation. Propp is useful, too, in encouraging a higher level of abstraction in thinking about *character* in film. Practitioners of other art forms have often been dismayed by audience interest in characters as if they were of flesh and blood: E. M. Forster, for example, referred to the figures in his

Figure 8 'Hero' and 'princess': Travis Bickle (Robert De Niro) and Iris (Jodie Foster) in *Taxi Driver* (US, 1976).

novels as 'word masses' and sought to direct reader attention towards formal patterns instead. Of course it is harder to dismiss characters in film narrative as, by analogy, mere image masses. The actor's stubbornly corporeal presence on screen – albeit flattened to two dimensions – serves to distract the audience from the artifice of cinematic character. Attempts to challenge an anthropomorphic understanding of character in film and reveal its constructedness have been mistrusted as weakening spectator identification on which narrative cinema relies and, by and large, have been confined to avant-garde and experimental filmmaking. One thinks of Godard's Brechtian work, where characters may be subject to a distancing external commentary. Note, too, the strain of cinematic experiment in which several actors play the same role, inhibiting any sense of character's 'naturalness'. Examples range from the Brazilian director Glauber Rocha's *A Idade da Terra / The Age of the Earth* (1980) – featuring Christ in variously 'Indian', 'black', 'revolutionary' and 'military' incarnations – to Todd Solondz's *Palindromes* (2004), where a young white female character is played by multiple actors of diverse age, sex and race.

Taking Propp's work as a template, however, it may be possible to interrogate the category of character in film without quite resorting to these directors' idiosyncratic techniques. Recall that his narrative model values characters in fairytales simply for their assigned status as one or more of the spheres of action. It is of no consequence that the 'donor' in one tale might be a toothless old woman and in another a magically speaking frog; the differences between these two figures fall away, since what matters is their identical role within story structure. By analogy, we should be less enticed by the flesh-and-blood distinctiveness of characters in film and more alert to their narrative function. Thus the different personalities, appearances and voices of Debbie in *The Searchers* and Iris in *Taxi Driver* become analytically insignificant next to their structural identity as, in Propp's terms, instances of 'the princess'. This may look a somewhat arid, impoverished response to cinematic narrative. To cite just one objection, it nullifies the elements of actor performance and image in a way that star studies, discussed in Chapter 7, would vigorously dispute. Can we afford to go straight to a conclusion about the typological identity of these two figures without at least pausing to consider the different cultural connotations of Natalie Wood who played Debbie and Jodie Foster who played Iris? Again, however, this Propp-inspired degree of abstractness has the advantage of allowing us to detect repetition across seemingly disparate narratives.

STOP and THINK

- As a first step in applying Propp's narrative schema to film, research his account of the fairytale's thirty-one functions and seven spheres of action. The fullest detail, including examples from particular Russian stories, is of course in *Morphology of the Folktale* itself; however, decent summaries of Propp's model are available elsewhere, as in Peter Barry's *Beginning Theory*, 2nd ed. (Manchester: Manchester University Press, 2002), pp. 226–31 and Nick Lacey's *Narrative and Genre: Key Concepts in Media Studies* (Basingstoke: Macmillan, 2000), pp. 46–53.

- Customisation of Propp's model is necessary if it is to be employed on film narratives set in different times and places from those characteristic of the Russian folktale. The 'magical agent' the hero receives, for example, is now unlikely to be a special ring or a talking animal; however, other items may still fulfil this structural function, as with Julia Roberts's lavish new clothing in *Pretty Woman* or the computer programs downloaded by Neo in *The Matrix* (1999). Once this updating has been achieved, consider whether Propp's narrative morphology is enlightening with regard to cinematic storytelling. Does it allow you to uncover the structuring principles not just of individual works but of groups of films?

- Because of the verbal material on which Propp worked, it is easy to point out ways in which his model is deficient for cinema. A Proppian approach reduces films to their bare narrative lineaments since it can have nothing to say about the material apparatus of cinema itself. However, a more pressing task is to assess whether it is also lacking on its own narratological terms. Wollen's groundbreaking essay on *North by Northwest* states how easily and productively the film accommodates 'Propp's functions and method of analysis in general' (*Readings and Writings: Semiotic Counter-Strategies*, p. 31). Yet Wollen also notes that by doubling the quest object Hitchcock's thriller introduces a complication not countenanced in Propp: the film's hero is not only pursuing 'the princess' but is after information, 'so that there is a mystery story interwoven with the quest story' (p. 32). Consider in what ways Propp's narrative schema fails to match the cinematic storytelling with which you are familiar. What can be learned from such structural disruptions or modifications?

Time and motion pictures

In *Morphology of the Folktale* Propp is adamant about the linearity of the narratives which he analyses. While he allows that not all fairytales include all thirty-one functions, he insists that those functions which appear in any given tale do so in strictly chrono-logical sequence. There is no wacky Russian story that begins with the hero ascending the throne and then works backwards, *Memento*-style. Such linearity is also dominant in cinematic story-telling. As David Bordwell notes, relatively few films engage in significant 'temporal reshufflings' (*Narration in the Fiction Film*, p. 33). Nevertheless, the fairytale's observance of an unvarying progressive chronology is clearly inadequate as a model of how many other films seek to represent time. Godard is not the only director to believe that a film should have a beginning, middle and end, 'but not necessarily in that order'.

Viktor Shklovsky, one of Propp's Formalist colleagues, provides a key concept for the analysis of time in narrative. Using Russian terms that have passed into the general critical lexicon, he differ-entiates between two narrative orders that may be identified in any work. *Fabula* has most often been translated as 'story', and refers to the setting-out of events in a narrative in their linear sequence, beginning with the chronologically earliest and concluding with the latest. *Syuzhet*, translated as 'plot' (sometimes 'discourse'), refers to events in the order – not necessarily linear – in which they are actually narrated by a text. Bordwell puts the distinction succinctly: '"Syuzhet" names the architectonics of the film's presentation of the fabula' (*Narration in the Fiction Film*, p. 50). Fabula and syuzhet are synchronised in films that are constructed according to linear principles. Perhaps more interesting, however, are cases of difference or discontinuity between these two narrative orders. A film may present events not in chronological sequence but by a more unruly time scheme, leaping forwards or back, and thereby observing what the French narratologist Gérard Genette terms *anachrony*. At the risk of piling Greek critical terminology on Russian, these temporal disruptions in film break down into two basic types: *analepsis* (flashback) and *prolepsis* (flashforward or foreshadowing).

Flashbacks were utilised as early as silent film: in the modern quadrant of Griffith's *Intolerance*, a brief flashback of the hero's handing-over of his gun confirms that he did not subsequently commit a murder. However, in American cinema at least, analepsis became more common from the 1940s, partly in the wake of *Citizen Kane*'s bravura experiments with time. As a device, it finds a more comfortable home in some genres than in others. Just as classic film noir has its stylistic signatures of low-key lighting and canted camera angles, so it is stencilled narratively by the flashback. Works such as *Double Indemnity* (1944), *Mildred Pierce* (1945) and *The Killers* (1946) begin in the narrative present, with the protagonist's disillusion or arrest, and then move into the past to reconstruct the course of his or her criminality and dangerous passion. In such circumstances analepsis has a clarifying effect, remorselessly filling in narrative blanks. Elsewhere, however, the flashback may have a less conservative application, serving to 'ambiguate' storytelling, so to speak, rather than tidy it up. This is indeed the case in *Citizen Kane*, where each new segment of the narrated past fails to clarify Kane's history because it provides evidence that runs counter to other flashbacks. Similarly, *Catch-22* (1970) follows Joseph Heller's source novel by cryptically flashing back to shots of an airman moaning that he is cold; the sense of temporal dislocation is intensified by bleached colour and muffled sound, and only towards the end of the film is there a more revelatory flashback of the man's mortal injuries.

Some films have sought to go beyond a relatively modest use of flashback and attempt a more thoroughgoing reversal of the usual beginning/middle/end schema. Of course none of these works runs strictly backwards. In his novel *Slaughterhouse-Five* (1969), Kurt Vonnegut imagines what a genuinely backwards film would be like. His hero watches a war movie in reverse and thereby turns it into something utopian, with airmen's wounds healing and the dangerous minerals that made bombs being safely restored to the ground. But even if this degree of reversibility is available only in fantasy, or through projectionist error, interesting cinematic experiments have been done that are oriented implacably towards the narrative past. Most sensationally in recent English-speaking cinema there is *Memento* (2000) – even though its director Christopher Nolan suggests that the film's narrative trajectory actually resembles a hairpin or Möbius strip, complicating any sense of pure reversal (James Mottram, *The Making of 'Memento'*, pp. 33–4). A less baroque instance of such structure occurs in the French director François Ozon's *5 x 2* (2004). With some debts to Harold Pinter's 1978 play *Betrayal* – itself filmed in 1983 – the film is organised as five long scenes between a married couple. Each of these segments moves forwards in the usual way but is placed chronologically earlier than the preceding one. Since *5 x 2* begins with the couple's divorce and concludes with their first meeting, it generates a sense of desolation that a more linear emplotment of the relationship might not have done.

The flashback is by now a familiar piece of film's storytelling grammar; where it is clearly marked off from the narrative present, it is accepted, even naturalised by spectators. However, the structurally opposite device of prolepsis is used less often and remains potentially disorienting. Whereas the flashback evokes the routine workings of memory, prolepsis has connotations of odder mental processes like prophecy and premonition, and thus seems genuinely uncanny. Unsurprisingly, then, it has sometimes been deployed by art cinema. In France, prolepsis occurs in such works as Chris Marker's short sci-fi film *La Jetée* (1962) and Alain Resnais's *La guerre est finie* (1968). Nicolas Roeg uses the device in

Don't Look Now (1973) precisely to show the protagonist's disturbing occult powers; on a smaller scale, he also employs prolepsis
during a long lovemaking scene, short-circuiting any simple spectator voyeurism by intercutting sexual activity with shots of the
couple's subsequent dressing. Such connotations of artistic experiment, however, do not mean that the flashforward is entirely
outside the grammar of mainstream film. In Sydney Pollack's
drama of the Depression, *They Shoot Horses, Don't They?* (1969),
anticipatory shots of the hero's later arrest are with a view to
bestowing a tragic weight upon the narrative present. Yet David
Thomson is vexed precisely by the film's handling of prolepsis,
writing that the 'brutal flashforwards' of Horace McCoy's source
novel 'chop in and out like a butcher's axe', but here are 'made
studied and mournful with pretty photography' (*The New
Biographical Dictionary of Film* (London: Little, Brown, 2002),
p. 690).

A film's syuzhet may revise not merely the order of events in the
fabula, but also their *duration* (or *speed*) and *frequency*. In his
classic books *Narrative Discourse* (1980) and *Narrative Discourse
Revisited* (1988), Genette considers these two facets of narrative
organisation. Taking literary fiction as his object of study, he notes
several possible permutations between narrative events on the one
hand and the time given over to their representation on the other.
At one extreme, narration may be greatly condensed by ellipsis or
summary, passing over events entirely or reducing them to insub-
stantial outline; at the other it may be considerably expanded by
description, when the text lingers over detail rather than immediately discharging its storytelling duties. In between these opposing
possibilities is a kind of normative narrating rhythm, neither too
hectic nor too dilatory: Genette terms this a narrative's 'constant
speed' and measures against it any variants in the pace of storytelling.

The cinematic equivalent of Genette's constant speed is a film
made in *real time*, in which the duration of events corresponds
exactly to their duration on screen. This strategy is generally used
to maximise tension within claustrophobic locations, from the
western town of *High Noon* (1952) and the jury room of *Twelve
Angry Men* (1957) to the eponymous setting of *Phone Booth* (2002)

and the doomed aircraft of *United 93* (2006). However, real-time filmmaking can also intensify reflection upon the textures of the moment, as in the Iranian work *Badkonake sefid / The White Balloon* (1995), centred upon a seven-year-old girl's interactions with various adults.

The real-time film is still a rare cinematic experiment, and more usual are works which variously accelerate or retard our sense of narrative speed. At one end of the spectrum films may condense time by employing the type of Hollywood montage considered in Chapter 2; or they may literally quicken action by use of fast-motion photography, whether for comic purpose (Tony Richardson's 1963 adaptation of *Tom Jones*), for maximising a chase scene's excitement, or for social critique (as in nauseously speeded-up footage of cars and city dwellers in Godfrey Reggio's 1983 environmentalist documentary, *Koyaanisqatsi*). On the other hand, time in cinema may be slowed down, even stilled. This tendency is taken to its furthest, indeed deathliest extent in the freeze frame (a topic for later discussion). Without aspiring to quite that degree of arrested temporality, filmmakers may employ slow-motion photography, again for a variety of reasons (contrast its elegiac use in *In the Mood for Love* with its vocation in the wildlife documentary for showing what is otherwise too fleeting for the human eye). Alternatively, a film may dwell upon the details of a scene, impeding narrative momentum. Consider the opening shot of Tarkovsky's *The Sacrifice* (1985), in which the camera's long pauses permit appreciation of the visual and sonic plenitude of the moment, not just of the official narrative action of a man and his son planting a tree.

A sense of time expanding is also achieved where a filmmaker employs overlapping editing, cutting together shots of the same event so that it lasts longer on screen than in actuality. Eisenstein uses this tactic in *October*, when a bridge is raised to prevent the revolutionary crowd's progress; this disruption to mundane temporal unfolding invites reflection on the image's political resonance. Besides affecting duration, overlapping editing offers a small-scale version of narrative repetition, and thus has implications for the further question of frequency in storytelling. Genette sketches out three possible narrative frequencies: *singulative* (narrating once something that happened once), *iterative* (narrating once something that happened many times) and *repetitive* (narrating many times something that happened once). Despite its origins in literary study, the model is again suggestive for cinema. Most films observe singulative narrative, moving from one unique event to another. Other works, however, modulate narrative frequency in either iterative or repetitive directions. Iterative storytelling might be deployed for reasons including narrative economy. At the other extreme, filmmakers may repeat single events for a variety of purposes, such as to indicate trauma or anxiety. Narrative recurrence may also denote the complexity and ambiguity of an event, its openness to multiple interpretations. The classic instance of this is Kurosawa's *Rashomon* (1950), during which a dead samurai (speaking through a medium), his wife, a bandit and a woodcutter variously reconstruct the event of the samurai's death. The film puts in crisis the activity of storytelling itself; as one character says: 'The more I hear, the more confused I am.' This problematising of narrative is ultimately not pursued in the First Gulf War film *Courage Under Fire* (1997), a Hollywood work that nevertheless models itself upon *Rashomon*, with Meg Ryan, implausibly, standing in for the dead samurai. Similarly, the Chilean film *Los Debutantes* (2003) presents narrative events in triplicate but appears more voguish than psychologically or philosophically penetrating.

STOP and THINK

• Take a small number of narrative films that you know well and consider relations in them between fabula and syuzhet. First, does the syuzhet in each case reproduce the fabula's chronological laying out of events, or does it significantly reorder this by flashback and flashforward? Second, is story-time accelerated (by ellipsis, Hollywood-style montage, fast-motion photography) or retarded (by freeze framing, slow-motion photography, overlapping editing, the camera's pausing upon scenic detail)? Third, are narrative events all shown singly, or are there also instances of Genette's iterative and repetitive frequencies? Assess the effects of the various temporal strategies in this narrative sample.

- Art cinema has a long tradition of fragmenting or complicating storytelling. Recently, however, narrative fracture has been loosened from such earnestly arthouse usage to become part of more mainstream cinema's repertoire. If the linear plot remains pre-eminent, there has also been a wave of films that flamboyantly rearrange narrative structure. Speaking only of cinemas of the Americas, this trend includes *Pulp Fiction* (1994), *Being John Malkovich* (1999), *Amores perros* (2000), *Donnie Darko* (2001), *Adaptation* (2002), *The Hours* (2002), *21 Grams* (2003), *Eternal Sunshine of the Spotless Mind* (2004), Tommy Lee Jones's modern bilingual western *The Three Burials of Melquiades Estrada* (2005) and *Babel* (2006). Among other things, these projects restore the prestige of the screenwriter, notably Charlie Kaufman (*Malkovich*, *Adaptation* and *Eternal Sunshine*) and Guillermo Arriaga (*Melquiades Estrada*, and his three scripts for the Mexican director Alejandro González Iñárritu: *Amores perros*, *21 Grams* and *Babel*). Evaluate your own responses to this strain of radically non-linear narrative, calculating the ratio of curiosity to boredom, engagement to frustration.

- Speculate on possible reasons for the emergence of this temporally and spatially complex storytelling. You might, hard-headedly, stress commercial motivations: the 'difficult' narrative's status as a niche product, not only at the cinema but in the home entertainment market, where its DVD version may be paused and repeatedly viewed. Or you might consider artistic motivations, as filmmakers seek to incorporate insights about time, identity and so on generated by contemporary physics and neuroscience. Or you might choose a socio-cultural explanation, linking the disappearance – or at least crisis – of the linear, unified story to Jean-François Lyotard's claim in *The Postmodern Condition* (1984) that, in the advanced contemporary West, former 'grand narratives' (God, reason, political emancipation and so on) have collapsed, making way for stories instead with a smaller claim on totality, clarity and authority.

The sense of an ending

Just as in literary scholarship, thinking about narrative trajectory within film studies has tended to neglect beginnings and middles and to focus instead upon endings. Where there is discussion of these earlier stages of cinematic narrative, it tends to be found in the specialist genre of manuals for aspiring screenwriters. Yet it is unsurprising that our chief attention has been directed towards the end, given a traditional expectation that it is here still-unresolved issues will be settled and a narrative's overall pattern and significance made explicit. As Edgar, the filmmaker protagonist of Godard's *Eloge de l'amour/In Praise of Love* (2001), puts it: 'It's strange how things take on meaning when the story ends.'

Godard's own film is careful even at the end not to yield unambiguous meanings. A corrosively satirical work, it bundles the drive to closure together with other strategies of mainstream cinematic storytelling as symptoms of Americanism to be resisted. The most conclusive, authoritative type of ending is indeed associated with classical Hollywood cinema; as Robert Stam says about this tradition's characteristic story arc: 'Everything becomes subordinated to a teleology as relentlessly purposeful as the Fate of classical tragedy' (*Literature and Film: A Guide to the Theory and Practice of Film Adaptation* (Oxford: Blackwell, 2005), p. 43). Merely to point out the salience of the ending for Hollywood, however, is not to deliver a knock-out blow against this tradition of film. Stam's own reference to tragic drama is suggestive: after all, the spectator of Sophocles's *Oedipus Rex* or Shakespeare's *Hamlet* is also agog from the beginning about how things will turn out, without such end-directedness leading critics to general conclusions about an impoverished art form. Where the Hollywood ending suffers is in the suspicion that it is too pat, too anally compelled to tie up loose ends, too preoccupied with warming or consoling its audience.

The classical Hollywood narrative often follows the simplified, tripartite model sketched by the French theorist Tzvetan Todorov. Here an initial state of *equilibrium* is provoked into *disequilibrium* by some complication or crisis – the crime film's unsolved murder or the musical's temporary separation of two lovers – before this interim situation yields to the phase of *equilibrium-restored*. For the moment, we can set aside the conceptual problem that any final equilibrium will be qualitatively different from the initial calm, and thus signifies realignment rather than 'restoration'. More to the purpose is to note the long history of trouble in the US for films that do not restore equilibrium convincingly enough. As early as 1928, the Swedish-born director Victor Sjöström's *The Wind* – a pessimistic prairie drama, ending in the heroine's desolation – was released by MGM with a hastily added optimistic coda. Following unease at preview screenings of *Blade Runner* in 1982, panoramas of a romantic mountainous landscape – actually shards of unused second-unit photography from Kubrick's *The Shining* – were bolted onto the film's dystopian, claustrophobic ending (an enormity only corrected by the Director's Cut ten years later). As recently as 2005, the American-released version of *Pride & Prejudice* included a final moonlit kiss between Darcy and Lizzie excised from the UK print. The British DVD edition includes this maudlin scene as an 'extra', so that the film, in a minor, still quite clunky way, begins to approximate a computer game with its multiple possible exits.

In certain circumstances, pessimistic endings may become as conventionalised as the Hollywood dénouement. Russia's taste for melancholia was so pronounced early in the twentieth century that Danish director August Blom added a tragic ending to *Atlantis* (1913) for that particular foreign market; conversely, the endings of several Russian films had to be deactivated of misery before being offered overseas. Such overt pessimism reinforces what might already be regarded as the deathliness of filmic conclusions, verbalised on screen by the appearance, ominously, of 'The End'. Narrative's tendency towards a stasis ultimately identical with death itself has been explored by Peter Brooks. In *Reading for the Plot* (1984), Brooks models narrative trajectory in literature according to Freud's 1920 essay 'Beyond the Pleasure Principle', which argues that life-affirming erotic impulses in humans are contested and ultimately subdued by the death drive. In *Death 24x a Second*, Laura Mulvey extends such thinking to cinema; indeed, she suggests its greater plausibility still for this medium, given the film ending's literal arrest of speed, its suspending of the movement of previously animated figures.

As Mulvey says, this deathly connotation seems intensified in films that conclude with a freeze frame; here what she calls cinema's 'aesthetic of stillness' appears absolute. The argument, however, is too generalised and risks detaching each instance of the freeze frame from its particular narrative and generic contexts. It is unlikely that spectators of *The Full Monty* (1997), which ends by freezing the joyous male striptease, left the cinema muttering about the triumph of the death drive. Similarly, morbid reflection may not have figured highly among patrons of *Wallace & Gromit in The Curse of the Were-Rabbit*, which concludes with one of the cartoon rabbits fixed in mid-air. Mulvey herself makes another point that concluding a film with a freeze frame may actually be *more* resistant to a sense of termination than other endings. After all, the device can leave narrative possibilities open and undecided, rather than resolving them in a single direction. Things are still 'up in the air' – literally so in *Wallace & Gromit*, and also in *Thelma and Louise* (1991), where the stilled closing shot of the car flying into the Grand Canyon defers, at least for a second longer, the destruction of the protagonists. At the end of Truffaut's *Les 400 Coups* (1959), a key work of the *Nouvelle vague*, the shot freezes the delinquent young protagonist as he stands in the surf off a beach and looks towards us; the moment seems suspended between several narrative possibilities, some of which are certainly alarming, but none of which is definitive. In this and many other cinematic instances, the tendency towards death that has been hypothesised for narrative seems complicated, if not thwarted. The triumph of 'conservative instincts', as Freud describes the death drive in 'Beyond the Pleasure Principle', is at least delayed. Although Freud intends 'conservative' in a metapsychological sense – to evoke the urge of the human species to return to its original, quiescent state – the term clearly has a political resonance also. If the stereotypical Hollywood ending might stand for the ideologically conservative position that everything is now defined and complete, other cinematic endings, including even some death-like freeze frames, evoke the alternative political possibility that the world is still up for grabs and open to reinvention.

STOP and THINK

• Return to the narrative films you used earlier to assess chronology, duration and frequency, and consider the implications of how they end. To use a phrase of the literary critic Frank Kermode, what 'sense of an ending' does each film provide? Do the final moments of these works evoke openness or completeness, ambiguity or clarity, unease or reassurance, frustration or bliss? What consequences follow from their specific modes of conclusion?

• Review the endings of films from different eras. The conclusion of an early gangster picture like *Public Enemy* (1931) might be set against Scorsese's *Goodfellas* (1990); or the ending of a classic American musical could be compared with *Chicago* (2002). Are there continuities between them? Or can we speak of a distinctively modern, or postmodern, ending? If you do detect a historical shift in cinematic endgames, explore the reasons – economic, cultural, ideological – for this.

Narrative and power

Fabula, *syuzhet*, *function*: the terminology introduced earlier in this chapter might seem to belong to a rarefied science of storytelling, given over to white-coated plotting of lines and grids in its objects of study. Yet, as the mere reference above to the variable politics of endings should indicate, narrative is worldly through and through. Suzanne Keen notes that, even from the beginning, the term *narrative* had socially charged rather than abstract or formalist connotations: when it entered common English usage in the mid-eighteenth century, it was as a name for statements lodged in court during legal disputes (*Narrative Form* (Basingstoke: Palgrave Macmillan, 2003), p. 1). Even away from such an explicitly contestatory situation as a case in law, stories are necessarily implicated in questions of power. This section, then, discusses aspects of power in specifically cinematic narrative, considering first the distribution of authority within narratives, before working outwards to review how film studies has theorised the spectator's own authority – or submissiveness – with respect to the stories told by cinema.

Two questions that Genette says are advisable to ask about any literary narrative – 'Who sees?' and 'Who speaks?' – are pertinent for film also. Because of the medium's ocular bias, the question of seeing, or perspective, is literal and urgent here. In much cinema, certainly within the mainstream tradition, *point of view* tends not to be explicitly marked. The camera lens generally frames the action without suggesting that the view which results is the property of a situated, bodily presence. Francesco Casetti proposes this be termed 'nobody's shot', which is misleading but nevertheless evocative of the sense that is generated of a disembodied perspective. More usually, the camera's unmarked seeing of this type is called an *objective shot* – again inadequately, since it actually emerges from a precise location in time and space and will be inflected by a specific purpose.

There is an alternative to the 'objective' regime in the so-called *subjective* or *point-of-view (POV) shot* which aims to mimic the optical situation of a figure within the narrative itself. Very early cinema sometimes put this shot to playful use: witness the English filmmaker G. A. Smith's *Grandma's Reading Glasses* and *As Seen Through a Telescope* (both 1900), which advertise their optical experimentalism by their titles. On the whole, the subjective shot is a quite lightly used variation in cinema, respecting Bernard F. Dick's sternly normative judgement that it 'should be restricted to specific scenes or sequences' and 'should never dominate a film' (*Anatomy of Film*, 4th ed. (Boston: Bedford/St. Martin's, 2002), p. 59). A rare attempt to organise an entire work by subjective shots is Robert Montgomery's Chandler adaptation, *The Lady in the Lake* (1946). Here, even in a kissing scene, the camera stands in for the private eye Philip Marlowe. Yet the film remains an oddball venture, rather than one which inaugurated other traditions of cinematic storytelling. It also exemplifies a prevailing use of the subjective shot not to rethink the internal politics of narrative – democratising diegetic space by offering a viewing position to characters that would more usually be fixed by the camera's objectifying gaze – but to maximise spectator sensation instead. In the horror film, say, subjective shots excitingly erase the distance between spectator and menaced protagonist (an effect that perhaps reaches an apotheosis in 1999 in the sustained handheld subjectivity of *The Blair Witch Project*).

If the power to see within film narratives is only seldom available to characters themselves, should we say the same about the power to speak or narrate (Genette's second question)? Immediately, we think of cases where some of a film's storytelling labour is delegated to a *voiceover* that is usually, though not always, spoken by a figure in the narrative itself. While the device is not consistently in favour, it has been institutionalised in certain genres, notably the classic film noir (as well as traditional documentary). However, any suggestion that the voiceover signifies a narrative revolt, a Pirandellian blow for freedom by characters against the oppressive, external narrating agency, instantly needs to be qualified. For while voiceover achieves a certain brief privilege, it still represents only one part of a film's total storytelling operation. Seymour Chatman's diagram of what he helpfully calls 'the multiplexity of the cinematic narrator' (*Coming to Terms*, pp. 134–5) shows that voiceover has to co-exist with sounds and music and thus cannot exert dominance even over the auditory channel, let alone control cinema's multiple *visual* effects. For such a first-person narrator to seize true narrative power in a film, as Stam points out, there would need to be 'relentless subjectification on almost all the cinematic registers: foregrounded presence in the shot, uninterrupted voiceover, non-stop point-of-view editing, constantly motivated camera movements, always marked subjective framing' (*Literature and Film*, p. 38).

Even in works possessing one, then, voiceover cannot convincingly be said to narrate. Yet exactly who or what does narrate in this medium has long vexed film studies. In *Logique du cinéma* (1964), Albert Laffay proposed that narration originates from '*le grand imagier*', the master of images. The later French critic André Gaudreault has a similarly gigantic storytelling presence in mind – albeit one not communicating exclusively through Laffay's visual channel – when he offers the somewhat inelegant term, 'the mega-narrator'. For David Bordwell, however, all such language goes too far in attributing cinematic narrative to a shadowy creative force, a kind of filmmaking Wizard of Oz. He argues in *Narration in the Fiction Film* that the question of narrator identity should actually be abandoned; a three-part model of cinematic storytelling – narrator/narrative/narratee (or receiver) – should be simplified to just the latter two terms. In a further twist of the theoretical spiral, Bordwell's provocative disappearing of the narrator has been criticised by writers including Chatman and Edward Branigan.

This debate might look like film studies' equivalent of the medieval theological dispute about how many angels can dance on the head of a pin. Certainly, trying to finger the cinematic narrator has led to some hair-splitting and moments of airless formalism. Yet the discussion is not without worldly consequences. In rejecting Laffay's and Gaudreault's hypothesis of a powerful storytelling machine, Bordwell mobilises the same objections he has to that 1970s film theory which evokes the spectator's submission to narrative and all its ideological works. We will consider this strain of ideology-critique in more detail in Chapter 8. Here we just note how Bordwell challenges such work for implying passivity, a fixed 'position', in receivers of film narrative. His own view is that 'A film ... does not "position" anybody. A film cues the spectator to execute a definable variety of *operations*' (*Narration in the Fiction Film*, p. 29). Defining precisely what these 'operations' are preoccupies Bordwell both here and in later work, as he sketches what he terms a 'perceptual-cognitive' account of film spectatorship. Not all of the spectator processes he outlines are necessarily or exclusively directed towards narrative engagement. However, the activities of problem-solving, hypothesis-building and inference are clearly fundamental in making sense of cinematic stories.

Bordwell's account of the spectator's relationship to narrative risks going both too far and not far enough. While he properly attempts to restore a sense of the viewer's meaning-generating activity in the face of the more morbid film theory, he overstates this, sometimes neglecting the powerful designs that cinema's storytelling machine has upon us. In other respects, however, his argument is rather shrunken. On cognitive grounds themselves, he neglects the emotional aspects of our involvement with narrative, as in empathetic bonds with characters: Bordwell's stress upon deduction and problem-solving is well-suited to modelling our response to the detective film but lacking in sensuous generosity as an account of how we watch and make sense of a melodrama. On non-cognitive grounds, too, Bordwell is open to critique. In emphasising feats of narrative comprehension, he pays little attention to other, less respectful things that might be done to film stories, such as taking them apart politically. He also generalises spectator responses, at a quite abstract level of shared mental functioning; variations in spectatorship – how audiences in different times and places interact dynamically with the same narrative – do not occupy him. For all its laudable empowering of the narrative viewer, then, Bordwell's schema urgently needs supplementing by the specific worldly emphases which cultural studies brings to discussion of film.

Analysing narrative: *21 Grams*

21 Grams is an exemplary case of 'transnational' cinema discussed in Chapter 9. Originally set in Mexico City, its story was transplanted to the US and placed in an oddly hybrid geography where Memphis suburbia appears to adjoin a Southwestern wasteland of dusty roads and grimy motels. The film's main creative personnel are themselves migrant across several nations, languages and cinematic forms. The cosmopolitan cast includes the British-born Australian Naomi Watts and the Puerto Rican Benicio Del Toro, while the editor is Californian, the composer Argentine, and writer and director both Mexican (Guillermo Arriaga and Alejandro González Iñárritu, respectively). But if the film evokes a contem-

porary transiting of film topics and styles across international
borders, it is principally of concern to us here because of its narrative form. Having worked previously on *Amores perros* and
subsequently on *Babel*, Arriaga and Iñárritu are patent-holders for
a kind of narrative triptych, in which a chance event precipitates
the constellation of three different stories.

To use terms introduced above, the syuzhet of *21 Grams* drastically disarranges its fabula. If we were to set out the fabula, the
film's chief events organised chronologically, it would look something like the following. Cristina Peck loses her husband and two
young daughters in a hit-and-run accident, caused by a reformed
convict Jack Jordan. The man's heart is transplanted into a mathematician, Paul Rivers, who becomes obsessed with discovering the
donor; he tracks down Cristina and begins an affair with her
(Figure 9). The two of them plot to kill Jack, who has abandoned

Figure 9 Paul Rivers (Sean Penn) and Cristina Peck (Naomi Watts) in
21 Grams (US, 2003).

his own family in guilt following the accident. However, Paul cannot commit murder; instead, his new heart giving out, he shoots himself and is rushed to hospital. There he dies but not before Cristina discovers that she is carrying his child.

All of this is the stuff of melodrama, if by 'melodrama' we understand that artistic mode propelled by vivid moral conflicts, passionately, even hysterically invoked emotions, and sensational events, including coincidences and stunning reversals. Jonathan Romney links *21 Grams* to the melodramatic form of the *telenovela*, a Latin American soap opera (*Sight and Sound*, March 2004: 16). We might also call it a 'transplant melodrama', thereby enlisting it in a highly specialised sub-genre which also comprises such films as the British *Heart* (1999) and Clint Eastwood's *Blood Work* (2002). Yet the emotional drive implicit in the fabula is complicated or rerouted by the extreme experimentation that occurs in the film's syuzhet. There is little prospect of the spectator's swooning in soap operatic excess, given the basic cognitive work she must continually do in order to grasp chronology and articulate one plot strand with another. Episodes of different temporal status are juxtaposed to disorienting, even giddying effect. These leaps in time cannot even with safety be described as 'flashbacks' or 'flashforwards', since both terms imply a stable narrative present – lacking here for the most part – around which either regressive or progressive movement may be coordinated.

Such extreme temporal disruption brings to mind a film such as *L'Année dernière à Marienbad* (1961). Yet with its vivid events and hectic pacing, not to mention the glamour of its Hollywood cast, *21 Grams* feels very distant from Resnais's modernist rigour. Equally, it resists in the end the parallels that seem possible with another radical narrative experiment: B. S. Johnson's novel *The Unfortunates* (1969), a book famously sold in a box, its pages not bound together but capable of assembly in any way the reader chooses. At times, Iñárritu's film seems motivated by a similar principle of artistic chance, with its scenes, too, comprising so much narrative raw material that awaits infinite forms of ordering. However, it becomes clear that the spectator's liberty among all these story fragments is only partial. Sequences in *21 Grams* are not combined according to chance but actually studded with directions for their eventual reassembly. Even before the events that definitively group characters together, figures from one narrative segment brush against those from others, as when Paul's wife sees the grief-stricken Cristina leaving hospital. Or actions, colours and objects may rhyme across scenes, as in a cut from Paul and his wife washing glasses to Cristina pouring herself a drink.

21 Grams is also marked by what Genette calls repetitive narrative. Certain moments are seen not once but several times, reappearing with the effect of fuller spectator comprehension. A case in point is the pre-credits sequence of a man smoking while a woman sleeps in bed; initially opaque, the episode can be narratively grasped by the time it recurs two-thirds of the way through the film. There are aural repetitions, too, notably of the final answerphone message left by Cristina's husband: routine or semantically insignificant when first heard, it is charged with poignancy when replayed much later by the grieving Cristina. And while the film's narrative generally proceeds at what Genette would term 'constant speed', there are also significant instances in which time is retarded. Slow motion evokes the possibility of heightened moments outside time's normally mindless flow: think, for example, of Cristina floating in the swimming pool, briefly redeemed from sadness.

Especially given their duplication in other work by Iñárritu and Arriaga, there is some danger that the multiple narrative rearrangements of *21 Grams* constitute a flamboyant stylistic signature, a form of cinematic niche marketing. However, this assault on routine chronology is ethically appealing in a film where characters are intermittently tempted by oppressively linear and finite modes of time. Jack, an evangelical Christian, denies the sense of time's plasticity by insisting that everything happens according to God's will; even if the film might in the end be said to provide a secularised endorsement of this – with seemingly disarranged episodes actually orchestrated by the filmmakers' preconceived logic – its frequent temporal jumps still resist any tendency towards narrative termination. As Jack's put-upon wife tells him: 'Life has to go on, with or without God'. Cristina's father uses the same argument when he disputes the terminal grief of her statement that 'Life does not just go on'. In the terms of Freud's 1917 essay, 'Mourning and Melancholia', Cristina is immobilised – 'paralysed', as she says – in a melancholic stage, rerouting her sense of bereavement into self-hatred (drinking, drug-taking, careless driving). The alternative, 'mourning' phase does not imply erasure of the loved one but a reconfiguring of loss within actions still directed outwards. Traversing ceaselessly across time, *21 Grams* seeks in its own movements to express this ongoing dynamic of loss and restitution, rather than an irrevocable course to tragedy.

Seeking a dignified retreat from his unhappy marriage, Paul says at one point: 'I want this to end well.' What might we say about the film's own ending? As he lies mortally ill in hospital with his failed second heart, Paul refers in voiceover to the '21 grams' that, apparently, are lost from the body at the moment of death. He goes on to muse not only about loss but also about survivals, what may be renewed or even freshly created by a death. We saw earlier that a character's voiceover affords only limited power, given the overall narrative apparatus of any film. Despite its nearly posthumous status here, however, Paul's voice does have a certain authority, not only in clarifying the otherwise obscure title but in even seeming to motivate the closing scenes. While he speaks, there is a montage of scenes in slow motion, some from the film's narrative past, but two from its future beyond his own death. In the first, Jack returns home to his family; then Cristina, pregnant with Paul's child, finally appears in a state of mourning, not closed-in melancholia, as she is shown able to enter her dead daughters' bedroom and nurse their belongings.

Jack's earlier intention to live 'alone' – seemingly abandoned at the end – is anyway a solipsistic impossibility in the Arriaga/Iñárritu universe. Paul's new heart, too, means that at the very core he is marked by the presence of another. The lines of narrative connection and collision in *21 Grams* hint at powerful human interdependency. Characters otherwise unrelated are liable, violently or erotically, to coincide with one another: the tattooed ex-con Jack can come into the same space as the suave mathematician Paul. Yet a point more theological or metaphysical than political seems being made by this narrative coming-together. Elsewhere in fiction and film – Dickens, say, or instances of film noir and the cinematic conspiracy thriller – complex plotting functions to disclose connections, within a single if hierarchised social structure, between different classes and spaces. By contrast, *21 Grams* is not particularly engaged by the social specificity of its figures: only a single reference to fractals, for example, denotes that Paul is a professional mathematician. The varied lives of these characters are not presented with political urgency, alerting us to problems of economic and social inequality. Instead, they are offered as all equally valuable in the sight of God or – its secular equivalent – in the filmmakers' humane vision.

Selected reading

Bordwell, David, *Narration in the Fiction Film* (London: Methuen, 1985).
    Boldly develops a 'perceptual–cognitive' account of the audio-viewer's processing of film narrative. Open to dispute but influential, eloquent and displaying Bordwell's customary pan-artistic, pan-philosophical erudition.
Bordwell, David, *The Way Hollywood Tells It: Story and Style in Modern Movies* (Berkeley, Los Angeles and London: University of California Press, 2006).
    Entertaining discussion of mainstream American cinema's storytelling from the 1960s to the present, arguing that the increased complexity and velocity of its plotting is continuous with classical film narration. In its historical range, both prequel and sequel to Thompson.
Branigan, Edward, *Narrative Comprehension and Film* (London: Routledge, 1992).
    Sophisticated, challenging study. Enters into debate with Bordwell's model of cinematic narration, and should also be read alongside Chatman.
Chatman, Seymour, *Coming to Terms: The Rhetoric of Narrative in Fiction and Film* (Ithaca: Cornell University Press, 1990).
    Thoughtful, lucid review of film's narrative processes relative to those of literary fiction. Chapter 8, on 'The Cinematic Narrator', offers a partial critique of Bordwell.
Kozloff, Sarah, *Invisible Storytellers: Voice-Over Narration in American Fiction Film* (Berkeley, Los Angeles and London: University of California Press, 1988).
    In need of updating and internationalisation but a well-researched survey of this key component of film's narrative repertoire (and sound regime).

Lothe, Jakob, *Narrative Fiction and Film: An Introduction* (Oxford: Oxford University Press, 2000).

A good place to start, offering a helpful overview of questions and terms in narrative theory. Sometimes privileges literary over cinematic narrative.

Mottram, James, *The Making of 'Memento'* (London: Faber and Faber, 2002).

Well-informed journalistic account of the genesis and reception of one of contemporary cinema's most ingenious narrative experiments.

Mulvey, Laura, *Death 24x a Second: Stillness and the Moving Image* (London: Reaktion, 2005).

Original, provocative reflections – shaped by Freud's theory of the death drive – upon cinematic endings: both the deathlike closures of the medium's narratives and, in the context of new digital technologies, the possible ending of film itself.

Stam, Robert, *Literature through Film: Realism, Magic, and the Art of Adaptation* (Malden, MA and Oxford: Blackwell, 2004).

Fascinating study of the adaptation of novels such as *Don Quixote* and *Robinson Crusoe* that raises questions about the fate of narrative when it traverses not only different media but highly divergent times and places.

Thompson, Kristin, *Storytelling in the New Hollywood: Understanding Classical Narrative Technique* (Cambridge, MA and London: Harvard University Press, 1999).

Extensive applications of an updated model of classical film narration – 'modern classicism' – to ten works from 1979–93, including *Alien*, *Tootsie* and *The Silence of the Lambs*.

Turim, Maureen, *Flashbacks in Film: Memory and History* (London and New York: Routledge, 1989).

Still the definitive study of cinematic analepsis. Theoretically ambitious, and both historically and geographically wide-ranging.

Wollen, Peter, *Readings and Writings: Semiotic Counter-Strategies* (London: Verso, 1982).

Essays of wide topical range, but especially recommended here for narrative concerns in '*North by Northwest*: A Morphological Analysis', 'Hybrid Plots in *Psycho*' and 'The Hermeneutic Code'.

Useful websites

www.jahsonic.com/CinematicTime.html.

This page on cinematic treatment of time serves as a portal to other resources on film and narrative; jumbles citations from Wikipedia together with refereed scholarship but includes much useful material.

www.kyushu-ns.ac.jp/~allan/Documents/CCEurope-05.html.

Essay that follows overview of Surrealism with an account of Buñuel and Dalí's disassembly of film narrative in *Un chien andalou*; especially good visuals.

5
Film and authorship

Although Godard's *Le Mépris* was considered in Chapter 3 for complexity of soundtrack, it also dramatises vividly the question of film authorship. Who, exactly, authors a film? Indeed, can we even speak of a film author in the way that we identify the creative force responsible for a novel, painting or symphony? In *Le Mépris*, Paul is hired for a film project because of his writing talents, previously directed elsewhere but now to be applied to a screenplay. However, his own claim to authorship of this film is compromised or merely partial, since he cuts a deferential figure next to its director (the actual German director Fritz Lang playing a version of himself). Lang already has a vision of the film he wishes to make; the final scene, when he orders shooting to begin, demonstrates that he also has a practical supervisory capacity, the kind of 'foreman's' authority ascribed to Ingmar Bergman by an observer of the making of *Winter Light* (1962).

However, any thought that *Le Mépris* is an assertion of the director's creative pre-eminence in filmmaking is premature. Lang, like Paul, is a hired hand on a project administered by the Hollywood producer Jerry Prokosch. The parable is close to home, since the real-life Lang's own career trajectory took him from German film in the 1920s to the more tightly regulated studio system of Hollywood. It is Jerry, and not Lang or Paul, who determines that the adaptation of Homer's *Odyssey* on which they are all working should include more nudity and be marked by levity rather than epic seriousness. If their film has an authorial signature, then, it appears to belong not to director or screenwriter but

instead to the producer (or to those corporate forces he represents). Yet the film Jerry envisages is itself not a product of some
autonomous imagination but, after all, an adaptation – however
free and vulgar – of a prior text. For all his swaggering sense of
answering to no-one, even this producer is caught up in an *intertextual* web over which he can make no absolute proprietary claim.

Le Mépris condenses several stages from the history of debate
over film authorship. Initially, in Paul's excitement at being
recruited for the Homer project, it recalls from earlier French film
history the notion of a scenarist's cinema, one in which the screenwriter is identified as chief author. By contrast, the concept of a
director-authored cinema of which Godard was a major proponent
is embodied in Lang's magisterial figure. Yet in its attention to the
structuring power exerted by producers and studio systems, *Le
Mépris* also anticipates subsequent challenges within film studies
to directorial autonomy – challenges that put into question such
casual attributions as this chapter's initial reference to *Godard's*
film. With uncanny prescience, the film shows, too, how theories of
intertextuality will disrupt all thinking about original or exclusive
authorship. It achieves this not only through the explicit drama of
how Homer's pre-existing text is to be adapted but, more fleeting-
ly, by showing a poster for Rossellini's *Journey to Italy* (1953), a
film to which *Le Mépris* itself is intertextually bound. The present
chapter contextualises and evaluates these shifts in theories of the
cinematic author.

Auteur studies: *Cahiers du cinéma* and other journals

'Little magazines' devoted to a particular field of study sometimes
exert a force larger than suggested by their mere circulation
figures. In Britain, the literary journal *Scrutiny* (1932–53) exhibited a passionate moral engagement with its subject that challenged
both genteel taste and mass culture, and energised the study of
English at all levels. The closest equivalent in film studies to such
an influential small publication is *Cahiers du cinéma*, first
produced in April 1951 by a group of Paris-based cineastes and
still in existence. During its heyday of the 1950s and 1960s, it was
not even the only film journal in France, having to compete with

rivals including the more politically aligned *Positif*. As a French-language magazine, it also seemed far removed from the film industry's centres of power in the United States. Yet in the first two decades of publication, *Cahiers* helped to invigorate and even transform not only the study of cinema but the cinematic institution more broadly.

Unlike most film periodicals, *Cahiers* was distinguished in its early years by being a journal of critic-practitioners. Many of its writers were also or would become directors of key *Nouvelle vague* films: Claude Chabrol, Jacques Rivette, Eric Rohmer and François Truffaut, besides Godard. A clear sense of continuity exists between these figures' critical and cinematic modes of practice. Their first films look like essays on cinema, just as their articles in the journal are implicitly sketches for future film projects. To read *Cahiers* in its early decades is to experience some of the most exhilarating writing ever produced about cinema. Though lacking the same advanced theoretical consciousness, the journal at this time fizzes with the medium-specific excitement of the 1920s generation of Russian writer-filmmakers gathered around Eisenstein. *Cahiers* writing is marked by suspect generalisation and lurid over-statement – 'cinema is Nicholas Ray' (Godard on a favoured US director in January 1958) – but scorched into the prose is a sense of the seriousness of film, the absolute commitment required by the medium. Such enthusiasm has sometimes led to charges of adolescent indulgence: for John Caughie, the journal in these founding years maintains 'a teenage romance' with the ideal of the creatively autonomous director (*Theories of Authorship*, p. 2); for Thomas Schatz, more scathing still, the *Cahiers* writers are at least partly responsible for having kept film studies in 'a prolonged stage of romantic adolescence' (*Film and Authorship*, ed. Virginia Wright Wexman, p. 91). While verbally similar, James Naremore's verdict that they are 'surely among the last romantics' is more generously intended (*A Companion to Film Studies*, eds. Toby Miller and Robert Stam (Malden, MA and Oxford: Blackwell, 1999), p. 16). This 'romanticism' consists not only in feverish outbursts from which soberly academic film studies should keep its distance but in forms of engagement and sensitivity from which anyone thinking about cinema can still productively draw.

Cahiers du cinéma in the 1950s and early 1960s is not graced by anything as systematic as a theory. Nevertheless, several propositions for the interpretation and evaluation of film can be identified from the polemics and informal manifestos that animate its pages. Broadly speaking, the journal in this period sought to

- legitimise cinema as an art commensurate with traditional aesthetic forms such as literature, painting, sculpture and music;
- locate film's artistic quality not so much in thematic contents as in formal elements, particularly the configuration of mise-en-scène;
- conceptualise the director, above all other figures, as a film's chief source of creativity and aesthetic distinctiveness;
- make evaluative distinctions between functionally competent directors (*metteurs-en-scène*) and those whose films are unified by a strong artistic signature (*auteurs*, French for 'authors').

None of these positions is entirely original. While there was certainly a tradition of aesthetic disregard for cinema – culminating in film's indictment by Adorno and other post-Second World War theorists as central to a banal, commodified mass culture – attempts had previously also been made to establish its seriousness as art. In the 1920s the Surrealist avant-garde embraced cinema alongside writing, painting and photography. In 1948, still a few years before the founding of *Cahiers*, Alexandre Astruc argued that cinema had finally lost its connotations of fairground spectacle and nickelodeon amusement, and was now legitimised as 'a form in which and by which an artist can express his thoughts, however abstract they may be, or translate his obsessions exactly as he does in the contemporary essay or novel' ('The Birth of a New Avant-Garde: La Caméra-Stylo', p. 18). Similarly, precedents exist for the *Cahiers* critics' valorising of the figure of the director. Besides Astruc's own metaphor of 'la caméra-stylo' ('camera-pen') – more likely to be wielded by the director than by other film personnel – the British filmmaker and critic Lindsay Anderson inquired into the possibility of a 'director's cinema' in the British journal *Sequence* in 1950. Anderson's journalism of the period even anticipates the *Cahiers* position that 'director's cinema' would be a party to which not all filmmakers are invited.

But if elements of *Cahiers*-thinking are visible earlier or elsewhere, this new group of French cineastes provided rhetorical verve and a certain critical mass. Their provocative reconceptualisation of film authorship is apparent as early as Truffaut's article, 'A Certain Tendency of the French Cinema', printed in the journal in January 1954. Here the chief object of attack is 'scenarists' films', the overmighty role played in French cinema by screenwriters. Where Truffaut criticises these screenplays for their swearwords, blasphemy, and anti-clerical and anti-militarist attitudes, he sounds more ready to man a church pew than a revolutionist's barricade: if the *Cahiers* generation is a very rough equivalent of the 'Angry Young Men' in English writing of the same period, it shares some of that grouping's blimpish tendency as well as its iconoclasm. More significantly, however, Truffaut's article also excoriates the cinema of screenwriters for its sheer literariness, its total inattention to the specific formal properties of the medium (particularly mise-en-scène).

By way of corrective, *Cahiers* maintained in its first two decades a strong emphasis upon the particularities of mise-en-scène, editing and sound. For the first time in the history of the medium, a collective of writers subjected the use of tracking shots, close-ups and so on to the level of scrutiny with which critics in other fields studied a sonnet's metaphors or a painting's brushstrokes. Even those later theorists who distance themselves from the *Cahiers* project frequently welcome its rerouting of attention from the contents or ostensible subjects of films to the dimension of form in which those contents are elaborated and transformed. Caughie nicely refers to the journal's promotion of 'a certain historically necessary formalism' (*Theories of Authorship*, p. 13). At times, to be sure, this heightened attention to mise-en-scène at the expense of other elements relevant to a film's critique is pushed to excess or even self-parody. One *Cahiers* writer admits that *Party Girl* (1958), directed by Nicholas Ray, 'has an idiotic story'; however – given its qualities of mise-en-scène – 'So what?' (*Cahiers du cinéma*, Vol. 2, p. 123).

Throughout, the *Cahiers* project is partisan and evaluative

rather than coolly analytical. Idiocies of narrative in *Party Girl* can
be forgiven because of Ray's accreditation already as an auteur.
While certain directors are damned by the journal as mere technicians, others are awarded auteur status on the basis of the
distinctiveness and unity of cinematic form detected across their
work. But much of *Cahiers'* influence consists in the identity of
those it invited into this pantheon. The pro-Americanism of these
selections can be exaggerated: Rohmer is not untypical in confess-
ing that his 'dearest masters' are Dreyer (Danish), Eisenstein
(Russian), Murnau (German), Renoir (French) and Rossellini
(Italian) (*Cahiers du cinéma*, Vol. 1, p. 93). Yet the journal's search
for auteurs went significantly wider and, besides Ray, elevated
other filmmakers from the Hollywood system, including Ford,
Hitchcock, Welles and Howard Hawks. No longer functionaries
within mass-produced cinema – Ford once complained to a studio
mogul that he felt like 'a piece-goods worker in the Hollywood
sweatshops' (Wexman, *Film and Authorship*, p. 8) – these directors
were reconceived as artists able to transcend the constraints of
formulaic filmmaking.

The energy and iconoclasm of *Cahiers* writing gained it an
international audience. In the United States Andrew Sarris's key
article, 'Notes on the Auteur Theory in 1962' was published by the
East Coast journal *Film Culture*. While his title was an inaccurate
translation of the *Cahiers* phrase, '*politique des auteurs*' – the
French term for 'policy' now systematised into 'theory' – Sarris
productively introduced auteurist thinking to America.
Meanwhile, in Britain, auteurism registered in the journal *Movie*,
founded in 1962 by a group of Oxford contemporaries. These
writers, too, promoted a new sensitivity to matters of cinematic
form and a notion of directorial authorship at the expense of soci-
ologically driven responses to film. If their work seems
unexceptionable now, that in itself is evidence of the universalisa-
tion of at least some auteurist precepts. At the time, however,
intellectual combat was bloody, with *Movie*'s interest in the director's organisation of mise-en-scène causing a feud with the BFI's
house journal, *Sight and Sound*.

STOP and THINK

- At different times and places in cinema, the figure of the director seems especially powerful, even insistent. Think, for example, of Alfred Hitchcock's cameo appearances in his films as if affirming personal ownership of them. Directorial recognition was similarly strong during the heyday of European art cinema in the 1960s and 1970s: spectators referred to films as 'the new Fellini' or 'the new Fassbinder', rather than distinguishing them by other criteria such as star, subject or even nation. Contemporary Hollywood, too, has been quick to exploit the branding potential of particular director names: 'Steven Spielberg's new movie' or 'the latest Michael Mann'. Across their several contexts, these director citations all function to specify with some confidence the source of cinematic authorship. Assess, however, whether it is plausible to equate the film director with such individualised artistic creators as the writer, painter or sculptor. Moments of heightened auteur visibility notwithstanding, how aware in general are you of directors? How strong a factor is knowledge of the director in what you choose to see? What place does this figure have in your critique of a film?
- Take any director with whose work you are familiar. Is it possible to identify recurrent patterns in his or her films? As the *Cahiers* writers and their successors argue, these may well be stylistic or formal consistencies; but they could also be thematic continuities (potentially even stretching across different genres). If such repetitive features can be detected, do they amount to marks of distinctively personal authorship, the directorial equivalents of Henry Moore's preoccupation with voids in sculpture or Jane Austen's signature irony about the genteel classes?
- Finally, list as many directors as possible. Then, giving reasons for your decisions, try to divide them between the *Cahiers* categories of cinematically distinctive auteurs and merely efficient *metteurs-en-scène* whose films seem to bear no personal trace. You may find more and more direc-

tor names proffering themselves for the more favoured category, making auteurism a currency as hyperinflationary as the German *Papiermark* in the 1920s; horrified at the prospect of just such a booming market in critical reputations, Godard spoke in elitist – and revealingly masculinist – terms about the need still to distinguish between 'the big boys and the little ones' (Jean Narboni and Tom Milne (eds), *Godard on Godard* (London: Secker and Warburg, 1972), p. 231). Or does this whole project of differentiating between directorial sheep and goats strike you as impossible, even undesirable?

The problems of auteurism

The success of auteurist thinking as promulgated by *Cahiers du cinéma* and other journals and books from the 1950s onwards can be measured institutionally. Inspired by cinema's new status as an art to be taken seriously and by canonisation of favoured film-makers from Europe and the US – occasionally from elsewhere, too, as in the case of Japanese directors such as Akira Kurosawa, Kenji Mizoguchi and Yasujiro Ozu – film societies and specialised exhibition venues sprang up in many places in the West. Festivals were inaugurated or reinvigorated. Auteurism played a significant part, too, in the establishment and consolidation of film studies itself, providing this new discipline with its core authors and texts. However, even as the evidence of auteurism's practical successes accumulated, it was increasingly subject to conceptual crisis and challenge. *Cahiers* itself interrogated the individualised, romantic notion of film authorship that had once been the journal's defining commitment. A snapshot of these intellectual shifts is provided by the trajectory of Jacques Rivette. Previously a major influence in identifying and exalting the director as a film's creative force, he could be heard, in 1968, rejecting as pernicious 'the idea that there is an auteur of this film, expressing himself. The only thing we can do in France at the moment is to try to deny that a film is a personal creation' (*Cahiers du cinéma*, Vol. 2, p. 319). What exactly caused such epochal changes of cinematic philosophy? In which ways did auteurism prove vulnerable to attack?

Playing parlour games
As noted above, auteurist writers tended to be governed by powerful enthusiasms and antipathies. Positively, their zeal brought a new sort of attention to the work of certain directors, including some formerly placed well below the salt. Less beneficially, whole bodies of cinema by others were excluded from serious discussion. Such blatantly evaluative criticism proved in the end an unstable basis on which to raise a new academic discipline. At its worst, auteurism could descend into cinematic parlour games, operating at a conceptual level only just above the saloon-bar value judgements we cheerfully make after watching a film. This tendency culminates in Sarris's book, *The American Cinema: Directors and Directions 1929–1968* (first published in 1968). In a veritable mania of evaluative categorisation, Sarris distributes two hundred mainly, but not exclusively, American filmmakers across eleven classes of achievement. At the apex of this critical hierarchy is the 'Pantheon', a sanctum into which only fourteen directors are invited. The names of other categories, too, evoke the vagaries of personal taste rather than a programme founded upon intellectual rigour: 'The Far Side of Paradise', 'Less Than Meets the Eye' and 'Lightly Likable'.

Sarris has suggestive things to say in passing about many of the directors he discusses. Yet his book also exposes conceptual and methodological crises in auteurism's evaluative project. Assessing directors and films against eleven categories of worth – or even two, as in the founding distinction between auteurs and *metteurs-en-scène* – looks more like idle diversion than a task for disciplined film scholarship. This is not, of course, to rule out in some puritanical spirit the making of all statements about the relative value of films and their makers: it would be an enfeebled discipline that left itself without the ability and willingness to say something like 'Orson Welles is a better director than Michael Winner'.

The collaborative art of film

According to the Australian director Fred Schepisi, 'The term "auteur" just denigrates everyone else's job' (*Sight and Sound*, January 2002: 12). Part of the riposte to auteurism consists in emphasising the collaborative – rather than individualistic – nature of film production. The director is generally not alone on a project but working alongside producers, designers, editors, cinematographers, composers, actors and perhaps screenwriters (to say nothing of all those technical personnel whose labour is apparent in the completed film). There are, of course, exceptional cases that more closely approximate the solitariness of the poet's garret or painter's studio: here the home movie model of production developed by the American experimentalist Stan Brakhage comes quickly to mind. In general, however, cinema is an extrovert rather than solipsistic art. As Michael Ondaatje puts it in his book of dialogues with Walter Murch: 'a film set resembles a beehive, or daily life in Louis XIV's court – every kind of society is witnessed in action, and it seems every trade is busy at work.' Murch adds suggestively that a director is 'the immune system of the film', her activity guaranteeing the effective functioning of all those involved in its creation (*The Conversations: Walter Murch and the Art of Editing Film* (New York: Knopf, 2002), pp. xi, 28). A key role, certainly, but strikingly less romantic than those early auteurist figurations of the director seeking to bring to fulfilment a purely personal vision.

The recognition of multiple creative presences in cinema has, oddly, not always led to the abandonment of auteurism as a conceptual model. Instead, having to mitigate the role of the director, critics have sometimes searched for alternative auteurs with respect to particular films. If not the director, then perhaps creative authority can be vested in some other figure? There are even moments of such redistribution of auteurist credentials in *Cahiers* itself: Rivette argues that, given his distinctive styles of movement and speech, the mid-century French star Jean Gabin is 'almost more of a director' than those formally credited with that function in his films (*Cahiers du cinéma*, Vol. 1, p. 37). Elsewhere, other cinematic figures besides actors have been nominated as putative authors. The American critic Pauline Kael fought a vitriolic battle with Sarris over her assertion that co-screenwriter Herman Mankiewicz, as much as Welles, was responsible for *Citizen Kane*. Claims of creative pre-eminence might also be made in specific instances for set designers (Ken Adam's 1960s James Bond sets), sound editors (Murch in *The Conversation* – 1974), choreographers (Lester Wilson in *Saturday Night Fever* – 1977), martial arts arrangers (Yuen Wo Ping in *The Matrix*) and many others. The increasing 'digitisation' of cinema leads some critics to identify contemporary wizards of computer-generated imagery (CGI), too, as auteurs, more responsible than their directors for the sheen and spectacle of films on which they work.

All of these suggestions preserve rather than destroy the model of singular film authorship: only the identity of the author is altered. Other film scholars, however, find appropriate a paradigm of *corporate* rather than individualised authorship. To what extent were directors in the classical Hollywood era conduits for the transmission of 'studio styles', as with the template for the Warner Bros. gangster film of the 1930s or the MGM musical of the 1940s? And what, too, both then and now, of corporations like Disney, proprietors of a version of animated film that is to be reproduced rather than modified by directors on specific projects? But while any such corrective to the auteurist 'autonomising' of the director is valuable, it is important not to overstate the counter-position. Otherwise, film production comes to look morbidly predetermined, without any possibility of material interventions and transformations by all those flesh-and-blood figures – not only directors – involved in the process itself.

Finally, collaborative film authorship may take forms very different politically from the corporate signature. Whereas Godard insisted in 1958 upon the director's solitary creativity – cinema 'does not mean teamwork. One is always alone; on the set as before the blank page' (*Godard on Godard*, p. 76) – he later abandoned this hierarchical model of production and became part of the Dziga Vertov collective (named after the similarly collaborative early Soviet filmmaker). Outside the US and Western Europe, notions of the isolate filmmaker have often proved ambiguous. Welcomed at times in the developing world as empowering the creative individual in the face of state censorship and other coercions, auteurism has also been mistrusted as politically reactionary. In Latin America in the 1960s *Ciné Liberation* rejected a director-centred form of production and promoted not merely equality on the set but, through discussion and rescripting, the active involvement of audiences themselves in the making of films. Here, as with Godard's collective, critique of a particular mode of authorship is connected to a more general suspicion of power.

The death of the author

Auteurism was also a casualty of investigations that took place generally into the etymological links between 'author' and 'authority', even 'authoritarianism'. From the late 1960s onwards, the most influential Western model of authorship – one which had been appropriated for film by *Cahiers* writers and others – came under attack as an agency of oppressive power. The two most vivid anti-authorial voices were heard in France. In May 1968, the French state was shaken to its foundations by the militant activism of students and industrial workers. Revolution was thus in the air as Roland Barthes produced his 1968 essay, 'The Death of the Author'; a year later the Paris cobblestones thrown by rioters had barely been replaced when Michel Foucault published 'What Is an Author?'. While aimed in the first instance at literary scholarship, these pieces had a reconstructive effect upon film studies also.

Forty years on, the title and substance of Barthes's essay still have the power to scandalise. In seven iconoclastic pages, he argues that the figure of the author is pernicious in its effects and analogous to the ultimate embodiment of authority, God. Our attempts to organise the reading of a literary text by authorial references – what we discover about the author's biography, what we surmise from the text about his intentions – are not only overly deferential but conceptually flawed. Instead, we should acknowledge that no author can thoroughly 'authorise' a text in the sense of regulating the meanings it will generate when it is out in the world. In addition, Barthes provocatively asserts that what is presumed by a romantic aesthetic tradition to be an author's fully original work is actually a weaving together of prior inscriptions: 'a text is made of multiple writings, drawn from many cultures and

entering into mutual relations of dialogue, parody, contestation'
(*Image – Music – Text* (New York: Hill and Wang, 1977), p. 148).
Barthes himself did not significantly extend this sense of intertextual fabrication to the case of cinema; his few articles on film are
quite auteurist, especially when discussing Eisenstein. Yet it is
clear that his arguments potentially transform the concept of cinematic authorship. While his deposing of original creation in favour
of a model of textual assemblage would seem to lend itself especially to some films – contemporary hybrids, say, such as
Tarantino's splicing together of spaghetti westerns, 1960s
American TV and Japanese pulp – it has the capacity to apply to all
cinema. Barthes's liberation of the reader in the wake of the
author's downfall also bodes well for the cinematic spectator, who
had been a subservient or totally neglected figure in auteurist
thought.

Foucault's essay is less verbally incendiary but equally far-
reaching in its implications. Among other things, it historicises the
concept of authorship itself: the model of a solitary producer of
artistic work, gifted with special powers, is shown not to be time-
less and universal but temporally and geographically specific.
Foucault argues that, displacing an earlier sense of communal
cultural production, the distinctive figure of 'the author' emerges
in the Renaissance and is aligned with a new ideology of individualism. While certain types of cultural work even in the modern
period remain relatively 'unauthored', privileged forms of expression such as literature are affixed with an authorial signature.
Relevantly for us, Foucault also considers how a particular attribu-
tion of authorship functions to unify what might otherwise appear
a disparate group of texts. The 'author-function' assumes three
main sorts of consistency across these texts: 'a standard level of
quality', 'a certain field of conceptual or theoretical coherence'
and 'a stylistic uniformity' (*Language, Counter-memory, Practice:
Selected Essays and Interviews* (Ithaca, NY: Cornell University
Press, 1977), p. 128).

Although Foucault does not mention cinematic authorship
itself, his essay has had a significant impact upon film studies.
Indeed, in Britain at least, film scholars proved far readier to
engage with Foucault – and Barthes – than their counterparts in

English departments, who tended to regard such strange continental imports with the suspicion of customs officers. We can
immediately see how the paradigm of authorial consistency identified by Foucault has operated in the treatment of favoured
directors by *Cahiers* and others. Simply recall from above the
critic's response to *Party Girl*: admittedly, the film's faulty plotline
causes a momentary problem, but Ray's pre-established status as
an auteur soon allows the work to be absorbed into a field of
conceptual and stylistic coherencies. The dangers of auteurism
functioning in this way as a grid laid dogmatically upon all films
signed by a given director did not entirely escape *Cahiers* itself.
André Bazin – a calming presence at the journal, alongside more
febrile colleagues – objected to evaluating each new movie by 'the
aesthetic portrait of the filmmaker deduced from his previous
films' (*Cahiers du cinéma*, Vol. 1, p. 256). We will return to this
problem at the end of the chapter, in discussing David Lynch.
Given the pre-formed 'aesthetic portrait' of Lynch, the understanding already established of his work's formal and thematic
constancies, what is to be done with a seemingly aberrant film
such as *The Straight Story* (1999)?

Author and genre
Near the start of 'What Is an Author?', Foucault lists several
conceptual categories that seem weak by comparison with 'the
solid and fundamental role of the author and his works' (p. 115).
Among these undernourished concepts is that of *genre*. This argument has a particular significance for film studies. As noted above,
there is a liberating quality in the recognition by *Cahiers* writers
and others of the artistic creativity of directors frequently
dismissed as part of Hollywood's genre-centred mode of film
production. The corollary of this position, however, is an implicit
or even frank dismissal of genre as conceptually unimportant in
the interpretation of film. Genre appears to signify little more
than a set of degraded formulae against which the auteur must
struggle in order to achieve her distinctively personal vision.
Barry Langford neatly summarises this strain of anti-generic
thought: 'Genre is thus in some measure the culture – like a Petri
dish – on which genius feeds, rather than meaningful material in

its own right' (*Film Genre: Hollywood and Beyond* (Edinburgh: Edinburgh University Press, 2005), p. 9).

With the crisis of auteurism, greater and more nuanced attention has been paid by film studies to the category of genre (topic of Chapter 6). Along with other institutional factors in film production, the genre system is re-evaluated as not simply a dead weight on artistic inspiration. For a brief moment, however, the discipline actually sought to combine the individualised emphasis of auteurism with the transpersonal implications of a concern with genre. This conjunction is especially evident in work on John Ford's westerns by the British critic Peter Wollen. Writing in the aftermath of Barthes and Foucault, Wollen can no longer with conviction present Ford as an author wholly and consciously in control of the meanings of his films. However, scrutiny of these westerns reveals a number of recurrent patterns beneath the surface (there are parallels here with the attention to deep narrative structure that, in Chapter 4, we saw Wollen practising in the case of Hitchcock). The films are found to be structured by a series of basic oppositions, such as that of nature/culture. However, instead of Ford's authorship consisting in a set of conceptual and stylistic aspirations clearly established by the director prior to filming, the sense of authorial presence that his westerns communicate is a retrospective construct or critical extrapolation. Given this shift away from the director's knowing control of his work, Wollen famously turns Ford into 'Ford' (other US filmmakers like Hawks and Samuel Fuller are similarly hedged about by inverted commas).

This type of film reading, known as *auteur-structuralism*, enjoyed only a brief intellectual heyday, around the turn of the 1960s. The convolutions involved in rendering flesh-and-blood figures as quotation mark versions of themselves proved too awkward to reorganise the discipline's approach to authorship. Auteur-structuralism had other problems, too, not least a largely thematic emphasis – as in Wollen's interest in antithetical conceptual pairings – that undid straight auteurism's recovery of mise-en-scène. Another weakness, however, was shared with auteurism itself: namely neglecting the spectator, that element in the film experience which was just about to get sustained critical attention for the first time. Even in the face of such critique, however, auteur–structuralism remains significant as a symptom of a tendency within film studies. Although its way of going about it may have been flawed, its attempt to preserve a sense of the author in the wake of theoretical shifts indicates a dynamic that will be repeated in following decades.

STOP and THINK

- Return to the director whose work you considered earlier from an auteurist perspective and reassess his or her films in light of the anti-authorial positions just discussed. Does it still seem appropriate to utilise the model of an individual's creative hegemony? Or is it more plausible in this case to speak of a collaborative process of authorship? If so, what are the key contributions made by others? Consider more generally the effect that awareness of the multiple creative forces engaged in film production has upon our sense of a director's authority. What metaphors might we need to figure the role of the director (besides the images cited above of foreman and immune system)?

- Many attempts to revalue and disperse authorship are interested in sustaining the category itself. However, consider applying the more radical anti-authorial critiques of Foucault and Barthes. In the attempt to posit a set of consistencies across the work of your chosen director, have you found the 'author-function' to operate as dogmatically and restrictively as Foucault says it does? Do his or her films also lend themselves to Barthes's text- rather than author-centred approach, one that relocates meaning-production from the consciousness of the director to the newly enfranchised spectator?

- Is the entire debate over whose signature to affix to a film – director's?, star's?, cinematographer's?, studio's? – tiresome and unproductive? Are there better things we could and should be doing in film studies? Is it time to shelve the whole problematic of authorship itself?

The rebirth of the author

The death of the auteur has proved to be greatly exaggerated. Since the impact upon film studies of Barthes's obituary for the author, there have been, to be sure, only sporadic returns to the version of romantic auteurism purveyed by *Cahiers du cinéma*. But the director-as-author is a persistent figure, surviving in mutated forms and multiple contexts. This section briefly discusses three critical approaches to film that have found the concept of authorship indispensable.

Analytic philosophy

Until fairly recently, the major philosophical influences upon film studies have been those same continental traditions that transformed the discipline of English: the structural Marxism of Louis Althusser, say, or versions of poststructuralist thought. However, writers from the alternative lineage of analytic philosophy have lately revisited familiar issues in cinema study, including representation, the image and the cognitive contents of spectatorship. In a brief but helpful essay, Paisley Livingston brings this kind of methodical, problem-solving approach to bear on authorship itself. His aim is to persuade by cautious and modest – rather than absolutist – lines of argument. In one gambit, he acknowledges that there are many other valuable things to do with a film besides searching for its authorial signature. He concedes, too, that any notion of directorial agency is vulnerable to recent theoretical attacks upon the notion of intentionality. Having given this much ground, however, Livingston argues for a recalibrated, souped-*down* model of authorship (one in which, incidentally, the spectator is not, as in classic auteurism, excluded from the film experience):

> If one recognises that an utterance can be both intentionally produced by someone and have meanings that are not all and only those intended by that person, then it follows that strong intentionalism is not entailed by a broad conception of authorship. We can identify someone as the author of an utterance without having to say that that person has authored each and every meaning (or significance) that the utterance manifests. ('Cinematic Authorship', p. 302)

On the basis of this 'weak' version of intentionality, Livingston seeks to rehabilitate an interest in film authorship. Despite other tasks facing the discipline, there are, he argues, some cases where deciding the question of authorship is of paramount importance.

Feminism

It has often been pointed out, with suspicion, that high theory evaporated away the figure of the author at precisely the moment when feminism was beginning to recognise and assess a previously neglected female authorial tradition. In film as in literary studies, feminist scholars have continued to be interested in the possibility of a distinctively female authorship. This does not entail a naïve return – only now in the name of women – to notions of a director's unimpeded creative agency. Like their male counterparts, women film authors are constructed by a complex set of social forces and have to speak through the institutions of cinema, including generic and narrative codes. Within this scaled-down model of authorship, however, interesting work has been done in retrieving a sense of the female cinematic voice. Women's authorial presence might register as moments of 'rupture' or 'excess' in what otherwise seem quite unexceptional films. Research of this kind began in the early 1970s with respect to the films of Dorothy Arzner, one of the very few female directors in classical Hollywood. However, it remains a viable approach to contemporary women filmmakers. Can a distinctively female authorship be detected in, say, Kathryn Bigelow's handling of the action idiom in *Blue Steel* (1990), *Strange Days* (1995) and *K-19: The Widowmaker* (2002)?

This interest in women's struggle for authorship may be combined with postcolonial concerns. Rather than taking *Bhaji on the Beach* (1993), *Bend It Like Beckham* (2002) and *Bride & Prejudice* (2004) as impersonally designed machines for signification set in motion by the spectator, it might be more productive to assess their director Gurinder Chadha's authorial voice as a British Asian woman. Even as he enthusiastically introduces a book of articles dismantling traditional notions of authorship, John Caughie warns about a thinning out of historical context that may result: in abandoning the sense of a flesh-and-blood author 'we remove the most accessible point at which the text is tied to its own social and historical outside' (*Theories of Authorship*, p. 3). There are many instances in which it would be intellectually and politically irresponsible simply to pronounce the death of the author and erase a director's biographical specificities. It is important to know, for example, that the Iranian film *Sib / The Apple* (1998) was directed by a 17-year-old woman Samira Makhmalbaf, making a bid for authorship in both a filmic and a broader culture hitherto under patriarchal rule.

Legal studies

Film authorship is not a matter fought over only in seminar rooms; it is disputed, too, in more immediately consequential venues. In a fascinating essay, Marjut Salokannel shows how the identity of a film's author provokes controversy and conflicting judgements in law courts across the world. She indicates a profound difference between European and British / American legal interpretations of authorship. In the system of civil law that prevails in the European Union, a conception of authors' rights takes precedence in disputes concerning the ownership and circulation of films, and creative control is vested in the figure of the director; as an EU directive of 1992 states: '*the principal director of a cinematographic work shall be its author*' ('Cinema in Search of Its Authors: On the Notion of Film Authorship in Legal Discourse', *Film and Authorship*, p. 166). While the law allows for the possibility that authorial rights may be extended to other key figures involved in a film, such as the writer of an original screenplay and composer of an original score, it never significantly weakens the director's creative claim. By contrast, the director enjoys few such privileges in the British and US system of common law, where legal contentions over a film are decided mainly through the instrument of copyright. Copyright is held to belong to the production interests responsible for financing a particular work; directors, like everyone else on the project, are regarded as 'hired hands' that cede primary rights to the producers in their contracts of employment. These rival models suggest that law can only multiply and perpetuate – rather than definitively settle – different interpretations of authorship that have long concerned film studies.

Digital auteurs

Disputes in law are a particularly vivid reminder of the commercial dimensions of film authorship. The figure of the director currently has high economic prestige. Directors' names are used as selling points for books in film studies: think of Wallflower's 'Directors' Cuts' series or Manchester University Press's 'British Film Makers' and 'French Film Directors' strands. Directorial signatures are also crucial in the marketing of films themselves, both mainstream and arthouse: Chapter 6 shows how the director's name was a significant component in the marketing of *Miami Vice* (2006), alongside star portraits, clues about genre and so on. Directors are frequently foregrounded, too, in the repackaging in video and latterly DVD formats of already exhibited films. A glance simply at *Sight and Sound* for September 2006 finds reviews of the following DVD sets: *Sam Peckinpah's Legendary Westerns*, *Louis Malle: Volume 2*, *Almodóvar: The Collection (Vol. 2)* and *The Errol Morris DVD Collection* (collecting three of this American filmmaker's documentaries). In all these cases the director's name is the chosen instrument of commercial branding. While it may be a marker of aesthetic distinction, it also functions to burnish the items' commodity value.

Even further opportunities have opened up in the video and digital eras for the promotion of the director as star. Video helped to create the phenomenon of 'The Director's Cut'. This release of a second, generally longer or significantly modified version of a previous film evokes a return to founding principles of auteurism. At last, the Director's Cut seems to promise, the author's vision can emerge in all its purity, finally freed from the limitations of producer imagination. This version of a film may also reassert the director's creative control over faint authorial efforts previously made by audiences themselves: the changes to *Blade Runner* mentioned in Chapter 4, after all, were introduced following adverse spectator evaluations on questionnaires issued during preview screenings.

Digitisation has offered another particularly potent means of reinforcing a director's creative authority. The 'Director's Commentary', included in the special features of many DVDs, blocks out much of a film's original soundtrack in order to allow the director's voice to clarify choices made during shooting. In one sense, this addition of speech strips the work of its absorptive power and would seem to demystify the director's role by reducing it to the performance of a series of technical processes. From another perspective, however, the Director's Commentary represents a consolidation of auteurism, not only mediating the relation between spectator and film but tending to inflect spectator interpretation in the author's preferred terms.

Spectators may, of course, choose to resist authorial coercions by not paying attention to such a commentary. Digital technology has also opened up creative possibilities for the viewer besides the director. During home viewing of a DVD, she may choose to disrupt the film's original coherence by tactics that range from freezing the frame to leaping discontinuously between scene selections. It might still seem far-fetched to describe such spectatorial re-editing of a film text as significant acts of 'authorship'. However, a major new development that has given the spectator authorial options of a sort is the extension to film topics of so-called *fan fiction*, also strongly elicited by other media like comic books and TV series. Of course spin-off fictions from film are nothing new and in their most professionalised form – the soul-destroying 'book-of-the-film' – are merely another merchandising exercise. Fan fiction, however, represents a significant, if qualitatively uneven upsurge of amateur creativity. It is also distinguished from deferential books-of-the-film by the unusual, sometimes provocative or even obscene actions and settings into which it introduces pre-existing film characters.

Here we consider only the best-known of these online fan forums, FanFiction.net, founded in 1998 (www.fanfiction.net). Not universally popular among devotees of the genre – its censorship regime is tighter and its quality control looser than some rival sites – FanFiction.net nevertheless illustrates vividly the sheer scale and variety of informal authorship spinning off from cinema (and other media). On the day of access to the site – 12 August 2006 – the sub-heading 'Movie' listed hundreds of films that have provoked fans' stories. The capacity of particular works to inspire spectator creativity varied enormously. *Rob Roy* (1995) was attached to only one story; by contrast, *Gone With the Wind* (1939) had generated 240 fictional responses, *Hannibal* (2001) 826 and *Van Helsing* (2004) 1,110. But vastly more inspirational than any other film has been *Star Wars* (1977), which on this site alone had been fictionally augmented, revised, even wildly transformed by no fewer than 16,376 contributions. What is important is not only the extent of such fan authorship but its sociability. On FanFiction.net and other websites, stories themselves are only one item in a discursive cluster, prefaced by a few words of authorial comment and precipitating countless reader reviews. A strong sense is given of a community continually making and remaking itself, often using a specialist language to further its distinctiveness (*gen*, *het*, *slash*, *fic*, *metafic*, *drabbles* and so on). While a film authored by others may have initiated all this creativity, the original work has, at least to some extent, been rewritten and displaced by such subsequent authorial effort. As in other areas of the discipline, film studies must go beyond the apparently pristine film text, here by tracking one of the many forms of its afterlife.

Like the 'generic communities' discussed in Chapter 6, it is important not to overstate the utopianism of online fan authorship; despite the rhetoric of universal internet access, digital poverty persists. We should also not exaggerate the effect of fan fiction: a host of unofficial stories about *Star Wars* may transfigure the text, but such textual modification occurs at informal, almost subterranean levels and will not cause George Lucas sleepless nights. But, at the same time, this appropriation by fans of rights to film authorship is a striking development – especially since, as noted above, it coincides with a revival or even extension of auteurist power vested in the director. Academia has been slow to catch up with the phenomenon of unofficial film authoring. However, a critical literature is developing. Henry Jenkins has been the major figure in establishing the cultural seriousness of fan fiction – initially with *Textual Poachers: Television Fans and Participatory Culture* (1992) and most recently with *Convergence Culture: Where Old and New Media Collide* and *Fans, Bloggers and Gamers: Exploring Participatory Culture* (both 2006). Other timely work includes Sheenagh Pugh's *The Democratic Genre: Fan Fiction in a Literary Context* (2005) and Karen Hellekson and Kristina Busse's edited collection, *Fan Fiction and Fan Communities in the*

Age of the Internet (2006). None of these studies is exclusively film-oriented, since fan fiction is generated by a range of media forms; each book, however, assesses the significance of the extension of digital auteurism from the filmmaker to spectators themselves.

Analysing authorship: David Lynch

'Once a name starts getting certain meanings attached to it', states the contemporary American director David Lynch, 'it can be good, or it can be, you know, really bad' (Chris Rodley (ed.), *Lynch on Lynch*, 2nd ed. (London: Faber and Faber, 2005), p. 29). As a name, 'Lynch' itself is more polysemic than singularly defined; a site of differences, not consensus. Positively, for his admirers, his signature marks a formally and intellectually adventurous film-making, work that engages in startling new ways with such major thematic fields as the dissolution of identity, the conjunctions of sex and violence, and the strangeness and threat of the spaces we inhabit. For his detractors, 'Lynch' is shorthand for the worst excesses of postmodernism, a cinema given to wilfully convoluted narrative, cartoonish characterisation and a facile tendency to shock. But the name of Lynch also circulates beyond these narrow filmic contexts. He has, for instance, released music albums, drawn a newspaper comic strip and had many painting and photography exhibitions. Chris Rodley, editor of a book of conversations with the director, notes too that by 1990 'Lynch had become an influential and fashionable brand name' (*Lynch on Lynch*, p. 191). This Lynchian logo does not simply attach itself to the primary film work – operating as a powerful marketing device for each new release and its later video and DVD formatting – but adds lustre elsewhere, notably in the ads Lynch has directed for such global corporations as Armani, Honda and Calvin Klein. The model of the cinematic auteur is tested in Lynch's case not merely by this proliferation of his name across other media texts but by his reliance on certain, near-permanent collaborators and by his positioning in disparate institutional contexts that include micro-scale, almost home-movie production (*Eraserhead* (1976) and the shorts preceding it), big-studio cinema (*The Elephant Man*

(1980) and *Dune* (1984)), independent film (the work from *Blue Velvet* (1986) onwards) and US network television (*Twin Peaks* (1989–91)). This section aims therefore not to offer another reading of Lynch but to consider how his work assists in theorising the authorship of film.

Recall Foucault's argument that the 'author-function' becomes operative when conceptual and stylistic uniformities are detected across a given body of work. Audiences familiar with Lynch's output from *Eraserhead* to *Inland Empire* (2006) may feel it relatively easy to identify such authorial consistencies here. A list of recurrent features of Lynchian mise-en-scène would include uncanny interior settings, chiaroscuro lighting, creepy tracking shots and – from the actors – a frequently stylised, non-naturalistic mode of performance. Lynchian sound practice is even more specialised. A kind of aural uncanny is produced, with classic pop ballads occurring in unexpected places and an unlocatable industrial hum subsisting with – or even muffling – dialogue. Character-types, too, are reused: women often come in schematic pairs – an ingénue posed against a devouring femme fatale – while a sinister male dwarf is common (Figure 10). With exceptions – early on, Victorian England in *The Elephant Man* and interplane-

Figure 10 The Mystery Man in *Lost Highway* (France/US, 1997).

tary space in *Dune*; lately, the Polish segments of *Inland Empire* –
Lynch places his action in stereotypical American geographies of
indeterminate, or heterogeneous, period. Thematically, also, there
are strong continuities: the characteristic Lynchian protagonist
has a porous, even dissolving identity and is liable to find him- or
herself menaced by uncanny occurrences at best, actual eruptions
of the demonic at worst.

Perceptions of the coherence of Lynch's author-function face
their greatest challenge with *The Straight Story*. In this work there
are no sinister doubles and moments of serio-farcical sexual
violence; the disquieting industrial throbs of *Eraserhead*, *Twin
Peaks* and *Lost Highway* (1997) give way to birdsong in the open
air of the American Midwest. The film centres upon the real-life
story of an elderly man who travelled to see his estranged brother
several states away, using for transport a lawnmower capable of a
highest speed of five miles per hour (Figure 11). For his erstwhile
critics, *The Straight Story* suggested the abandonment of Lynch's
alienating form of cinema in the interests, finally, of humane character study. Many of the director's adherents, however, treated the
film as a betrayal or perversion of his cinematic distinctiveness.

Figure 11 The lawnmower man in *The Straight Story* (France/UK/US,
1999).

Although these responses are antithetical, each shows the operation of a preconceived auteurist persona – what Bazin calls the
already-established 'aesthetic portrait of the filmmaker'. So, too,
do the frequently ingenious attempts that have been made to align
the film, after all, with other films directed by Lynch. Some critics
point to the road as echoing a key location in *Wild at Heart* (1990)
and *Lost Highway*. Others argue that Lynch's uncanny denota-
tions of space carry across into *The Straight Story*: here a key
exhibit is a shot which tilts gracefully from lawnmower to sky and
returns to the road to find, bizarrely, that the slow-moving vehicle
has advanced only a few metres. Most audaciously, Rodley
suggests that, far from representing something alien or newly
additive in the director's work, the film is actually *'pure* David
Lynch' (*Lynch on Lynch*, p. 246), its central premise of the family
reunion offering in admittedly concentrated form elements of
sweetness and sentiment that had always been present, if usually
complicated or ironised. Though this is a useful insight, its keen-
ness to affiliate the new film with the old again suggests the
dangers of reducing interpretive resources simply to an auteurist
optic.

Even if *The Straight Story* is put to one side, however, the totality or purity of Lynch's auteurism across his other work is still
open to question. Intertextually, for example, his films carry traces
of significant precursors, including *The Wizard of Oz*, *Sunset
Boulevard* (1950) and Hitchcock's *Rear Window* (1954). Original
inscription perhaps needs to be reconceived, in Barthesian terms,
as rewriting or textual collage (a point reinforced by the films'
sampling of *music* too, from Roy Orbison to German techno).
There is also the sense that, in its mode of production, Lynch's
cinema is deeply collaborative. Michel Chion's study of the director states at the outset a challenge to romantic auteurism and a
desire to reckon with 'the multiplicity of collaborators (in particular, the actors)' (*David Lynch* (London: BFI, 1995), p. xi). Lynch's
repertory company of performers themselves extends from 'character actors' like Jack Nance and Harry Dean Stanton to stars
including Laura Dern (*Blue Velvet*, *Wild at Heart* and *Inland
Empire*) and Kyle MacLachlan (*Dune*, *Blue Velvet*, *Twin Peaks* and
the spin-off cinematic feature *Twin Peaks: Fire Walk with Me*

(1992)). Besides working with co-writers on some projects, Lynch is indebted to regular collaborators in editing, cinematography, sound and production design. Above all, perhaps, there is Angelo Badalamenti, who has composed the music for all his work from *Blue Velvet* to *Mulholland Dr.* (2001). *Twin Peaks* is unthinkable without Badalamenti's bass guitar chords over the credits and disconcerting jazz fragments throughout; so, too, his music powerfully stencils the cinematic films. That the creative relationship between Lynch and Badalamenti is co-authorial rather than traditionally hierarchical seems confirmed by the extra-cinematic musical albums and performances on which they have combined.

Collaboration can, of course, take less attractive forms than this quasi-familial mode of production. Lynch's involvement with US network television is a case in point. Not swayed by the charisma of his brand name, ABC rejected the pilot he made for a noir Hollywood mystery, resulting in the material's reshaping and extending for the cinema release, *Mulholland Dr.* The imprint of this network is also apparent on *Twin Peaks* itself. Despite its TV provenance, *Twin Peaks* has been embraced as part of the authentic Lynchian canon: besides repeating key stylistic tropes, it observes such thematic consistencies as demonic visitation and a sense of the sordidness underlying American small-town normality. But it is far from straightforward to attribute the programme to Lynch's authorship, even to the scaled-down authorial model indicated above. ABC's own imperatives were registered in their insistence that the murderer of Laura Palmer be revealed earlier than Lynch intended, and also in their decision to cancel the show after two series, thereby 'writing' an ending different from that projected by Lynch himself. Other factors, too, make it difficult to view *Twin Peaks* in the light of romantic auteurism. From the outset, the project was a co-originated one, designed by Lynch and the TV dramatist Mark Frost. Lynch's hands-on control was actually modest: he directed only the pilot and six episodes of the twenty-nine that followed; his writing involvement was similarly reduced and dispersed. Though he has spoken of his frustration at not being able to author the whole of *Twin Peaks*, the programme actually evokes a different, more distanced – in fact, *franchised* – model of auteurism. The bodily presence of the auteur himself was no longer required; instead, 'Lynch' became a formal and thematic signature that could be 'forged' by the thirteen other directors recruited by him to help deliver the project as he imagined it.

Across Lynch's career, there are certainly indications that he shares classic auteurism's belief in the power of directorial expression: since *Dune*, for instance, he has secured the right to 'final cut' on all his cinema releases. Yet he also makes many pronouncements investing the spectator – that figure often overlooked by auteurism – with interpretive freedom. The narrative enigmas of *Lost Highway* and *Mulholland Dr.*, in particular, would seem to demand solution in the director's preferred terms; however, Lynch himself speaks democratically of the spectator's liberation by such complex structures. Where he refers at one point to the author of a book one might be reading, he sounds positively Barthesian: 'It doesn't matter what he thought. It could be interesting, but it doesn't really matter. What I would be able to tell you about my intentions in my films is irrelevant' (*Lynch on Lynch*, p. 29). Not for Lynch, then, the DVD 'Director's Commentary' that affirms a singular creative voice. His works for film, TV and other media are, instead, occasions that precipitate the multiple, frequently conflicting discourses of others.

Here we turn for the last time to 'What Is An Author?'. Foucault distinguishes between on the one hand a standard authorial class including novelists and on the other what he calls 'initiators of discursive practices'. Someone belonging to the first group is 'basically never more than the author of his own text' (p. 131); however, someone in the second category – a Marx or a Freud – 'authors' not merely his or her particular texts but a mass of commentary, critique and elaboration subsequently performed by others. While the distinction has some legitimacy, it is nevertheless overstated: the novelist – in this case the filmmaker – may also provoke significant textual productivity. Lynch, in the final analysis, seems an author of precisely this kind. Of course a good deal of the output that accumulates around his work is relatively low-level: endless fan exchanges on the connection of Fred Madison and Pete Dayton in *Lost Highway*, and the like. But as well as initiating fairly mundane problem-solving, 'Lynch' can generate ideological contests. The sheer strangeness and opacity of his work – *The Straight Story* excluded – opens it to variant, even fiercely opposed readings. To take just one instance: his films have become a privileged site for debate about the politics of postmodern culture, with Brian Jarvis in *Postmodern Cartographies* (London: Pluto Press, 1998) aligning them with the agenda of the American New Right and Slavoj Žižek in *The Art of the Ridiculous Sublime* (Seattle: University of Washington Press, 2000) seeing in them a radical ideology-critique that prepares the ground for leftist resurgence. The point on this occasion is not to choose between these antithetical readings; instead, what is important is to recognise how an author-based approach to Lynch's work may go beyond exalting its maker, or cataloguing its formal and thematic continuities, and become energised by real-world implications.

Selected reading

Andrew, Dudley, 'The Unauthorized Auteur Today', *Film Theory Goes to the Movies*, eds Jim Collins, Hilary Radner and Ava Preacher Collins (New York and London: Routledge, 1993), pp. 77–85.
Elegant, economical reflections, best read after engaging with texts below by Corrigan, Hillier and Wollen.
Astruc, Alexandre, 'The Birth of a New Avant-Garde: La Caméra-Stylo', *The New Wave*, ed. Peter Graham (London: Secker and Warburg, 1968), pp. 17–23.
Brief but suggestive and pioneering article, first published in 1948, on film as a medium for directorial expressiveness.
Braddock, Jeremy and Stephen Hock (eds), *Directed by Allen Smithee* (Minneapolis: University of Minnesota Press, 2001).
Highly original attempt both to extend and dismantle auteur theory by applying it to those botched or low-grade films released by their directors under the approved US pseudonym. A creative, irreverent intervention in authorship studies.
Caughie, John (ed.), *Theories of Authorship: A Reader* (London: Routledge & Kegan Paul/BFI, 1981).
Well-contextualised essays representing both auteurism and the advanced theoretical ripostes produced in the late 1960s and 1970s. Valuable, but of its time and in need of supplementing by materials in Gerstner/Staiger and Wexman.
Corrigan, Timothy, *A Cinema Without Walls: Movies and Culture After Vietnam* (London: Routledge, 1992).

The chapter on 'The Commerce of Auteurism: Coppola, Kluge, Ruiz' offers valuable insights into how three contemporary directors, of diverse national and artistic backgrounds, manage and modulate their status as auteurs.

Gerstner, David A. and Janet Staiger (eds), *Authorship and Film* (New York and London: Routledge, 2003).

Lively and productive essays, exploring mainly US instances of authorship across a wide textual and contextual range – from classical Hollywood to marginal US cinemas such as African American independents and the avant-garde.

Hillier, Jim (ed.), *Cahiers du Cinéma: The 1950s* (London: Routledge & Kegan Paul, 1985).

Exemplary collection of articles, interviews and roundtables, buzzing with early auteurist excitement. Besides writings by such critic-practitioners as Godard and Truffaut, the book includes Bazin's measured overview of this approach to film, 'On the *politique des auteurs*'.

Hillier, Jim (ed.), *Cahiers du Cinéma: 1960–1968* (London: Routledge & Kegan Paul, 1986).

Edited with similar scrupulousness, and vividly mapping tensions and collapses in auteurist thought as the whiff of cordite is smelt in French intellectual and political life.

Livingston, Paisley, 'Cinematic Authorship', *Philosophy of Film and Motion Pictures: An Anthology*, eds Noël Carroll and Jinhee Choi (Malden, MA and Oxford: Blackwell, 2006), pp. 299–309.

Thoughtful attempt to re-examine the problem of authorship from the perspective of analytic philosophy.

Sarris, Andrew, *The American Cinema: Directors and Directions 1929–1968* (Chicago: University of Chicago Press, 1986).

Originally published in 1968 and a pinnacle of US auteurism, restating the faith in this approach to film which Sarris first voiced in 'Notes on the Auteur Theory in 1962'.

Truffaut, François, 'A Certain Tendency of the French Cinema', *Movies and Methods: An Anthology*, ed. Bill Nichols (Berkeley and Los Angeles: University of California Press, 1976), pp. 224–37.

Powerful early strike (1954) in the auteur wars, best placed alongside Astruc's article and the first volume of *Cahiers* selections.

Wexman, Virginia Wright (ed.), *Film and Authorship* (New Brunswick, NJ and London: Rutgers University Press, 2003).

Stimulating collection of essays, tracing shifts in film authorship across a wide range of institutional and ideological contexts.

Wollen, Peter, *Signs and Meaning in the Cinema*, 4th ed. (London: BFI, 1998).

Crucial volume in film studies broadly and auteur theory narrowly: 'The Auteur Theory', first published in 1969, is augmented and revised by both the 'Conclusion (1972)' and the much later 'Afterword (1997)'.

Useful websites

www.myweb.tiscali.co.uk/jeanrenoir/FilmDirectors.htm.

Very useful resource, assembling links to a mass of articles on directors – many non-Anglophone – from Chantal Akerman to Fred Zinnemann.

www.sensesofcinema.com/contents/directors/index.html.

Similarly international in focus and offering engaging surveys, from an auteurist perspective, of directors ranging alphabetically from the American experimentalist Peggy Ahwesh to Zinnemann.

www.davidlynch.com.

Fascinating official site, allowing assessment of the many facets of Lynch's auteurist identity now (from radical artist to salesman of 'signature' coffees).

www.britishfilm.org.uk/lynch.

Quite detailed tracking of Lynch's shifting 'author-function' across work from *Eraserhead* to *Wild at Heart*.

6

Film and genre

Imagine coming across a film that has already been running for an hour. The screen shows a middle-aged man in baseball cap and overalls walking into a cavernous, sparsely lit space, from the ceiling of which chains descend and water trickles. He is searching for a missing cat. Other than his calls to the animal, no dialogue occurs in the scene. On the soundtrack, however, there is an initially muffled yet intensifying heartbeat, which could be the diegetic noise of an engine but might also be non-diegetic and indicative of the protagonist's emotional state.

How do we begin to make sense of, or *place*, this sequence? Rather than specifying it microscopically, we might choose among the broader categories proposed by Alan Williams in his article, 'Is a Radical Genre Criticism Possible?' (*Quarterly Review of Film Studies* 9, 2 (1984): 121–5). For Williams it is helpful to assign films to one or other of three large-scale classes: narrative, experimental or avant-garde, and documentary. With these permutations in mind, a spectator might cautiously decide that the sequence belongs to narrative. It does not exhibit the problematical spatiality or temporality, or the self-referring cinematic technique, which are taken to be signatures of the experimental work. Nor does it seem to belong to the documentary mode (though the option might be kept open that the film is an unusual report on working conditions in a decommissioned factory or engine room).

These classifications, however, are too capacious and unrefined to offer more than minimal comprehension of the scene. While Williams reduces the number of cinematic *genres* to three, we need to mobilise our knowledge of many more, treating each one as a schema or set of expectations to be placed against this sequence and then either discarded or ratified. The method should eventually trigger recognition; as Jacques Derrida says: 'there is no genreless text' ('The Law of Genre', *Acts of Literature*, ed. Derek Attridge (London and New York: Routledge, 1992), p. 230). But to which genre might this scene be assigned? Some options seem to rule themselves out fairly quickly. While the western is historically elastic – extending not only to the car and machine gun of *The Wild Bunch* (1969) but even to TV and gay sub-culture in a variant such as *Brokeback Mountain* – it is usually associated with a particular geographical setting which seems far removed from this sequence. Similarly, it is unlikely the scene is part of a musical. Even if chiaroscuro, industrially located musicals are possible – witness Lars von Trier's *Dancer in the Dark* (2000) – the protagonist's world-weariness here does not suggest a man about to burst into song or dance. Perhaps, too, the scale and idiosyncrasy of the sets makes us conclude we are not watching a porn movie. Yet even in coming to this judgement, it is as well not to be too hasty. The Italian theorist Umberto Eco notes that a porn film consisting entirely of sexual couplings would be intolerable, and that therefore the genre has a structural need for mundane activity such as people driving or travelling in lifts: 'Go into a movie theatre. If, to go from A to B, the characters take longer than you would like, then the film you are seeing is pornographic' ('How to Recognize a Porn Movie', *Movies*, ed. Gilbert Adair (London: Penguin, 1999), p. 164). Where the protagonist dawdles in the sequence under discussion, then, he might actually be providing one of porn's breathing spaces.

Yet the scene's technical assurance and evident expense encourage us to continue searching Hollywood's system of genres for more convincing paradigms. A war film, maybe, given the air of threat and the interior that could be that of a bomb-damaged building? Or perhaps a noir variant of the crime film, given the low-key lighting and the tight close-ups on a seedy protagonist? However, there are stronger possibilities still. In particular, the camera's creeping through this murky space, the slow accumulation of tension and the heartbeat's gaining in volume may persuade us to correlate the sequence – at least provisionally – with the schema of the horror film. This tentative judgement is vindicated shortly afterwards: first by the horror genre's customary false climax – the missing cat suddenly lunges at the protagonist – then by its pay-off, as a monstrous figure appears from above and kills the man.

The discussion of this scene from Ridley Scott's *Alien* (1979) shows how the concept of genre in film studies is both indispensable and unsatisfactory. Genre usefully breaks up the generalised stuff of narrative into recognisable patterns organised by choices in plotting, character-type, mise-en-scène, soundtrack and other elements. This type of classification is supple and informative compared with many other film cataloguing systems, such as those early brochures in which works offered to exhibitors were grouped merely according to different running lengths. Organising films by genre is also more generously inclusive than organising them by particular directors or stars (approaches covered in Chapters 5 and 7). Less pleasingly, however, genre criticism has traditionally had problems in defining and stabilising the categories with which it works. It is poorly equipped for the discussion of hybrid generic artefacts – a matter of consequence to *Alien*, which is a fusion of horror and sci-fi. Genre study's taxonomic bands also seem unwieldy when confronted by sub-genres, briefly lived film cycles and so on. Additionally, this approach to cinema is tainted by its lack of international focus, by what Robert Stam calls its '*Hollywoodcentrism*' (*Film Theory: An Introduction* (Malden, MA and Oxford: Blackwell, 2000), p. 129). While there is a dense literature on the US western and musical, the Anglophone reader will struggle to find studies of such distinctively non-American genres as the Italian *giallo* (a merging of horror, crime and sex), the German *Heimatfilm* (a form dating from the 1950s, sentimentally depicting rural life) or the Hindi *mythological* (spectacularly rendering India's epics and legends).

Despite listing genre's numerous conceptual deficiencies, Stam argues that it is still an 'explanatory cognitive instrument' (p. 129). Similarly, for the literary theorist Franco Moretti, genres are helpful, even revelatory so long as they are understood not as fixed, unchanging categories but as 'temporary structures'

(*Graphs, Maps, Trees: Abstract Models for a Literary Theory* (London and New York: Verso, 2005), p. 14). With these cautious methodologies in mind, the remainder of this chapter sketches out some of the uses of a genre-based approach to film.

Taxonomies of film genre

To a greater extent than some other areas of film criticism, the study of genre has invited the application of scientific method or, at least, scientific metaphor. Shortly, we will see attempts to model a genre's development in terms of evolutionary biology. While the discipline still awaits its Linnaeus, the fact that *genre* shares an etymological root with *genus* has also encouraged writers to believe that the film genre system can be laid out with the precision of botanical and zoological classifications. Tempting though these approaches are as a way of giving film studies a clear and defensible method, however, they immediately fall foul of the categorical slipperiness and promiscuity of genres themselves.

An immediate problem is the lack of consensus in identifying the core element of film genres. From time to time, plausible candidates have emerged for this common molecular material that, distributed differentially across genres, might divide them one from another like biological species. In 'On the Iconography of the Movies' (*Movie* 7 (1963): 4–6), Lawrence Alloway suggested that film studies might take a lead from art history, specifically from Irwin Panofsky's concept of *iconography*. Just as convention stabilises the depiction of certain objects in some types of painting but not in others – a lamb carries meaning in a religious picture but would be puzzling in a seascape – so, by analogy, significant things, figures and actions might be dispersed across different film genres. Taken up by Ed Buscombe and other cinema scholars, Alloway's proposal has the merit of specifying film's visual element as the domain in which particular generic status is asserted. It is also clear that the iconographic method works well with respect to certain genres. What is a western but a repository of icons from six-shooters and leather chaps to tumbleweed and swinging saloon doors? See one of these things on screen and it is likely we are watching a western or, at least, a film that intends some imitative or parodic relation to the western genre. Other genres also marshal significant objects in this way. A bare-chested man wearing sandals and carrying a sword and shield tends, on the whole, to make us feel we are viewing an epic rather than a crime film. Similarly, a submarine is part of the visual repertoire of a war movie but rarer in the 'teenpic'. Yet while the method of icono- graphic differentiation is intermittently effective, it breaks down in the face of genres that are less strongly marked by particular images. What are the key icons of comedy, say, or romance? Icons that appear safely assigned to one genre may also migrate to another. A man wearing a sharp suit could belong equally in a gangster film and a musical. A lawnmower looks like an icon of comedy (of a suburban sort) but, as noted in Chapter 5, may stray into a road movie.

The iconographic approach does not have the necessary range and precision to support a grand theory of genres. As evidenced above, in the shifting grounds for generic assignment of the scene from *Alien*, film genres are actually defined by an incoherent range of criteria rather than by their different instantiations of some- thing they all have in common. Some genres are specified according to contents (the war film). Others are defined by a recurrent locale (the western or the road movie). Still others are categorised by their foregrounding of the protagonist (the gang- ster film or the biopic). Most obviously in the case of the musical, genres may also be distinguished by performance style. Nor does this exhaust the list of differentiating criteria, since several more genres are named for their vivid emotional, even visceral effects upon the spectator: horror comes immediately to mind but so too does the melodramatic spectacle variously referred to as the 'weepie' or 'tearjerker'. In *Moving Pictures* (1997), Torben Grodal attempts to go beyond these special cases and classify *all* genres – now reduced in number to eight – according to different mental and emotional reflexes they prompt in the spectator. Rather awkwardly, however, he retains some familiar labels such as horror, while also proposing such new, not always convincing groupings as 'lyricism' and 'schizoid fictions'. For all its boldness, Grodal's intervention remains somewhat marginal in film genre theory; and we are left with the present, conceptually unsatisfactory state of affairs in which, as crazily as relating a carrot to a python, one genre distinguished for its emotional effect may be placed in the same system as one denominated by its protagonist-type.

This is hardly the basis for an orderly taxonomy that would pass muster with a zoologist or botanist. Facing defeat on this larger scale, critics have sometimes retreated to individual genres and attempted instead to offer stable definitions of these. Some of the earliest film genre criticism, by André Bazin and Robert Warshow, is heavily marked by this effort of purification. In the first of two pioneering essays on the western, Bazin refers to the genre's 'essence' and represents this kind of film as a coherent, self-contained entity which has no need to mingle with other genres (for example, the detective movie). Any such interfusion is described ahistorically as 'contamination' of the western's abiding purity, rather than as a possible means of advancing and enriching the genre. While Bazin's second essay does allow for developments in the western, these are still presented as a fall from the 'definitive stage of perfection' already achieved in *Stagecoach* (1939) (*What is Cinema?*, Vol. 2, p. 149). This essentialising tendency – offering a static, ideal conception of a filmic category – is also evident in Warshow's important essay on the gangster genre.

At its worst, such an approach seems the work of genre police, vigilantly patrolling a film category for signs of immigrant or deviant forms (recall Derrida's '*law* of genre'). The prescriptive tendency that runs through genre theory from the literary criticism of Aristotle and Horace onwards is apparent once more. But Bazin and Warshow are also suspect on evidential grounds. In achieving their particular configurations of the western and the gangster movie, they succumb to that besetting weakness in film genre study which Barry Langford terms 'endemic critical selectivity' (*Film Genre: Hollywood and Beyond*, p. 135). Warshow's account of the gangster film is based upon a worryingly small sample of three works, two from the early 1930s, the other from 1947; he thus ignores a host of other productions that might have unsettled his conception of the genre's 'essence'. And while Bazin casts his net more widely over the western, he too deduces generic shape from a very limited archive (notwithstanding the practical difficulties he faced in post-war France in obtaining materials for analysis). Although genre criticism promises to be more hospitable to the *mass* of films than the director-based approach to which it is often opposed, it thus runs the same risk of casting many works into oblivion.

We should not feel snootily superior to these early genre critics. Their work has the permanent value of having opened up the study of popular film in an era of the medium's marginalisation. In addition, selectivity in genre study is not safely a thing of the past but, as discussed shortly, a contemporary problem too. Nevertheless, it is clear that attempts in the lineage of Bazin and Warshow to distil the 'essence' of any single genre are likely to fail. Even those genres that seem peculiarly self-contained – those to which film genre study has devoted much of its labour – prove to be quite leaky categories. Although the western, say, is on the face of it very cogent in iconic repertory, character-types and plot structures, it is still open to mutation and hybridisation. As well as hosting a carnival of sub-generic forms – parodic westerns like *Blazing Saddles* (1974), musical westerns like those starring Gene Autry either side of the Second World War, horror westerns like *Ravenous* (1999) – its icons and plots may be reconfigured when they travel into non-US productions (the Italian 'spaghetti' western most famously but also films including *Fah talai jone / Tears of the Black Tiger* (Thailand, 2000) and *The Proposition* (Australia, 2005)). And this still says nothing about the western's disguised presence in other genres: think only of how the genre's key trope of the frontier has relocated to sci-fi (*Star Wars*) or the war film (*The Deer Hunter* (1978)).

Only in the most shoddily run zoo can a llama mate with a penguin; yet in cinema interbreeding may occur between species as far apart as porn and the rock concert documentary (Michael Winterbottom's *9 Songs* (2004)). Zoological law cautions against the lamb lying down with the lion; but there is no cinematic fiat to prevent seemingly the most opposed genres from combining, as when Roberto Benigni fuses comedy and Holocaust drama in *La Vita è bella / Life is Beautiful* (1997) (Figure 12). In case such hybrids seem merely a tendency of the postmodern moment, note that as long ago as 1935 *The Phantom Empire*'s story of a cowboy singing in deepest space blended sci-fi, the western and the

Figure 12 Generic fusion: comedy meets Holocaust drama in *La Vita è bella/Life is Beautiful* (Italy, 1997).

musical. Taxonomists of film genre thus have to face the bad news that an elegant classificatory system is impossible. The genres that comprise it can only ever be provisionally identified, since they are always subject to combination with and redefinition by other filmic categories. As Rick Altman wittily describes this potential for mutation: 'In the genre world ... every day is Jurassic Park day' (*Film/Genre*, p. 70).

STOP and THINK

- Compile your own list of film genres, which should be as exhaustive as possible. Many genre surveys, including those by Langford and Neale, settle on somewhere between twelve and fifteen categories. Other attempts, however, at doing the arithmetic of genres arrive at a much higher figure. What is your own total? Might any of your suggestions be collapsed into a broader category – as sub-genres of the action-adventure film, say – or would such compression be conceptually imprecise? This initial inventorying is best carried out with others, so there are several mappings of the genre system to compare. Assess whether it is possible to conclude from this exercise if genre definition is a matter of ongoing cultural dispute or, rather, amenable to scientific consensus.

- Choose any genre from your list. Aiming again at exhaustiveness, inventory everything you would expect to find in this category of film. Such features may extend across the textual range: familiar types of plot structure, protagonist and iconography, as well as marked tendencies in mise-en-scène (horror's subjective tracking shots) and soundtrack (romance's dreamy saxophone for love scenes). Do these attributes suggest it is possible to speak of the genre's 'essence' or 'typology'? Or is the genre so subject to historical change and infiltration by other categories as to be taxonomically unstable?

- Stick with this genre and analyse your own demands as a spectator. Do you always expect the conventions on your list – however provisional they may be – to be observed? Or do you hope for generic reinvention, even sabotage? Consider how specific examples of the genre negotiate between predictability and novelty, tedium and disorientation.

Threads, prisms, maps

Dissatisfied by the stasis implicit in a taxonomic model, other writers evoke a sense of film genres' mobility and dynamism. Paul Watson is typical of many cinema scholars in noting how the concept of genre magically brings together various constituencies that might be kept apart in other areas of the discipline. In his metaphor, genre is 'the golden thread' connecting producers, critics and audiences, all of whom have an interest in the definition and circulation of categorising terms (*An Introduction to Film Studies*, 3rd ed., ed. Jill Nelmes (London: Routledge, 2003), p. 151). Although helpful in its sense of genre as a mediating force between territories of production and reception, however, the figure of the thread overstates the clarity and tidiness of genre processes. Watson's alternative metaphor – genre as 'conceptual prism' – is more promising and indicates how the situations of diverse groups engaged in film will materially affect how they look at specific genres and at the genre system as a whole. Even so, the image still does not quite capture a sense of these constituencies' continuous and competing efforts at genre construction. For this, we can turn to Rick Altman, who has been the most eloquent opponent of static, decontextualised understandings of genre. 'The process of genre creation', in his words, 'offers us not a single synchronic chart, but an always incomplete series of superimposed generic maps' (*Film/Genre*, p. 70). At first glance, a map might appear as inert as the discredited taxonomic model of film genres. Altman's metaphor has two advantages, however: first, geographical study has long demonstrated that any cartography is not a rarefied intellectual act but an attempt at power or control emerging from somewhere particular in culture; second, Altman speaks not of a single map but of overlapping, sometimes clashing generic cartographies produced by the film industry, critics and spectators (including fan communities).

For writers such as Steve Neale, genre study should be centred upon the industry's own promotion and maintenance of categorising terms. This is itself no easy task and requires the tracking of genre references not only through the archives of studios and production companies but through the masses of publicity material they send out into the world. An interest in the industry's marketing of genres demands also a suppler, case-specific terminology. While the dozen or so broad categories familiar to us are still of use, we should adjust our sights to take account of *subgenres* and smaller-scale *cycles* of film made over quite brief periods (an example is the recent return of the historical seafaring adventure: *Pirates of the Caribbean* three times (2003–7), *Master and Commander* (2003), the BBC's lavish *To the Ends of the Earth* (2005)). In Neale's view, an adequate genre criticism is only possible when this documentation of the production side has been achieved: 'it is only on the basis of this testimony that the history of any one genre and an analysis of its social functions and social significance can begin to be produced' (*Genre and Hollywood*, p. 43).

Other film scholars, however, argue that a strong industrial emphasis of this kind risks exalting just one of several forces involved in genre construction. Echoing Altman, Christine Gledhill suggests in 'Rethinking Genre' (*Reinventing Film Studies*, eds Gledhill and Linda Williams (London: Arnold, 2000), pp. 221–43) that film constituencies other than studio moguls have not only a stake but, at least partially and variably, a certain power in how genres are defined. Critics, spectators and cultist fans, as well as production publicists, contribute to the '*intertextual relay*' in which any film is embedded and its genre status established. The concept of the 'intertextual relay' derives from Gregory Lukow and Steven Ricci's essay, 'The "Audience" Goes "Public": Inter-Textuality, Genre and the Responsibilities of Film Literacy' (*On Film*, 12 (1984): 29–36), which argues that a film is not assigned to a given genre simply on the basis of the textual elements it delivers to audiences during screenings. Before and after the film's exhibition, numerous discourses and events also serve a classificatory purpose.

It is undeniable that the film industry itself is the major generator of this intertextual array. As the weight and saturation of its marketing exercises increase, so, proportionately, the genre-creating potential of other constituencies declines. Who can compete with the industry's discursive arsenal of cinema trailers, foyer displays and posters, TV and radio commercials, newspaper and magazine previews, merchandising tie-ins and dedicated websites? A trip during the time of writing to the local multiplex – only one of the industry's many publicity venues – quickly disclosed this power to shape the generic image of a film, and hence the terms of that film's reception. Commercial material was in evidence for the then-imminent *Miami Vice*. Much of the movie's targeted audience was likely to have no recollection – perhaps even no knowledge – of its progenitor TV series (1984–89). The nature of the publicity exhibited in the cinema foyer, however, gave clear generic clues about *Miami Vice* the film without ever using words like 'crime', 'detective' or 'thriller'. In two corners stood life-size photographs of its three main stars – Colin Farrell, Jamie Foxx and Gong Li – looking cool with their guns and shades. On the wall was a poster sending out related if slightly different generic signals. Here the woman had been excised, with the resulting image of just Farrell and Foxx evoking such mixed-race detective buddy films as *48 Hrs.* (1982) and the *Lethal Weapon* franchise (1987–98) (Figure 13). The poster further signalled the film's generic status by identifying its director Michael Mann as responsible for *Heat* (1995) and *Collateral* (2004), but saying nothing about his non-crime credits such as *The Last of the Mohicans* (1992) and *Ali* (2001). Such detailing of the industry's publicity effort for *Miami Vice* does not preclude the possibility that scholars and other spectators might assign the film to different categories. To a genre of 'Florida movies', perhaps, alongside such works as *Key Largo* (1948), *Body Heat* (1981) and *Miami Blues* (1990)? But even if this kind of alternative generic mapping is still possible in theory, it palpably, at least at the moment, lacks institutional force.

In attending to intertextual relays of this kind, genre criticism

Figure 13 Genre signalling in a poster for *Miami Vice* (Germany/US, 2006).

joins in the project evident elsewhere in the discipline to dethrone the film text itself as the chief object of study (recall from Chapter 3, say, interest not merely in a film's produced sound but in the ambient soundtracks generated by audiences themselves). But the concept of the intertextual relay is more immediately valuable here in offering hope of some challenge to the industry's power to determine generic definitions. For, despite the brief case study above, not all the discursive materials surrounding a film are issued and circulated by producers themselves. There are the interventions of film reviewers, not simply confirming a studio's preferred label ('the best comedy this year'), but potentially generating new terminology of their own ('gross-out comedy'). And while academic film critics might seem very low down the intertextual food chain, they too have had their successes in struggles over genre. The story is familiar of how feminist scholars gathered certain films from classical Hollywood into a productive category of 'melodrama' that did not correlate with the industry's understanding of the melodramatic. The flow of generic definitions is not uniformly from industry to academia but may even be reversible. In the 1940s and early 1950s Hollywood thought it was making 'crime' or 'detective' films when it put seedy private eyes into mean streets where it was always raining. Yet critical activity over the last three decades has reassigned these works to a category called 'film noir'. A further twist sees this categorising term appropriated from academia by the industry itself and used to add allure and commodity value in the publicity for such works as *The Last Seduction* (1994) and *L.A. Confidential*.

Generic communities, or the strange case of the cycling film

So far, in discussing the intertextual relay that extends around a film and helps to shape its generic identification, we have considered producers, reviewers and academic critics but said nothing about the creative role of audiences. Yet, as Henry Jenkins suggests, 'Fandom generates its own genres' (*Textual Poachers: Television Fans and Participatory Culture* (London and New York: Routledge, 1992), p. 279). Genre assignment is not adequately imaged as a case of industrial might encountering spectator passivity; despite the undoubted weight of the industry's publicity, audiences themselves are active combatants in the genre wars. At a fairly non-institutional level, spectators find a variety of communicational outlets to produce 'word-of-mouth' about a film. But more energised and institutionally grounded types of audience response are also possible. Altman writes interestingly about what he terms 'generic communities' (*Film/Genre*, pp. 156–64), defined as social clusters or fractions that organise themselves around enthusiasm for a particular kind of film. The conversations that these groups have are not only semantically valuable in disclosing something about the genre in question but socially enriching in affirming the groups' sense of well-being and togetherness. Altman goes so far as to argue that, especially in the contemporary West, 'it is possible for genre to stand in for an absent community' (p. 187).

To see one such tiny community at work, consider the case of 'cycling films'. While video stores and the like are accustomed to placing films among a relatively small number of film categories, genre classifiers do not have to be so parsimonious. A precedent for more finely calibrated genre recognition exists in the American Film Institute (AFI) index for the 1930s, which lists no fewer than sixty-one varieties, including 'boxing', 'jungle' and 'newspaper' films (Neale, *Genre and Hollywood*, pp. 241–2, 255–6n.). Although some of these categories are transport-related – 'automobile racing' and 'aviation' films – there is no recognition in that historical moment of the existence of the cycling film. But that such a genre may be constructed from subsequent film archives across the world is shown by the researches of Séamus King, editor of an online cycling journal, *Byke Kultuur Never*. The results can be found on the website http://uk.geocities.com/mikstar123.films.html (accessed 21 July 2006).

In King's hands, the cycling film is shown to have both long historical pedigree and broad geographical reach. His list extends chronologically from a mistitled and misdated British film, *6 Day Racer* ('the 1940s') – presumably this is *6 Day Bike Rider* (1934) – to a Japanese animation of 2003, *Nasu: Summer in Andalusia*. Far from sharing genre criticism's usual vice of Hollywoodcentrism, the cycling archive includes items from Brazil, China, Finland,

Hungary, Iran, South Africa, Vietnam and other nations. There is a good-natured autism, even mania at work in King's cycle-centred study of each of these films, rather as if someone set out to read *Lady Chatterley's Lover* purely for its detail about a game-keeper's working practices. Normally, de Sica's *Ladri di biciclette / Bicycle Thieves* (1948), for example, would be reflected through the prisms of Italian neo-realism and humanist cinema; it becomes a different thing when looked at with an eye for handle-bar and saddle design (Figure 14). What is especially striking is that categorising all these works as 'cycling films' cuts across their previous, institutionally approved generic identities. The new genre omnivorously swallows examples of many film categories: animation (*Father and Daughter* – Holland, 2000); comedy (*Jour de Fête* – France, 1949); crime (*BMX Bandits* – Australia, 1983); parody (*Ladri di saponette / The Icicle Thief* – Italy, 1989); romance (*A Boy, a Girl and a Bike* – UK, 1949); the teenpic (*Rad* – US, 1986); and the (male) weepie (*American Flyers* – US, 1985).

King does not generate this new generic grouping merely in a

Figure 14 'The cycling film': *Ladri di biciclette / Bicycle Thieves* (Italy, 1948).

spirit of abstract scholarly inquiry. To borrow another term from Altman, he aims to enhance 'lateral communication' among cyclists in Britain and beyond at a time when more immediate modes of communality may be under threat. Of course the strength of this gesture towards generic community still needs careful measurement. By its editor's own admission, *Byke Kultuur Never* is a somewhat irregular journal; it appears at imprecise intervals, and its eccentricity can be gauged by the fact that one issue includes a recipe for cooked squirrel. Other British cycling outlets apparently regard it with bemusement, even suspicion. Even so, its pages on cycling films suggest it is not without institutional connections, or without grounding in something larger than one man's idiosyncratic enthusiasms. King includes details of this genre community's interacting in face-to-face – not merely electronic – ways during the annual festival of cycling films held at the Phoenix Theatre, Leicester. This festival might be put together with other public validations of the genre, such as the bike-directed movie reviews carried by a well-funded American cycling education website: http://chibikefed.org (accessed 26 July 2006). None of this intertextual activity amounts to proof that universally agreed generic reassignment is imminent for *Bicycle Thieves* and the other works; yet it does suggest that fans can, as Jenkins says, be productive genre critics. At the same time, we should be cautious not to overstate any such generic community's force. The film industry's own mechanisms of genre definition are so powerful as to put limits on the revisionary work that even the most ardent fandom can achieve.

STOP and THINK

- Reconstruct as thoroughly as possible the 'intertextual relay' of any current film. This entails research across multiple domains, from newspapers and magazines to street posters and websites. Assess the strength of the industry's own genre signalling in this instance: do publicity materials tend to mark emphatically or, on the contrary, minimise the film's generic status? In either case, why? Bearing in mind the various user groups that make up the intertextual relay – producers, critics, spectators and so on – assess whether consensual genre definition of this film is achieved. Do production and reception interests form a single generic community here, agreed upon the film's categorical designation? Or is there evidence of dissension, with the film subject to alternative generic mappings? One possibility is for printed and internet fanzines to evade the industry's potent intertextual mechanisms and generate new perspectives on the work.

Genres and history

In *Graphs, Maps, Trees*, Franco Moretti offers another suggestive metaphor for genres. He calls them 'Janus-like creatures, with one face turned to history and the other to form' (p. 14). Genre critics should therefore turn cubist themselves, looking both at sets of formal conventions that define different film-types and at what these conventions signify historically. Yet even to put the genre researcher's tasks like this is to introduce a false dichotomy between form and history. Apparently 'formal' or 'internal' elements of a genre are not isolated from historical processes but, on the contrary, saturated by them. To take a particularly clear, if familiar example: the very features that lend the western its formal systematisation – distinctive protagonists, frontier settings, particular objects, extreme long shots of landscape – are heavily mediated by American histories of race, gender and nation. And, as we have seen, they are not timelessly fixed but subject to modification in the genre's ongoing life.

Genre criticism, then, should be historicist through and through. Several commentators, however, point out the deficiencies of many attempts to write the history of film genres. Altman is especially troubled by a tendency to reach for biological models when narrating generic change. There are two preferred analogies: a developmental language that likens a genre's course to that of a human life and – more grandly, if very loosely – an evolutionary language describing a genre's shift from life-generating novelty to predictability and ultimate extinction (*Film/Genre*, pp. 21–2). We will suggest in a moment how the evolutionary parallel might be fortified. Here we can just agree with Altman and others about the problems of applying a model of finite biological development to a messily unfinished cultural process such as film genre construction. It is striking how often genre critics working in this vein have been tempted by a tripartite schema. For Thomas Schatz, in *Hollywood Genres* (1981), a genre's three stages are 'experimental' (before it has a recognisable identity of its own), 'classical' (when its conventions have stabilised and are at their most coherent) and 'formalist' (when it has outlived its original purpose and conventions are no longer unself-consciously reproduced but, rather, openly cited, even parodied). Writing in the same period, Richard Dyer proposes a comparable trajectory (*Movie* 75 (1981): 1484). Only the names given to the three phases differ: Dyer suggests that a film genre is successively 'primitive', 'mature' and 'decadent', these labels seeming to add a note of moral judgement to Schatz's more aesthetically based terminology.

No-one should deny the partial usefulness of this type of schema. At the very least, the sense of change which it promotes encourages genre criticism to move beyond taxonomic stasis. The developmental model also allows for the suggestive grouping of films that might otherwise appear as individual texts (Bazin, anticipating Schatz, collates westerns he calls 'classic' – *What is Cinema?*, Vol. 2, p. 150). At the same time, however, a fixed trajectory is flawed as a model of generic history. Dyer, Schatz and others sketch a single line of development for genres without considering how this might be complicated by the heterogeneous fates of sub-generic categories. The worryingly unilinear pattern they propose has little to say about deviant films that are either, using Dyer's language, 'decadent' before their genre's time or still 'mature' at a time when the genre's death has been pronounced. In addition, what can this developmental model do with films in which the supposedly separate generic phases co-exist? Take Spielberg's *Saving Private Ryan*. With its virtuous US hero and drive towards a heroic ending, it rejects counter-cultural anti-militarism and still resembles the works of its genre's classical moment. Yet its visceral footage of the Normandy landings also

signals a consciously *late* or 'post-classical' war film, one antago-
nistic towards the falsifying conventions of earlier Second World
War movies like *The Longest Day* (1962). Things become more
complex still when we sense from Spielberg's co-produced TV
series *Band of Brothers* and Scott's *Black Hawk Down* (both 2001)
that the handheld camerawork and rapid cutting of *Saving Private
Ryan* are not the war film's dying breath but already stabilising as
its new conventions. Such oscillations between generic past and
future clearly throw into crisis a unilinear film history.

The problem with the evolutionary model of film genre studies
is not so much that it is used at all, as that it has not been used
rigorously enough. When critics suggest that a parallel for generic
history can be found in evolution, they tend to do so on the basis
of quite sketchy understandings of Darwin. This results in the
limited and linear historical pathways indicated above. Moretti,
however, having done the serious reading in evolutionary biology,
sketches out how this model might still be appropriate for grasping the extent and variety of a genre's history. Although he writes
in a literary critical context – trying to renovate what he regards as
that discipline's moribund paradigms – his work in *Graphs, Maps,
Trees* is suggestive for film studies also. Rather than discussing
only those novels written in England from 1700 to 1900 that have
since been accorded classic status, he constructs a diagram of the
totality of novelistic production during this period. Forty-four
categories of fiction in all are identified. In an echo of the AFI's
heterogeneous genre index from the 1930s, cited above, the list
includes varieties usually overlooked by scholarship, such as
'nautical tales', the 'ramble novel' and the 'sporting novel'.
Moretti borrows a term from evolutionary theory to suggest that
the history of 'the novel' should not be mapped as a single trajectory but as a 'diversity spectrum' comprising multiple variants
that undergo distinct processes of alteration, fusion and sometimes extinction. There are lessons here for a much more complete
mapping of a film genre's 'evolution'. As just one possible research
programme, consider how a 'diversity spectrum' might be
constructed of the action–adventure genre, mapping the rates and
forms of development of its many variations from swashbucklers
through disaster films to cinema's own 'nautical tales'.

Whether it draws upon evolution or some other conceptual model, the history of any genre cannot be written without regard to broader historical processes. Even as a category of film seems to follow its own dynamics, these are already socially overwritten. Works like *Saving Private Ryan* and *Band of Brothers* that reinvigorate the Second World War movie at a time when it seemed to have disappeared originate not as some purely formal manoeuvre but as part of post-Vietnam recuperation in the US, a desire in critical times to restore a sense of America's muscular virtue. Generalising from this example, we can read historical significance in the waxing and waning of particular genres and sub-genres (an exercise that will be repeated in Chapter 7 with reference to the rise and fall of specific stars). Like the canary once taken down a mine, a genre is an unusually sensitive instrument for measuring changes in the atmosphere.

At the same time, care is needed in correlating generic changes with larger socio-cultural shifts. It is possible to be much too crude and direct in asserting a genre's capacity for historical revelation. The emergence of film noir, for example, has been traced retrospectively to social factors such as the beginnings of Cold War paranoia and a post-war crisis in American masculinity following women's unprecedented entry into the workforce. In Darwinian terms, the genre is 'selected' to register those concerns at that historical juncture. Yet we should not overstate the genre's diagnostic power with respect to America in the 1940s and early 1950s; at the same time as brooding crime films of this type were produced, Hollywood continued to release comedies and musicals that gave a somewhat different sense of the nation. The ideological implications of a genre also shift: by the time of a contemporary noir like *L.A. Confidential*, those features of plotting and mise-en-scène that emitted gender anxieties in the 1940s survive largely as lucrative cinematic fetishes.

Critics of mass culture sometimes speak darkly of the conservative tendency of the Hollywood 'genre system' as a whole (irrespective of superficial differences among film categories). But even if specific political valencies may be attached to genres at particular moments, it is perversely anti-historicist to argue that these are total or permanent. Progressive impulses might be registered at times in the most seemingly retrograde generic products. Consider the utopianism manifested in some musical or animated films by an exhilarating sense of movement and transformation that clashes with the conservative politics that may be officially expressed in them. And, as noted earlier, the ideological significance of genres – as of any filmic feature – is not universally agreed but, rather, is the stuff of ongoing dispute between different generic communities.

STOP and THINK

- Franco Moretti argues that 'a genre exhausts its potentialities – and the time comes to give a competitor a chance – when its inner form is no longer capable of representing the most significant aspects of contemporary reality' (*Graphs, Maps, Trees*, p. 17n.). Do you agree with his Marxist perspective that symptoms of social transformation may be detected in the rise and fall of particular genres?

- Return to the list of genres you compiled earlier and consider which of them are particularly prominent now and, in a Darwinian sense, well-adapted to the present. Conversely, which genres seem weakened, only sporadically produced, perhaps about to vanish (if only temporarily)? Speculate on the causes of this respective generic empowerment and enfeeblement.

- Can film genres ever die? Since apparently the most moribund kind of film can be unexpectedly reactivated, it may be advisable to avoid terminal thinking here. If a genre does not actually re-enter production, it may still be sustained at the level of reception, through fan activity. With respect to the old AFI index, however, where now are the categories of the 'Northwest' film and the 'travelogue'?

The end of genre?

From the late 1960s, literary scholars have shown an enthusiasm for terminations, pronouncing the death of the author and the death of the novel among other fatalities. Getting into this apocalyptic mood, some film critics have recently argued that genre is dead as both a category of production and a schema of reception. Here we will mention just two of these obsequies for the film genre system. In the relevant section of a well-known cinema textbook – Jill Nelmes's *An Introduction to Film Studies* – Paul Watson sounds the death knell for the very concept he is discussing. He draws on Andrew Darley's thesis, in *Visual Digital Culture: Surface Play and Spectacle in New Media Genres* (2000), that contemporary Hollywood production is no longer bound to spectators in the kind of contractual arrangement that requires it to deliver a number of story-types clearly differentiated by the conventions they follow and the expectations they generate. Instead of these discrete categories, there is now a trans- or post-generic cinema that Watson summarises as 'the blockbuster, special-effects movie, event cinema, spectacle cinema, summer movie, even action cinema' (p. 159). Generic motifs from the previous Hollywood are currently combined in multiple, heterogeneous ways that go beyond the fashioning of relatively straightforward hybrids (the comedy thriller, say). In Watson's conclusion, 'genre' is now inadequate as a term for 'capturing the artistic and economic complexity of contemporary Hollywood' (p. 166).

Watson also alludes briefly to Jim Collins's work on genre and the new post-generic settlement. Collins's influential essay, 'Genericity in the Nineties: Eclectic Irony and the New Sincerity', included in his co-edited collection *Film Theory Goes to the Movies* (London and New York: Routledge, 1993), argues that contemporary Hollywood has developed two opposing ways of negotiating the concept of genre. The first of these – 'the new sincerity' – sees a filmmaker trying valiantly to return to some generic archetype or essence (examples include *Field of Dreams* (1989) and *Dances With Wolves*). On the other hand are those films that openly, even exuberantly acknowledge the artifice of all genres and the possibil-

ities this opens up for ceaseless play across their former boundaries. This second mode of filmmaking Collins calls 'eclectic irony'
or 'ironic eclecticism': examples include *Batman* (1989) and *Back
to the Future III* (1990). Although his essay sometimes suggests
the two options are equally viable, it is clear to which one he is
drawn. In his account, the new sincerity presumes a naïve spectator and stands for backwards – indeed backwoods – thinking; by
contrast, eclectic irony plugs into the 'sophisticated hypercon-
sciousness' (p. 248) of a media-aware spectator and manifests
energy and playfulness.

Undoubtedly, Watson, Darley, Collins and others identify an
important tendency in contemporary Hollywood (and beyond:
consider, say, the delirious fusion of horror, sci-fi, comedy and the
stuff of other genres in *Gwoemul/The Host*, successfully exported
from South Korea in 2006). Old genre labels can indeed seem as
cumbersome as boxing gloves when attempting to handle with
categorical precision 'the summer movie' or 'event cinema'. The
problem, however, is the breathtaking generalisation that tends to
follow from identifying this new type of blockbuster. Here the
'endemic critical selectivity' of which Langford convicts earlier
genre critics like Bazin and Warshow returns with a vengeance.
The work of post-generic writers tends to privilege an equally
small number of titles: in addition to the films mentioned in
Collins's article, American favourites include *Moulin Rouge!*, the
Scream franchise and Tarantino's generic collages. The sheer
dazzle of this small corpus of films appears to have distracted
attention from the more routine genre production that still goes
on in mainstream US cinema and elsewhere. For every ironically
eclectic and self-referring film, after all, there is a new Jennifer
Anniston comedy.

Powerful ripostes to the more excitable pronouncements of the
death of film genre can be found in several places, including the
closing pages of Neale's *Genre and Hollywood*. Nevertheless, any
reassertion of the category of genre for film studies should not be
taken as indicating it is in rude health and beyond conceptual
reproach. Rather, it is still open to modification at both macro-
scopic and microscopic levels. In *Film Genre*, Langford argues for
at least some use of *modes*, larger organising categories – such as

melodrama – under which several, traditionally differentiated genres might be productively gathered. At the other extreme, it would be helpful to reach to a sub-atomic level in genre study and identify sub-genres or briefly lived and geographically disparate micro-categories of film. Something of this scaled-down sort is attempted in the case study that follows.

Analysing genre: the high school movie

Is 'the high school movie' a genre, possessing the same conceptual value as the western or war film? Lacking the longevity and supportive apparatuses of such genres, it is, at present, still the subject of definitional dispute. Much of this controversy is carried on through popular fan discourses rather than substantial academic study. Traditionally, however, those books and articles that do discuss the high school movie tend to categorise it as a sub-genre of a larger generic field variously called the 'teenpic', 'teen movies' or 'the cinema of adolescence' (to borrow the title of David Considine's 1985 book). In Timothy Shary's *Generation Multiplex: The Image of Youth in Contemporary American Cinema* (Austin: University of Texas Press, 2003), 'school' is identified as one of five sub-categories of the teenpic alongside 'delinquency', 'horror', 'science' and 'romance/sexuality'. While giving significant attention to such high school movies as *Clueless* (1995), Roz Kaveney takes a similarly expansive approach to visual representations of adolescence in *Teen Dreams: Reading Teen Films and Television from 'Heathers' to 'Veronica Mars'* (New York and London: I. B. Tauris, 2006).

Yet if the high school movie is regarded by some as too particularised to substantiate its own genre, it is evidently considered by others as too large and incoherent and already dividing. With tongue only partly in cheek, the critic Howard Feinstein announces the birth of 'a new genre' he calls 'the high school massacre film' (www.indiewire.com/movies/movies_031027eleph .html: accessed 30 July 2006). The key text to which he devotes most of his genre manifesto is Gus Van Sant's *Elephant* (2003), an oblique response to the Columbine High School shootings in Colorado in April 1999 when two students murdered twelve classmates and a teacher before killing themselves. However, he finds three other instances of the new genre: two feature films – *Home Room* (2002) and *Zero Day* (2003) – and Michael Moore's muck-raking documentary, *Bowling for Columbine* (2003). And this is without considering whether the category has a longer history: we might reference the 1976 'exploitation' film, *Massacre at Central High*.

Feinstein's high school massacre film looks too small for generic status; the series of movies of this type released in 2002–3 is more a cycle prompted by momentarily heightened anxiety about gun use in the US. At the other end of the scale, the broad category of the teenpic is poorly equipped to register the distinctiveness of the high school movie. Cautiously, then, we assume here that the latter is a genre. This follows the lead given by Robert Bulman in the fullest study of the category to date: *Hollywood Goes to High School: Cinema, Schools, and American Culture* (New York: Worth, 2004). Although one of the high school movie's strongest claims to genre accreditation is its regular geographical setting – compare the western – Bulman actually contests this homogeneity of space at the outset by subdividing his materials according to three differ-ent educational locations: urban, suburban and private schools. Each of these settings is then correlated with a particular themat-ic preoccupation: respectively, the role of the teacher, social conformity and class division. At this early stage in the high school movie's generic consolidation, however, such a geographical and sociological grid risks rigidity. It is also fairly unresponsive to the genre's formal specificities: Bulman writes as an academic sociolo-gist rather than film scholar, and his book appears in a non-cinematic series entitled 'Contemporary Social Issues'. Without denying the value of this pioneering work, it is clearly in need of augmenting. Research priorities for genre study of the high school movie might include the following:

1. *Conventions*. Although searching for a genre's recurrent plot structures, character-types, settings, icons and so on often leads to uninspired taxonomic work, it can also be productive in the case of a newly recognised genre. The provisional inven-torying of a set of high school movie conventions at any one moment will allow subsequent, historically significant shifts to

register. A convention-based approach that is alert to history might explore, say, mutations in the character-type of the teacher or changes in the value of rock music on the soundtrack.

2. *'Genrification'*. Altman's dynamic model of genre creation – the process he calls 'genrification' – might be used to theorise the emergence of the high school movie. *Film/Genre* describes how a previously *adjectival* variant of a larger film category may become significant enough to warrant a *substantive* category of its own (as when 'the western comedy' threw off its subservience to the comic parent genre and produced 'the western'). The high school movie perhaps develops in this way from modification of the teenpic to autonomous genre. It is by now sufficiently strong to have generated its own host of sub-genres. Research might follow Moretti's genre study by constructing a diversity spectrum of all these, recording and comparing their respective rates of development. Sub-generic variants of the high school movie include: adaptation (*10 Things I Hate About You*, based on *The Taming of the Shrew* – 1999); arthouse (*Elephant*); comedy, from black (*Heathers* – 1999) to gross-out (the *American Pie* series – 1999–2003); documentary (Frederick Wiseman's cinéma-vérité *High School* – 1968); horror (*The Faculty* – 2000); musical (*Grease* – 1978); noir (*Brick* – 2005); parody (*High School High* – 1996); sci-fi (*Donnie Darko* – 2001); and the social problem film (*Blackboard Jungle* – 1955). This list does not include romance, which operates across several of these sub-genres as well as authorising its own. As with the high school movie's own emergence, some adjectival variants here might, in the unfolding genrification process, eventually bid for autonomy. Feinstein's high school massacre film is a premature attempt to claim this.

3. *Auteurism*. One of the attractions of genre study is its promise to attend to the totality of films rather than to a privileged few. At this early stage of discussing the high school movie, however, there may be scope to consider how the genre sometimes functions as a way for younger directors to exhibit stylistic and narrative bravura. At the level of cine-

matic form itself, they thereby demonstrate the same lack of conformity exhibited by many of their protagonists. Besides Richard Kelly's *Donnie Darko*, examples of the young auteur's high school movie include Todd Solondz's *Welcome to the Dollhouse* (1995), Wes Anderson's *Rushmore* (1998), Terry Zwigoff's *Ghost World* (2001) and – outside the US – the Swedish director Lukas Moodysson's *Fucking Åmål/ Show Me Love* (1998).

4. *Ideology*. Assessing the ideological force of the mass and range of high school films requires nuanced studies rather than generalised claims. Like the literary *Bildungsroman*, the genre might appear genetically disposed to conservatism, narrating the manufacture of adult conformists from the inchoate stuff of teen desires and anxieties. Yet there may be space too for narratives at an angle to American patriarchal and consumer society (the sheer opacity of *The Virgin Suicides* (1999), say, or the revenge fantasies of *Heathers* (Figure 15)).

5. *Generic communities*. Who watches – and for what purposes – high school movies? While young fans themselves are attached to some part of this genre's production – particularly its horror and comic variants – it is striking that there is also a

Figure 15 'The high school movie': *Heathers* (US, 1989).

type of high school movie that seems engineered at least partly for post-teen consumption. Arthouse spectators relish the elaborate tracking shots of *Elephant*, or enjoy spending what the French social theorist Pierre Bourdieu terms *symbolic capital* as they get the references to *Othello* in *O* (2001) and Jane Austen's *Emma* in *Clueless*. Overlapping, sometimes competing genre communities thus gather around strains of the high school film.

6. *Internationalism*. Like much genre study in general, the discussion above is too American-centred. Even if the high school movie has a cultural centrality in the US not always replicated in other countries, the internationalisation of study of this genre will be productive. A start on such comparative work is made by Timothy Shary and Alexandra Seibel's co-edited *Youth Culture in Global Cinema* (Austin: University of Texas Press, 2006) – despite the volume's sense of teen film extending, again, beyond the particularities of the high school genre.

Selected reading

Altman, Rick, *Film/Genre* (London: BFI, 1999).
  Engaging, sophisticated attempt to rethink the question of genres in film, developing a 'semantic/syntactic/pragmatic' approach adequate to their mutability and their status as objects of constant cultural contestation.

Bazin, André, *What is Cinema?*, Vol. 2 (Berkeley, Los Angeles and London: University of California Press, 2005)
  Important, in this context, for the pioneering genre criticism of 'The Western, or the American Film *par excellence*' and 'The Evolution of the Western'.

Grant, Barry Keith, *Film Genre: From Iconography to Ideology* (London: Wallflower, 2006).
  A lucid, economical and up-to-date overview of the topic.

Grant, Barry Keith (ed.), *Film Genre Reader III* (Austin: University of Texas Press, 2003).
  Indispensable collection of articles, heftier still than previous editions published in 1986 and 1995. Essays come from a variety of periods and critical positions, and include both overarching and single-genre reflections.

Grodal, Torben, *Moving Pictures: A New Theory of Film Genres, Feelings, and Cognition* (Oxford: Clarendon Press, 1997).

Sophisticated, demanding instance of a cognitive approach to genre, offering an alternative to historical and sociological studies by aligning each film-type with a particular emotional effect and mode of mental functioning.

Langford, Barry, *Film Genre: Hollywood and Beyond* (Edinburgh: Edinburgh University Press, 2005).

Less internationalist than its subtitle promises but a lively survey of the shifting, entangled histories of genres from the western and the musical to pornography and the Holocaust film.

Lusted, David, *The Western* (Harlow: Longman, 2003).

Fresh, comprehensive overview of one of the most intensively studied genres, particularly valuable in extending the canon upon which generic claims are based (as in a chapter on the frequently neglected silent western).

Neale, Steve, *Genre and Hollywood* (London and New York: Routledge, 2000).

Slightly drier in manner than Langford but formidable in scholarship; offers extended bibliographical essays on coverage to date of Hollywood's genres, identifying its lacunae and proposing a new programme of historically richer 'cross-generic and multi-cyclic' study.

Neale, Steve (ed.), *Genre and Contemporary Hollywood* (London: BFI, 2002).

Stimulating, up-to-the-minute essays, exploring the modulation of many traditional genres since the 1970s, as well as the emergence of cycles such as the legal thriller and the Shakespeare adaptation.

Schatz, Thomas, *Hollywood Genres: Formulas, Filmmaking and the Studio System* (New York: Random House, 1981).

Important study of classical Hollywood's genre system, albeit one that needs supplementing by Langford and Neale (and by Schatz's own later work).

Warshow, Robert, *The Immediate Experience: Movies, Comics, Theatre and Other Aspects of Popular Culture* (Cambridge, MA and London: Harvard University Press, 2002).

Reissue of a posthumous publication from 1962 and especially valuable here for 'The Gangster as Tragic Hero' and 'The Westerner'.

Useful websites

www.filmsite.org/genres.html.

Tends towards a cheerfully populist tone and an American bias, but nevertheless gathers much useful material on the history of genres and sub-genres.

www.jahsonic.com/FilmGenre.html.

Wildly inconsistent – mixing commercialism with scholarliness, fillers from Wikipedia with quotations from Altman and Stam – but, at its best, lively and with a more internationalist eye than the site above.

7
Star studies

24 August 2006: under the headline 'Mission over for Mister Impossible', *The Guardian* carries on its front page a story that says much about contemporary American film stardom. The report describes a catastrophic collapse in relations between business mogul Sumner Redstone and star Tom Cruise. Redstone, chairman of Viacom which owns Paramount Pictures, is so exasperated by Cruise's recent conduct that he is cutting him loose from any connection with the studio. Viacom is ending the arrangement that aimed to bind Cruise to Paramount by paying his production company $10m annually and giving it office facilities in Los Angeles.

This brief story registers a shift in Hollywood's geopolitics, as the mighty studios of yesteryear have been repositioned as merely part of larger entertainment and media conglomerates. It also hints at a current modality of film stardom that differs significantly from the version which prevailed in classical Hollywood. Mention of Cruise's own production company is evidence of a fairly recent tendency for stars themselves to develop and manage projects, offering some respite from the near-feudal working arrangements of actors during the studio era. At the same time, however, the *Guardian* article shows the persistence of the view that the star is an item of capital, a corporately deployed asset that, if not absolutely a commodity itself, is certainly central to the film industry's commodity output. While Cruise has delivered profits for Paramount in the past – notably in the first two *Mission: Impossible* films (1996 and 2000) – it has been noted by the Viacom chief that ticket sales for his vehicles are in decline: the star's brand appeal is waning. Significantly, Redstone, as quoted in the article, does not attribute this falling-off to what we might call textual factors, that is to say, changes in the nature of Cruise's star presence in the films themselves. Instead, he refers accusingly to passages in the star's off-screen life that conflict with his winsome persona rather than straightforwardly reinforcing it. Cruise has lately given a series of public performances that evoke not so much mainstream Americanness as eccentricity and intransigence. The newspaper cites his 'jumping the couch' while declaring his love for Katie Holmes to Oprah Winfrey; the circus surrounding the birth of the couple's daughter; and Cruise's militantly asserted Scientology, as when denying the value of medication in treating psychological conditions such as post-natal depression.

For all its transitory news value, the episode is helpful as a way into many of the topics that concern this chapter. In a merely implicit way, the *Guardian* piece indicates that, like the concept of genre, film stardom is a phenomenon best investigated not through a single critical optic but by a multi-stranded approach, here measuring the star's effects upon the several domains of industrial production, textual composition, ideological formation and audience response. This chapter begins by placing the star system in shifting production contexts from its beginnings in Hollywood and elsewhere to the looser articulations of today. It then considers the construction and implication of a star's persona, that system of meanings around an actor felt to have badly malfunctioned in Cruise's case. One element of stardom, however, which is actually understated in the newspaper is our intense investment in people like Cruise, the emotional and psychic bonds which attach us to film stars. Thus the chapter will recognise the audience's powerful involvement in the star system, and assess ways used to conceptualise this engagement that have ranged from psychoanalytic accounts of the spectator to ethnographic surveys of fans. Finally, a film star's presence on the front page – the *Guardian* report is accompanied by a large photo of Cruise, all glittering teeth – would seem to indicate the continuing cultural centrality of this type of figure; a film actor still looks, in Christine Gledhill's words, like 'the ultimate confirmation of stardom' (*Stardom: Industry of Desire*, p. xiii). Nevertheless, we will also examine recent shifts in the balance of power between film stars and stars in other domains, including sport.

Political economies of film stardom

In an essay on Prince as an example of film and music crossover, Lisa Taylor rejects two well-established forms of star studies. She criticises both textually based readings of a star's persona and ethnographic surveys of fan response to stars for their neglect of film's commercial imperatives. For Taylor, these two approaches give too great a weight in determining the meaning of stardom to, respectively, the alert critical viewer and the enthusiastic fan. She suggests instead that stars be embedded in a more industry-centred account of film that, borrowing from social studies, she calls *political economy*: 'political economy approaches, which find it unfeasible to isolate the film "text" from the rest of its multi-media production-line, offer the most useful perspectives' ('"Baby I'm a Star": Towards a Political Economy of the Actor Formerly Known as Prince', *Film Stars: Hollywood and Beyond*, ed. Andy Willis, p. 158). Taylor's own conceptual framework is not without costs: it may efface film too completely in the 'institutional production of commodities' (p. 160), and absolutise the power of the production side rather than recognising the role also played by critics, spectators and fans in shaping the meanings and directions of cinema. Nevertheless, her emphasis upon the film star as primarily a commercial construct is salutary and a good place to start here.

There is nothing inevitable about cinema as a star-centred medium. Just as with narrative in Chapter 4, the star system is historically and geographically contingent rather than something encoded in film's DNA. Strains of non- or even anti-star cinema have always existed: think of the amateur performers assembled by Eisenstein and others during the early Soviet era, or the communally generated political films of Latin American *Ciné Liberation* mentioned in Chapter 5. The emergence of a star system is certainly not synchronous with the beginnings of film itself as a medium. Instead, cinema's first fifteen years or so saw it generally promoted for its technical enchantments; interest was centred in the sheer optical wonder of figures moving on a screen rather than in questions of who exactly they were. While stars already existed in adjacent fields such as theatre, music and dance, film seemed less hospitable to charismatic personality. However, the growing complexity of film narratives that allowed more scope for virtuosity in performance provoked audience interest in the identity and, eventually, the off-screen life of actors themselves.

Given the centrality of Hollywood to our thinking about stars, it is striking that Ginette Vincendeau calls Max Linder, the French comic performer, 'the world's first film star' (*Stars and Stardom in French Cinema*, p. 42). Linder's name appeared in French film publicity as early as 1909, a year before evidence of an incipient star system in the United States. The first American film star is often taken to be Florence Lawrence, poached from the well-established Biograph studio by an independent producer and introduced in a blaze of sensationalist advertising in March 1910. However, film historians including Janet Staiger and Richard deCordova have shown convincingly that, although she was the most vividly promoted early star in America, Lawrence was not actually the first: some months before her unveiling, other studios had not only disclosed the names of their previously anonymous actors but were already enmeshing them in publicity campaigns that included foyer display cards and press advertisements. Soon enough, these rudimentary ventures in star promotion were augmented by actor credits in the films themselves, by slides of the performers for showing between reels and – off-screen – by fan magazines and fan clubs.

Internationally, star systems in the first half of the twentieth century took different forms. Nations like France and England lacked the established studio network and high film output that could have tied actors into lengthy, exclusive contracts. Instead, performers were more liable than their US counterparts to move between assignments in cinema and theatre. The political economy of stardom in these countries was thus a cottage industry compared with the advanced capitalist apparatus represented by the star system which prevailed in mainstream US cinema from the 1920s to the early 1950s. Typically, actors in Hollywood during this period would be signed up by studios on closely confining seven-year contracts and then deployed in a series of films for which they were considered suitable according to body and personality types. Studio moguls would remodel stars like any other element of fixed capital at their disposal: an actor might lose performative variety (as when MGM responded to fan suggestions by placing Clark Gable in tough-talking heroic roles) or even his or her given name (as when Lucille Le Sueur was christened 'Joan Crawford' following a studio-organised magazine competition). Despite their allure – most intensely epitomised on screen by the close-up – stars were actually embedded in a system of production akin to the Fordist capitalist regime then turning out standardised consumer products like cars, radios and refrigerators. Ominously, they were not only implicated in commodity output but were themselves infected by the logic of commodification. Walter Benjamin writes in 'The Work of Art in the Age of Mechanical Reproduction' that the film actor has no more contact with the audience that will view the finished work than 'any article made in a factory'. He goes on to argue that the 'The cult of the movie star, fostered by the money of the movie industry, preserves not the unique aura of the person but the "spell of the personality", the phony spell of a commodity' (*Illuminations* (New York: Schocken Books, 1968), p. 231).

Barry King speaks of a film star's 'persona work', the efforts made to establish, systematise and sometimes modify an image that is portable across a career ('Embodying an Elastic Self: The Parametrics of Contemporary Stardom', *Contemporary Hollywood Stardom*, eds Thomas Austin and Martin Barker, p. 60). During the classical Hollywood era, the star largely relinquished such persona consolidation to his controlling studio. Public appearances were arranged and fan clubs established with a view to reproducing a star image already vividly communicated by on-screen performance. The aim was to minimise precisely the kind of disruption to persona stability lately glimpsed in the case of Tom Cruise. Such a coherent image functioned first of all as a form of branding for films themselves, helping to specify their generic status and thus mobilise a particular audience; it could, however, also extend beyond cinema itself and be incorporated into the advertising of other commodities. Although prospects for multi-media and cross-market synergy were more limited in this period, the glamour and charisma of stars were still utilised in a variety of commercial tie-ins, from clothing, cosmetics and toiletries to movie memorabilia like photographs and magazines. Bearing out Taylor's thesis, it would be a much depleted star studies that, even in the studio era, focused solely upon the evidence of film texts themselves and thereby omitted the star's extension across other elements of the capitalist production-line.

The commercial exploitability of the star has increased exponentially in recent decades. From the 1950s onwards, however, Hollywood has also witnessed a relative 'autonomising' of the star compared with the restrictive labour conditions of the classical era. The collapse of the studio system under economic and legislative pressures discussed in Chapter 9 has led to looser, more provisional arrangements between actor and production interests. 'Persona work' becomes less a controlling producer's responsibility than the star's own labour (albeit delegated to specialist technicians of promotion and publicity). At the level of film production itself, the star is now perceived not so much as a fixed item of capital under singular ownership as a package offered to various users just for the duration of particular projects. Geoff King writes that stars are converting themselves 'into their own franchise properties', over which the forces of production may exercise only intermittent and imperfect control ('Stardom in the Willennium', *Contemporary Hollywood Stardom*, p. 68). This perhaps exaggerates current stars' power: even redefined as franchise properties, star personas are still vulnerable to the kinds of corporate decision-making that prevailed in the studio era. Jim Carrey might have an economic autonomy unimaginable during the 1930s but, given his particular 'brand' of comic idiosyncrasy, would still struggle to interest makers of a swashbuckling adventure. Yet even if King overstates the case, he describes an important recent adjustment in stardom's political economy.

It is no coincidence that Taylor works up her corrective view of star studies in the course of a study of Prince. As a significant player in both film and music industries, he is an example of what Geoff King calls 'synergistic property' ('Stardom in the

Willennium', p. 63). King's own essay in the Austin and Barker collection is on another major embodiment of film/music crossover, Will Smith. Figures of this type seem to extend the already considerable commodity output of the star system. However, two points are worth making. The first is the historical observation that, while now massively boosted and able to operate across multiple platforms in advanced media society, the synergistic star is not an entirely new phenomenon. From earlier Hollywood, we need only think of the musical and cinematic crossings of such disparate figures as Bing Crosby and Elvis Presley. Second, it needs to be stressed that the synergistic performer can fail as well as succeed. In their carefully detailed studies, Taylor and King demonstrate not only that the commercial performances of Prince and Will Smith are patchy rather than uniformly profitable but also that the rewards of success have been unevenly and complicatedly distributed across a multitude of corporate interests. Thus a political economy approach to contemporary stardom needs precision in tracing how this is expressed in a commercial period more complex than the studio era.

The making and meaning of star personas

In his indispensable book, *Stars*, Richard Dyer suggests that a film star's image is composed by four different types of 'media text': *promotion*, *publicity*, *films*, and *criticism and commentaries* (p. 60). Although he writes that 'Inevitably, the films have a distinct and privileged place in a star's image' (p. 61), his placing them third in the list of media texts tends to undermine rather than confirm this priority. Such downgrading of the actor's on-screen work in the process of star manufacture is repeated in Dyer's subsequent study, *Heavenly Bodies*:

> A film star's image is not just his or her films, but the promotion of those films and of the star through pin-ups, public appearances, studio hand-outs and so on, as well as interviews, biographies and coverage in the press of the star's 'private' life. Further, a star's image is also what people say or write about him or her, as critics or commentators, the way the image is used in other contexts such as advertisements, novels, pop songs, and finally the way the star can become part of the coinage of everyday speech. (pp. 2–3)

It is clear from this just how heterogeneous and dispersed are the forces implicated in star-making. The process is so multiply centred, rather than singularly controlled, that even the individual fan, or at least groups of fans, may feel enfranchised with respect to determining the image of a particular star. We will explore the place of the spectator in 'star discourse' in the next section. Significantly, however, Dyer adds in *Heavenly Bodies* that this discourse is 'not an equal to-and-fro' (p. 5). In star-making, as with the process of 'genrification' considered in Chapter 6, some interests have more definitional power than others.

For the moment, the question of the precise ratio between those forces that constitute a star's image can be set aside in order to discuss instead this image's meaning for both performer and the culture at large. How exactly we label the cluster of associations that gather around a film star is fraught with difficulty. As evidenced above, Dyer tends to favour 'star image'; other theorists, however, refer more frequently to either 'star persona' or 'star text'. Although these terms have their particular nuances, they are also fairly interchangeable: each phrase is also calculatedly non-anthropomorphic, indicating that what concerns star studies is not the flesh-and-blood performer as such but the array of meanings that she generates across platforms that, as Dyer acknowledges, extend from the film work itself to advertisements, posters and fan exchanges.

Are the meanings produced by particular stars fixed or, on the other hand, unstable and open to modification? Barry King's distinction between two modes of film performance offers a starting point here. In his essay, 'Articulating Stardom' – included in Gledhill's collection *Stardom: Industry of Desire* – King distinguishes what he calls *personification* from *impersonation*: in the first of these performative styles, the personality of the star is flagrantly and continuously exhibited, regardless of role; the impersonating actor, on the other hand, is felt to dissolve her personality into the particularities of each character being played. This sort of distinction is useful for separating a force of personification like Schwarzenegger from an inveterate impersonator like Dustin Hoffman. However, it is rare for a star to become so immersed in an impersonatory performance that his or her pre-established star image ceases to be recognised and activated by the audience. As he acknowledges, King's distinction is not so much between banal stardom on the one hand and proper acting on the other, as between two different ways of being a star.

Whatever a star's performative tendency, the question remains of how solidified is his or her persona across the course of a career. For some observers, stardom as such imposes a crushingly narrow set of references upon the actor. John Sayles notes wittily that 'A woman alone at night who answers the doorbell to find Peter Lorre on the front steps is in for a different evening than one who finds David Niven' (*Thinking in Pictures: The Making of the Movie 'Matewan'* (Cambridge, MA: Da Capo Press, 2003), p. 46) (Figures 16 and 17). Lorre, a whey-faced, physically squat actor associated with macabre roles from German Expressionist cinema onwards, is positioned here as the antithesis of the elegant, lean Niven, a figure who epitomised mid-century English suavity. In Sayles's reading, however, these two very different stars are equally marked by invariant associations assembled across their bodies of screen work, as well as through the multiple other media texts identified by Dyer. From such a perspective, the film star typically carries these meanings like a second skin. While this permits the actor brand identity, an opportunity for niche market-ing, it may also seem a restriction on performative range. Film history is thus full of examples of stars trying to resist this short-circuiting of what they might signify: consider Robin Williams's efforts to break out of his man–child comic–sentimental persona by taking grimmer roles in *Insomnia* and *One Hour Photo* (both 2002). It would be an inert model of stardom that did not allow for the possibility of a star's subtle modifications across a career. Barry King writes that, rather than being simply deposited in each new film, a star's 'persona is differentially activated in successive roles' ('Embodying an Elastic Self', p. 47).

The matter of star persona, however, is too culturally important to be discussed simply in the vocabulary of acting. We have already seen how a political economy approach articulates film stardom with the manufacture of commodities from movies themselves to CDs and perfumes. Another major tradition in star studies draws upon semiotics and ideology critique in attempting to disclose the

Figure 16 David Niven as the British diplomat Sir Arthur Robertson in
55 Days at Peking (US, 1963).

social significance of particular star personas. What might the
flourishing or even the failure of a given star indicate about values
and beliefs in the culture in which it occurs? In *Violent America*
(1971), Lawrence Alloway describes film stars as 'maximised
types', suggesting that they embody in heightened fashion ways of
being and behaving that are possible in their society. Dyer argues
in *Stars* that Alloway neglects the possibility of a star's struggle

Figure 17 Lobby card showing Peter Lorre as the child murderer Hans Beckert in *M* (Germany, 1931).

against or even rejection of her dominant image; nevertheless, he refers himself to 'social types', aiming similarly to go beyond a concern with stars as individuals and to assess the culturally diagnostic value of their personas.

Stars carry an ideological charge in their faces and bodies, their ways of speaking and moving, their trajectory in the film plots with which they are most commonly associated. To return briefly to two actors named above: Lorre's persona was especially 'fitted' for 1930s German cinema's, then American film noir's, communication of cultural anxiety, even paranoia. Similarly, Niven's brand of urbanity expresses the late-imperial white Englishman's confidence (even if it looks alien from the vantage point of contemporary multicultural Britain). Star readings of this kind are especially interested in what their objects of study reveal about prevailing constructions of gender, race and class. For example, Yvonne Tasker, Susan Jeffords and others have done influential work in correlating the rise of cinematic masculine 'hard bodies' like Schwarzenegger and Stallone in the 1980s with the period's anti-feminist backlash and Reaganite reassertion of US might abroad. The later obsolescence of this maximised type then occurs not because of the stars' perceived acting deficiencies but because their version of masculinity comes to seem, in another historical conjuncture, strident, hysterical, even risible. A similar account can be given of shifting feminine types in US cinema. From such a perspective, the relative decline of Demi Moore might owe less to her skill levels as an actor, or even to Hollywood's relentless favouring of younger women, than to the insecure social status of the muscular, narcissistic version of femininity she has exhibited in places ranging from her performance in *G.I. Jane* (1997) to her *Vanity Fair* nude cover portraits. This form of ideologically oriented interpretation also suggests that particular African American performers have been selected for stardom by Hollywood on grounds that extend beyond their dramatic abilities. Take the consolidation of Sidney Poitier during the 1960s as the first major black star in US cinema. Handsome, clean-cut, well-dressed, Poitier played such instances of officialdom as a teacher in *To Sir With Love* and a doctor in *Guess Who's Coming to Dinner* (both 1967); his rise to prominence coincided with the realignment of American racial politics by significant Civil Rights legislation. While his stardom is certainly to be read positively – installing a black presence at the heart of mainstream US entertainment and giving him roles outside the stereotypes of aggressive criminality and demeaning servitude – Poitier's unthreatening appearance and embodiment of individual rather than communal advancement suggest that his selection as a star also figures the limitations of Civil Rights reformism. One African American critic describes Poitier as 'the model integrationist hero', and notes that other black actors of the period, with edgier connotations or less classical beauty, struggled to emulate his success (Donald Bogle, *Toms, Coons, Mulattoes, Mammies, and Bucks: An Interpretive History of Blacks in American Films*, 4th ed. (New York and London: Continuum, 2000), p. 175). This case also demonstrates that the ideological value of a star is liable to be a contentious rather than consensual affair: the Black Panther activist would have deciphered Poitier's star semiotic very differently than a well-intentioned liberal white constituency.

Theorists indebted to the tradition of ideology critique have argued that film stars take on a *pedagogic* function, instructing us in socially preferred forms of being. Without being 'role models' in any banal or explicit sense, their personas play a particularly vivid part in ideological reproduction. Yet caution is needed when making this argument. The risk with some star readings is that they overstate the educational force of a given actor's persona. Even as the popularity of Schwarzenegger and Stallone, say, seemed evidence of their effective instruction in an aggressive masculinity, many fans took these movies with a pinch of salt, while other audiences ignored them completely and looked elsewhere – including to other male stars – for advice on how to be a man. Most far-reachingly, some critics have argued that stars resemble myths in their capacity to reconcile – at an imaginary level – rival socio-cultural tendencies that otherwise seem incompatible. In *Movie Crazy*, Samantha Barbas writes that the appealing personality of the early American star Mary Pickford enabled her to negotiate between Victorian and twentieth-century models of femininity; similarly, in *Heavenly Bodies*, Dyer argues that Marilyn Monroe winningly embraced in her persona two opposing 1950s discourses about American female sexuality. For all their ambition and interest, however, such claims again risk concentrating too much cultural authority in the figure of a single film star.

STOP and THINK

John O. Thompson has developed an effective means of recognising and evaluating star personas. In 'Screen Acting and the Commutation Test', first published in *Screen* 19, 2 (1978): 55–69 and reprinted in Gledhill's *Stardom: Industry of Desire*, pp. 183–97, Thompson argues that star studies might profitably adopt an exercise used in the phonological branch of linguistics. The so-called 'commutation test' involves phonologists in introducing changes of sound into a given utterance with a view to assessing whether these also produce change in the utterance's meaning; the exercise thereby allows recognition of the distinctive, meaning-bearing qualities of linguistic items that might otherwise be overlooked. Although Thompson's argument for how the method could work in film studies is subtle, he essentially proposes that in this new version of the commutation test stars themselves are the elements subjected to change. If the actual star of a particular work is substituted in imagination by another star, what then happens to the film's meanings?

Thompson revisits his work self-critically in 'Beyond Commutation – A Reconsideration of Screen Acting' (*Screen* 26, 5 (1985): 64–76). For our purposes, however, the richly productive aspects of his original article are assumed. Before attempting your own imaginary commutations of one star for another, you might consider some instances of recasting that occurred in film history itself. So, how would *Speed* (1994) have changed with the original choice Halle Berry playing the Sandra Bullock part? What would have happened to *Panic Room* (2002) if Nicole Kidman had, as the producers hoped, been able to fill the role eventually taken by Jodie Foster? And what would be different about *American Beauty* with the preferred Tom Hanks, not Kevin Spacey, playing the lead?

Then carry out some star substitutions of your own. You might start by commuting two actors who already seem quite close in star persona: for example, replacing Stallone by Schwarzenegger in the *Rocky* series (1976–2006). As with certain phonological substitutions, is this a case of a change at the level of expression that procures no equivalent change at the level of meaning? Or are significant modifications achieved even by this replacement of one chunk of laconic muscularity by another? As you go on, strive to be more drastic in your recasting decisions; what would be the effect if Hugh Grant played the Brad Pitt role in *Fight Club* (1999), or if Tom Hanks and Audrey Tautou were replaced as the questing duo of *The Da Vinci Code* (2006) by Samuel L. Jackson and Dame Judi Dench? While such imaginary substitutions may be amusing, they are not frivolously intended; in each commutation you perform, assess what it indicates about the meaning and portability of particular star personas. Building upon the auteur debates discussed in Chapter 5, this exercise may also allow you to evaluate the star's contribution to cinematic authorship.

Seeing stars

On 23 August 1926 the Italian-born star of silent film Rudolph Valentino, celebrated for such exotic spectacles as *The Sheik* (1921) and *The Eagle* (1925), died of septicaemia, aged thirty-one. A week later, his funeral mass took place in New York. As the cortege moved towards the church, the sidewalk mise-en-scène was as exotic and melodramatically charged as episodes from Valentino's own film work. A crowd of 100,000 people – many wearing black and weeping – lined the streets. Valentino's lover Pola Negri, who fainted several times during the funeral, had rivals in both quantity and quality of mourning among many of the star's fans; indeed, she was exceeded in grief by several of them. Although reports of a nationwide, even global pandemic of suicide attempts prompted by Valentino's premature death have been exaggerated, some fans did take their devotion to him to the point of seeking to end their own lives in a kind of star suttee. In London, a 27-year-old actress, surrounded by photographs of him, committed suicide by poisoning just two days after he had died; later in 1926, a young American mother seriously wounded herself by shooting, similarly carrying out her bid for oblivion amidst an informal shrine of images of the star. Given Valentino's androgynous features and performance style, and the camera's lingering upon his male beauty, many gay men in the United States and beyond also reacted in charged ways to his death.

This episode is worth recalling for a number of reasons. First, it is a salutary reminder that celebrity culture is not a recent invention: dispersed by print, telegraph and radio, news of Valentino's death had the same impact as a contemporary star episode that would be most powerfully disseminated by internet, TV and mobile phone. Second, the passionate mourners of Valentino alert us to a possible puritanism in star studies. For all their value, both political economy and semiotic approaches operate at some distance from the spectator's encounter with stardom. Cinema stars, after all, are frequently the site of our most intense engagement with the medium. If film can animate us in multiple ways, it is still likely to be the star's appearance on screen that stirs the profoundest response. Watching and thinking about particular stars, the spectator is traversed by powerful desires and aspirations – as well as by feelings of antipathy and estrangement. Without isolating all this affective substance from the economic and ideological materials already considered, an adequate star studies still needs to take it fully into account. We should also introduce something that has been largely missing in the chapter to date, namely a sense of *the star's body*. Reference to commodities and personas does not quite capture the extent to which audience engagement with the star is a tumultuously corporeal, even carnal matter.

Various conceptual frameworks have been proposed for analysing the dynamic between audience and star. One major tradition draws upon psychoanalytic approaches that have been influential elsewhere in film studies. Much of this psychoanalytic modelling of the spectator has a strong feminist inflection, and so a fuller assessment of its explanatory power will be deferred until the next chapter. Here, however, we might point out that work in this vein discusses the spectator's interaction with narrative film spectacle in such terms as *narcissism*, *voyeurism* and *fetishism*. Although many writers argue it is characters, not stars, which provoke such psychosexual dynamics, these figures in a narrative are of course powerfully instantiated by stars themselves. So, for example, the male spectator may be enlisted by the vividness of screen presence in narcissistic identification with a film's male star: he rides wish-fulfillingly with Clint Eastwood and thereby finds an idealised version of self (possibly making problematic his post-film re-entry into a more mundane identity). The male viewer's watching of female stars, on the other hand, may be more complex and ambiguous. Concealed – usually – in the dark, he has the advantage of voyeuristic scrutiny of them. However, this version of star studies also proposes that the male subject faces the terror of his own castration in the figure of the female star on screen and seeks to control such anxieties by strategies like breaking up her body into fetishised objects. Film history is full of examples of the female star 'morselised' in this way: the legs of Betty Grable in the 1940s, the breasts of Jayne Mansfield in the 1950s and, more recently, the lips of Julia Roberts (her 'major lippage', to quote *Wayne's World*).

The psychoanalytic account of star spectatorship is less empowering of *women* as viewing subjects, restricting them to such unattractive options as passive or even masochistic identification with the put-upon female clotheshorses that have often adorned narrative cinema. So, while Jackie Stacey's important study, *Star Gazing* (1994) continues to use a partially psychoanalytic language, it also registers its distance from this conceptual paradigm. The book exemplifies an important alternative tendency in star studies, namely surveys of fan response that draw upon ethnographic models established in the social sciences. Stacey was not the first writer to approach real spectators and ask them what they make of stars, rather than relying upon abstract and homogenising theories of reception: in the final chapter of *Heavenly Bodies*, Dyer uses letters sent him by fans to explore how the persona of Judy Garland had been important to gay men growing up in a still homophobic post-war United Kingdom. Stacey's project, however, is on a much bigger scale and at a far higher level of methodological self-consciousness. The second half of her book assembles and evaluates the several hundred responses she had after placing requests in two British women's magazines for readers to contact her with memories of their favourite Hollywood female film stars of the 1940s and 1950s. All of this affective material she then categorises as either 'cinematic identificatory fantasy' or 'extra-cinematic identificatory practices'. Each of these two basic ways of relating to stars has a spectrum of intensities; for example, cinematic identificatory fantasy begins most restrainedly with 'devotion' to the star and passes through stages of 'adoration', 'worship' and 'transcendence' before concluding in a state of 'aspiration and inspiration' where the star's image induces in the spectator a 'desire to transform the self and become more like the ideal' (*Star Gazing*, p. 159). Extra-cinematic identificatory practices, the term indicating responses to a star that have more worldly consequences, start with 'pretending' and intensify into 'resembling', 'imitating' and finally 'copying'. These practices involve progressive realignment of the spectator's face, hairstyle, body, voice, movement and whole way of being to accord with those of the emulated star.

Criticisms can certainly be made of *Star Gazing*. A doctrinaire psychoanalytic approach might question the interpretive value of the letters and questionnaires on which Stacey relies: as self-conscious, written-up materials, they may not capture all of the messiness of spectatorial engagement with stars. The book is also restricted in evidentiary range. First, it uses only female spectators from the chosen period, rather than including men as well (contrast the mixed-sex sample in Annette Kuhn's own venture into ethnography, *An Everyday Magic*). Stacey also asks her respondents mainly about female stars, thereby restricting potentially fascinating evidence of their interaction with male idols of the time. Finally, she chooses to omit British and other non-American stars from the discussion, a decision which reinforces the Hollywoodcentrism that is already an unfortunate aspect of star studies. These problems notwithstanding, *Star Gazing* offers a model for spectator-centred work on stars that subsequent writers have built on by compiling and interpreting both qualitative and quantitative surveys of audience response.

Unsurprisingly, given that Stacey's evidence is drawn from the Second World War and just after, analysts of contemporary film stardom need to add to the array of identificatory fantasies and practices she outlines. Her respondents are all relatively genteel older women when they communicate with her, and the types of yearning which they recall having been activated by their favourite stars seem, on the whole, containable rather than transgressive or anti-social. In this sample of fans, there are certainly no stalkers. A contemporary star studies, however, may wish to say more about a broad spectrum of pathological star worship, the extreme case here being John Hinckley, who developed a morbid interest in the child star Jodie Foster, pursued her relentlessly by letter and phone call, and eventually tried to assassinate President Reagan in March 1981 in a colourful attempt to get her to notice him. Similarly, the erotic dimension of our engagement with stars is often sublimated in Stacey's book. But in an essay on current internet constructions of star image, Paul McDonald refers not only to websites that solicit the voyeuristic fan by showing photographs grabbed of stars in various states of nudity but also 'fake nude' sites that allow the user to digitally manipulate materials that make it appear the star is naked or even involved in degrading sexual acts ('Stars in the Online Universe: Promotion, Nudity, Reverence', *Contemporary Hollywood Stardom*, pp. 29–44). Though McDonald overstates the spectator power this manifests – 'Fake nudes are members of the audience using technology to take control over the stars' (p. 38) – he usefully identifies the significant underside of officially promoted star images. Forums designed to regulate and commodify audience engagement with stars – approved fan clubs, bland celebrity interviews, tours of Hollywood homes that began in the 1920s – are countered by others in which less hygienic and respectful constructions of the star may circulate.

STOP and THINK

• How, precisely, would you characterise your engagement with film stars? The rapture in the voices of Stacey's respondents is striking: 'Stars were fabulous creatures to be worshipped from afar, every film of one's favourite gobbled up as soon as it came out', or 'I was completely lost – it wasn't Ginger Rogers dancing with Fred Astaire, it was me' (*Star Gazing*, pp. 143, 146). Although these women are recalling cinemagoing in the specific conditions of austere, post-war Britain, can you recognise *yourself*, even faintly, in their sentiments? Does a language of 'worship' still have resonance, as you think about your interaction with film stars; or does it hint at an uncomfortable, even disturbing loss of self-control?

- Use Stacey's broad categories of 'identificatory fantasies' and 'extra-cinematic identificatory practices' to chart the forms of your own 'star gazing'. If these seem private fantasies, not necessarily having any measurable effect on the world, calculate their intensity according to Stacey's scale of devotion, adoration, worship, transcendence and aspiration/inspiration. If your responses to stars seem better described as 'practices', locate these similarly in a range of intensities from pretending through resembling and imitating to copying. Many of Stacey's terms imply a same-sex interaction, the female spectator affected by the female star. However, star fantasies and practices may equally operate across sexual boundaries: think only of the woman enthusiastic about Brad Pitt who joins one of his fan clubs.

- Meditating upon one's relationship with favourite stars is perhaps best done discreetly, since it is likely to involve a measure of self-psychoanalysis, the disclosure of deep desires and aspirations. And not only positive affects but, potentially, also repulsion or hostility: spectator-centred approaches to star studies neglect the significance of our *dislike*, even *hatred*, of certain screen icons. While the scrutiny of your psychic engagement with stars might not indicate another Hinckley in the making, it may still restore a sense of those unruly, even erotic dimensions of spectatorship that are sometimes excised from star studies.

- Finally, it is vital that the several conceptual paradigms employed in star studies do not become estranged from one another. Stacey creates an overlap between psychoanalytic and political economy approaches where she shows how spectators' fantasies about stars may be expressed materially in forms of *consumption*. Sensitively, she does not convict her respondents of ideological dupery when they recall happily making star-inspired purchases: the young typist in subdued post-war England who bought a colourful, star-modelled dress might, in an admittedly limited, problematic way, have been rebelling against oppressive gender codes. In turn, consider if and how your own feelings for film stars are affirmed in acts of consumption. How big a factor, to begin with, are particular stars in your choice of which films to watch? Do your affective ties to a star prompt other purchases?

National and transnational stars

Even as he introduces a collection of essays on British film stars, Bruce Babington acknowledges that Hollywood has 'unquestionable status as the paradigmatic site of stardom' (*British Stars and Stardom*, p. 3). The hegemony of mainstream US cinema is such that its stars have achieved more global reach than figures from other national film industries. Nevertheless, a Hollywood-centred approach to stardom should be contested or at least complicated, rather than uncritically reproduced. Postcolonial sensitivity to diverse local cultures, together with changes in film production and distribution that have internationalised the appeal of many non-US stars, make it more important than ever to recalibrate the dominant, American-centred model of star studies.

Nations, as briefly noted earlier, construct different versions of film stardom. The British star system is not merely tinier than that of the US but determinedly less strident; it flaunts what Babington calls 'an ideologically meaningful reserve' (p. 20). In France, the star system has a more patriotic connotation – its icons sometimes serving the purpose of cultural nationalism against incursions by Anglophone film – but it too takes relatively discreet public forms. Not all non-US cinemas, however, promote their stars in understated fashion. Here the case of Mumbai-based Indian cinema – Bollywood – is especially striking. Vijay Mishra notes that, from the early 1950s onwards, Bollywood has foregrounded charismatic performance in its films: 'Popular cinema in

India, perhaps even more so than in Hollywood, became the cinema of the star rather than the cinema of the director or the studio' (*Bollywood Cinema: Temples of Desire* (New York and London: Routledge, 2002), p. 126). India and the Indian diaspora have thus nurtured a star system that, in terms of publicity and intense spectator interest, rivals or even outstrips that of Hollywood itself. Yet this vast apparatus of stardom is still invisible to many people worldwide: readers of *The Guardian* on 4 August 2006, for instance, may have been surprised to see a lead-in that referred to 'the world's biggest film star' followed by a profile not of Cruise, Hanks or Pitt but of current Bollywood's major male icon, Shah Rukh Khan (Figure 18). Besides familiarising itself at a basic level with the personnel of non-US, particularly non-Anglophone film stardoms, a newly globalised star studies will also need to produce detailed comparative examination of these systems. To give only one example: Mishra suggests that Bollywood stars are differentiated from those of other nations not only by filmic centrality bordering on a sense of authorship but by a distinctive performance style that sets great store on adeptness in 'song and dialogic situations' (p. 127).

In addition to considering a wider range of national stardoms, star studies should do more to explore the case of the charismatic transnational performer. The star that leaves an indigenous cinema in order to find success in Hollywood is a long-established figure. However, economic developments including the globalisation of media spectacles have accelerated a trend for stars to work across a number of different national cinemas: if the contemporary non-US star migrates to America it may no longer be a one-way trip. Take the case of Ewan McGregor. Although a Hollywood icon – notably via three *Star Wars* films (1999–2005) – he is not restricted to this particular star identity; British works like *Nora* (2000) and the Scottish-set *Young Adam* (2003) indicate his mobility across not only multiple cinematic idioms but also different versions and levels of stardom. Perhaps more interesting still are cases of actors who work outside their own first languages as well as their national cinemas. One striking European instance of such linguistic and cultural crisscrossing is Penélope Cruz, who moves between commercial American projects and her role in

Figure 18 'The world's biggest film star': Shah Rukh Khan in *Asoka* (India, 2000).

Spain as an 'Almodóvar girl'; analysis of her star image needs to do detailed work on how it is inflected by this cosmopolitanism.

Given America's current gaze towards the potent economies of the Pacific Rim, it is unsurprising that major Asian stars, too, have been drawn to work in the US. Again, however, it is important to stress the potential reversibility of their trajectories. This capacity for reverse migration, or indeed for a series of geographic dislocations, can be glimpsed in the recent careers of several stars of Hong Kong cinema. Note Michelle Yeoh's passage from a Bond role in *Tomorrow Never Dies* (1997), through very different interpretations of the Chinese martial arts tradition in the international *Crouching Tiger, Hidden Dragon* (2000) and the Hong Kong *Fei ying* (2004), before gravitating back to Hollywood, specifically to a kind of Hollywood Orientalism, in *Memoirs of a Geisha* (2005). This latter role in particular suggests the potential risk of a non-US star's persona being repackaged by Hollywood as exotic commodity. Similar questions might be asked about the American use of figures like Jet Li, Chow Yun-fat and the comically adept Jackie Chan, who collectively evoke for the US a more supple action hero than that provided by behemoths like Stallone and Schwarzenegger and their indigenous successors. In each of these cases, however, there may be reciprocal interaction between US cinema and non-US star, rather than simply the former's reshaping of the latter; the 'host' cinema, as well as the incoming actor's persona, is liable to readjustment.

Tiger, not James, Woods

In 1990, Christine Gledhill acknowledged the glitter of pop and sports stars, yet still felt able to claim that cinema provides 'the ultimate confirmation of stardom'. Writing ten years later, however, Christine Geraghty was not quite so sure: 'We need to look at stars in a context in which film stars may struggle for prominence' ('Re-examining Stardom', p. 183). As a response to this situation, Geraghty offers a tripartite model of film stardom. Two of the categories she introduces – the star-as-professional and the star-as-performer – are generally defined by cinematic performance itself and thus distinct from other sites of stardom.

However, Geraghty also identifies the star-as-celebrity, a film star whose fame is affirmed not so much by the cinema work as by a mass of other media texts – gossip column entries, magazine interviews, advertisements and so on. Here, clearly, is a kind of stardom in which film performers may lose some outline and mingle promiscuously with figures from other, non-cinematic fields. Just as people easily forget that David Beckham plays football or Charlotte Church makes records, so the fact that Liz Hurley appears in movies is not necessarily significant given the repetition of her celebrity across countless media platforms.

Even the star-as-professional and the star-as-performer may now operate in a world in which film stardom has become less culturally central. Geraghty makes the point that, in contemporary production conditions far removed from the conveyor belt of the studio era, Hollywood films, at least, take a long time to emerge and are thus 'a relatively inefficient way of delivering fame compared with some other formats' (p. 188). This is of course less relevant to the film star-as-celebrity, for whom screen performance is anyway more incidental to her status. Nevertheless, Geraghty is right to suggest the greater speed and flexibility now of other vehicles of stardom. The ceaseless spectacle provided, say, by today's 'sports-industrial complex' has kept performers like Tiger Woods and Michael Jordan more continuously in public discourse than their cinematic counterparts. The ubiquity of such figures in media texts and their hyper-attractiveness to advertisers suggest that the ratio of power between sports and film stardoms has changed from a time like the 1960s, when Paul Newman's beauty on screen was hardly to be out-dazzled by the sensible sweaters of US golfer Arnold Palmer.

Just as the political economy of sports stardom increasingly rivals in magnitude its cinematic counterpart, so, too, there has been a rise in the sports star's ideological power. Earlier we saw the importance of film stars in exhibiting in attractive ways socially favoured gender and race identities; it is at least arguable that this role in ideological reproduction has substantially devolved upon sports – and music and TV – stars. In Britain recently no male film star – indigenous or otherwise – has negotiated versions of masculinity in as complex a way and with as many effects, liberating besides commodifying, as David Beckham. British university courses teach the cultural semiotics of Beckham; there is no comparable programme of Brad Pitt studies. Consider, too, the relative contributions of film and sports stars to American debates about race. Black movie performers have often been strongly implicated in these: not only Poitier, but earlier figures like Stepin Fetchit and Lena Horne, and later stars like Eddie Murphy, Denzel Washington, Samuel L. Jackson and Halle Berry. However, it is debatable whether the more contemporary African American film stars have been as central to explorations of black identity as Jordan and other NBA (National Basketball Association) players, Tiger Woods in golf and the Williams sisters in tennis.

Unsurprisingly, sports studies now emulates work on film by producing semiotic and ideological readings of its stars. Take a volume like David L. Andrews and Steven J. Jackson's edited collection, *Sports Stars: The Cultural Politics of Sporting Celebrity* (London and New York: Routledge, 2001). Repeating the asceticism of some film star studies, this book's contributors ignore the possibly progressive implications of their subjects' breathtaking grace, finesse and athleticism; instead, they explore the contemporary sports star's roles in expanding commodity culture and reinforcing conservative ideology. From this perspective, the images of black sportspeople like Woods function in the US to consolidate, rather than dislodge, an unequal racial status quo; as in the case of Poitier, such individual success stories inhibit awareness of the need for structural social change.

Analysing stars: Johnny Depp

'You will not like me.' Improbably, these words are uttered by Johnny Depp, speaking direct to camera as the seventeenth-century Earl of Rochester in *The Libertine* (2004). The remark is hostile in tone; the character does not ingratiate himself, and Rochester refuses to show remorse even as his body fails after a lifetime of licentiousness and anarchy. There are resonances here for Depp's own positioning in contemporary popular culture. The part of 'libertine' seems made for him, given his circulation through gossip columns, muckraking biographies and paparazzi-snapped photographs. Rochester's anti-authoritarianism – what, anachronistically, we might term his counter-cultural energy – also fits with the star persona Depp has developed over an acting career that began by playing a dreamy youth in *A Nightmare on Elm Street* (1984). However, when Rochester tells the spectator at the start of *The Libertine*, 'I do not want you to like me', he chronically misjudges the charismatic effect of Depp's performance style. Depp's 'likeability' is now a major phenomenon, and this section aims to track its effects across commercial domains, ideological formations and fan cultures.

As a star, Depp is unusually or multiply positioned. If his astonishing dramatic range excludes him from one of the three modes of contemporary film stardom identified by Geraghty – the star-as-professional, who is associated with an invariant character-type, often in a single genre – he can be aligned with the other two: the star-as-celebrity and the star-as-performer. Although discussion of Depp's seriousness as an actor has never been totally suppressed, his celebrity has often been carried by vehicles other than screen performances themselves. Newspaper, magazine and TV reports of famous girlfriends, trashed hotel rooms and assaulted photographers all evoke a type of fame that does not require validation by the labour of film acting. This media intensity abated when Depp retreated to France with his partner Vanessa Paradis and their children. Yet his identity of star-as-celebrity is still liable to reactivation: magazines have lately annulled his hellraiser status and repositioned him as an ungrateful exile who fails the stringent tests of American patriotism post-9/11. The existence of at least seven popular biographies of Depp, plus an image archive augmented at each glittering premiere, suggests the durability of this version of his film stardom. By contrast, there are only two books that privilege his acting career itself, giving nuanced attention to his performance style and its cultural significance. As Depp ages, there might be a shift in the terms of attention, a closer focus upon his operations as star-as-performer. For the moment, however, he continues to migrate across categories of film stardom: like Brando, Hoffman or Pacino in intensity and detail of screen performance, yet with a celebrity's buzz.

Despite his professed distaste for cinema's marketing machine, Depp is of course a key commercial player. Thus the political economy approach to stardom invoked by Taylor, McDonald and others finds plenty to say here. On the whole, Depp, with his established fan base, has functioned to underwrite the viability of a relatively small-scale, independent cinema. Diverse, comparatively low-budget projects like *Finding Neverland* (2004) or *The Libertine* itself are made more likely by his inclusion as a key item in the 'package' constructed by filmmakers and put to possible financial backers. In these instances, Depp exhibits the newer film star's ability to franchise out his persona on a project-by-project basis. However, he has also emulated classical studio relationships between star and director such as those of John Wayne and John Ford, or Katharine Hepburn and George Cukor, by making five films with Tim Burton after the successful *Edward Scissorhands*: *Ed Wood* (1994), *Sleepy Hollow* (1999), *Charlie and the Chocolate Factory* (2005), *Tim Burton's Corpse Bride* and *Sweeney Todd* (2007). Besides consideration of its commercial strategy, this director/star symbiosis also invites study through an auteurist optic: to what extent is Depp a co-author of Burton's films?

Since 2003, Depp's commercial dimension has been complicated by his involvement with the larger-scale, mainstream project represented by the three *Pirates of the Caribbean* films. The films themselves occupy a kind of interim stage in a multi-format series, succeeding the Disneyland ride that was their point of origin and preceding lucrative extra-cinematic elaborations such as the *Pirates* computer games. Unlike other of the films' stars, Depp has lent his voice to these games. Any account of his political economy, then, needs to reckon with a partially mainstream as well as independent stardom, and also with its synergistic exploitability in non-cinematic media.

The big-budget success of the *Pirates* films has only to a certain extent 'mainstreamed' Depp's persona. By and large, his star image still signifies oddity, ethereality, angularity with respect to the customary world. Yet his ease and grace of performance, and the beauty of his looks, ensure that such unusualness rarely communicates itself to audiences as disturbing or repellent. Just the opposite in fact. Murray Pomerance notes that while many of the parts Depp plays justify 'categorisation of his on-screen personality as other, it is also true that he manages to draw himself to us as a distinct familiar.' He is 'chameleon-like', yet 'globally accessible (both aesthetically and in marketing)'; his strangeness on screen is 'entirely a cosy and comprehensible strangeness' (*Johnny Depp Starts Here* (New Brunswick, NJ: Rutgers University Press, 2005), pp. 30–1). 'Otherness' is of course a capacious category, so we will concentrate here on just three components of his idiosyncratic persona: counter-culturalism, 'Europeanness' and a redesigned masculinity.

Despite a birth certificate saying Owensboro, Kentucky, it is arguable to what extent Depp is still an *American* film star. Much of his work since 2000 has been playing non-American characters. Before considering those, it is noticeable that even the US parts he plays are often figures not recognised by officially endorsed national narratives. If Tom Hanks signifies the virtue of patriotic, small-town America, Depp's roles tend to expose that world's stultifying, even coercive properties. This could not be clearer when he plays icons of US counter-culture, such as the Beat writer Jack Kerouac in the TV film, *The Source* (1999) and versions of the drug-inspired journalist Hunter S. Thompson in both *Fear and Loathing in Las Vegas* (1998) and *The Rum Diary* (expected 2009). Elsewhere, too, with ambiguous exceptions like his undercover FBI agent in *Donnie Brasco* (1997) and possessed space commander in *The Astronaut's Wife* (1999), he has specialised during the US-centred films in the nation's casualties and renegades. To cite just three examples: the failed Hollywood director, Ed Wood; the title role in *Edward Scissorhands*, combining in his appearance and behaviour such US 'others' as artist, punk, African American and person with disability; and the figure adrift in the Old West in *Dead Man* (1995), until, significantly, he establishes a connection with the white nation's other, the Native American (note that Depp's own ancestry is part Cherokee).

'William Blake' – the name of the character he plays in *Dead Man* – evokes the visionary spirit of English Romanticism. The role thus serves as a bridge between Depp's American-centred and European-oriented work (another intermediary of this kind is his US incarnation of Don Juan in *Don Juan DeMarco* (1995)). Fully

Europeanised roles include an Irish character in *Chocolat* and a Romany in *The Man Who Cried* (both 2000). But if Depp is becoming a European film star, perhaps, more specifically still, he is becoming a *British* one. Besides Rochester in *The Libertine*, the evidence for this includes his opium-addicted Victorian detective in *From Hell* (2001) (Figure 19); his version of J. M. Barrie in *Finding Neverland*; and, most colourfully, his performances as Captain Jack Sparrow in the *Pirates of the Caribbean* films. In *Pirates* Depp's voice is famously modelled on that of Keith Richards of the Rolling Stones, suggesting an anglophile fondness for the nation's older cultural monuments which he also exhibited by appearing in the farewell series of the BBC comedy, *The Fast Show* (2000). All of this European work indicates that, at the time of writing, Depp has mutated into a figure with a distanced, even exilic perspective on the United States; he echoes earlier Americans abroad, like the writers Fitzgerald and Hemingway in France after the First World War.

Although a pin-up figure of his cinematic generation, Depp by no means embodies a standardised heroic masculinity. At times, his on-screen gendering is ambiguous, as with hints of effeminacy

Figure 19 Johnny Depp as Inspector Abberline in *From Hell* (US/UK/Czech Republic, 2001).

in both *Finding Neverland* and – his voice evoking Michael Jackson – *Charlie and the Chocolate Factory*. He is a contemporary of Tom Cruise and Keanu Reeves, yet does not emulate their kinetic action styles; instead, Depp's characters on screen are often withdrawn, given more to interiority than decisive intervention in the world. Think, for example, of the blocked writer Mort Rainey on his sofa in *Secret Window* (2004), or Inspector Abberline sinking into an opium trance in *From Hell*. Even in roles seemingly predicated upon action, he tends to exhibit thoughtful detachment: recall how in *Donnie Brasco* he stands by while beatings occur, or how in the *Pirates* films he buckles his swash less than Orlando Bloom. This poise and distance, however, rarely congeals into narcissism on screen. In contrast to the near-invulnerability of other leading Hollywood men, Depp is characterised in performance by a capacity to be wounded or even die: he just fades away at the end of films like *Dead Man* and *From Hell*. Even his physical beauty is subject to concealment, disfigurement or outright corrosion in much of his film work. He wears quaint spectacles in *Sleepy Hollow*, is bald in *Fear and Loathing in Las Vegas* and loses parts of his face to syphilis in *The Libertine*.

Fan cultures that gather around Depp often downplay such signs of passivity, effeminacy and woundedness, and read in him instead an idealised masculinity. His fandom differs from many academic responses by giving considerable weight to his public appearances as well as – or even instead of – the film work. Websites devoted to Depp – all of them unofficial – house a constantly updated and annotated archive of images of him gathered at premieres and other occasions. Fans also express their passion by writing stories or poems in which, miraculously, their surrogate selves have encounters – sometimes sexual – with Depp. Yearning with respect to a star is clearly as intense as during that earlier cinematic culture explored by Stacey; here, verbatim, are examples from www.johnnydeppweb.com (accessed 12 August 2006):

- He is a God Deppism ain't just a disease it's a religion, my religion an i really believe it i am a true Deppist.
- i love johnny depp so much i would die for him (no joke).
- i would deff break up wit my boyfriend for johnny.

Exasperated by such statements, someone else posts: 'Jesus, people get a life.' Yet it seems as if the 'Deppists' already *have* a life, consisting in extremely powerful, indeed all-consuming identificatory fantasies and practices (always allowing, of course, for the fact that the internet's anonymity licenses extremely inventive performances of self). While it is tempting to dismiss all of this as debased adolescent emotion – confirmation of the worst fears of critics of mass culture – it is as well to remember that intense identification with Depp speaks powerfully of a desire for something other than mundane experience, a desire that may have progressive rather than simply reactionary implications. Perhaps to a greater extent than other leading men of his generation, Depp seems equipped to fulfil stardom's utopian potential. His is not a static and coercive version of masculinity but a plural, plastic one (even many of the ardent website contributors admire not only his looks but his versatility across a wide performative range). He is also a figure whose stardom transgresses gender boundaries, hinting at their anachronism: alongside Depp's heterosexual female fans should be set his gay fandom, including the none-too-coyly named New York hardcore band, Gay for Johnny Depp.

Selected reading

Austin, Thomas and Martin Barker (eds), *Contemporary Hollywood Stardom* (London: Arnold, 2003).

Interesting, methodologically varied essays. Besides analysing such flesh-and-blood stars as Jodie Foster and Robin Williams, models of film stardom are extended to Jar Jar Binks in *The Phantom Menace* and Woody and Buzz in *Toy Story*.

Babington, Bruce (ed.), *British Stars and Stardom: From Alma Taylor to Sean Connery* (Manchester: Manchester University Press, 2001).

Along with Vincendeau's volume, a helpful, engaging corrective to Hollywood-centred star studies: covers an historical range from the 1910s to Kenneth Branagh and Emma Thompson.

Barbas, Samantha, *Movie Crazy: Fans, Stars, and the Cult of Celebrity* (New York and Basingstoke: Palgrave Macmillan, 2001).

Overstates the role of fans in 'star discourse' but offers a very readable account of responses to stars in the US either side of the First World War.

Dyer, Richard, *Heavenly Bodies: Film Stars and Society* (Basingstoke and London: Macmillan, 1987).

A practical companion to Dyer's *Stars*, testing its insights in extended, illuminating studies of Judy Garland, Marilyn Monroe and the mid-century African American film, theatre and singing star Paul Robeson.

Dyer, Richard, *Stars*, 2nd ed. (London: BFI, 1998).

The foundational text of modern star studies (first published in 1979); still hugely productive, despite subsequent challenges to its combination of semiotics, sociology and ideology critique. This second edition includes valuable updating material by Paul McDonald.

Geraghty, Christine, 'Re-examining Stardom: Questions of Texts, Bodies and Performance', *Reinventing Film Studies*, eds Christine Gledhill and Linda Williams (London: Arnold, 2000), pp. 183–201.

Suggestive attempt to reconceptualise star studies for the twenty-first century, including exploration of the film star's affiliations with other figures in celebrity culture.

Gledhill, Christine (ed.), *Stardom: Industry of Desire* (London and New York: Routledge, 1991).

Pioneering collection, gathering formative work on stars by Richard deCordova, Barry King, John O. Thompson and others. Still valuable, though needs supplementing by newer materials like Austin/Barker and Willis.

McDonald, Paul, *The Star System: Hollywood and the Production of Popular Identities* (London: Wallflower, 2000).

Lucid, highly informed account of the US star system from its beginnings to its mutations in contemporary digital and celebrity cultures; a very accessible way into thinking about the history of Hollywood stardom.

Stacey, Jackie, *Star Gazing: Hollywood Cinema and Female Spectatorship* (London and New York: Routledge, 1994).

Groundbreaking study of British women's responses to American female stars during the 1940s and 1950s; conceptually rich and challenging, but also moving in its inclusion of these neglected spectators' voices.

Vincendeau, Ginette, *Stars and Stardom in French Cinema* (London and New York: Continuum, 2000).

An attractive variation upon American-centred star studies, consisting of well-informed, engaging essays on French stars from Max Linder to Juliette Binoche via Brigitte Bardot, *Nouvelle vague* performers, Depardieu and others.

Willis, Andy (ed.), *Film Stars: Hollywood and Beyond* (Manchester: Manchester University Press, 2004).

Not quite so far from America as the subtitle promises – lively pieces on Branagh, Jackie Chan and Cynthia Rothrock's Hong Kong martial arts films notwithstanding – but still a set of vivid, accessible essays.

Useful websites

www.filmbug.com.

More popular than scholarly but wide-ranging in its encyclopaedia of stars and – through its fan forums – revealing about the terms of our contemporary responses to screen icons.

www.shef.ac.uk/f/frenchfilmstars/home.html.

Lacking post-2002 entries but, with many biographies and filmographies of French stars, a promising antidote to the Hollywood fixation of much star study.

www.usindiainfo.com/filmstars.htm.

Assembles information on numerous Indian stars: besides this database function, however, is even more valuable as evidence of the intensities of Indian fandom.

8
Film and ideology

In an essay on the African American film *Boyz N the Hood* (1991), Robyn Wiegman refers to a 'now clichéd, polysyllabic referent "genderraceclass"' ('Feminism, "The Boyz", and Other Matters Regarding the Male', *Screening the Male: Exploring Masculinities in Hollywood Cinema*, eds Steven Cohan and Ina Rae Hark, pp. 174–5). Wiegman acknowledges that this portmanteau category may be salutary for feminist thinkers: the reference to 'gender' activates interest in the complexities of masculinity alongside those of femininity, while the rest of the newly coined term helps to correct any previous feminist neglect of racial and class differences that fracture the apparently unified category of 'Woman'. However, there also dangers in this new conceptual constellation. On the one hand, attempts to maintain a productive sense of interconnection between gender, race and class sometimes deteriorate into hierarchical thinking, with one term prematurely given overmighty, determinate status. On the other, the conglomerated word cannot always hold, with the result that each item in this triplet may still become detached from the others, thereby repressing a sense of the complexity of our construction as social subjects. The problems are exacerbated when we appreciate that even such a generous formulation as 'genderraceclass' is insufficient to evoke the full range of ideological domains in which we are situated. At the very least, we need also to consider sexuality and speak, more inelegantly still, of 'gendersexualityraceclass'.

The present chapter aims to introduce gendersexualityraceclass in film studies. It will sketch out some major lines of inquiry regarding ideology and social subjectivity in cinema and suggest areas for further study. At the same time, we should note that categories of gender, sexuality, race and class have already been operational in this book. Recall such topics as female costume and body positioning in *In the Mood for Love* (Chapter 1); the feminisation of film editing, relative to directing and cinematography (Chapter 2); female authorship, given scepticism about the unique cinematic signature (Chapter 5); and stars' embodiment of culturally normative – or sometimes dissentient – modes of gendered, sexual, racial and class identity (Chapter 7). Other areas of film study previously discussed are also traversed by this chapter's concerns; think, say, of the frequent gendering of Hollywood genres, by which a supposedly 'masculine' generic repertoire of westerns, action and war films is set against a 'feminine' one of musicals, romances and melodramas.

Class struggle – and the struggle for class – in film studies

'The history of all hitherto existing societies', declare Marx and Engels at the start of the *Communist Manifesto*, 'is the history of class struggles'. With the indefinite postponement of a classless utopia since they wrote these words in 1848, their insight into structural social hierarchies and antagonisms has continued to motivate the political activism of generations of men and women. In addition, of course, it has underpinned theoretical work across a host of disciplines. Yet the presence of class as an analytical category within film studies itself has been tenuous and intermittent. Certainly, critical writings can be cited that focus explicitly and unashamedly upon this topic. Note such frank titles as Fredric Jameson's 'Class and Allegory in Contemporary Mass Culture: *Dog Day Afternoon* as a Political Film' (1977; reprinted in *Signatures of the Visible* (London and New York: Routledge, 1992)), or the chapter on 'Class, Race, and the New South' in Ryan and Kellner's frequently class-oriented *Camera Politica: The Politics and Ideology of Contemporary Hollywood Film* (1988). At other moments, however, film studies' engagement with structures and dynamics of class has been either abandoned altogether or subsumed by overly generalised accounts of *ideology*. This

conceptual neglect has coincided with the new – and necessary –
promotion of such previously ignored fields as gender, sexuality
and race. Given these developments, then, David E. James could
anxiously entitle an essay of the late 1990s: 'Is There Class in this
Text?: The Repression of Class in Film and Cultural Studies' (*A
Companion to Film Theory*, eds Toby Miller and Robert Stam
(Malden, MA and Oxford: Blackwell, 1999), pp. 182–201).

Even before turning to film texts themselves, however, the discipline should already have class lodged near its centre. Questions of
film consumption will be considered in detail in Chapter 10; for
the moment, we can just note that the class status of film spectatorship has been at issue since the medium's beginning. At the
level of production, too, inequalities in access to educational,
financial and technological resources powerfully shape who gets to
make cinematic representations in the first place. Thus even
sympathetic portrayals of, say, the British working class are more
likely to come from filmmakers personally originating outside that
social fraction than from directors or writers located within it.
This structural imbalance is replicated at a global level.
Proletarianised within the world economic system, many nations
in Africa, Asia and Latin America still lack the financial and
cultural infrastructures necessary to support significant film
industries, and so are more liable to be the objects of others' representation than significant producers of representation themselves.
It remains to be seen whether lower-priced digital equipment and
new forms of distribution will help to counteract such inequalities
in cinema's domestic and international class systems.

Marxist critics have analysed the part played by film in class-
divided societies. Important early contributions here include
Kracauer's assessment of the ideological effects of popular
cinemagoing in Weimar Germany, and Adorno and Horkheimer's
Dialectic of Enlightenment (1947) which scourges 'the culture
industry' – prominently including cinema – for its commodification of art and its key role in manufacturing conformist citizens.
Building upon such work, Marxism was a major strand in the
paradigm that came to dominate film studies by the 1970s. Yet to
reread writings from this period now is not always to encounter
the heightened sensitivity that might be expected to questions of

class in cinema; instead, there is frequently a discourse that floats abstractly away from the materiality of specific class struggles and from the sheer suffering of those without social power. This oversight occurred as Marxist theorists sought to develop an ever more elaborate and total account of film's ideological instrumentality. Writers associated with the newly radicalised *Cahiers du cinéma* in France and with the journal *Screen* in Britain drew conceptual substance particularly from the French structural Marxist Louis Althusser. For Althusser, the reproduction of unequal social orders is achieved not only at the point of a gun or policeman's baton but, more subtly, by the operations of a wide range of institutions he calls Ideological State Apparatuses (ISAs), such as the church, the media and the arts (including cinema). Ideologically saturated, the dominated subject within a class-unequal society thereby misrecognises, *Matrix*-style, her actual place in it, and consents imaginatively to the terms of oppression.

Althusser's work leans upon the psychoanalysis of his French contemporary Jacques Lacan. In particular, Lacan's theory of *the mirror stage* – the phase when an infant derives an illusory sense of wholeness and self-sufficiency by gazing at his reflection in a mirror – was taken up by Althusser as a suggestive way of thinking about the adult subject's ideological formation. Such tropes of mirrors, images and gazes made Althusserian ideology-theory especially transmissible to film studies. Yet in borrowing terms and concepts from Althusser and Lacan, Marxist writers on film in the late 1960s and 1970s also imported these thinkers' tendency to pessimism. Thus some of the canonical texts of Marxist film theory tend to present cinema as a kind of perfected machine for the reproduction of bourgeois ideology and, by extension, class-divided society. In 'Cinema/Ideology/Criticism', a 1969 editorial for *Cahiers du cinéma*, Jean-Luc Comolli and Jean Narboni admittedly allow for the possibility of some filmmaking that will disrupt the spectator's usual ideological quietude. Any such radical gestures, however, occur against the grain of the medium's disposition towards a reactionary effect: 'the classic theory of cinema that the camera is an impartial instrument which grasps, or rather is impregnated by, the world in its "concrete reality" is an eminently reactionary one. What the camera in fact registers is the

vague, unformulated, untheorised, unthought-out world of the
dominant ideology' (*Film Theory and Criticism: Introductory
Readings*, 6th ed., eds Leo Braudy and Marshall Cohen (New
York: Oxford University Press, 2004), p. 815). Still more fatalistic
is Jean-Louis Baudry's argument in a much-anthologised essay,
'Ideological Effects of the Basic Cinematographic Apparatus'
(1970). For Baudry, the specific properties of different films – 'the
forms of narrative adopted, the "contents" of the image' (*Film
Theory and Criticism*, p. 364) – can generally be set aside as of little
analytical significance. Rather, film's ideological function is
fulfilled by the optics of the viewing situation itself: the spectating
subject is like the Lacanian infant, repressing awareness of the
constructed, illusory nature of the images gazed upon and instead
occupying a position from which they appear intelligible and, as it
were, 'natural'. Baudry refers to 'the ideology inherent in perspective' (p. 357), and indeed aligns cinema as a technology for
capturing and making sense of the world with the notion of
perspective developed by Renaissance painting in the West.

Baudry's argument that film carries the virus of ideology in the
very optical systems of projection and spectatorship makes it difficult to imagine how a politically oppositional cinema could come
into being. Though his essay is in the service of a militantly
intended criticism – 'ideology' is a recurrent term – it is very
unworldly. To a lesser extent, the same stricture applies to the
Comolli/Narboni article and to other writings from this significant wave of Marxist film theory. Along with differences in the
institutional locations and social experiences of film spectatorship,
the contents of particular film texts are in danger of effacement in
favour of a more unitary, abstract account of cinema as an ideological practice.

Later film scholars working with the category of class have
tended therefore to produce a finer-grained textual analysis. Some
of these readings are in support of films that seek to disrupt the
old ideological order and evoke a new one by breaking with the
language of narrative cinema. This historically and geographically
dispersed tradition of radical filmmaking extends from Soviet
montage experiments through such examples as collectively
produced Latin American cinema and Godard's mid-career work

to the uncompromising practice of the French husband-and-wife team Jean-Marie Straub and Danielle Huillet. However, analysis has also focused on films – as different as those by Ken Loach in Britain and Ousmane Sembene in Senegal – that expose specific class inequities by still using the resources of narrative. Beyond this concern with politically engaged cinema, however, a class-based approach can find suggestive things to say about strategies of representation in virtually any film. What are the ideological implications of the ways in which particular social classes are cinematically staged and narrated?

Several recent studies listed in this chapter's bibliography suggest that such analysis is not obsolete. Far from sharing the voguish suspicion in parts of the West that class is now superseded as a concept, Paul Dave unabashedly uses its subdivisions to organise *Visions of England: Class and Culture in Contemporary Cinema* (2006). Dave's chapters focus successively upon representations in modern English film of the upper classes, middle classes, working classes, the underclass and the lumpenproletariat. This enterprise looks less like the last spasm of a dying Marxist approach to film than its forceful re-articulation, only equipped now with greater textual sensitivity and an awareness of the multiple articulations of class with other domains. As Chuck Kleinhans puts it: 'Today Marxism seems most dynamic when it combines its analysis of class with an analysis of gender, race, national, post-colonial, and other issues raised by progressive social-political movements' ('Marxism and film', *The Oxford Guide to Film Studies*, eds John Hill and Pamela Church Gibson (Oxford: Oxford University Press, 1998), p. 111).

STOP and THINK

- Compared with the current fashionability of theories of gender, sexuality and race, a vocabulary of class may appear antiquated, as rusted – at least in the West – as the factories in which it once circulated. To what extent is sensitivity to representations of class an element of your film spectatorship?

- Consider how cinema has represented a particular class and its interaction with other social fractions. You might, for example, assess images of the contemporary English working class generated by films like *Brassed Off* (1996), *The Full Monty*, *Billy Elliot* (2000) and Shane Meadows's *Once Upon a Time in the Midlands* (2002), *Dead Man's Shoes* (2004) and *This Is England* (2006). Or – joining class questions to those of ethnicity and nation – what constructions of the Latino underclass in the US borderlands are produced by Jennifer Lopez's pre-fame vehicle *Selena* (1997), Loach's *Bread and Roses* (2000), and the already-mentioned *Lone Star*, *Traffic* and *The Three Burials of Melquiades Estrada*?

- Do the narratives of class in films with which you are familiar tend to reinforce or undermine existing social orders? Particular films might, say, present a sympathetic portrayal of working classes, yet still withhold a militant social analysis. A work like *The Full Monty* perhaps falls under this heading: despite moments of pathos, it orchestrates as warm, comic narrative the loss of formerly solid class – and gender – identities. Even so, the men's mastering and performing of the striptease might still stand, however faintly, as a figure for renewed class coherence and struggle.

A very short history of gender in film studies

'Down with sexism, up with women!'
Although evaluations of masculinity have always been crucial to cinema – witness audience response from the early twentieth century onwards to a succession of male screen icons – approaches to gender in film studies itself initially centred upon images of women. Writers early in the1970s extended to film 'second-wave' feminism's polemical force and anti-patriarchal scrutiny. Where Kate Millett's *Sexual Politics* (1970) had excoriated female representation in literary texts, a number of American feminists attempted such a critique of cinematic women. First was Marjorie Rosen, in *Popcorn Venus: Women, Movies, and the American Dream*

(New York: Coward, McCann and Geoghegan, 1973). A year later, more influentially, came Molly Haskell's *From Reverence to Rape: The Treatment of Women in the Movies*. In a series of decade-by-decade overviews, Haskell traces a trajectory from the stultifying gentility of film's early representation of women to the blatant rape fantasies of works such as Sam Peckinpah's *Straw Dogs* (1971). A chapter on post-1974 cinema, added for the book's second edition in 1987, speaks of an 'Age of Ambivalence', which denotes some improvement but not enough to cause Haskell to retitle her study.

For all its pioneering significance, *From Reverence to Rape* has an odd, slightly embarrassing place in feminist film studies. Written by someone who worked primarily as a magazine film critic, it was open to challenge – and condescension – by academics in the discipline. Most damagingly, the book has been exposed for its impoverished representational model. Like Rosen's text, it is concerned in quasi-sociological fashion with *images* or *stereotypes* of women on screen, which, without methodological self-consciousness, it correlates with what it understands as women's actual experiences; the book thus lacks a complex sense of cinema as a system of fabrications and constructions, rather than mere reflections. Compared with later feminist scholars' psychoanalytic nuances, it is also limited in its account of the interactions of female viewers with on-screen spectacle. Yet to read *From Reverence to Rape* now is to recover a sense of its invigorating qualities. Unsophisticated or not, that strain of criticising images or stereotypes which it exemplifies has not perished but is still activated by women – by subordinated classes and ethnic and sexual minorities too – who deplore existing representations of themselves and seek more 'positive' ones. Haskell also writes in an iconoclastic spirit that is not always exhibited by feminist film studies. Without succumbing to facile anti-intellectualism, it is important to reiterate that the kind of polemical verve she typifies is as vital as advanced theoretical production to the carrying-on of political struggle. Her book has the fierceness, the satirical vigour, the vivid rallying cries – like the phrase heading this section – that recruit people to causes. For a flavour of Haskell's writing, consider this summing-up of the supposedly 'great women's roles' of

Anglo-American cinema in the 1960s and early 1970s:

> Whores, quasi-whores, jilted mistresses, emotional cripples, drunks.
> Daffy ingenues, Lolitas, kooks, sex-starved spinsters, psychotics.
> Icebergs, zombies, and ballbreakers. That's what little girls of
> the sixties and seventies are made of. (*From Reverence to Rape*,
> 2nd ed. (Chicago and London: University of Chicago Press, 1987),
> pp. 327–8)

Theories of the spectatrix

In 1989 a special issue of the radical film journal *Camera Obscura*
appeared under the title of 'The Spectatrix'. This verbal coinage
indicates how feminist film theorists, going beyond Rosen and
Haskell's primary interest in on-screen images of women, increasingly regarded the situation of the female spectator herself as a key
point of intervention. Here the inaugurating document is Laura
Mulvey's essay 'Visual Pleasure and Narrative Cinema', first
published in *Screen* in Autumn 1975, collected in book form in
1989 and long a staple of anthologies of film theory.

Mulvey presents a pessimistic, even morbid account of the
female spectator's place as it is constructed by mainstream narrative cinema. She considers the interaction in film of three kinds of
'look': the camera's look at characters in the diegesis (narrative),
the characters' looks at each other and, finally, the spectator's look
at the screen. Although she indicates that these variously sited
gazes exist in a state of 'shifting tension' (*Visual and Other
Pleasures*, p. 19), her essay also suggests that, for male subjects at
least, they may be continuous or homogeneous. Thus a male character in the diegesis prompts a camera movement by gazing
desiringly towards a female; the resulting image of her body is
then, in an uninterrupted visual series, gazed upon with pleasure
by the male spectator. According to the depressingly binary system
sketched by Mulvey, 'pleasure in looking has been split between
active/male and passive/female' (p. 19). Where the male character
in mainstream film exemplifies activity and controls the operation
of looking, the on-screen woman can only connote '*to-be-looked-
at-ness*' (p. 19). Unlike her complacent male counterpart, then, the
woman spectator is left in an invidious position, offered either a
masochistic identification with such a passive female object of

desire or tangled up in the complexity of cross-gender identification with active on-screen men.

As Mulvey's essay develops, the situation of males – both spectators and diegetic characters – appears less assured than all this might suggest. While man might indeed be the origin of looking, what he gazes upon has the potential to induce not pleasure but panic. Specifically, from the essay's psychoanalytic viewpoint, the anxiety is one of castration: the female body – so central to the visual regime of most cinema – provides an 'image of the bleeding wound' (p. 14). Faced by the need to avert such devastation of masculine authority, mainstream film turns, in Mulvey's argument, to two strategies: *voyeurism* and *fetishistic scopophilia*. The first of these operations involves a frequently sadistic treatment of the on-screen woman that is conveyed by her narrative trajectory as well as her visual representation itself, and may be relished by male characters and spectators alike. Scopophilia, on the other hand, refers to morbid sexual excitation by looking, and the fetishistic variant identified by Mulvey occurs when specific parts of the woman's body or props associated with her become abstracted as objects of psychic investment (we return here to Jayne Mansfield's breasts or Julia Roberts's lips, mentioned in Chapter 7).

Writers on masculinity argue that Mulvey overstates the power of such visual and narrative practices to assuage male castration anxiety. Just like his on-screen counterpart, the male spectator may subsist in a state more lastingly precarious than Mulvey's theory of patriarchal cinematic signification seems to countenance. Even by her own account, certain mainstream films may also *expose* – rather than uncritically reproduce – regimes of voyeurism and fetishistic scopophilia. She mentions Hitchcock's *Rear Window*, *Vertigo* (1958) and *Marnie* (1964), all of them investigations of the perils besides pleasures of 'the male gaze'. She might equally have cited Michael Powell's *Peeping Tom* (1960), which looks like a prophetic cinematic companion to her thesis. Here Mark, a young cinematographer, films the death throes of women as he kills them with the sharpened point of his movie camera's tripod. Mulveyan tropes abound: the protagonist *looks* obsessively – through windows as well as viewfinders

– and his actions literalise the anti-female violence which
Mulvey sees at the heart of cinema's gaze (Figure 20). Yet
Peeping Tom finally demonstrates the *failure* rather than triumph
of a patriarchal scopic regime. 'Whatever I photograph, I always
lose', Mark states in an admission of unappeasable lack; and the
film ends not with another female victim but with his impaling
himself on the tripod.

Nevertheless, such instances of narrative cinema's capacity for
auto-critique were insufficient for Mulvey at the time of the
'Visual Pleasure' essay. The section of her book in which this
piece appears is called 'Iconoclasm', and she speaks frankly about
wanting to smash the institution of mainstream film because of
the depth and power of its patriarchal logic. Synchronically,
then, with her earliest academic writing, she made a series of
films with Peter Wollen – *Penthesilea* (1974), *Riddles of the Sphinx*
(1977) and *Amy!* (1979) – that aimed to disrupt normal cinematic looking and to project a feminist gaze. These works employed
the strategies of avant-garde or experimental cinema and were
shown outside commercial circuits. Other feminist filmmakers
produced similar interrogatory work, which they exhibited in
settings where the film texts themselves were amplified by

Figure 20 The murderous male gaze in *Peeping Tom* (UK, 1960).

printed materials, lectures and consciousness-raising discussions among spectators.

Yet feminism's embrace of 'counter-cinema' was limited as a political strategy. It struck too austere, even puritanical a note and risked appealing only to elite constituencies of cineastes rather than to a mass female audience. Thus feminist work, post-'Visual Pleasure', frequently addresses mainstream films and attempts to find in relation to them positions of empowered or at least less drastically compromised female spectatorship. Mulvey's own later writing includes efforts in this direction. In 'Afterthoughts on "Visual Pleasure and Narrative Cinema" inspired by King Vidor's *Duel in the Sun* (1946)', she utilises another part of Freudian theory to suggest that it is indeed possible for women viewers to identify with active male protagonists in film. As they do so, they return imaginatively to a 'phallic' phase of sexuality, that primal moment open to both male and female subjects but, Freud argues, repressed by the latter in their progression to conventional feminine identity. However, Mulvey insists that such phallic identification can only be fleeting and precarious: 'for women (from childhood onwards) trans-sex identification is a *habit* that very easily becomes *second nature*. However, this Nature does not sit easily and shifts restlessly in its borrowed transvestite clothes' (*Visual and Other Pleasures*, p. 33).

This sense of constraints upon the spectatrix carries across to other work in the feminist psychoanalytic vein, such as Mary Ann Doane's important essay, 'Film and the Masquerade – Theorising the Female Spectator' (*Screen*, 23 (1982): 3–4, 74–87). Drawing upon Joan Riviere's account of womanliness as not biologically rooted but performative – a type of *masquerade* – Doane argues that the female spectator may only be mimicking femininity, rather than inhabiting it uncritically, when she identifies with the passive, conventional versions of women on screen. Like Mulvey's transvestism, Doane's masquerade grants a little more space to female viewers. Both moves, however, only enlarge the perimeters of a cage or prison; feminist psychoanalytic study of cinema tends, for all its conceptual finesse and diagnostic power, to leave intact a sense of patriarchal rule. (There are clear echoes of pessimistic Marxist work at the same time on the bourgeois cinematic apparatus.)

The trials of psychoanalytic feminism

Psychoanalytic feminism in film studies has come under increasing scrutiny in the past two decades. Cognitive film theorists, for example, argue that psychoanalysis overstates the importance of unconscious processes within spectatorship to the detriment of concern with preconscious and conscious ones. As noted in Chapter 4, cognitivism sometimes takes a depoliticised form, as when describing the mental operations at work in our understanding and decipherment of narrative films. Elsewhere, however, it may have a more obviously social implication. Take Flo Leibowitz's essay, 'Apt Feelings, or Why "Women's Films" Aren't Trivial', included in the key counter-psychoanalytic anthology, *Post-Theory* (1996). Like psychoanalytic feminists, Leibowitz assumes the value of that strain of female-centred melodramas produced in Hollywood either side of the Second World War. However, her account of why these films give pleasure bypasses psychoanalytic processes such as masochism and stresses instead the ethical lesson of their presentation of female suffering and self-sacrifice. Audience identification with these wounded on-screen women occurs consciously rather than unconsciously; at this level of spectatorship, indeed, gender differences themselves may be suspended:

> there is a limit to the degree these films are gendered. Both men and women can feel sad when rotten things happen to nice people, which is what happens in these films, and in that respect the term "women's film" is a misnomer. Certainly the point of view of a film is in the film. But ... gender isn't an intrinsic part of point of view, and ... the gendering of imaginative pleasures is not intrinsic to imagination. (*Post-Theory: Reconstructing Film Studies*, eds David Bordwell and Noël Carroll (Madison: University of Wisconsin Press, 1996), p. 227)

Although Leibowitz signals an affinity with feminist concerns by taking as her topic such a key 'female' genre, it may be felt that, in propositions like this one, she decisively moves away from feminism. However, film theorists of avowed feminist militancy have also sought to redirect attention from unconscious to conscious elements of spectatorship. The African American feminist bell hooks makes a vital intervention with her essay, 'The Oppositional

Gaze: Black Female Spectators' (first published in 1992 and subsequently much anthologised and discussed). hooks objects that feminist accounts of the spectatrix are deeply compromised: 'Feminist film theory rooted in an ahistorical psychoanalytic framework that privileges sexual difference actively suppresses recognition of race, re-enacting and mirroring the erasure of black womanhood that occurs in films' (*Reel to Real*, p. 205). Crisscrossing high-theoretical discourse, autobiographical reflection and reportage on her community, hooks argues that, in viewing mainstream narrative films, black female spectators resist all types of identification (whether sadistic or masochistic, cross-dressing or masquerading). This claim is not without problems. It risks essentialising opposition to images as black women's only mode of film viewing, neglecting those mechanisms of enticement by and identification with screen spectacle which psychoanalytic feminism has done much to expose. Nevertheless, on very different grounds to cognitivism's critique of psychoanalysis, hooks similarly opens up the possibility that women may have more varied and conscious engagements with film.

The hints of ethnographic method in hooks's essay – 'Most of the women I talked with felt that they consciously resisted identification with films' (p. 203) – have been elaborated by other writers. Still within the context of African American female reception of film, Jacqueline Bobo has talked to viewers about Spielberg's *The Color Purple* (1985). Her findings – presented in *Black Women as Cultural Readers* – differ significantly from hooks's thesis of this particular group's resolutely oppositional gaze at mainstream cinema. While the African American women Bobo speaks with are mindful of the film's lacunae, they tend not to follow many academic commentators and even journalistic reviewers in indicting it for racism; instead, they testify to a sense of empowerment by its spectacle, its representation of figures with whom they can actively associate. Again there is a danger of focusing only upon articulated conscious responses and neglecting unconscious ones; in addition, as with all social science experiments of this type, Bobo's presence as an academic among these audience clusters has a complicating effect on the generation of evidence. Nevertheless, her study helps to develop ethnography as an adjunct – if not downright alternative – to psychoanalysis in accounting for female film spectatorship. So, too, does Jackie Stacey's *Star Gazing* – discussed in Chapter 7 – which operates in the very different context of a group of white Englishwomen's responses to Hollywood stars of the post-war era. Stacey carefully works through the elaborate systems of feminist psychoanalysis, rather than dismissing them. She still insists, however, that the psychoanalytic tendency to posit a singular viewing position constructed by the film text – a constrained, even frozen stance at that – reduces the sheer variety and agency of women's responses to cinema.

Recent decades, then, have seen a dispersal of feminist work in contrast to the psychoanalytic moment of the 1970s and early 1980s. A previously exclusive methodology is now more likely to be coordinated with approaches including the ethnographic and racially sensitive ones sketched above. It is also suggestive that many of the major scholars of that feminist psychoanalytic wave are now engaged in other areas of film studies. Consider here just a few representative careers. Mulvey and Doane have both been concerned recently with the temporality of cinema: Mulvey's latest book, *Death 24x a Second* (2006) explores the effects on spectatorship of the arresting of film time – as by the DVD's pause facility – while Doane also discusses film's alternating stillness and velocity in *The Emergence of Cinematic Time: Modernity, Contingency, the Archive* (2003). Meanwhile, Annette Kuhn has turned to several strands of research, including an ethnographic survey of cinemagoing in the already-mentioned *An Everyday Magic: Cinema and Cultural Memory* (2002); global film in the co-edited *Screening World Cinema* (2006); and – displacing the film text altogether – photography in another work of co-editorship, *Locating Memory: Photographic Acts* (2006). Such heterogeneous interests may look like displacement activities, compensating for the ideological fervour that animated feminist theory – and film-making – in that earlier phase. Equally, however, this turn to other things may indicate that at least some feminist interrogations – of the screen images of women or the gendering of audiences – have now been 'mainstreamed' and consolidated as part of the common sense of film studies.

From man to masculinities

If women have long been the focus of gender-oriented film study, there has been an explosion of interest since 1990 in what John Beynon calls 'cinematic man' (*Masculinities and Culture* (Buckingham and Philadelphia: Open University Press, 2002), p. 64). Some earlier, prototypical researches into screen masculinity should be mentioned: Joan Mellen's critique of images of men in westerns and cop films in *Big Bad Wolves: Masculinity in the American Film* (New York: Pantheon, 1975), say, or Steve Neale's appropriation of elements of Mulvey's psychoanalytic framework in 'Masculinity as Spectacle: Reflections on Men and Mainstream Cinema' (*Screen*, 24, 6 (1983): 2–16). Yet such texts looked isolated intellectual efforts until Cohan and Hark assembled many writers for *Screening the Male: Exploring Masculinities in Hollywood Cinema* (1992). The plural in this book's subtitle is significant: where masculinity had previously been regarded as unproblematic – in Cohan and Hark's words, 'unperturbed' and 'monolithic' (p. 3) – developments in gender studies now registered a sense of its fracturing and multiplicity. Theorists such as Judith Butler – in *Gender Trouble: Feminism and the Subversion of Identity* (1990) – go far in uncoupling masculinity and femininity from male and female biology respectively, and reconceptualising them as cultural constructions. If womanliness is a masquerade, so, too, is 'manliness'. Masculinity is from this perspective 'dramaturgical', its status akin to that of a theatrical performance. Other metaphors, too, are available to get at this sense of the contingent and inessential in gender identities: Murray Pomerance refers to gender as 'sartorial', suggesting that masculinity, like femininity, is a suit of clothes that may be put on and taken off at will (*Ladies and Gentlemen, Boys and Girls*, p. 307).

Valuable though this language of theatricality and costume is, it risks ignoring the inequalities among rival fabrications of masculinity in any society. Employing a politically more alert vocabulary, Beynon refers to the struggle in particular cultural conjunctures between 'hegemonic masculinity' and 'subordinate variants' (p. 16). Various screen masculinities may themselves contribute either to the reinforcement of culturally dominant models of how to be and look a man, or to their critique and subversion. At the time of his death in 1926, Rudolph Valentino was hugely popular with cinema audiences but viewed with suspicion by some sections of US culture; his star image looked dangerously androgynous and exotic, threatening the reproduction of sturdy white American masculinity. By contrast, a closer correlation existed between the cinematically popular masculinity of John Wayne and the gender norms of the US more broadly before and after the Second World War. The screen muscularity associated with Schwarzenegger, Stallone and others in the 1980s has perhaps an ambiguous political status, seeming both a riposte to and a risible denial of a whole host of developments that had brought into crisis a once-hegemonic blue-collar American masculinity (the decline of manufacturing and concomitant growth of a service economy; the rise of a 'feminised' consumerism; the impact of the women's and gay movements).

Because of the precariousness of this buttoned-up, 'hypermasculine' image, newer versions of Hollywood masculinity by contrast often favour volubility and emotional expressiveness. For all its progressive potential, this development should not be regarded as unequivocally liberating. Susan Jeffords points out that, where previous male icons offered intimidating displays of action and physical prowess, later screen men have sometimes been equally dominant in the realms of nurturing and sensitivity (think of the rebranding of Schwarzenegger's character between the first two *Terminator* films, or of the caring father substituting for a demonised African American motherhood in *Boyz N the Hood*). Thus qualities culturally coded as 'feminine' – at least in the West – may float away from female bodies themselves and be appropriated by men as part of an expanded masculine repertoire. Of course the opposite process may also occur, with the cultural stock of masculinity open to female adoption (as by the gun-toting Linda Hamilton in *Terminator 2* or Sigourney Weaver in *Alien*). Indeed, Mulvey notes that, through the figure of the strong, 'phallic' woman, 'the power of masculinity can be used as postponement against the power of patriarchy' (*Visual and Other Pleasures*, p. 37). By her own account, however, this is only a last-ditch tactic, and one which merely puts a female face on aggressive masculinity rather than doing away with masculine systems altogether.

Finally, it is important to recognise the dangers of ethnocentrism in analyses of men in cinema. Geographical and cultural restrictions blight the field of masculinity studies generally: 'There is a problem in looking at masculinity in other places because most of the literature about masculinity is about British and American men by British and American men and women' (*Masculinities and Culture*, p. 62). In the case of cinema, however, there have been signs of increased interest in non-Anglo-American masculinities. Much of this has been carried out under the umbrella of star studies: Ginette Vincendeau's *Stars and Stardom in French Cinema*, for example, considers how actors such as Jean Gabin, Jean-Paul Belmondo, Alain Delon and Gérard Depardieu have embodied shifting versions of what it is to be a man in France. Yet film studies still needs to invest more heavily in comparative surveys of masculinity. What are the hegemonic and subordinate forms of masculinity in Iranian cinema? In Nigerian or Brazilian or Polish or Australian cinemas? How are such national masculinities reshaped by Hollywood importation or by the cultural crisscrossings that mark transnational film?

STOP and THINK

- Assess the strength of the claim by Mulvey and other feminist theorists that the gaze of mainstream cinema is gendered and operates in the interests of patriarchy. Do films you have watched bear out the thesis of a generally male scopic power – enjoyed by male diegetic characters and spectators alike – or do they complicate, or even contest, this patriarchal rule over the visual? To what extent, and in what particular contexts, do males on screen also suffer the fate of 'to-be-looked-at-ness' which Mulvey tends to reserve for females?

- Consider the range of your identifications with characters in narrative film. Does identification tend to respect gender allegiances, so that female spectators identify primarily with on-screen females and male with male? Or is this too rigid as a model of our engagement with cinemat-

ic protagonists? Are there at least some instances in which
the imagination violates lines of sexual difference, so that,
in temporarily cross-dressing fashion, male spectator
becomes aligned with female character and female with
male? Do such fluid identifications occur more frequently
in some genres than in others?

- Consider variations in screenings of the male. In moving
from older to newer Hollywood films, what are some of the
key developments in the embodiment of masculinity, and
how socially progressive do you judge those shifts to be?
Similarly, what variations occur – and, again, with what
ideological valency – as you juxtapose masculinities in
American or British film with versions of the male proposed
by other national cinemas?

Queering cinema

Interest in gay and lesbian representation in cinema is currently
supported by an institutional apparatus of university courses and
conferences, dedicated journals and specialist film festivals. By
contrast, work on the subject that appeared in the 1970s and early
1980s was piecemeal, individualist, sometimes even idiosyncratic.
A notable precursor text is Parker Tyler's *Screening the Sexes:
Homosexuality in the Movies* (New York: Holt, Rinehart and
Winston, 1972). Tyler was an inventive poet and novelist, besides
wide-ranging film critic; his interests in American avant-garde and
non-Anglophone cinemas ensured that the book on screen homosexuality covered such heterogeneous examples as Andy Warhol's
underground films and Fellini's work from Italy. This eclectic
referencing – allied to a vivid prose style – produced a readership
that was cultic rather than general. More successful as an overview
of gay and lesbian cinematic representation, then, was Vito Russo's
The Celluloid Closet: Homosexuality in the Movies, published first
in 1981, revised in 1987 (New York: Harper and Row) and adapted
as an informative documentary film in 1995. Like Rosen and
Haskell's early feminist work, Russo's study tends towards image-
critique. In exhaustive detail, he documents variously overt or
coded screen representations of homosexuality and interprets

them as a reflection of homophobic formations in society at large.

The Celluloid Closet performed particularly important work in restoring gay men and lesbian women to visibility in classical Hollywood's output. From 1930 to 1967, mainstream US cinema was subject to the rule of the Motion Picture Production Code (colloquially, 'the Hays Code'). Certain activities such as adultery and murder were subject to restricted representation; other behaviours – including miscegenation and profanity – were excised from the screen entirely. But although the Code contains a lexicon of conservative America's phobias, it nowhere speaks the word *homosexuality*; instead, this is implied in such vague formulations as 'sex sins' and 'impure love'. However, even as the Code thereby condemns homosexual identity to total exclusion from American screens, the repeated, denunciatory terms it uses to do so hint at hysteria, an anxiety that policing action might not be successful. And, indeed, Russo uncovers much evidence of homosexuality in mainstream American films of this period – expressed, for example, in narrative ambiguities or styles of performance or types of costume and hairstyle. Such work of decrypting in *The Celluloid Closet*, however, tends not to be affirmative, but in the cause of identifying a virulently prejudicial culture both on- and off-screen.

Subsequent writers influenced by *queer theory* – a conceptual move discussed below – have contested Russo's approach to classical Hollywood cinema. Rather than simply reading off negative stereotypes of homosexuality from the screen, they have activated a very different type of spectatorship. A space for queer pleasure and desire – not just for critique – is opened up. Particular star images have been important loci of imaginative investment by non-straight audiences and critics. Consider how Rock Hudson's outing as gay following his death from AIDS in 1985 has prompted spectators to review screen performances – notably in melodramas directed by Douglas Sirk and sex comedies co-starring Doris Day – that had once seemed impeccably heterosexual. Similarly, knowledge of Montgomery Clift's troubled sexual identity – complicating his status as a male pin-up of the post-war period – becomes a factor in both the critical interrogations and audience fantasies initiated by his screen work. In the western *Red*

River (1948), say, it adds to already existing textual hints that the relationship of his character to the older John Wayne is not only an oedipal struggle but an undeclared love affair. Here the woman the two men officially compete for mediates their desire – still unspoken, of course – as much as she drives them apart.

Readings of this sort are interested not only in revisiting clearly promising genres like melodrama but in 'queering' such bastions of mainstream heterosexual cinema as the western, the war film and the buddy action movie. However, it is important to hesitate before routinely eroticising all same-sex bonds in cinema; awareness of the concept of the *homosocial* is crucial here. More than any other writer, the queer theorist and literary scholar Eve Kosofsky Sedgwick has mobilised this idea, taking the homosocial to refer to any cultural situation in which same-sex relationships are endowed with the highest emotional and symbolic value. Such formations are not bound to be eroticised and, indeed, are often stridently heterosexist in their explicit utterances (as with all-male cultures in the genre of the western pre-*Brokeback Mountain*). Productively, however, Sedgwick also undermines 'homosocial/homosexual' as a stable binary opposition, referring instead to 'the potential unbrokenness of a continuum between homosocial and homosexual – a continuum whose visibility, for men, in our society, is radically disrupted' (*Between Men: English Literature and Male Homosocial Desire* (New York: Columbia University Press, 1985), pp. 1–2). This insight can be carried across from Sedgwick's literary context and used to evaluate images of male friendship in individual films or even whole genres that seem to flaunt a no-nonsense heterosexuality. And, though Sedgwick argues that lines between erotic relationship and non-erotic bonding are anyway more permeable for women – not so nervously insisted upon as by male culture – this conceptual framework can also be applied to female buddy films. Are we legitimised in reading the bond between Thelma and Louise, say, as a version of lesbian desire? Or is that inappropriately to eroticise a different kind of sisterliness?

Gay and lesbian writers on film still do a variety of things. Russo-like critique of Hollywood's negative stereotyping of gays and lesbians is far from dormant: recall protests like those over

Sharon Stone's psychopathic bisexual character in *Basic Instinct* (1992). Other critics construct canons of films avowedly about non-straight experience, from work by gay precursors including Jean Genet in France and Warhol and Kenneth Anger in the US to such proponents of post-1985 'New Queer Cinema' as Todd Haynes (director of *Far From Heaven* – discussed below), Derek Jarman, Isaac Julien, Jennie Livingstone, Rose Troche and Gus Van Sant. This later wave of filmmaking is marked by formal variety – from camp to self-conscious intellectuality, narrative obliquity to melodramatic excess – and has correspondingly diverse ideological implications. The name given to this loose cinematic grouping also suggests its correlation with queer theory which has been intellectually prominent – especially in the West – over the same period. Queer theory actually resists as dangerously fixed and normative a previous identity politics' defining of 'gay' as the opposite of 'straight'; instead, it argues that all sexual and gendered identities are complex, mutable, merely provisional. In the process a larger number of behaviours and positionalities than before is gathered under the sign of queerness. Benshoff and Griffin write that the term 'queer' in this new sense is intended not only to

> acknowledge that there are many different ways to be gay or lesbian, but also to encompass and define other sexually defined minorities for whom the labels 'homosexual' and/or 'heterosexual' are less than adequate: bisexuals, cross-dressers, transgendered people, interracial couples whether homosexual or heterosexual, disabled sexualities, sadomasochistic sexualities whether homosexual or heterosexual, etc. Even heterosexuals can be queer – the so-called *straight queer* – because queer as a theoretical concept encompasses all human sexual practices while rejecting the opposing binary hierarchies of sexuality and gender that currently govern our understanding of them. (*America on Film*, pp. 328–9)

The outcomes of this conceptual turn are multiple and complex. Filmmaking in the era of queer theory – from the camp excesses of *The Adventures of Priscilla, Queen of the Desert* (1994) to the tragedy of transgender in *Boys Don't Cry* (1999) – certainly evokes a riot of sexual and gender identities that exceeds the definitions proposed by straight society and hints at a more polymorphously perverse future. Looking backwards – as to classical Hollywood – queer approaches also subvert many cinematic texts that propagandise for heterosexuality and demonise same-sex or transgressive erotics. Yet queer theory may also incur significant costs, both political and intellectual. The sheer expansion of queerness noted by Benshoff and Griffin risks abandoning prematurely certain types of gay and lesbian identity politics. Such euphoric sense of diffusion and diversity can also neglect ongoing inequalities between queer cultures: the poor and disabled black cross-dresser has fewer advantages than the gay white male professor with tenure at an American university. From our narrower perspective, there is the question of to what extent the provocative models of queer filmmaking and film theory influential in the West can be generalised across non-Western situations. In certain Asian or African societies, to attempt a queer reading of an old national classic or to put on screen erotic experiences other than those of normative heterosexuality might be, quite literally, a matter of life and death.

STOP and THINK

- Consider some problems of defining 'gay' and 'lesbian' film. If a choice is made to define these categories by subject matter – the representational primacy of same-sex erotic experience – then they embrace many works made by people of heterosexual orientation: Robert Aldrich's *The Killing of Sister George* (1968), or John Sayles's *Lianna* (1983), or Stephen Frears's *My Beautiful Laundrette* (1985) and *Prick Up Your Ears* (1987). This expansionist principle counters the notion that ability to speak here can only derive from gay or lesbian affiliation itself. Of course such 'gay' and 'lesbian' films, certainly including Aldrich's, may be more than usually prone to circulating negative rather than progressive images of same-sex erotics. An alternative categorising logic, then, states that gay and lesbian film is only produced by gay and lesbian filmmakers. This assembling of a canon of gay- and lesbian-authored works boosts homosexual identity politics more broadly. However, this taxonomic strategy raises the problem of what to do with films that fulfil the author-criterion but are seemingly not interested in same-sex issues (Haynes's *Safe* (1995), or Van Sant's *Finding Forrester* (2000)). Can we still find in their narrative and formal tendencies evidence of 'queer' authorship (recalling Chapter 5's point about emphases or fractures in films directed by women that may disclose a distinctively female authorship)?

- Explore some of the formal varieties of queer filmmaking. You might range from the perverse drag aesthetic of John Waters's *Pink Flamingos* (1972) through lavish homoerotic spectacle in Jarman's *Sebastiane* and avant-garde documentary in Julien's *Looking for Langston* (1988) to the fragmented post-AIDS narratives of Haynes's *Poison* (1991). Are some strategies more politically and aesthetically effective than others? Are these strategies distinctive to a campaigning gay filmmaking, or open to adoption elsewhere, so that we might speak of a queering of cinema more generally?

- Evaluate Sedgwick's thesis that there is a continuum – rather than a clear divide – between the homosocial and homosexual. Take a number of films in which same-sex relationships are paramount and consider through homosocial and homosexual optics how these bonds are represented. Many buddy films suggest themselves here (including the already-mentioned *Miami Vice*: the two male cops have the alibi of heterosexual attachments but maybe these lack the richness of their same-sex bonding?).

- Consider films from cultures in which homosexual relationships are formally prohibited. What strategies have filmmakers developed to hint at these? How plausible or useful in the context of these other national cinemas is the type of queer textual reading sketched above?

Unthinking racism in film studies

Umberto Eco writes in a sharp satirical essay that Native Americans may alleviate the 'dire' social conditions facing them by working as 'movie Indians'. Helpfully, he outlines the many behaviours they must master to succeed in the film world:

Attacking the Stagecoach

In any attack on a stagecoach, always follow the vehicle at a short distance or, better still, ride alongside it, to facilitate your being shot.

Restrain your mustangs, notoriously faster than coach horses, so you won't outstrip the vehicle.

Try to stop the coach single-handed, flinging yourself on the harness, so you can be whipped by the driver and then run over by the vehicle.

Never block the coach's advance in a large body. The driver would stop at once.

('How to Play Indians', *Movies*, ed. Gilbert Adair (London: Penguin, 1999), p. 160)

In witty fashion, Eco demonstrates how Native Americans have been diminished by Hollywood's images and narratives. Instead of being represented as daring, strategic and wise – all qualities, among others, authenticated by the historical record – they have traditionally been confined on screen to idiocies like those listed above. Eco's article stands as a relatively playful contribution to the project of image-critique, which, as in the domains of gender and sexuality, dominated initial coverage of race in film studies and continues to be important. Screen caricaturing of Native Americans became a subject of angry protest during the upsurge of indigenous people's activism in the US in the 1960s. Contemporaneously, powerful critiques of filmic stereotypes of African Americans began to emerge. Here an important early intervention was made by Donald Bogle in *Toms, Coons, Mulattoes, Mammies, and Bucks: An Interpretive History of Blacks in American Films*, first published in 1973 and cited in the previous chapter. This book argues that, in mainstream US cinema, African

Americans have been restricted to a demeaning repertoire of five character-types: the compliant Tom, buffoonish Coon, the tragic Mulatto, the buxom, smothering Mammy and the violent Buck. As well as memorialising the depressingly stunted careers of earlier generations of black actors, Bogle's text has contemporary resonance: Eddie Murphy, say – electric and unpredictable in *48 Hrs.* and *Beverly Hills Cop* (1984) – seems in later films like the *Nutty Professor* franchise (1996–2000) to be rehabilitating the figure of 'the Coon'. Such analysis of African American and Native American stereotypes in cinema has also been adapted for many other racial and ethnic communities. Consider, for example, Italian American exasperation at the persistence of the screen gangster, or Latino protests against films like *Falling Down* (1993), or contemporary Arab vigilance against Hollywood's emphasis on the cruel terrorist, or Salman Rushdie's excoriation of British cinema and TV representations of India that seem contractually obliged to include a quota of 'cruel-lipped princes and dusky slim-hipped maidens' (*Imaginary Homelands: Essays and Criticism 1981–1991* (London: Granta, 1992), p. 88). At the time of writing, Kazakh officialdom is objecting to what it believes to be Sacha Baron Cohen's act of ethnic stereotyping in *Borat: Cultural Learnings of America for Make Benefit Glorious Nation of Kazakhstan* (2006).

As with resistance to stereotypes of gender and sexuality, the critique of cinematic images of race and ethnicity has served valuable purposes. Not the least of its achievements has been simply to put the topic of race on the agenda of film studies, after its earlier neglect not only by auteurist approaches but by the discipline's first investments in psychoanalysis. Robert Stam acknowledges, too, the legitimacy of demands by previously disadvantaged racial and ethnic communities that, in the interests of 'representational parity', they be given more 'positive' film versions of themselves (*Film Theory: An Introduction* (Oxford: Blackwell, 2000), p. 275). Recall from a moment ago the sense of liberation experienced by black female spectators while watching what they perceived as plausible sorts of African American women – neither Mulatto nor Mammy – in *The Color Purple*. However, Stam also exposes the conceptual and political limitations of racial and ethnic 'image studies'. To appeal for more 'positive' representation of the people of a community tends in the first place to assume that such a community is monolithic and that its 'essential' qualities may be quite readily instantiated by figures on screen. Furthermore, as Stam argues, the project of criticising images or stereotypes is sometimes appeased by a more benign portrayal of *individuals* belonging to a racial or ethnic grouping; such limited focus means that a racially oriented film studies might still leave unchallenged 'larger configurations of power' in cinema (p. 276). The often bracing rejectionism of image-critique inhibits it, too, from exploring the ambivalences and contradictions of audience response to representations of non-hegemonic races and ethnicities. None of this is to declare the analysis of stereotypes obsolete; to be effective, however, it must become, in the words of Isaac Julien and Kobena Mercer, 'conjunctural' or 'context-oriented'. Julien and Mercer share Stam's unease about blind spots in the 'theory of the stereotype' but insist it can still be productive if used with precision 'to explain how and why certain ethnic stereotypes are at times recirculated' ('De Margin and de Centre', *The Film Cultures Reader*, ed. Graeme Turner (London and New York: Routledge, 2002), p. 361).

Racially and ethnically sensitive approaches to film, however, have taken other forms besides the negativity of image-critique. In the first instance, institutional resources – books, journals, university courses, exhibition spaces, film festivals and niche production of videos and DVDs – have been devoted to identifying and consolidating instances of minority filmmaking. Here we might cite attempts to construct a canon of Black British films or African American films or works by Latino Americans. A film like *Smoke Signals* (1998) – written, produced and directed by Native Americans – prompts optimistic thoughts of a whole range of counter-cinemas generated by numerous racial and ethnic minorities. However, celebration of this sort – while important and invigorating – should not be uncritically indulged. For a start, it may rest on the essentialist claim that progressive images of a given racial community are guaranteed if they are produced by a filmmaker who shares its pigmentation; such thinking has disturbing echoes of racism itself, since it homogenises any minority

grouping and ignores how it is fissured by differences of class
status, gender position, sexual orientation and so on. A sympto-
matic case here is Spike Lee's 1992 biopic of Malcolm X. After
this project had been provisionally allocated to the liberal white
director Norman Jewison, Lee fought hard to take it over, arguing
on suspiciously essentialist grounds that only an African American
could do justice to such a key figure in black US history. However,
in a polemical response to Lee's eventual work, bell hooks asserts
that 'there is no visual standpoint or direction in *Malcolm X* that
would indicate that a white director could not have made this film'
(*Outlaw Culture: Resisting Representations* (London and New York:
Routledge, 1994), p. 157). hooks's critique of conservative tendencies in the film is well-judged. Less compelling, however, is her
own essentialist implication that blackness and whiteness in the
US each comes equipped with an irrevocable, singular viewpoint.
Recent work on race – including race in cinema – has demonstrated that there can be no clear correlation of this kind between
epidermal colouring and ideological position.

Besides investigating variations within specific minority groupings, race theory since the 1990s has shown an increased interest in
the category of 'whiteness' itself. Often regarded as a sort of non-
race, a neutral non-ethnic field against which the ethnicities of
others play themselves out, white is now conceptualised as a racial
construction itself; moreover, while dominant in much of human
history, it is also exposed as permeable and entwined with other
racial categories. Richard Dyer's *White* (1999) represents an
important application of such theoretical work to the specific case
of cinema. Whiteness studies can augment – or even reorient
entirely – existing approaches to questions of race in film texts and
histories. Take the suggestion that the first African American
figure to appear on screen in the United States was Uncle Tom, in
a 1903 adaptation of Harriet Beecher Stowe's novel. Image-
critique would rightly highlight the significance of America's
cinematic portrayal of its black citizens beginning with a servile
figure. The role was not even played by an African American but
by a white performer in blackface: here a political economy
approach would be valuable, too, disclosing the limited opportunities at that time – and indeed well beyond – for non-white actors

in mainstream US cinema. In the wake of whiteness studies, however, interpretation might also register the psychic complexities – besides social stereotyping and economic discrimination – apparent in this white resort to blackface. The actor leaves the circumscriptions of his genetic identity and, at least for the duration of a film, enters another racial grouping. As he 'performs' this cross-racial manoeuvre, and as the mainly white audience of the period sees the performance occurring, there may well be feelings of excitement and desire. Toni Morrison's *Playing in the Dark* (1992) has explored in a literary context white America's fascination with black, its partial self-construction by another ethnicity. Her analysis can readily be extended to cinema: for an example, see *Reinventing Film Studies* (eds Christine Gledhill and Linda Williams (London: Arnold, 2000)), in which Sharon Willis discusses Tarantino's attempt to make a white-produced cinema 'pass' as belonging to a distinctively black aesthetic. Similarly, white in the US sees itself partly through the prism of red in the genre of the western. In many film cultures beyond America, too, discussions of the complex entanglements of whiteness with other races will be fruitful.

Like the discussion of class, gender and sexuality, then, current racially- and ethnically-centred work in film studies draws upon a range of strategies and vocabularies. If the project of image-critique has, necessarily, not yet been abandoned, the gaze at minority representation on screen is now not exclusively 'oppositional' (to recall hooks's term). As well as refusing certain images, minority spectators themselves may be prompted to fantasies of power by representations produced not only by their own communities' filmmakers but even, on occasion, filmmakers from 'outside'. Whites' cinematic spectatorship, too, may not simply reiterate a singular racial identity and hegemony but might involve – albeit sporadically and uncertainly – a measure of cross-racial identification.

Finally, in a more utopian spirit still, we might consider whether cinema is better equipped than other media to project a *post-racial* future. When Paul Gilroy seeks evidences of that truly cosmopolitan imaginary he calls 'planetary humanism', it is significant that he turns not to other cultural artefacts but to films –

specifically to films like *Independence Day* (1996) and *Men in Black* (1997), in which multiracial coalitions form in the face of extraterrestrial threat. He writes that 'it is impossible to overlook the fact that this crop of movies expresses real and widespread hunger for a world that is undivided by the petty differences we retain and inflate by calling them racial' (*Between Camps: Nations, Cultures and the Allure of Race* (London: Penguin, 2000), p. 356). At this historical juncture, thoughts of a post-racial dispensation may look like the flimsiest utopianism. There is also the risk that Gilroy generalises too rapidly from the narrative peculiarities of a couple of Hollywood movies, repeating the error of stereotype-studies by focusing upon individual characterisations at the expense of attention to larger – and persisting – patterns of racial and ethnic inequality in cinema and beyond. For all its danger of premature optimism, however, Gilroy's mode of positive interpretation is suggestive, even exhilarating. Perhaps as indispensable now as the earlier, negative tradition of image-critique was in its moment, it offers at least a glimpse of a future beyond the racism that has marked not only much film but the discourse of film studies itself.

STOP and THINK

• In the study of racial and ethnic representations in cinema, critique of stereotypes has a long, pugnacious history. Assess whether it is still needed by considering recent filmic images of a particular race or ethnic community. You might explore, say, how the Japanese are portrayed in a wave of post-1980s US films, including *Black Rain*, *Pearl Harbor* (2001), *Kill Bill: Vol. 1*, *Lost in Translation* (2003), *The Last Samurai* (2003) and *Memoirs of a Geisha*. Do these works reproduce or contest Hollywood's earlier, 'Orientalist' stock of images of the Japanese (fanatical, sadistic killers; inscrutable masters of samurai wisdom; women of mysterious, exotic allure)? Even if free of such stereotypes, do they produce a new set of conventional representations of Japan instead? Or you could examine the portrayal of British Asian communities in such films as *My Beautiful*

Laundrette, *Sammy and Rosie Get Laid* (1987), *My Son the Fanatic* (1997), *East is East* (1999) and works by Gurinder Chadha cited in Chapter 5. These films bring to visibility communities largely absent from earlier British cinema: do they do so without recourse to recurrent and limited character-types? More generally, consider how adequate analysis of stereotypes is as an approach to race and ethnicity in film.

- A previous section notes how psychoanalytic models have complicated the sexual politics of film spectatorship, theorising the possibility of cross-gendered identification between viewer and character. By analogy, to what extent is *cross-racial* or *cross-ethnic* identification achieved in the watching of narrative films? If such mobility across boundaries does occur, are its effects inevitably – and durably – positive? Or are there limitations as well: for example, might such transgressing of racial and ethnic lines happen only in the contained time and place of film viewing and have no discernible effects upon power relations in the larger, extra-cinematic world?

- With vivid results for fields like film studies, theory has lately detached gender identity from biological substance and redefined it as 'fabrication' or 'performance' or 'masquerade'. To what extent can a similar account be offered of race and ethnicity? Can these identities, too, be perceived as mutable cultural constructs rather than as biologically predetermined? Where in film is there evidence of such 'culturalist' conception of racial and ethnic identity?

- Evaluate Paul Gilroy's choice of film examples to illustrate the emerging post-racial imagination. He is not uncritical of *Independence Day* and *Men in Black* – noting, for example, the 'product placement' (pp. 355–6) that betrays their high capitalist origins – yet still wants to stress their 'transethnic' scope. Do you share his affirmative reading of these Hollywood blockbusters? Are there other films – perhaps also from cinematic traditions beyond Hollywood – that project, in Gilroy's terms, a future beyond racial categorisations? Or, rather than functioning in this utopian way, does cinema strike you as, more dismally, a medium in which racial divisions are deep-rooted and by which they are perpetuated?

- 'Racism often travels in gangs, accompanied by its buddies sexism, classism, and homophobia' (Ella Shohat and Robert Stam, *Unthinking Eurocentrism: Multiculturalism and the Media*, p. 22). Test this proposition with regard to a number of films. Is one sort of oppression typically congruent with others, as Shohat and Stam argue, or are the domains of class, gender, sexuality and race more jaggedly related? A case study of these ideological intersections follows below.

Analysing ideology: *Far From Heaven*

Edward Said has written about the process whereby ideas, like people, travel from one geographical and historical setting to another. Such transiting of thoughts takes a number of forms, including 'acknowledged or unconscious influence, creative borrowing, or wholesale appropriation' (*The World, the Text, and the Critic* (London: Faber and Faber, 1984), p. 226). For Said, it also involves four distinct moments or phases: first, 'a point of origin, or what seems like one', in which an earlier text or conceptual formation is recognised as a source for subsequent adaptations; second, 'a distance traversed', with the arrival of ideas into a new environment; third, 'a set of conditions' in this different location that determines whether the imported ideas are embraced or resisted; and, finally, the transformation of the original ideas, how their meaning is altered when inserted in 'a new time and place'.

Said's essay is ultimately concerned with the movement of some concepts in twentieth-century European Marxism. Nevertheless, its thesis of travelling ideas and the changes that occur to them in transit can also be productive here. When Todd Haynes directed *Far From Heaven* in 2002, many reviewers noted the film's closeness to one of Douglas Sirk's melodramas, *All That Heaven Allows*

(1955). Besides borrowing the earlier work's paradisal title, Haynes took over its basic scenario. In *All That Heaven Allows*, a bereaved, middle-class white woman scandalises her children and the country-club set to which she belongs by falling in love with her gardener. In *Far From Heaven* – set in the same period and milieu as Sirk's film: Hartford, Connecticut in 1957 – the female protagonist Cathy (Julianne Moore) teeters on the verge of a similarly scandalous liaison with her own gardener, Raymond (Dennis Haysbert) (Figure 21). But while Haynes's film is structurally indebted to Sirk's, it is far from a straightforward repetition or remake: to begin with, Cathy is not widowed, even if she is in a sense bereaved because of her deteriorating marriage. In the course of *Far From Heaven*, her husband Frank (Dennis Quaid) discovers his homosexuality and eventually leaves home to begin life with a male partner. A further twist on the premise of *All That Heaven Allows* is that the gardener differs not only in class terms from his employer but racially too, since Raymond is African

Figure 21 Transgressing racial and class boundaries: Cathy Whitaker (Julianne Moore) and Raymond Deagan (Dennis Haybert) in *Far From Heaven* (France/US, 2002).

American. Here it becomes clear that the trajectory between Sirk's work of 1955 and Haynes's of 2002 is not direct and unimpeded but mediated by another film made in the intervening years: Rainer Werner Fassbinder's *Angst essen Seele auf / Fear Eats the Soul* (1974). Fassbinder explores the relationship that develops between a white German woman and a Moroccan guest worker who is culturally subordinate to her when they first meet ('German master; Arab dog' as the man says). In Said's terms, Sirk's ideas have already been subject to one sort of transit and revision before they travel further into *Far From Heaven*. Representation in Haynes is thus highly self-conscious, rather than naive; his film is a kind of *palimpsest*, a new document about class, race, gender and sexuality in which the traces of earlier cinematic interventions in these domains can still be read.

Revisiting the American 1950s from a contemporary vantage point, *Far From Heaven* opens to critique the period's ideologies without overcoming them entirely. Some modern liberties are taken: verbally, these include one use each of 'fucking' and 'homosexual' ('That word!' as Cathy exclaims). In general, however, the film does not flamboyantly violate the limitations of its periodised suburban world. For example, although Haynes is a key figure in American 'New Queer Cinema', he hardly offers here a celebratory or carnivalesque version of gay identity. While the merely coded or tacit evidences of homosexuality in the world of Sirkian melodrama are now made explicit, the homoerotic is still lacking in narrative prominence. Moreover, the composition of Frank's early scenes of homosexual longing evokes angst rather than a sense of enriching discovery. These episodes occur at night-time, the chiaroscuro lighting of a gay bar and Frank's office after hours hinting at moral shadiness; the musical score, too, takes on a louche, jazzy quality when he is on screen, compared with more harmonic orchestral arrangements elsewhere in the film. Yet though an image-critique approach to sexuality in cinema might be severe on *Far From Heaven* – not only because of the shadowy Frank but because of the effeminate, cravat-wearing art critic – the film also gives grounds for optimism. Notably, its narrative arc refuses the option of what a doctor consulted by Frank calls 'heterosexual reconversion'; rather than following the prescribed course of psychotherapy, 'hormonal rebalancing' and even electro-shock treatment, Frank leaves the sham of his marriage. Near the end, he is also shown in an apartment with his male lover. While this relationship exists in merely the faintest outline, it still connotes a kind of partnership and so contrasts with the infinitely deferred heterosexual union of Cathy and Raymond.

If this openly gay outcome is unimaginable within melodramas of the post-war period, the fate of Cathy, on the other hand, is all too aligned with their sense of suffering femininity. Not all histor-ical dramas reproduce the gender politics of their settings: at the end of *The Scarlet Letter* (1995) – set in seventeenth-century New England – Demi Moore tears off the stigma of sinful woman that her Puritan community has pinned upon her and sets off for a sexually liberated life underwritten less by historical scholarship than by present-day popular feminism. Yet, even in a film made fifty years after the events it narrates, Cathy is not given the power to escape bourgeois suburbia. Instead, she lives in a state of inau-thenticity, as when, disguised by dark glasses and a headscarf, she travels to tell Raymond it is 'not plausible' for them to be friends. Or the camera registers her thwarted desire – early on glancing wistfully at a heterosexual couple embracing on a bench, later sobbing alone in bed. Despite the film's historical retrospect, there are still words it cannot say and narrative dénouements it cannot will. In an essay on Sirk, Laura Mulvey allows that post-war melo-dramas of the type he directed fulfilled an important function in admitting previously ignored female desires to the screen. However, she also insists that any cinematic space which thereby opens up for female fantasy is highly restricted: 'Hollywood films made with a female audience in mind tell a story of contradiction, not of reconciliation. Even if a heroine resists society's overt pres-sures, its unconscious laws catch up with her in the end' (*Visual and Other Pleasures*, p. 43). Such laws apply as severely to Cathy as to any melodramatic heroine of the past; her suffering, however, accrues still more pathos, since it is implicitly juxtaposed with the whole post-Sirkian history of increasing – if still compromised – women's freedoms.

The rules against miscegenation that were included in the Hays Code also seem reactivated by *Far From Heaven*. While Raymond and Cathy's friendship is the most emotionally rich in this otherwise artificial, status-obsessed world, it is still confined in its possible intensities and directions. In other respects, however, the film mobilises a current racial sensibility in its representation of African Americans. When a white suburbanite at a party declares that 'There are no Negroes in Hartford', the camera pans militantly to a nearby black waiter holding a tray of drinks. Raymond himself is a notably sensitive, engaging figure, impossible to fit into the typology of demeaning African American figures on screen that Bogle has devised. Though hardly a radical in matters of race, he has sufficient pride in his community not to ingratiate himself in the style of an 'Uncle Tom'. He is also endowed intellectually: as well as possessing a degree in business, he has enlightened opinions on modern art. At an exhibition where the white bourgeoisie cluster for reassurance around the least challenging figurative paintings, Raymond speaks intelligently to Cathy about the colours and patternings of a Miró. But of course narrative limits still apply. Though an image-critique approach here would detect progress in Raymond's outwitting of stereotypes, the film is unable to move beyond this sensitive redesign of individual characters and sketch out larger transformations in US racial politics.

Responses to Raymond within the narrative are *overdetermined* in the sense of arising from multiple forces rather than any single cause. Whether spotted by Cathy's neighbours in her garden, or glimpsed with distaste in the art gallery, he signifies the otherness of class as well as race. As Shohat and Stam suggest, racism may be quite congruent with classism; and Raymond's behaviour scandalises the bourgeoisie for its violation of both ethnic and class demarcations. Yet *Far From Heaven* itself entertains some nervousness about detailed engagement with the lower orders. For while Raymond is currently defined by occupation as working-class, he seems only temporarily or accidentally situated there (unlike, say, Cathy's African American maid, whose perspective is scarcely articulated). Although he is denied full exploitation of his business degree by racial prejudice, he nevertheless owns a shop selling plants: gardening serves only to supplement his income. With his knowledge of modern art, he also has access to

Bourdieu's 'symbolic capital', that familiarity with vocabularies of advanced taste that may sometimes compensate for – rather than simply being identical with – control of economic capital itself. This intellectuality is also present in Raymond's prototype in *All That Heaven Allows*, the gardener Ron Kirby (Rock Hudson). While Ron does not proffer his views on the Abstract Expressionist painting then in vogue, he espouses a radical philosophy of repudiating society and living with nature that he derives from the nineteenth-century American Transcendentalist writer Thoreau. By comparison, Raymond's plant shop is a muted, petit bourgeois project, suggesting that Sirk's ideas may sometimes be resisted or moderated by Haynes rather than invariably developed in progressive directions.

All That Heaven Allows requires Ron's symbolic punishment – sustaining serious injuries in an accident – before he can cross boundaries of class (and age) and achieve a life with the film's female protagonist. Yet even this muted, only partially optimistic conclusion does not seem feasible in the successor films by Fassbinder and Haynes. In *Fear Eats the Soul*, differences of ethnicity – and age again – are so great that the couple drifts apart: the final image is of Emmi by the unconscious Ali's hospital bed. In *Far From Heaven* the period setting's ideological norms are so substantially in place that contact across divides of race and class can only be tentative and incomplete. Menaced by both white and black communities for incipient miscegenation with Cathy, Raymond departs with his young daughter to begin a new life in Baltimore. In a reprise of *Brief Encounter* (1945), the female protagonist remains in suspended desire on a railway platform while the male leaves by train. Nevertheless, even this negative development may be recuperated for a politically progressive reading. The film denies itself the false consolation of a personalised solution to structural inequities of race and class; only a radical social shift, it would seem, can establish the space in which friendship between the likes of Cathy and Raymond is not only 'plausible' but unremarkable. *Far From Heaven*'s final shot gestures symbolically towards such an ideological renewal. Whereas the film's opening credits appear against autumnal red and gold leaves – their gorgeousness almost overpowering, like the smothering floral décor in *In The Mood for Love* (Chapter 1) – the last image has in its foreground a branch of white blossom.

Selected reading

General

Benshoff, Harry M. and Sean Griffin, *America on Film: Representing Race, Class, Gender, and Sexuality at the Movies* (Malden, MA and Oxford: Blackwell, 2004).

A very productive way into this chapter's concerns, in the context of American cinema; wide-ranging, clear, attractively constructed.

Codell, Julie F. (ed.), *Genre, Gender, Race, and World Cinema: An Anthology* (Malden, MA and Oxford: Blackwell, 2007).

Ample – occasionally even unwieldy – collection of materials. Very extensive in its primary coverage, discussing films from Hollywood, minority American traditions, Europe and – anticipating a concern of Chapter 9 – 'world cinema'.

Class

Bodnar, John, *Blue-collar Hollywood: Liberalism, Democracy, and Working People in American Film* (Baltimore and London: Johns Hopkins University Press, 2003).

Thoughtful survey of representations of the working class in US cinema. Films discussed, from the 1930s to the 1980s, include *The Grapes of Wrath*, *It's a Wonderful Life*, *A Streetcar Named Desire* and *Raging Bull*.

Dave, Paul, *Visions of England: Class and Culture in Contemporary Cinema* (Oxford: Berg, 2006).

Excellent restoration of class to centre-stage in film studies: vivid, up-to-the-minute and supported by wide textual reference.

James, David E. and Rick Berg (eds), *The Hidden Foundation: Cinema and the Question of Class* (Minneapolis: University of Minnesota Press, 1996).

Invigorating attempt to keep this topic on film studies' agenda, with essays on US, Soviet and Chinese cinemas, besides general reflections (including an earlier version of James's essay, 'Is There Class in this Text?').

Rowbotham, Sheila and Huw Beynon (eds), *Looking at Class: Film, Television and the Working Class in Britain* (London: Rivers Oram Press, 2000).

Covers film and TV representations in the second half of the twentieth century, and offers a valuable British counterpart to Bodnar's US-centred study.

Ryan, Michael and Douglas Kellner, *Camera Politica: The Politics and Ideology of Contemporary Hollywood Film* (Bloomington and Indianapolis: Indiana University Press, 1988).

A very accessible, spirited instance of political film interpretation, surveying the ideological implications of two decades of Hollywood output in such genres as horror, fantasy, war, sci-fi, the western and the disaster movie.

Gender studies

Clover, Carol J., *Men, Women and Chainsaws: Gender in the Modern Horror Film* (London: BFI, 1992).

The best title in film studies, and an engaging, sophisticated study of the psychodynamics of our spectatorship of sub-genres such as slasher and rape revenge films.

Cohan, Steven and Ina Rae Hark (eds), *Screening the Male: Exploring Masculinities in Hollywood Cinema* (London and New York: Routledge, 1993).

Pioneering, still vital collection; is usefully complemented now by post-1993 and international materials, but stimulatingly explores constructions of masculinity across a wide generic range, including musicals, epics, horror and action films.

Kaplan, E. Ann (ed.), *Feminism and Film* (Oxford and New York: Oxford University Press, 2000).

Very generous, well-contextualised sampling of feminist theoretical and critical writings on cinema from the early 1970s.

Mulvey, Laura, *Visual and Other Pleasures* (Basingstoke and London: Macmillan, 1989).

Includes not only the foundational 'Visual Pleasure and Narrative Cinema' but revisions and developments of the argument in such pieces as 'Notes on Sirk and Melodrama' and 'Afterthoughts on "Visual Pleasure and Narrative Cinema" inspired by King Vidor's *Duel in the Sun* (1946)'.

Pomerance, Murray (ed.), *Ladies and Gentlemen, Boys and Girls: Gender in Film at the End of the Twentieth Century* (Albany: State University of New York Press, 2001).

Uneven in quality but pleasingly eclectic in range; includes lively essays on such diverse topics as Tom Cruise's polymorphous appeal, screen women and motorbikes, and gender representations in Hong Kong and Iranian cinemas.

Spicer, Andrew, *Typical Men: The Representation of Masculinity in Popular British Cinema* (London and New York: I.B. Tauris, 2003).

Good example of the new masculinity studies, covering post-war British film lucidly and informatively.

Thornham, Sue, *Passionate Detachments: An Introduction to Feminist Film Theory* (London: Arnold, 1997).

The story of feminist film study's first three decades is a familiar one but Thornham tells it with clarity and spirit. An ideal companion volume to both her own and Kaplan's anthologies.

Thornham, Sue (ed.), *Feminist Film Theory: A Reader* (Edinburgh: Edinburgh University Press, 1999).

Only slightly less chunky than Kaplan's selection, and another excellent, helpfully signposted way into this area of film study.

Sexuality

Benshoff, Harry M. and Sean Griffin (eds), *Queer Cinema: The Film Reader* (London and New York: Routledge, 2004).

Very useful collection of essays, demonstrating the impact of queer approaches upon such key domains of film studies as authorship, genre and spectatorship.

Benshoff, Harry M. and Sean Griffin, *Queer Images: A History of Gay and Lesbian Film in America* (Lanham, MD: Rowman and Littlefield, 2006).

Needs supplementing by international materials but very comprehensive and up-to-date.

Doty, Alexander, *Flaming Classics: Queering the Canon* (London and New York: Routledge, 2000).

Invigorating rereadings from a queer perspective of six familiar films: *The Cabinet of Dr. Caligari* from German Expressionism, and *The Wizard of Oz*, *The Women*, *The Red Shoes*, *Gentlemen Prefer Blondes* and *Psycho* from Anglo-American cinema.

Dyer, Richard, *Culture of Queers* (London and New York: Routledge, 2002).

Lively collection of essays; topics range from Rock Hudson's star persona to Fassbinder's films, and gay pornography to Charles Hawtrey of the *Carry On* series.

Farmer, Brett, *Spectacular Passions: Cinema, Fantasy, Gay Male Spectatorships* (Durham, NC and London: Duke University Press, 2000).

Sophisticated, provocative theorisation of the range and mobility of gay male spectators' interactions with – mainly Hollywood – narrative cinema.

White, Patricia, *unInvited: Classical Hollywood Cinema and Lesbian Representability* (Bloomington: Indiana University Press, 1999).

Valuable complement to Farmer's text, investigating the tacitly lesbian spectatorship activated by earlier Hollywood melodramas and horror films.

Race

Bobo, Jacqueline, *Black Women as Cultural Readers* (New York: Columbia University Press, 1995).

Fascinating example of ethnographic reception studies; as well as chapters on *The Color Purple* discussed above, explores audience evaluation of the more experimental African American feminist film, *Daughters of the Dust* (1991).

Courtney, Susan, *Hollywood Fantasies of Miscegenation: Spectacular Narratives of Gender and Race* (Princeton: Princeton University Press, 2005).

Densely researched study of mainstream American film's ambivalent representation of cross-racial contacts, from 1903 to 1967's *Guess Who's Coming to Dinner*.

Denzin, Norman K., *Reading Race: Hollywood and the Cinema of Racial Violence* (London and Thousand Oaks, CA: SAGE, 2002).

Valuable survey of recent representations of minority communities in US film, and assessment of the possibility of 'a new racial aesthetic'.

Dyer, Richard, *White: Essays on Race and Culture* (London and New York: Routledge, 1997).

Key contribution to 'whiteness studies'; embraces other aesthetic fields, such as painting and photography, but packed with insightful discussion of how whiteness is privileged by all cinema's registers – from narrative organisation to lighting of actors' faces.

Gormley, Paul, *The New Brutality Film: Race and Affect in Contemporary Hollywood Cinema* (Bristol and Portland: Intellect Books, 2005).

Usefully complements Courtney, by exploring racial constructions in later US films including *Menace II Society*, *Reservoir Dogs* and *Se7en*.

hooks, bell, *Reel to Real: Race, Sex and Class at the Movies* (London and New York: Routledge, 1996).

Vigorous responses by this major African American feminist to a wide range of films, including Spike Lee's work and *Pulp Fiction*; includes, too, the key essay, 'The Oppositional Gaze: Black Female Spectators' (available also in Thornham's feminist anthology).

Shohat, Ella and Robert Stam, *Unthinking Eurocentrism: Multiculturalism and the Media* (London and New York: Routledge, 1994).

Indispensable for its analytical finesse, polemical urgency and global sensibility; explores the functioning of racist and imperial tropes in films of very wide provenance, and assesses the chances for anti-racist cinema.

Vera, Hernán and Andrew M. Gordon, *Screen Saviors: Hollywood Fictions of Whiteness* (Lanham, MD: Rowman and Littlefield, 2003).

Attempts to bring to visibility Hollywood's construction of whiteness, through case studies of many films from *Gone With the Wind* to *The Matrix*. Suggestive and very accessible.

Useful websites

www.ejumpcut.org.

The home of *JUMP CUT: A Review of Contemporary Media* (now published electronically, following its printed history from 1974–2001). Internationalist in focus, containing accessible articles from an avowedly 'non-sectarian left, feminist, and anti-imperialist' position. Access is free.

www.uiowa.edu/~commstud/resources/GenderMedia/tvfilm.html.

Handy database, archiving materials on questions of gender, sexuality and race in cinema; mainly – though not exclusively – American in coverage.

www.wsu.edu/~amerstu/pop/race.html.

A lively, polemical site, gathering together accounts of retrograde racial and ethnic politics in US film and TV.

www.let.uu.nl/womens_studies/anneke/filmtheory.html.

Thoroughly referenced survey by Anneke Smelik of feminist film theory from the early 1970s to the mid-1990s; serves as a helpful abridgement of Thornham's book-length study.

www.gseis.ucla.edu/faculty/kellner/essays/filmpoliticsideology.pdf.

Douglas Kellner's acute, energetic essay on US cinema in the 1980s offers a good introduction to ideologically oriented film study.

9

Film production

How should film studies demarcate its areas of interest? Historically, the discipline's focus has fallen upon the particularities of film texts themselves. Lately, however, some scholars in the field have sought to distance themselves from such 'textual reductionism' (Toby Miller et al., *Global Hollywood 2*, p. 43). The authors of a book on the economics of contemporary world cinema – a book more likely to cite the *F.T.* than *E.T.* – propose that attention to the formal specificity of films be aligned with 'an account of *occasionality* that details the conditions under which a text is made, circulated, received, interpreted and criticised' (*Global Hollywood 2*, pp. 41–2). In previous chapters, we have witnessed this expansionist imperative in some established domains of film study: remember, say, how analysis of composed soundtrack is augmented by interest in noises occurring in various sites of film reception, or how 'generic communities' try to make their understandings of particular genres stick in real-world institutions. However, this chapter and the next aim at more concentrated and systematic extra-textual discussion. Chapter 10 considers the last three activities in Miller et al.'s inventory of concerns for a reconfigured film studies: the geographically and historically dispersed work of 'receiving', 'interpreting' and 'criticising' that goes on during film consumption. First, though, we explore some variations in 'making' and 'circulating', or film production and distribution. An account of cinema's most powerful site of production is followed here by discussion of two major non-Anglophone cinemas and assessment of to what extent, in an increasingly globalised media economy, film creation is still usefully thought of in national terms.

The interest that such an approach shows in diagrams of corporate ownership or graphs of film exports should not, however, be taken to imply abandonment of detailed textual work. Instead, film studies has to shuttle constantly between text and context. There can, anyway, be no clear separation of these levels: product placement in a film – focusing for a little too long on the protagonist's brand of watch or car – is just a particularly unsubtle instance of the many enfoldings of commercial imperatives into textual composition itself. Thus the present chapter concludes by studying a film that registers tendencies in the contemporary global economy not only in its mode of production but in its formal and narrative specificities.

Hollywood

In some stern pages, Mitsuhiro Yoshimoto indicts film studies as 'a distinctly mono-cultural discipline in which Hollywood cinema dominates more than ever'. While economic globalisation holds out the prospect of a diffusion of filmmaking cultures – 'a polycentric imagining of the world, where no single centre monopolises the production and circulation of audiovisual images' – this sense of dispersal is, Yoshimoto argues, not yet reflected in film studies itself. Instead, the discipline is prone to a 'false universalism', its formulaic expressions of interest in cinemas from around the world not matched by provision of significant institutional resources for their study (*Theorising National Cinema*, eds Valentina Vitali and Paul Willemen, pp. 257, 260). Thus anyone beginning an account of production with Hollywood, rather than with non-US cinemas, would seem to risk furthering the already entrenched Americanisation of film studies. Yet Hollywood is a more complex, less parochial object of inquiry than Yoshimoto allows. First, it should not be viewed, pessimistically, as a juggernaut incapable of diversion: its products may be open to multiple, often irregular uses, whether by constituencies in the US or by film cultures elsewhere in the world. Second, relations between the US film industry and its global others are not unidirectional, since Hollywood's formal and narrative strategies – even its selection of key creative personnel – are subject to influence from elsewhere. Finally, though 'Hollywood' is useful shorthand, the term assumes too readily a singular mode of production and thereby neglects the historical shifts and internal differentiations of American popular cinema.

'Classical' Hollywood

Southern California was already a locus of entrepreneurial activities when the film industry, drawn by factors including low land prices and the availability of dry, sunlit conditions for year-round shooting, arrived there early in the twentieth century. Previously, most American filmmaking had occurred nearer the financial hub of New York City; however, westward cinematic migration was wholesale and rapid. In 1909 D. W. Griffith relocated from the east, and in 1913 Cecil B. De Mille, future maestro of Roman and biblical epics, began his career by shooting a western, *The Squaw Man* in what David Thomson calls 'the frontier village of Hollywood' (*The New Biographical Dictionary of Film* (London: Little, Brown, 2002), p. 218). A cluster of studios of varying scale quickly cohered into 'classical' Hollywood, a filmmaking system most often regarded as operating from the end of the First World War into the 1950s.

In David Bordwell, Janet Staiger and Kristin Thompson's *The Classical Hollywood Cinema* (1985), 'classical' appears without scare-quotes; instead, the authors argue, Hollywood films of this period are governed by codified principles of composition that suggest parallels with the classicism of other art forms. For writers such as Richard Maltby, however, 'classical' is suspect as a qualifying term in this context precisely because of its primarily stylistic and formal connotations and its erasure of the sheer money-making drive of Hollywood. Maltby proposes the alternative of 'commercial aesthetic', a phrase which, usefully, does not overlook the artistic sensibility of popular American cinema but also stresses the irrepressible profit motive of each film project. Similarly, some scholars have questioned the adequacy of 'the studio system' as a synonym for this phase of Hollywood's history, given that the term risks detaching production from those other arms of the industry by which film companies maintained their grip over markets in the US and beyond. The so-called 'Big Five' – MGM, Paramount, RKO, Twentieth-Century Fox and Warner Bros. – were, in the language of business theory, examples of *vertical integration*: they controlled not only the means of production but also channels of distribution and, through ownership of many of the most profitable cinemas in America, exhibition. At a lower level of corporate organisation, the 'Little Three' – Columbia, United Artists and Universal – produced and distributed films but relied upon deals with the larger studios to get them into cinemas. Below these were the tenants of 'Poverty Row': companies like Republic and Monogram – the latter the dedicatee of Godard's *A bout de souffle* – which owned no distribution or exhibition facilities but produced westerns and other genre movies.

In their mode of making films, the studios of the classical Hollywood era invite at least partial analogies with contemporaneous industries of mass-production. Suitably modified and glamorised, the practices of the Fordist assembly line seemed transferable to film manufacture. Each film project advanced through a series of specialist units housed within the same organisation; items of fixed capital such as sets were efficiently adapted for repeated use; as noted in Chapter 7, even stars – seemingly less malleable – were rationalised, typically tied into exclusive seven-year deals with particular studios and reduced to personas replicable across a body of screen work. According to Hollywood's many critics, such streamlined, industrial-scale output was ill-equipped to generate subtle and distinctive works. From within the system, Bette Davis, one of its great female stars, complained that it was suitable only for making sausages. At the level of intellectual critique, the German Marxists Theodor Adorno and Max Horkheimer took classical Hollywood as representative of the twentieth-century 'culture industry'. In *Dialectic of Enlightenment* they argue that it shares the tendencies of other commercial aesthetics such as popular music and radio broadcasting to standardise products and manufacture passive respondents. Like the car industry, Hollywood ruthlessly suppresses questions of quality or value in favour of a logic of quantities:

That the difference between the Chrysler range and General
Motors products is basically illusory strikes every child with a keen
interest in varieties. What connoisseurs discuss as good or bad
points serve only to perpetuate the semblance of competition and
range of choice. The same applies to the Warner Brothers and Metro
Goldwyn Mayer productions. But even the differences between the
more expensive and cheaper models put out by the same firm steadi-
ly diminish: for automobiles, there are such differences as the
number of cylinders, cubic capacity, details of patented gadgets; and
for films there are the number of stars, the extravagant use of technology, labour, and equipment, and the introduction of the latest
psychological formulas. (*Dialectic of Enlightenment* (London: Allen
Lane, 1973), pp. 123–4)

From this perspective, the formal, narrative and generic variations among classical Hollywood's output are distinctions without
a difference. A social problem picture of the 1930s is functionally
equivalent to a musical of the late 1940s; a gangster film is homol-
ogous with a comedy. The same aesthetic structures and same
reactionary ideology are carried, like spoors, by each film made
within this context of production. However, Adorno and
Horkheimer depart from the richest Marxist tradition by criticising this bit of popular culture without simultaneously attempting
to salvage its progressive potentials. Though their negative argument is expressed with sophistication, it effectively restates what
Maltby identifies as a familiar 'vulgar Marxist' position on
popular US cinema: 'Hollywood's enslavement to the profit
system means that all its products can do is blindly reproduce the
dominant ideology of bourgeois capitalism' (*Hollywood Cinema*,
p. 45). Yet even if much of classical Hollywood's output indeed
leans towards conservatism, its details may allow still for radical or
subversive inflections. This possibility of counter-use applies also
to the products of the re-engineered filmmaking system that
emerged in Hollywood after drastic industrial, economic and
social changes in the late 1940s and early 1950s.

'Post-classical' Hollywood

In 1948, the power of the Hollywood studios was weakened by a
Supreme Court judgement against Paramount. Independent
exhibitors had alleged monopolistic behaviour by those studios

which owned cinemas as well as production and distribution interests; they objected, too, to such practices as *block booking*, whereby
exhibitors in the independent sector were required to buy a slate
of a major's films in order to obtain those likely box office successes which they really wanted. The uncoupling of highly profitable
exhibition activities from production/distribution in the wake of
the court ruling was to have a significant impact upon the strategy
of many Hollywood studios. Yet, even before this legal verdict,
there were signs of trouble for the US film industry. American
audience figures had, in fact, peaked in 1946; under way was a
decline in cinema attendance that would become precipitous in
coming decades until the beginnings of revival in the late 1970s.
Various reasons have been offered for this national loss of the
cinemagoing habit. The most facile suggestion is that movies were
simply ousted by their precocious sibling, television. However,
numbers of cinema spectators began to fall well before the time of
widespread TV ownership. We should look, then, to larger structural changes in the United States, notably to rising affluence that
precipitated a flight from urban centres well-stocked with cinemas
to new suburbs that lacked this amenity. In addition, as Geoff
King notes, money that once went towards cinemagoing was
increasingly diverted into providing for the large numbers of
baby-boom children or distributed across a wider range of leisure
activities, including DIY and gardening besides television (*New
Hollywood Cinema*, p. 25).

Scholars still dispute the extent to which 'post-classical'
Hollywood differs from the mode of film production consolidated in the first half of the twentieth century. Maltby argues that
the nature of the product, at least, was fairly unchanged: if two
films made in Hollywood almost eighty years apart are
juxtaposed, they will still 'have more in common with each
other than either does with contemporary European art cinema,
documentary, or avant-garde film' (*Hollywood Cinema*, p. 8). Yet
for other writers, the specifications of post-1950 US popular
cinema are so altered from what came before as to amount to
a paradigm shift. Without discounting the continuities between
an older, 'frontier' Hollywood and a contemporary, 'global'
one, we emphasise here a number of breaks in their respective

forms of corporate organisation, business modelling and textual composition:

1. *Corporate organisation.* Declining audience figures, loss of control over exhibition and a scaling-down of production left the once-autonomous studios vulnerable to takeover bids. For a period, they offered a source of glamour to companies in unrelated fields: in 1969, the acquisition of Warner Bros. brought much-needed glitter to Kinney National Services, a company otherwise known for owning car parks and funeral parlours. Subsequent takeovers or mergers, however, have repositioned film studios in more plausibly organised business networks. The abandonment of corporate regulation under Reaganomics even permitted some return to the classical era's vertically integrated pattern, with a major wave of cinema acquisition by production interests beginning in 1986. But a more common move has been towards *horizontal integration*: increasingly, the old studio names figure in multimedia conglomerates alongside music, publishing, internet, amuse-ment park and other entertainment interests. Thus Columbia is the film production arm of the Japanese electronics giant, Sony; Warners brings a filmmaking capacity to an empire otherwise comprising the publishing group Time and the US internet service provider AOL; and so on. The diffuse hold-ings of these companies indicate the traditional film object's loss of centrality within the US leisure economy.

2. *Business modelling.* The 'feature film business no longer exists in its own right', argues Maltby (*Hollywood Cinema*, p. 189). Although Hollywood has from its inception sought to exploit any ancillary commercial opportunity, box office returns them-selves remained at the heart of the classical era's business model. Increasingly, however, the American popular film industry regards cinemagoing as only one among many profit-making possibilities. Maltby writes that studios construe movie production as 'the creation of "filmed entertainment" software, to be viewed through several different windows and transported to several different platforms maintained by the other divisions of diversified media corporations' (p. 190). The income of today's Hollywood film derives not only from

cinema audiences but, to a significant extent, from the cinema experience's prolongation and refashioning in such other exploitable formats as DVD and video, computer games, soundtrack albums, cable and network TV screenings, amusement park rides and numerous promotional tie-ins. Even a film yielding the base metal of poor viewing figures at the multiplex may still be alchemised into gold by such multimedia synergy. In addition to looking towards post-theatrical venues of film consumption, Hollywood producers have come increasingly to rely for profits upon box office performance overseas. To take one example: King reports that *Godzilla* (1998) derived approximately $220–250m. of its total takings of $385m. from exhibition abroad (*New Hollywood Cinema*, p. 62). This ratio of non-US to US revenues typifies Hollywood now: in 2004, $15.7 billion of the industry's global box office of $25.24 billion, or 62 per cent, was earned outside the United States. Overseas audiences are also able to view Hollywood's products much more rapidly than before. The domestic model of TV-advertised *saturation* release of a film – largely replacing an earlier pattern of gradual, or *platform*, release (major cities first) – has been internationalised; the launch of blockbusters, in particular, is now a synchronised worldwide event. As well as a practical measure to deter video piracy, this move indicates Hollywood's contemporary globalisation (a tendency reflected also in the industry's out-sourcing of some elements of production and its recourse to co-financing deals with non-US partners).

3. *Textual composition.* The classical Hollywood studio's model of filmmaking – in which each activity of pre-production, production and post-production was performed in-house – has yielded to a looser, more devolved process (encouraging some commentators to enlist the film industry as part of a general shift from Fordist to flexible, post-Fordist forms of manufacture). Hollywood production now is best figured not as the maintenance of an assembly line but as differentiated involvements in a range of niche projects. Developers of a film idea seek to elicit studio interest with a particular *package*: a given star's or director's guaranteed participation, say, or an

already known narrative (one based perhaps on a popular novel or comic strip). The level of the studio's financial commitment and/or creative intervention, however, will fluctuate from case to case.

Several writers have argued that this loss of centralisation in contemporary Hollywood's production regime is replicated in the films it makes. Compared with classical Hollywood's integrated narratives, newer works are, for these scholars, marked by a high degree of disarticulation: storytelling coherence is subordinated to the display of lavish spectacle or to the showcasing of elements with high synergistic potential, such as a film's musical score. Justin Wyatt makes the case with particular force, referring to 'modular' filmmaking in *High Concept: Movies and Marketing in Hollywood* (Austin: University of Texas Press, 1994). Yet, like those arguments for the disappearance of genre discussed in Chapter 6, the thesis is overstated. While contemporary Hollywood may indeed give a new prominence to hyperkinetic visuality or sonic overload, this should not imply the depletion of narrative drive. The notion of modular filmmaking extrapolates too quickly from a handful of blockbusters and prematurely consigns to history a storytelling mode that is one of the distinctive markers of Hollywood production and a source of continuity across its classical and post-classical periods.

STOP and THINK

- In their manifesto for a film studies freed from exclusive attention to the particular qualities of the text, Miller et al. observe that 'Institutions do not have to be arid areas of study, and the links to everyday life are real' (*Global Hollywood 2*, p. 43). Do you agree that the discipline is vitalised by exploration of the commercial, industrial and legal parameters of a given filmmaking institution (like Hollywood)? Are there risks, as well as rewards, in this reoriented film studies? How, exactly, should we combine our observations of a film's formal details with the data we gather from such sources as studio archives, government records and newspaper financial pages?

- Assess the extent to which Hollywood constitutes a national cinema, comparable, say, to Iranian or Swedish or Turkish cinemas. Historically sensitive responses are important here. Maltby argues that the sense of American cultural location is especially attenuated within contemporary, internationalised Hollywood, and that this may allow national status to devolve upon other kinds of filmmaking in the US. Specifically, blue-collar dramas with modest export potential – like Billy Bob Thornton's *Sling Blade* (1996) – may compose 'an American national cinema, in a sense that has not previously applied to Hollywood's product' (*Hollywood Cinema*, p. 223).

- Maltby's reference to indigenous blue-collar cinema may be put alongside several full-length studies that valuably revive a sense of non-Hollywood US traditions. In *American Independent Cinema* (New York and London: I. B. Tauris, 2005), Geoff King focuses on post-1980 challenges to Hollywood's formal, ideological and commercial norms – besides noting the mainstream sector's renewal of itself through appropriating personnel and stylistics from the independents. *Underground U.S.A.: Filmmaking Beyond the Hollywood Canon*, edited by Xavier Mendik and Steven Jay Schneider (London: Wallflower, 2002), has a broader historical remit and assesses the transgressive quality of such non-Hollywood US cinemas as radical black filmmaking and low-budget porn and horror production. Most expansive of all is David E. James's *The Most Typical Avant-Garde: History and Geography of Minor Cinemas in Los Angeles* (Berkeley, Los Angeles and London: University of California Press, 2005), a wonderful archaeology of almost a century of alternative American film cultures. Here Los Angeles becomes a conflicted space, one of Foucault's heterotopias: no longer reducible only to Hollywood but somewhere that also houses traditions of counter-filmmaking.

Beyond Hollywood: two examples

Reinforcing Yoshimoto's point about the pre-eminence of Hollywood in film studies, Stephen Crofts says in the same volume that 'Film scholars' mental maps of world film production are often less than global' (*Theorising National Cinema*, p. 53). Periodically, certain non-Anglophone cinemas have been taken up in the United Kingdom and United States as the focus of research activity and the syllabi of university and high school courses: older examples include Soviet montage, German Expressionism and the French *Nouvelle vague*; newer equivalents might be the dynamic popular cinemas of Japan and Korea. Such cinematic cosmopolitanism is welcome but limited. In the first instance, these gestures beyond Hollywood clearly represent only a start in compiling an atlas of world film production; vast areas of the globe remain relatively unmapped, at least by Anglophone centres in the discipline. Where, say, are the cartographies of Mauritanian or Peruvian film? Second, the cinemas selected for such study are typically marked by formal innovation and/or political radicalism that may be used as sticks with which to beat Hollywood's purportedly conservative aesthetic. As a result, more popular or generic production even in nations falling within the gaze of film studies emanating from Anglo-America may continue to be neglected: there are, for example, few surveys of French comedian Coluche's films to set alongside the archive of work on Godard's deconstruction of narrative cinema.

This section provides the merest sketch of the type of cinematic cartography that is badly needed. Again, there is an issue of selectivity: just two non-Hollywood cinemas are considered and those only briefly. Countless other filmmaking centres might have been chosen: why not study stylistic and industrial practices in Finland or Scotland, or in Nigeria, where the unimaginatively dubbed 'Nollywood' hybridises traditional narrative forms with rapid, improvisatory production and straight-to-video distribution? Nevertheless, these two particular case studies usefully allow us to raise larger questions of sub-national, national, regional and global film cultures that will be explored later in the chapter.

Bollywood

While Bollywood has an increasingly global reach, it is also an instance of sub-national film. There is a regrettable tendency by spectators outside India to collapse the nation's filmmaking into this single tradition of Hindi popular cinema. Yet Bollywood's productivity is matched by the fertility of many other Indian film-making cultures, which utilise various regional languages and sometimes very different formal idioms. Rachel Dwyer and Divia Patel cite such traditions as Telugu and Tamil popular film production in the south of the country, and arthouse traditions in Bengal – home of India's most celebrated auteur to date, Satyajit Ray – and Malayalam-speaking Kerala. Nevertheless, while rela-tivising Bollywood in this way, Dwyer and Patel also allow that because of features including its use of Hindi – India's official language – it has perhaps a stronger claim than its rivals upon the title of 'national cinema of India' (*Cinema India: The Visual Culture of Hindi Film* (London: Reaktion, 2002), p. 8).

Bollywood, as indicated by its initial letter, is centred upon Bombay (now Mumbai). In his novel *The Moor's Last Sigh* (1995), Salman Rushdie pays lyrical tribute to Bombay as India's bastion of multiculturalism, right back to its beginnings as 'the bastard child of a Portuguese-English wedding': 'In Bombay all Indias met and merged. In Bombay, too, all-India met what-was-not-India.' These fusions can be traced in the subjects, forms and industrial structures of Bollywood itself. Certainly, the influence of Hindu epic and drama has been paramount: *Raja Harischandra* (1913), the first sustained narrative in Indian cinema, inaugurated a tradi-tion by taking its story from part of Hinduism's sacred text, the *Mahabharata*. The *devotional* and the *mythological* – centred upon saints and foundational Hindu myths – remain important, distinc-tive Bollywood genres. What Vijay Mishra evokes as Bollywood's chief presentational mode – 'an erotic economy of the look and the counterlook' between spectator and spectacle (*Bollywood Cinema: Temples of Desire*, p. 9) – can also be affiliated at least partly to Hinduism, since it echoes the religious practice of *darshan* which requires rapt contemplation of an object of veneration. Yet Bollywood's frontal presentation to the viewer borrows, too, from other, non-Hindu forms of staging – such as British proscenium arch theatre and Parsi drama – and is always liable to be diverted from sacred to secular objects.

If Hollywood's 'cinema of attractions' has been located by scholars in an early, soon superseded moment, its Bollywood equivalent, according to Dwyer and Patel and other writers, has proved more durable. Without by any means abandoning narrative, Bollywood abstracts or even fetishises certain visual and auditory elements. Emphasis falls upon the spectacular properties of setting and costume. Star charisma is foregrounded, recalling the point made in Chapter 7 that Bollywood's star system has a wattage outdoing the American version. Music and dance, too, may float free from the strictest exigencies of plotting. This disarticulation of formal elements makes Bollywood a frequent object of critique, not least among Indian intellectuals. The Bombay-born Rushdie himself speaks, at times, for this culture of distaste. In his monograph on *The Wizard of Oz*, he makes a qualitative distinction between this product of the Hollywood system and Bollywood films, which, though undeniably enjoyable, are 'trashy' and elicit a pleasure 'something like the fun of eating junk food' (*The Wizard of Oz* (London: BFI, 1992), p. 13). At the same time, however, he consistently and exuberantly alludes in his fiction to this cinema's vibrancy. Gibreel Farishta, one of the protagonists of *The Satanic Verses* (1988), is a major Bollywood star (when India became the first nation to ban this novel, it was for offences against Islam rather than local film). And in *The Moor's Last Sigh*, Rushdie's narrator evokes Bollywood, in all its lavishness and generic mixture, as an 'Epico-Mythico-Tragico-Comico-Super-Sexy-High-Masala-Art'.

Bollywood has also struggled to achieve serious scrutiny because of its dependence upon melodrama, a mode that in the West has connotations of vulgar, often feminine taste. Using the language of the French film theorist Christian Metz, Mishra writes that 'Bombay Cinema is itself a genre that is primarily a sentimental melodramatic romance ... it is a grand syntagm (*grande syntagmatique*) that functions as one heterogeneous text' (*Bollywood Cinema*, p. 13). Mishra's totalisation is useful, allowing detection of a continuous melodramatic register across an otherwise expansive generic array. Nevertheless, it is important to recognise too the diachronic – time-bound and mutable – aspects of Bollywood besides its synchronic or systemic character. At a technical level, for instance, it has, from 2000, made greater use of synchronised rather than dubbed sound. Partly in response to developments in Western consumer culture, it now shows an increased interest in displays of the well-groomed male as well as female body. Its subjects, too, have expanded to include such topics as domestic violence and colonial history. There are also the beginnings of exploration of the vast Indian diaspora: Bollywood has supplemented its traditional domestic locations by filming in overseas spaces, including London and – as in the Shah Rukh Khan vehicle, *Kal Ho Naa Ho* (2003) – New York City.

Diasporic India is not only a topic for contemporary Bollywood but an increasingly important market. Reflecting what Mishra terms 'Bombay Cinema's new global aesthetics' (*Bollywood Cinema*, p. 269), its films circulate outside India in numerous venues and formats: theatrical exhibition in multicultural cities, cable TV screenings, DVD and video releases, and sales of sound-track CDs. Bollywood thereby offers constituents of the Indian diaspora a version of the homeland, a type of 'imagined communi-ty' – to recall Benedict Anderson's phrase – within which they may or may not choose to situate themselves. At the same time as they reach out to spectators of Indian descent, Bollywood films are also dispersed across contexts and platforms that give them a func-tion as signifiers of 'Indianness' for a wider audience. Such exhibition is by no means restricted to situations of concentrated viewing: Indian restaurants in nations including the United Kingdom may display stills from Bollywood classics or even project sequences, stripped of contextualisation, while people eat. Cinema thus joins food itself in serving up a particular, invented India for foreign consumption. Yet while 'invention' is not synony-mous with 'falsification', and Bollywood production is poorly served by the application of absolutist notions of cultural authen-ticity and inauthenticity, it remains important to evaluate the effects of its images of India upon both the home country and nations beyond.

Hong Kong

Hong Kong cinema both resembles and differs from Bollywood. From its beginnings – with the less than action-packed narratives of *Right a Wrong with Earthenware Dish* and *Stealing the Roasted Duck* (both 1909) – it, too, has shown a susceptibility to heterogeneous influences: what David Bordwell calls 'a scavenger aesthetic' (*Planet Hong Kong: Popular Cinema and the Art of Entertainment*, p. 11). Besides borrowing from American musicals, French crime thrillers and the Cantonese movie tradition in China, Hong Kong filmmaking, according to Esther Yau, has been shaped by such historically and geographically disparate extra-cinematic sources as classic ghost stories, contemporary Chinese martial arts novels and computer graphics (*At Full Speed: Hong Kong Cinema in a Borderless World*, p. 11). Bordwell adds that it also cannibalises the current Hollywood blockbuster: visual and musical passages of American action pictures like *Speed* and *Die Hard* (1988) are rapidly reprocessed by the lower-budget Hong Kong system.

Again like Bollywood, the film output of Hong Kong is liable to be totalised and construed as 'itself a genre ... one heterogeneous text' (to recall Mishra's perception of the unity of Hindi cinema). Many observers take spectacle and action relatively freed from narrative binding to be Hong Kong's signature. Bollywood's foregrounded song and dance routine is substituted by an extended scene of combat – martial arts or otherwise – that showcases qualities of strength, athleticism and quick-wittedness. Yet emphasis upon the spectacular, hyperkinetic properties of Hong Kong cinema can be misleading. If there is freestanding spectacle in the work of Wong Kar-wai, for example, it is of a chic, glossy sort very different from the brashness and populism – the 'circus aesthetic' (Bordwell, *Planet Hong Kong*, p. 220) – of Hong Kong's action movies. Although the action genre is undeniably crucial to both the local film economy and export markets, it hardly exhausts the totality of production. One of the several risks of construing this cinema as solely a line of descent from Bruce Lee through Jackie Chan, Chow Yun-fat and Andy Lau to Jet Li is that it overly *masculinises* the tradition. How, if such a narrative of Hong Kong film prevails, are we to recognise the 1980s and 1990s work of the female director Ann Hui? How can an action-oriented account perceive and value the local cinema's 'mundane, esoteric, woman-ist, queer, and communitarian moments and voices' (Yau, *At Full Speed*, p. 25)?

Cinematically, Hong Kong is located in a number of concentric geographies. In the innermost ring, it has the status of a national cinema. Though open to an eclectic mix of formal models from elsewhere, Hong Kong's film industry has been able to absorb these and still seem assertively indigenous. Bordwell reports how, historically, local cinemagoers' taste has favoured local products, to the extent that many Hollywood successes – including *Mrs Doubtfire* (1993), *Forrest Gump* (1994) and *The Lion King* (1994) – have failed at the Hong Kong box office (*Planet Hong Kong*, p. 34). However, as well as national in its spatial connotations, Hong Kong film, to a greater extent than Bollywood, should also be defined as a *regional* cinema. Its most complex neighbourly rela-tions, of course, are with the People's Republic of China (not least since 1997, when Beijing assumed sovereignty over Hong Kong at the conclusion of British colonial rule). Stylistic, industrial and commercial ties, however, exist with other nations in East Asia: with Taiwan, for example, as a source of finance and with Japan as not only a significant market but also home of the region's main competitor film industry. Creative personnel, too, may be drawn from throughout Pacific Asia, confirming Yau's sense of the complex 'ethnoscape' of current Hong Kong filmmaking (*At Full Speed*, p. 11).

Any mapping of Hong Kong cinema must recognise, finally, its *global* character. Again, this is apparent at the level of the industry's ethnoscape: note simply the Australian Christopher Doyle, who has done stunning work as Wong Kar-wai's cine-matographer on such films as *Chungking Express* (1994), *In the Mood for Love* and *2046* (2004). In evaluating the consequences of Hong Kong's insertion into a globalised film economy, it is important to avoid the two extremes of uncritical celebration and morbid pessimism. Certainly, it is hard not to be depressed when acknowledging the level of competition that, since the mid-1990s, Hong Kong cinema has faced in both its local and regional markets from a more aggressively exporting Hollywood. As a result, production has dwindled in volume and profitability; previous euphoria about Hong Kong as a power-house of Asian filmmaking equipped to resist American cinematic imperialism has had to be moderated. Even so, the current terms of film trade are by no means entirely weighted in favour of the US. A notion of *reverse colonisation* – developed by the literary critic Stephen Arata for the quite different purpose of reading Bram Stoker's novel, *Dracula* – may usefully be adopted here to discuss Hong Kong's incursion into Hollywood. If, in imperial fashion, Hollywood holds sway over Hong Kong – its products penetrating not only local auditoria but the imaginations of local spectators – then, reciprocally, Hong Kong film is now near the heart of Hollywood. Inelegantly, but valuably, Bordwell refers to a contemporary 'Hongkongification of American cinema' (*Planet Hong Kong*, p. 19). At the time of his book's publication in 2000, he could cite such developments as US recruitment of actors like Jackie Chan and directors like Tsui Hark, Ringo Lam and, above all, John Woo; the importation of Hong Kong talent has continued since, with opportunities for other performers such as Jet Li. Textually, too, Hollywood is proving subject to influence by Hong Kong aesthetics, especially those of the action genre. Think, for example, of combat choreography in the *Matrix* trilogy (1999–2003) and Tarantino's *Kill Bill: Vol. 1*. And if Hong Kong cinema has long been adept in recycling the Hollywood blockbuster, the process was reversed in 2006 when Martin Scorsese's Oscar-garlanded *The Departed* transposed to Boston the Hong Kong hit *Mou gaan dou/Infernal Affairs* (2002). All of this reverse colonisation comes at a price, whether confirming a narrowly action-oriented version of Hong Kong filmmaking or offering resources to renew a jaded Hollywood cinema and boost its export potential, including in East Asia itself. Nevertheless, such transactions do, at least, indicate that globalisation in the film economy is not simply a narrative of spreading US dominance.

STOP and THINK

- Return to Stephen Crofts's claim above that 'Film scholars' mental maps of world film production are often less than global.' Drawing upon your film-viewing experiences and other sources of knowledge, construct a personal cartography of world cinema. Which parts of the world can be mapped in reasonable detail? Which areas, by contrast, are sketchy in outline, or even entirely blank? Suggest reasons for this geographical patchiness.

- What problems do we face when viewing films from diverse cinema cultures, especially those of non-Anglophone nations? Crofts writes that 'Without cross-cultural contextualisation – a broadly educational project – foreign distribution of national cinemas ... will tend to erase the culturally specific' (*Theorising National Cinema*, p. 53). To what extent has contextualisation of the sort Crofts advises been an element in the circulation of 'foreign' films with which you are familiar?

- The French theorist Jean-François Lyotard claims that 'Eclecticism is the degree zero of contemporary general culture: one listens to reggae, watches a western, eats McDonald's food for lunch and local cuisine for dinner, wears Paris perfume in Tokyo and "retro" clothes in Hong Kong' (*The Postmodern Condition: A Report on Knowledge* (Manchester: Manchester University Press, 1984), p. 76). Leaving to one side this passage's reckless generalisation in favour of the affluent, is eclecticism, more narrowly, the 'degree zero' of contemporary film culture? Bordwell suggests it might be when he notes the emergence, in the video/DVD era, of 'a World Film' comprising 'Japanese anime, Indian melodramas, Italian horror, Mexican masked-wrestler films, Indonesian fantasies, and other off-centre media materials from various countries' (*Planet Hong Kong*, p. 96). From this perspective, 'World Film' or 'world cinema' risks – again – the annulment of cultural specificity: disparate non-Anglophone film cultures become valuable in the West for their capacity to tickle the palates of consumers unsatisfied by Hollywood. But perhaps this is too pessimistic, and neglects cultural and political enrichments that may follow as spectators in Leeds or Philadelphia venture beyond the domestic film product to watch Hayao Miyazaki's *anime* or Dario Argento's strain of Italian horror? Offer your own assessment of the benefits and/or costs of the West's current modelling and consumption of 'world cinema'.

National and transnational film

'Having a nation', writes Ernest Gellner, 'is not an inherent attribute of humanity ... nations, like states, are a contingency, and not a universal necessity' (*Nations and Nationalism*, 2nd ed. (Malden, MA and Oxford: Blackwell, 2006), p. 6). Conceptually, nations are porous, owing their existence to questionable feats of fabrication rather than to some unimpeachable logic. Nevertheless, though hoping to map other – and better – political terrains upon which people might gather, Gellner also has to acknowledge that the sense of national belonging is by now globally widespread and psychologically deep-rooted: 'A man without a nation defies the recognised categories and provokes revulsion' (p. 6).

By analogy, can we imagine a film that has no country? A film that, as Gellner would wish to happen to people themselves, is not primarily identified as belonging to one or other of those domains we call 'nations'? For our narrower purposes here, we should follow political theorists like Gellner in asserting the contingency of national categorisation. There is nothing inviolable about the tendency to ascribe films to particular nations, as happens now in contexts ranging from magazine listings and festival programmes to books that take as their subject 'French' or 'British' or 'Egyptian' cinema. Valentina Vitali and Paul Willemen show that early in the twentieth century, at least, a film's point of national origin was not the most pressing concern for distributors and exhibitors: 'The main way of differentiating product lines was provided by the name and, eventually, by the reputation of companies that produced films in different national territories' (*Theorising National Cinema*, p. 1). At a conceptual level, Andrew

Higson suggests that the category of the nation may be insufficiently flexible to deal with all of the geographies of interest to
film studies: 'the contingent communities that cinema imagines
are much more likely to be either local or transnational than
national' (*Transnational Cinema*, p. 23). Rather like the concept of
genre discussed in Chapter 6, then, 'the nation' risks being simultaneously too large and too small for the discipline's needs. At one
extreme it lacks the power of magnification necessary to recognise
local, *intra*-national filmmaking cultures. How adequate is a unifying model of 'Belgian cinema' when discussing the provincially
situated, French-language work of the Dardenne Brothers,
including such films as *Rosetta* (1999) and *L'Enfant* (2005)? Or
what can a notion of 'Spanish cinema' do with Spain's distinctive,
often militantly separatist Basque film tradition, one that extends
from features to Julio Medem's successful documentary *La Pelota
vasca. La piel contra la piedra / Basque Ball: The Skin Against the
Stone* (2003)? At the other geographical extreme the category of
the nation is too small to account for certain itineraries of film
production, distribution and exhibition. In a moment we will
consider work that is not only produced in *transnational* circumstances but takes intercontinental shifts of peoples, languages and
ideas as its thematic preoccupation. Here we just briefly acknowledge how a fixation upon nations also inhibits the recognition of
other cinematic cartographies: those instances where commonali-
ties in adjacent states allow national cinemas such as Hong Kong's
to achieve *regional* status, or where historic ties of language and
culture across the globe produce something like *diasporic* films (a
phenomenon illustrated by *Bombón el Perro* (2004), a work set in
the Patagonia region of Argentina, directed by the Buenos Aires-
born Carlos Sorin, but also an Argentine / Spanish co-production
that has circulated throughout the Spanish-speaking world).

Yet even as we indicate the impoverishing effects of 'the nation'
in film studies, we need simultaneously to acknowledge the
concept's indispensability (recall, again, the provisional usefulness
of the idea of genre). Just as Gellner acknowledges the difficulty of
thinking outside national configurations, so too, from within film
studies, Higson cites the nation's 'helpfulness as a taxonomic

labelling device, a conventional means of reference in the complex
debates about cinema' (*Transnational Cinema*, p. 16). To attribute
films to particular nations may be enlivening as well as harmful.
Most importantly, it can identify a locus of cultural resistance to
the directly colonial or otherwise hegemonic force of other states.
As Chapter 8 noted, certain countries in the developing world that
lack the resources to build indigenous film industries remain at the
mercy of others' cinematic representations; thus there would be
more positive things to do with a film labelled 'from Chad' or
'from Paraguay' than piously to point out the artifice of national
boundaries. Similarly, a film described as 'Palestinian' – for
instance, *Paradise Now* (2005) – should not elicit in the first
instance a political science lesson in the flaws of the nation as a
construct; instead, given the observation of the actor-director
Mohammed Bakri that 'We have no film schools and we have no
studios ... because we have no country' (*The Guardian*, 12 April
2006), the consolidation of a self-styled Palestinian national
cinema would be occasion for celebration.

Focus upon films' national origins also discloses historical shifts
in production. At different times, a number of non-American
industries have been dominant in world markets. In 1907, Mihir
Bose reports, 40 per cent of films shown in the US were from the
one Paris studio alone. Bose adds that French cinematic rule was
still apparent in 1910 when feature films released in Britain
'included thirty-six from France, twenty-eight from the US, and
seventeen from Italy, well ahead of the fifteen from Great Britain
and four from Denmark, Germany and elsewhere' (*Bollywood: A
History*, p. 61). Such modest US share of world film trade was, of
course, not to last. Miller et al.'s *Global Hollywood 2* is a finely
detailed study of the mutually reinforcing commercial, legal and
political strategies by which the hegemony of American popular
cinema has been achieved during the twentieth and early twenty-
first centuries (the authors briskly reject the notion that such
global penetration is owing to textual quality alone). The correla-
tive of Hollywood's upsurge has been a shrivelling of many
'indigenous' or 'national' film industries elsewhere. A blizzard of
dismal statistics produced by Miller et al. includes the fact that,
over the period 1945–2000, the combined European film indus-

tries declined by eight-ninths (*Global Hollywood 2*, p, 10). As noted above, even a self-confident indigenous film culture like Hong Kong's also proved vulnerable, by the end of the twentieth century, to a newly globalised Hollywood.

Nevertheless, to repeat, it is important not to absolutise the power of America in today's world cinematic system. By way of challenging the bleakest diagnosis of US cultural imperialism, we might acknowledge the extent to which this particular culture of production is itself inflected by other nations. Whether providing finance or plausible locations or elements of production, these countries, at least to an extent, 'de-Americanise' American film. If such developments are far from uniformly benign – Hollywood is interested in rerouting production beyond US borders to avoid higher labour costs and more heavily unionised workforces at home – neither are they completely lacking in progressive potential. We noted earlier Hollywood's 'Hongkongification', and the variously exhilarating and disquieting effects of this. A similar ambivalence is evoked by the post-2000 'Latinisation' of US cinema. Over this period, many directors who made their reputations in Central and South America have worked within the US system. As well as Iñárritu (discussed in Chapter 4), consider just two other representative trajectories. First, the Brazilian Walter Salles – best-known for *Central do Brasil / Central Station* (1998) and *Diarios de motocicleta / Motorcycle Diaries* (2004) – went to the United States to make the Japanese-influenced horror film *Dark Water* (2005). Second, the Mexican Alfonso Cuarón has followed his successful indigenous film *Y tu mamá también* (2001) with two US/UK productions: *Harry Potter and the Prisoner of Azkaban* (2004) and *Children of Men* (2006). These and other instances might be regarded as neo-colonial appropriation of non-US resources to revivify a flagging domestic film product; from another perspective, however, they hold out at least some hope of lodging an outsider, even 'Third-Worldist' sensibility within Hollywood itself.

Reflecting on such personal itineraries and also on the circulation of favoured products of 'world cinema' through Western markets – recent examples would include *Y tu mamá también*, *Amores perros*, *In the Mood for Love*, *Hero* and the 2005 Korean film *Oldboy* – Elizabeth Ezra and Terry Rowden propose that film is now 'borderless' (*Transnational Cinema*, p. 5). However, it seems premature to be welcoming – or deploring – the arrival of a completely cosmopolitan cinema: the national, in cinematic terms, has not wholly given way yet to the transnational. Note the residual appeal of homelands for at least some of the creative personnel cited in this chapter who have worked in US or broader English-language filmmaking: for example, Cuarón's *México '68* – due in 2009 – is a Spanish-language production, shot in the director's home country and with a subject that has primarily indigenous appeal rather than any obvious translatability to other markets. Indeed, Ezra and Rowden moderate their initial assertion by acknowledging that the extent of 'cinematic mobility, like human mobility, is determined by both geopolitical factors and financial pedigree' (p. 5). Uneven distribution of cultural and economic power determines not only the movements of stars, directors and other creative talents across the world cinema system but also the potential that any particular film has to travel beyond its place of origin.

Suggestively, Ezra and Rowden add that transnational flows are not merely apparent in circumstances of film production and distribution but figure among the narrative concerns of an increasing number of films. Migration and diaspora, they write, have become prominent 'as themes within transnational cinema texts themselves' (p. 7). Such is powerfully the case in the film that provides this chapter's case study.

Analysing production: *In This World*

In This World (2002) narrates the difficult, often covert journey of two Afghan youths from a refugee camp in northern Pakistan towards their intended destination of London. A red line periodically traced on a map summarises Jamal and Enayat's progress: overland from Pakistan to Iran and Turkey; by boat to Italy; then, following the death of Enayat in asphyxiating conditions at sea, Jamal's onward travel to France by train and, finally, to England by the underside of a lorry (Figure 22). Apart from relatively brief scenes in an Istanbul cutlery workshop, the dockside at Trieste, the

Figure 22 Transnational cinema: Jamal Udin Turabi in *In This World* (UK, 2002).

Red Cross refugee camp at Sangatte, and a London mosque and café, the film is set in Asia. Only a little English is heard, mainly during an early voiceover informing us about worldwide numbers and conditions of refugees; instead, the dominant languages are Pashto and Farsi. The cast is drawn from non-professionals encountered along this cosmopolitan itinerary, especially from local populations in Pakistan, Iran and Turkey.

Given these features, is *In This World*, in any meaningful sense, a *British* film? One piece of evidence for this is the country of birth of both the director Michael Winterbottom and the writer Tony Grisoni. However, these are flimsy grounds on which to build an argument for any film's national identity: by the same token, Wolfgang Petersen's *Troy* (2004) is a German movie and Michael Curtiz's *Casablanca* (1943) part of Hungary's cinematic canon. For a more convincing sign of *In This World*'s Britishness, then, we might cite the fact that much of its budget came from the BBC and the UK Film Council. Yet in assessing matters of national provenance, the criterion of financing, too, is not beyond challenge: after all, David Lynch's *The Straight Story* and *Inland Empire* were substantially financed by the France-based Studio Canal Plus, yet it would be perverse to think of them as 'French films' in the same way we apply this term to the work of Jacques Tati.

Attempting to find more solid grounds for the national categorisation of films than those utilised above, Paul Willemen suggests that 'the issue of national cinema is ... primarily a question of address, rather than a matter of the filmmakers' citizenship or even of the production finance's country of origin' (*Theorising National Cinema*, p. 36). From this perspective, *In This World* seems 'addressed' to a British – and more largely Western – audience, aiming to advance spectator understanding of the nature and scale of human displacements caused by such actions as the US bombing of Afghanistan in the wake of 9/11. Though the English-language voiceover is heard only briefly, its occurrence at a key early moment appears to identify the film as primarily a speech act for British reception. At the same time, however, it is not far-fetched to consider *In This World* as *an instance of 'Third World' cinema*. Aesthetically, politically and industrially, it demonstrates affinities with the conventions of liberationist, Third World filmmaking as these have been sketched out in such epochal manifestos as 'For an Imperfect Cinema' (1969) by the Cuban Julio Garcia Espinosa and 'Towards a Third Cinema' (1969) by the Argentine filmmaker-theorists Octavio Getino and Fernando Solanas. Consider, for example, how Winterbottom's film largely forgoes high-budget glossiness and follows Espinosa's demand for a kind of aesthetic 'poverty' that echoes the poverty of people in front of the camera; while *In This World*'s colour palette is rich at times – supplied by sunsets or the gold of sand dunes – there are also sparsely lit night scenes, examples of staccato camerawork and, throughout, no fetishisation of the perfect image. The film might similarly be recruited to Getino and Solanas' 'Third Cinema', a form of cinema which refuses in equal measure both the commercial Hollywood product and an auteurist or art tradition principally associated with Europe. Though a fictional narrative, *In This World* has the atmospherics of undercover, propagandist documentary. Guards patrolling the snowy Iran/Turkey frontier at night are seen through infra-red equipment, as if surreptitiously; certain interiors are barely lit at all, evoking an attempt to avoid detection by authority. A sense of engagement with topical concerns is advanced by the use of exclusively non-professional performers, who play characters quite adjacent to their 'real' selves. Winterbottom also used a very small production crew, based in the first instance in a rented Pakistani bus; he thus fulfilled the Third-Worldist imperative of reducing as far as possible the distance between the guild of aesthetic specialists on the one hand and the poor or dislocated peoples who are the objects of representation on the other.

Yet, tempting though they are, Third-Worldist analogies for *In This World* should in the end be resisted; both textually and contextually, the film is marked still by First World privilege. To begin with, it emerges from an established – if, by Hollywood standards, modestly funded – culture of production; the BBC's involvement also guarantees it TV screening to add to its exhibition in venues mainly identified with what Getino and Solanas call 'Second Cinema'. Winterbottom says, too, that while the itinerary of filming usually resembled the narrated journey as closely as possible, everyone's life was sometimes made more comfortable by use of flights to replace portions of overland travel; again in evidence, then, is a well-resourced film industry rather than the hand-to-mouth, indigenous ones evoked by Third Cinema's theorists. Such relative privilege can, at moments, be detected in the text itself. Although the use of infra-red, for example, aptly suggests an operation of insurgent counter-surveillance, it also cannot help but speak of Western technological advantage.

Favourable terms of trade – economic and cultural – are most apparent in the film's very subject matter. Winterbottom and his collaborators achieve a geographical scope that it is difficult to see being replicated at present by many Iranian or Pakistani filmmakers. The transnationalism of *In This World*, then, is politically ambiguous, connoting inequality as well as progressiveness. Here a more general point made by Ella Shohat and Robert Stam is apt. They argue that where First World filmmakers seem to possess a greater ability than their colleagues in the developing world 'to float "above" petty nationalist' concerns', this is not because of their richer imaginations but, much more materially, because they can 'take for granted the projection of a national power that facilitates the making and the dissemination of their films.' Third World filmmakers, by contrast, frequently lack the 'substratum of national power' on which to base more internationally expansive projects (*Unthinking Eurocentrism: Multiculturalism and the Media* (London and New York: Routledge, 1994), p. 285). Without in any way wishing to affiliate Winterbottom with 'the imperial imaginary' that Shohat and Stam critique so forcefully, we may still observe that *In This World* originates in the kind of advanced cinema culture they speak of, and that it is precisely this stable national foundation which licenses the film's movements beyond Britain.

However, it would be both unfair and inadequate to leave the discussion there. Instead, more positively, we can draw upon another distinction, this time provided by two documentary filmmakers. John Hess and Patricia F. Zimmermann distinguish between types of transnational or cosmopolitan imagination. On one side is what they call 'corporatist transnationalism', usually associated with profit-maximising multinational companies as they extend across ever more national boundaries and in the process flatten local economic and cultural forms ('global Hollywood' itself is a striking example of transnationalism of this kind). But on the other side is the resistant practice Hess and Zimmermann call 'adversarial transnationalism', a mode of cross-cultural engagement that identifies with those displaced and dispossessed by catastrophic military-industrial adventures during the late twentieth and early twenty-first centuries. If *In This World* cannot, in the end, be a bona fide Third-Worldist film, it is certainly constructed on adversarial transnationalist principles. The film, for instance, configures travel across borders as trauma rather than as First World-style leisure. While London still serves as a destination, Jamal's arrival there is treated cursorily; the city is now less an imperial centre than another node in a complex global network. Even the film's closing credits are set against patches of irregularly painted wall that, from a certain perspective, look like maps and so suggest the protagonists' ongoing displacement rather than a sense of settled location.

In This World, finally, asserts an adversarial stance by its representation of what the postcolonial media scholar Hamid Naficy calls 'the westering journey'. For Naficy, the mapping of westward movement across borders has become a major preoccupation of filmmakers exiled or otherwise relocated from the developing world. Winterbottom's interest in this cinematic trope is also apparent in a later film, *The Road to Guantanamo* (2006; co-directed by Mat Whitecross). Here, indeed, he augments Third-Worldist explorations of this topic. Naficy writes that the westering journey is typically one 'of escape, emigration, or exile' (*An Accented Cinema: Exilic and Diasporic Filmmaking*, p. 225); he thereby omits the westering journey of *imprisonment* – precisely Winterbottom's theme in this later film. Like *In This World*, *The Road to Guantanamo* has a topic and geographical range that testify to a well-established centre of film production, one better resourced than filmmaking in the spaces it takes for its subject. Both films, however, engage with the world in committed ways that anticipate a productively rather than dangerously borderless cinema.

Selected reading

Hollywood

Bordwell, David, Janet Staiger and Kristin Thompson, *The Classical Hollywood Cinema: Film Style and Mode of Production to 1960* (London and New York: Routledge, 1985).

Work of classic status itself, though its version of the Hollywood paradigm has been subjected to modifications and challenges by later writers such as Maltby.

Grainge, Paul, *Brand Hollywood: Selling Entertainment in a Global Media Age* (London and New York: Routledge, 2007).

Timely, intricately detailed account of contemporary Hollywood's multiple strategies of commodification. A good example of film studies' post-textual turn.

King, Geoff, *New Hollywood Cinema: An Introduction* (London and New York: I. B. Tauris, 2002).

Explores New Hollywood's stylistic, industrial and ideological departures from – and continuities with – the classical studio system; well-informed, judiciously argued and enjoyable.

Maltby, Richard, *Hollywood Cinema*, 2nd ed. (Malden, MA and Oxford: Blackwell, 2003).

Wrist-breakingly extensive, and close to the last word on Hollywood's 'commercial aesthetic', with exhaustive description of this production centre's industrial, technological, ideological, formal and stylistic particularities.

Miller, Toby, Nitin Govil, John McMurria, Richard Maxwell and Ting Wang, *Global Hollywood 2* (London: BFI, 2004).

Extended version of a text first published in 2001; a densely researched, politically vital account of Hollywood's global penetration – and, more optimistically, of attempts worldwide to develop forms of 'counter-power'.

Neale, Steve and Murray Smith (eds), *Contemporary Hollywood Cinema* (London and New York: Routledge, 1998).

Lively studies arranged by categories of 'historiography', 'economics, industry and institutions', 'aesthetics and technology' and 'audience, address and ideology'; a helpfully detailed set of additions to King's overview.

Bollywood

Bose, Mihir, *Bollywood: A History* (Stroud: Tempus, 2006).

Betrays, at times, its author's lack of specialist film expertise; but a handy, anecdotally rich journalistic account to set alongside the more challenging academic studies of Dudrah, Mishra and others.

Dudrah, Rajinder Kumar, *Bollywood: Sociology Goes to the Movies* (London and Thousand Oaks, CA: SAGE, 2006).

Sophisticated, engaging exploration of not only Bollywood film texts themselves but their diverse contexts of reception, including in the Indian diaspora.

Ganti, Tejaswini, *Bollywood: A Guidebook to Popular Hindi Cinema* (London and New York: Routledge, 2004).

Lucid and helpful introduction.

Kaur, Raminder and Ajay J. Sinha (eds), *Bollywood: Popular Indian Cinema through a Transnational Lens* (London and Thousand Oaks, CA: SAGE, 2005).

Wide-ranging responses to Bollywood's geographical representations and transmissions; offers, in its attention to Bollywood in the global economy, a suggestive companion to Morris et al.'s book on Hong Kong cinema.

Mishra, Vijay, *Bollywood Cinema: Temples of Desire* (New York and London: Routledge, 2002).

Combines enthusiasm and erudition, Western film theory and local knowledges, in exploring conceptual, formal and ideological questions raised by 'Bombay Cinema' over some seventy years.

Hong Kong

Bordwell, David, *Planet Hong Kong: Popular Cinema and the Art of Entertainment* (Cambridge, MA and London: Harvard University Press, 2000).

Bordwell at his most unbuttoned. Rooted exuberantly in the specific, but also taking Hong Kong cinema – especially its action genres – to exemplify the vitality and achievement of popular film more broadly.

Morris, Meaghan, Siu Leung Li and Stephen Chan Ching-kiu (eds), *Hong Kong Connections: Transnational Imagination in Action Cinema* (Durham, NC and London: Duke University Press, 2006).

Fascinatingly tracks the modes of travel of Hong Kong's action genres through the cinemas – and broader popular cultures – of nations including Australia, France and the US.

Stringer, Julian, *Blazing Passions: Contemporary Hong Kong Cinema* (London: Wallflower, 2007).

Economical, accessible, up-to-date; a very convenient starting point.

Teo, Stephen, *Hong Kong Cinema: The Extra Dimensions* (London: BFI, 1997).

Lucid, chronologically ordered account of the first nine decades of Hong Kong production; needs supplementing by Stringer's more up-to-date material.

Yau, Esther C. M. (ed.), *At Full Speed: Hong Kong Cinema in a Borderless World* (Minneapolis and London: University of Minnesota Press, 2001).

Lively collection of essays, offering culturally detailed responses to such figures as Jackie Chan, Tsui Hark, Ann Hui and Wong Kar-wai, as well as assessments of Hong Kong cinema's place in the contemporary global mediascape.

National and transnational film

Ezra, Elizabeth and Terry Rowden (eds), *Transnational Cinema: The Film Reader* (London and New York: Routledge, 2006).

Essays registering the impacts of transnationalism everywhere from the film text itself to fan cultures and contexts of production. Strikes a judicious balance between critique and optimism.

Grant, Catherine and Annette Kuhn (eds), *Screening World Cinema: A 'Screen' Reader* (London and New York: Routledge, 2006).

Valuable, diverse sampling of two decades of writings from *Screen* on questions of national and transnational cinema.

Naficy, Hamid, *An Accented Cinema: Exilic and Diasporic Filmmaking* (Princeton: Princeton University Press, 2001).

Fascinating explorations of a body of formally varied and politically complex work by filmmakers displaced from the developing world; mediates very productively between contextual and textual specificities.

Vitali, Valentina and Paul Willemen (eds), *Theorising National Cinema* (London: BFI, 2006).

Impressively wide-ranging collection, covering many national cinemas as well as testing the continuing viability of notions of 'the national' in an era of increasingly globalised film production.

Useful websites

www.fafo.at/download/WorldFilmProduction06.pdf.

Detailed and illuminating statistics – broken down by nation – on recent trends in global film production and distribution; discloses, for example, that Cyprus released one feature film in 2005, as against the US's 699.

www.columbia.edu/cu/lweb/indiv/africa/cuvl/video.html.

With a few exceptions, African nations are excluded from the statistics above of world film output; this site offers links to numerous resources – some commercial rather than scholarly – on African cinema and TV.

www.digitalhistory.uh.edu/historyonline/hollywood.cfm.

Helpful, neatly organised materials on Hollywood's commercial and aesthetic development from early in the twentieth century.

10
Film consumption

Places and experiences

Here is a passage from the beginning of *The Moviegoer* (1961), a novel by the American writer Walker Percy:

> It reminds me of a movie I saw last month out by Lake Pontchartrain. Linda and I went out to a theatre in a new suburb. It was evident somebody had miscalculated, for the suburb had quit growing and here was the theatre, a pink stucco cube, sitting out in a field all by itself. A strong wind whipped the waves against the seawall; even inside you could hear the racket.

Binx Bolling, the novel's narrator and film fan, eventually gets round to a summary of what the cinema was showing: 'The movie was about a man who lost his memory in an accident and as a result lost everything.' Before turning to these textual matters, however, he is careful to supply the geographical, architectural and social coordinates of his act of moviegoing. While most of the cinemas Binx attends in the novel are in busy parts of New Orleans, this one, by contrast, has an unpopulated, semi-rural location. The building is not simply an inert, affectless backdrop to his film spectatorship but, as 'a pink stucco cube', engages the senses with its own properties of colour, texture and shape. No clear demarcation exists between exterior and interior spaces: the auditorium is a liminal zone, mixing together the soundtrack of the film about the amnesiac with the noise of waves from outside. And just as the film text loses some of its autonomy in the face of these peculiar environmental conditions, so its prestige is weakened by the evidence Binx gives of moviegoing's *extra*-textual motives. He is at the cinema, after all, as part of a seduction routine with his secretary.

This episode from *The Moviegoer* serves as a reminder of what film studies has all too frequently excluded from its field of inquiry, namely the complex spatial and social architectures within which any act of film consumption occurs. Writing about the patrons of very early film exhibition, Ian Christie makes the point that their viewing decisions were not, in the main, textually motivated: 'They went to the biograph, the cinematograph, the moving pictures, the nickelodeon: it was a *place* and an *experience* long before identifiable works and their makers emerged to claim their niche in history' (*The Last Machine: Early Cinema and the Birth of the Modern World* (London: BBC Educational, 1994), p. 8). The only difficulty with this formulation is that it might imply that valuing the space and activity of film consumption alongside or even above engagement with the text itself is something which faded away as soon as there was promotion of such textual elements as star, director and genre. On the contrary, spectators continue today to make powerful extra-textual investments in the places and experiences of reception.

Film studies has been slow to respond to such situated spectatorship and to generate detailed cartographies of consumption. The 'screen theory' that prevailed in the discipline from the 1970s sets aside as conceptually unimportant the particularities of different viewing sites and shrinks the space of reception to little more than a line joining the spectator's eye and the contents of the projected image. While this approach yields sophisticated accounts of the absorptive power of spectacle, they come at a price. The positing of a standard, textually constructed viewing position represses, among other things, awareness of unequal access to the very sites of consumption in which that textual operation must occur. For some African American cinemagoers of the 1930s, say, forced to use a rear door to reach a racially segregated balcony, the idea that specificities of reception space can be ignored when calculating film's ideological effects might seem odd indeed. Screen theory's cramped geography also neglects a host of other spaces beyond the cinema auditorium itself that are encountered during film consumption. Think only of the sumptuous lobby of a 1930s picture palace, or the multiplex's out-of-town location amidst arterial roads and retail parks, or the familiar contours of the living-room in which much film-watching now occurs.

Despite this previous reluctance to 'place' spectators, film studies may now be developing a geographical imagination. Here a significant book is *The Place of the Audience: Cultural Geographies of Film Consumption* (2003), by Mark Jancovich and Lucy Faire, with Sarah Stubbings. This study charts the history of film exhibition sites in Nottingham – from fairgrounds and churches to art cinemas and multiplexes – and argues forcefully that a text-centred approach to film cannot account for all of the connotations which attendance at these varied venues has had for patrons. At times, Jancovich et al. go very far in erasing the specificities of film texts themselves: particular movies that played at the Metropole appear insignificant next to this cinema's meanings as a built space. While the book corrects an exclusively textual model of spectatorship, then, it risks substituting another sort of one-sidedness and failing to follow Henry Jenkins's more dynamic suggestion that film reception studies should explore 'the relationship between the films' content and their consumption contexts' ('Reception Theory and Audience Research: the Mystery of the Vampire's Kiss', *Reinventing Film Studies*, eds Christine Gledhill and Linda Williams (London: Arnold, 2000), p. 178).

Annette Kuhn's *An Everyday Magic: Cinema and Cultural Memory* (2002) comes closer to fulfilling this remit. Like Jancovich et al., Kuhn is indebted to cultural geography and shows heightened sensitivity to particular film reception sites (here, the picture palaces and neighbourhood fleapits of 1930s Britain). However, such extra-textual interests are subtly combined with awareness of what goes on in films themselves. Kuhn assesses, for example, the extent to which cinemagoers of the period could reproduce in off-screen geographies Fred Astaire and Ginger Rogers's fluid movements through screen space. As well as blending cultural geography, textual criticism and a modified screen theory, *An Everyday Magic* also draws upon the *ethnographic* evidence provided by a set of interviews with older people who recall their cinemagoing experiences. With this crisscrossing of methodologies, Kuhn's book is a striking instance of the '"mixed genres" of writing' that Jenkins argues will characterise the 'new' reception studies (p. 177).

Since *The Place of the Audience* also makes use of ethnographic data – gathered from questionnaires given to contemporary Nottingham filmgoers – this is an opportune moment to consider ethnography's value in studies of film reception. Some early research into cinema audiences is, in method and tone, very close to classic anthropological work on patterns of behaviour in traditional societies. Take the Mass-Observation programme to gather information about Britain's cinemagoing habits at the time of the Second World War. If one of the project's research methods was a questionnaire allowing cinemagoers to express their own thoughts, another was surveillance work in which the observer resembles a pith-helmeted traveller coming across a strange tribe. From 'Report on Cinema Queue' (May 1940): 'As the queue moves forward those men behind obs. [observer] who had been talking to a man by the kerb have to talk louder to make themselves heard ... They are exchanging trivialities, "What are you doing with yourself?" "Seen Bert lately?" and so on' (*Mass-Observation at the Movies*, eds Jeffrey Richards and Dorothy Sheridan (London and New York: Routledge & Kegan Paul, 1987), p. 190). This blatantly externalised perspective on cinemagoers has no equivalent in the work of current scholars like Jancovich et al. and Kuhn.

Nevertheless, Richard deCordova has questioned even sensitive, self-conscious uses of ethnography within film reception studies. Like the anthropological research from which it takes its protocols, an ethnographic approach to consumers of film – interviewing or surveying them – raises the question of how 'the subjects of this research can escape becoming its object, constituted in an interpretive gesture by the researcher in relation to his/her agenda, identity, and desires' ('Ethnography and Exhibition: The Child Audience, the Hays Office, and Saturday Matinees', *Moviegoing in America: A Sourcebook in the History of Film Exhibition*, ed. Gregory A. Waller, p. 160). Besides this problem of unequal observer/observed relations, ethnography of film audiences holds other dangers. Jancovich et al. rightly point out that it has often generated aberrant results because of 'an over-concentration on fan cultures', leaving more 'casual' spectators relatively unstudied (*The Place of the Audience*, p. 27). Even an expansively conceived ethnography yields little information about the commercial forces usually responsible for exhibition, and so is of only partial value to research into film as an industry. A cultural geographic approach to the spaces of film consumption may also be deficient in this respect, risking fetishisation of their particularities to the detriment of concern with the organised economic interests behind such reception sites as cinemas and home computer screens. Nevertheless, it is this chapter's contention that, integrated where necessary with other approaches like textual analysis and political economy, cultural geography and ethnography offer exciting routes ahead for film studies. What follows are, first, brief surveys of categories of film reception site – pre-theatrical, theatrical and post-theatrical – and then a case study of one particular venue.

Cinema before cinemas

Jancovich et al. argue that 'film consumption has never been fully defined or fixed, but has been in a constant process of contestation and transformation' (*The Place of the Audience*, p. 37). If we are struck by the current plurality of reception spaces – from multiplex to mobile phone – this was no less the case in film's earliest period. With the quite tardy development of specialised exhibition venues – the *OED*'s first instance of *cinema* used in an architectural context comes from *Punch* in 1913 – films were shown at first in a heterogeneous array of sites. Prefiguring possibilities in our own spectatorship, the earliest consumption of all was enacted by a relatively isolate subject. Parlours equipped with Thomas Edison's coin-operated Kinetoscope machines opened in the United States from 1894: patrons peered into the interior of the device as brief footage of a popular entertainer or everyday scene spooled by, illuminated by a filament bulb. Although this invention enjoyed a brief vogue, its modelling of film consumption as a solitary activity doomed it to obsolescence. The cinematograph devised by the Lumière Brothers had the distinct advantage of being able to render film a material for public exhibition rather than peephole spectatorship; as Louis Lumière wrote: 'the projected images may be viewed by a large number of spectators all at once' (*Letters: Auguste and Louis Lumière*, ed. Jacques Rittaud-Hutinet (London: Faber and Faber, 1995), pp. 32–3).

Film was highly mobile across sites of public projection during this early period. When the Lumières demonstrated their cinematograph at the Salon Indien of Paris's Grand Café on 28 December 1895, the occasion was conceived less as populist amusement than as scientific edification for the bourgeoisie; class – and imperial – privilege was amply stated by the room's décor of elephant tusks and finely carved bamboo. Soon, however, the Lumière cinematograph attracted patrons who came not to study its optical specifications but to be entertained by the novelty of the images it projected. Film's early associations with popular culture were confirmed by its exhibition in venues including fairgrounds, amusement parks, travelling shows, and also vaudeville theatres where short works featured on the bill of fare alongside songs, recitations, acrobatics and performances by trained animals.

Yet it is important to note that many of these exhibition spaces remained subject to class stratification. Consider some evidence in Rudyard Kipling's short story 'Mrs Bathurst' (1904) – a terrifying parable, incidentally, of the dangers of absorption by screen spectacle. Film exhibition here has strongly popular, even carnivalesque connotations, occurring in a circus in Cape Town and alternating with other amusements like 'the performin' elephants'. Nevertheless, the space is still marked by status differentiation: Kipling's narrator records that some spectators pay more for better seats near the back. Social inequality of this sort could also be seen in the *nickelodeons* that represent film's first dedicated exhibition sites. These enterprises emerged in the US from 1905 and were usually housed in 'a converted cigar store, pawnshop, restaurant, or skating rink made over to look like a vaudeville theatre' (Douglas Gomery, *Shared Pleasures: A History of Movie Presentation in the United States*, p. 18). Offering wooden chairs or benches facing a smallish screen in a sparsely decorated room, nickelodeons had all the trappings of cheap, working-class entertainment (deriving their name – as did their British equivalent, *penny gaffes* – from a relatively low admission charge). Yet research by Gomery and other historians has shown that to consider the nickelodeon simply as a domain of poorer classes is to neglect the fact that then, as now, film consumption was traversed by social differences, even antagonisms. While nickelodeons attracted the nickname of 'democracy's theatre', they were frequently located in the wealthier districts of such American cities as New York.

Spaces of cinemagoing

Purposefully constructed venues of film exhibition – *cinemas*, in other words – began to supplant improvised, often ramshackle sites like nickelodeons shortly before the First World War. The subsequent century of cinema-building in the West has generated many variants, including picture palaces, humbler neighbourhood picture houses, art cinemas, multiplexes and IMAX theatres. An adequate evaluation of the cultural significance of these diverse sites would require many full-length studies. Ideally, research of this sort would also acknowledge its likely Occidentalism and develop comparative geographies and ethnographies of film consumption around the world. With our space limited, however, we sketch two particularly important shifts that have occurred in the physical and cultural architectures of Anglo-American cinemagoing.

'Optical fairylands'

Robert C. Allen writes that many spaces of current film consumption are 'phenomenologically impoverished' ('From Exhibition to Reception: Reflections on the Audience in Film History', *Moviegoing in America*, p. 304). He has particularly in mind a contrast between the functional, shed-like multiplex of today and the lavishly designed 'picture palaces' that began to emerge in the US, Britain and elsewhere during the 1910s. Such buildings were 'spectacles of consumption in themselves' (*The Place of the Audience*, p. 114), their glamour rivalling or even outstripping the spectacular properties of what they showed on screen. Picture palaces appealed to patrons by a combination of exotic architecture (flamboyantly quoting Egyptian, Greek, Gothic, Italianate and other building styles), cathedral-sized foyers and auditoria, and opulent internal decoration, with few expenses spared on carpeting, mirrors, chandeliers and paintings. As Siegfried Kracauer wrote in 1926: 'to call them *movie theatres* [*Kinos*] would be disrespectful' (*The Mass Ornament: Weimar Essays* (Cambridge, MA and London: Harvard University Press, 1995), p. 323). Instead, they were, in Kracauer's words, 'optical fairylands' and 'palaces of distraction' (Figure 23).

The critical tenor of that last phrase is evident in many accounts of cinemagoing produced during the first half of the twentieth century. For Kracauer himself, picture palaces of the type he saw in Berlin were not so much utopian spaces as sites for the reproduction of reactionary politics. With organised religion declining, these cinemas offered a new source of opiates for the people, their architecture evoking 'the lofty and the *sacred* as if designed to accommodate works of eternal significance – just one step short of burning votive candles' (p. 327). While Kracauer acknowledges

Figure 23 The Plaza Cinema, Northam, Southampton, c. 1932.

the role played by film *contents* in shaping the conservative social values of the 'Little Shopgirls' or 'Little Miss Typists' – his revealingly gendered and class-inflected terms for the cinematically gullible – he also insists on the determining effects upon spectator consciousness of the place and experience of cinemagoing itself. The design of the picture palace colludes with textual phenomena to induce a kind of political slumber in its patrons. C. Day-Lewis – father of Daniel – makes a similar point in a 1938 poem, 'Newsreel'. As Europe starts to burn, the cinema functions, in Day-Lewis's sardonic words, as 'the dream-house', 'this loving/Darkness a fur you can afford'.

Such critiques from the period accord with some work by recent film scholars on the ideological dangers of an opulent cinemagoing experience. Historians of reception like Miriam Hansen and Judith Mayne have described the movement from the nickelodeon era to that of the picture palace as a kind of fall. Where the rougher-hewn nickelodeons and penny gaffes allowed for boisterous collective spectatorship – even for an alternative 'public sphere' in which socially marginalised subjects including women and immigrants could find a place – the grander cinemas that came afterwards initiated a more conformist type of film consumption. Free to marvel at the splendid fixtures and fittings, the spectator at the picture palace was also subject to certain disciplines (a precursor to that *disciplinisation* of the contemporary multiplex patron we will consider in the next section). As an example, audience conversation while a film played – an aspect of nickelodeon culture – was frequently frowned upon in the newer, more controlled exhibition spaces.

There is, however, something one-sided about accounts of the picture palace as a reliable agency of conservatism. To begin with, this critique is sometimes based upon a suspect idealisation of the reception conditions that came earlier; Janet Staiger has been especially prominent in arguing that the talk which occurred in the nickelodeon was not necessarily progressive but also liable to be desultory or trivial. If the nickelodeon is one of Foucault's heterotopias – a space capable of sustaining different, even conflicting cultures – so too, Kuhn suggests, is the picture palace. Kuhn locates the picture palace or *supercinema* in both 'a real and accessible world' with depressingly finite boundaries *and* in 'the worlds of fantasy and imagination' (p. 141). Against the Little Shopgirl hypothesised by Kracauer – a simple dupe of the picture palace's grandeur – we might place someone like Muriel Peck, one of the 1930s cinemagoers whose testimonies enrich *An Everyday Magic*. She recalls: 'To go to the Astoria was like going to wonderland ... The décor was Moorish ... High up there were doors and balconies which were illuminated during the interval and one fully expected a beautiful princess to emerge with her prince' (p. 141). Was Ms Peck a victim of the commodification of cinemagoing? Perhaps. A solitary subject rather than the communally engaged figure yearned for in Kracauer's and Day-Lewis's critiques of picture palace spectatorship? Maybe. But to adhere only to this negative perspective would be as facile as it is insulting. The sense of wonderment that Muriel Peck and other spectators experienced as they left behind constrained, everyday circumstances and entered the early twentieth-century picture palace was, in its small way, a model for any utopian politics.

'Gated communities'

While some observers lamented the raucous nickelodeon's displacement by the picture palace, many more have spoken with a deep sense of loss about the picture palace's own supersession by another wave of cinema-building. The *multiplex* – an unostentatious box containing not one but many screens – emerged in the United States during the mid-1960s. Gomery records that the first 'fourplex' was built in Kansas City in 1966, the first 'sixplex' in Omaha, Nebraska in 1969 and the first 'eightplex' in Atlanta in 1974 (*Shared Pleasures*, p. 97). Since then, the number of screens under a single roof has continued to multiply, culminating in the post-1990 *megaplex* that typically houses between twenty and thirty auditoria (each with a seating capacity of around two hundred). This model of cinema design has also been streamed to many other nations. Consequently, debates over multiplex construction in these non-US localities sometimes take as one of their themes the desirability or otherwise of an increased Americanisation of public space. Jancovich et al. report that Nottingham's local press portrayed the arrival of a multiplex in

1988 as an 'American invasion of the city' – albeit benign (*The Place of an Audience*, p. 201). Before cultural geographers and ethnographers study how the multiplex is negotiated by its users, then, there is certainly need of a political economy approach that will show the involvement of powerful US corporations in the worldwide development and management of cinemas of this type.

The multiplex offers a very different version of public space from the picture palace. Where the latter was usually located at the heart of the urban area, the multiplex is often situated near traffic nodal points in outlying districts of a town or city; it is thus much less accessible by spectators without cars. With its functional architecture, it also seems unlikely to appeal to its users as an object of imaginative investment. Sixty years on, Muriel Peck can still vividly recall the marble flooring and fountain in the foyer of her favourite picture palace; their contemporary multiplex equivalents – not quite such propitious materials for nostalgia – would be a sea of grey carpet and a large cardboard cut-out of Harry Potter. In addition, the multiplex lobby typically contains payment kiosks, videogame machines, posters for forthcoming attractions and, of course, the refreshment counters.

At the multiplex, the spectator is positioned as a consumer not only of film but of a whole array of other goods. It is important not to overstate the novelty of this: whether selling drinks and snacks or sheet music of featured songs, cinemas have traditionally sought to develop other revenue streams besides admission charges themselves. In an intensification of this process, however, the newest, largest multiplexes tend to decentre the film-watching experience itself and to conceive their multiple screens as merely part of a much larger merchandising and recreational enterprise. While not wanting to push the analogy too far, Charles Acland sees the emergence of something like a 'gated community' in such venues as Universal CityWalk in Orlando, Florida, which situates a multi-screen cinema in an integrated, controlled environment of restaurants and shops (*Screen Traffic: Movies, Multiplexes, and Global Culture*, p. 149). An example closer to home for the British reader is the StarCity complex in Birmingham, opened in 1996 by George Clooney and containing, at the time of writing, a 24-screen cinema alongside such other attractions as a tapas bar,

Mexican and Indian eateries, a bowling alley and Europe's largest casino. Cinemagoing is thus relocated from the public sphere of city streets around the picture palace to a specialised consumer zone where the non-purchasing classes are not welcome. StarCity's cinema performs a further privatisation by designating three of its screens as 'Gold Class': on payment of a price higher than for other auditoria, customers get electronically operated reclining chairs, extra leg room, side tables for drinks and snacks, and access to an exclusive bar.

As with the picture palace, however, it is important not to over-state any regressive tendencies in the multiplex. StarCity, for example, preserves within its consumer enclave traces of older, carnivalesque sites of film exhibition: funfairs and firework displays are held there, offering a more collective experience than is available in the economically segregated Gold Class screens. In addition, the venue is not racially encoded as all-white. Reflecting Birmingham's multi-ethnic population, some of the site's restaurants include halal meat on their menus, while the cinema itself features Bollywood movies. Even if such developments might still be read in pessimistic fashion as merely extending the consumer class beyond its traditional white caucus – simply varying the ethnicity of that 'bourgeois (cinemagoing) subject' that Acland argues is produced by multiplexes (*Screen Traffic*, p. 202) – they are nevertheless progressive when set against the racial monoculture of filmgoing earlier or elsewhere in Britain.

Any plausible assessment of the politics of multiplex attendance needs to be nuanced rather than either blandly optimistic or morbidly despondent. Take the relationship between discipline and freedom in these cinemas. While the multiplex experience might seem a whirligig of unfettered consumption, it is also one in which the spectator is subject to various forms of monitoring and control. Again, this is not unprecedented: earlier cinemas may have had only a rudimentary disciplinary apparatus at their disposal – a manager surreptitiously watching patrons, an usher insisting on silence in the auditorium – yet still sought to check the most liber-tarian spectatorship. However, it is possible to detect in the multiplex a huge increase in institutional power over filmgoers:

The policing of ushers, the presence of security cameras, the regiment of scheduling, and the overt appeals to decorum in film trailers (feet off the seat in front, no talking, cell phones and pagers off, etc.) are indices of the intense interest in encouraging civility and reducing the prospects for impromptu (and economically unproductive) interventions. (*Screen Traffic*, pp. 231–2)

To this list we might add newer, still more ominous on-screen notices about video piracy. Recognition of the multiplex's authoritarian regime leads Acland, somewhat uncritically, to espouse the radical potential of indecorous behaviours: talking on a mobile phone or putting feet on the seat in front may, after all, express complacent egotism at the expense of bonds of sociability. Nevertheless, there is something energising in this attempt to redeem the multiplex for progressive politics, to locate vivid communal life in a space that critics have often written off as merely functional and capitalistic. Even if multiplexes evoke a public sphere in disrepair compared with the riotous communality of earlier film exhibition spaces, they still gather people together and so faintly signify, in Acland's words, 'a dream of global collectivity' (p. 243). Like the picture palaces that Rebecca Solnit wonderfully calls 'island republics' (*Motion Studies: Time, Space and Eadweard Muybridge* (London; Bloomsbury, 2003), pp. 245–6), the multiplex continues – albeit imperfectly and intermittently – to provide its audiences with a model of solidarity that suggests an alternative to dominant social forms.

STOP and THINK

- Evaluate the claim that it is important to consider both the places and the experiences of film consumption. How vitalising – or limiting – do you judge extra-textual research of this sort to be? How should it be integrated with discussion of film texts themselves?

- Robert C. Allen describes setting his university students the task of uncovering the archaeology of film exhibition in their home towns: 'A student can be wonderfully empowered by becoming the world's leading expert on the history of film exhibition in Shelby, NC' ('From Exhibition to

Reception', p. 305). What is revealed by localised studies of
this kind? What research tools are needed, and how reliable is each as a source of evidence?

- Ethnographies of reception accumulate evidence from film
  viewers themselves. What instruments are useful in such
  research? What are the strengths and weaknesses of each
  of these investigative resources? Given that an ethnographic approach to spectatorship brings into closer than
  usual contact the people being studied and the people
  doing the studying, do you see any ethical and intellectual
  problems with the researcher's role?

- Try an experiment in which you observe how spectators
  behave in any cinematic setting (to avoid threats of litiga-
  tion or physical violence, it is preferable to perform this
  exercise on a group of friends). Log behaviours with the
  patience and eye for detail of the Mass Observation of
  cinemagoing during the 1930s. What issues of power and
  principle are at stake in such research? What of value is
  uncovered by this ethnographic scrutiny? What are the
  limitations of analysing film consumption by such
  methods?

Home looking

Janet Staiger suggests that, in thinking about where films are
consumed, it is important not to be fixated by exhibition venues
themselves: while a film might be materially exhibited within the
four walls of a multiplex auditorium, the space of its reception is
liable to be much more diffuse and heterogeneous. Consumption
of *Star Wars*, say, may be extended across a number of post-
theatrical settings: the bar afterwards in which you discuss the film
with friends, or the university seminar room in which you
discourse about the semiotics of R2D2, or the Internet forum on
which you post a piece of fan fiction about the previously unsuspected sexual fantasies of Han Solo. Even such a catalogue of sites,
however, needs supplementing if it is to capture the massively
extended reception space of certain films. Take controversial

works from *A Clockwork Orange* (1971) and *Last Tango in Paris* (1972) to the Cronenberg *Crash* (1996) and *Brick Lane* (2007). In each of these cases the film circulates well beyond bricks-and-mortar exhibition venues, dispersing across the less concrete geographies of parliamentary debate, newspaper editorialising, policymaking statement and so on. It is 'consumed' or 'received' by people who may actually have watched little – or even none – of it.

Having acknowledged the diffuseness of post-theatrical film consumption, we must nevertheless give systematic attention to one increasingly important locus of spectatorship: *the home*. In a brief but evocative essay, 'Leaving the Movie Theater', Roland Barthes juxtaposes cinematic viewing with the experience of watching a film on TV at home. The mingling of strangers in dark, comfortable conditions that occurs at the cinema induces in him a state close to hypnotic immersion, 'a veritable cinematographic cocoon'; domestic film spectatorship, by contrast, holds 'no fascination; here darkness is erased, anonymity repressed; space is familiar, articulated (by furniture, known objects), tamed'. Here, too, the 'eroticism' associated with cinema spaces is 'foreclosed' (*The Rustle of Language* (Oxford: Blackwell, 1986), p. 346). Barthes is writing at a time before development of home theatre systems equipped to fill a living-room with enormous, high-definition images and all-enveloping, multiplex-quality sound. Nevertheless, his celebration of the cinema's immersive pleasures damns in advance the very phenomenon of domestic film reception, which is compromised in his eyes by familiar surroundings, mundane distractions, above all by *light*.

But while admiring Barthes's erotics of cinema space, we should not follow him in regarding domestic film consumption as necessarily impoverished. Evaluation of the psychology, sociology and economics of home spectatorship requires careful accumulation of detail rather than mobilisation of a simple spatial binary in which the cinema is good and the home is bad. Here Barbara Klinger's *Beyond the Multiplex: Cinema, New Technologies, and the Home* (2006) is especially helpful. Klinger resists what she describes as 'the value-laden dichotomy that has continually regarded home film exhibition through a comparative lens' (p. 3). Complaints

about a lack of absorptive power in domestic exhibition overlook
the fact that cinemas, too, with their distractions like audience talk
and loud snack consumption, will not always draw the spectator
into a blissful, womb-like environment. Klinger also addresses the
somewhat different argument that watching films in domestic
settings produces a passive, even anaesthetised type of viewer; she
suggests instead that 'All viewers – including couch potatoes – are
implicitly active', even if it is true that home spectators' engagement with the screen 'does not necessarily translate into a
progressive political position' (p. 11).

Where Barthes is primarily concerned with the experiential
quality of domestic spectatorship, we might start, more hard-
headedly, with its *economics*. As noted in Chapter 9, Hollywood has
for some time understood that theatrical screening of a film, far
from being an end in itself, is simply one stage in the film's pack-
aging and repackaging for different exhibition formats. Much of
this profitable reformatting is for home consumption. At first,
home spectatorship was limited to tuning into movies as they were
broadcast on terrestrial television. Centres of film production
including Hollywood quickly conquered hostility to TV, recognised an exploitable market when they saw one and, from the
1950s, began selling their backlists for television exhibition. The
subsequent emergence of cable networks – some housing dedicated movie channels – raised the price that studios could charge for
their works to be shown in a home setting. Increasingly, however,
consumption by home viewers has been less beholden to others'
scheduling decisions and has taken the form of renting or
purchasing films made available in a number of portable formats.
The video recorder emerged during the 1970s and gradually
became an indispensable consumer item; by 1992, revenues from
the sale of films in videocassette form were outstripping cinema
box office returns in the United States. And although one of the
videocassette's several successor technologies – the laserdisc –
endures mainly as a specialist archiving medium, there has been a
mass-market triumph for another: the DVD, or digital
video/versatile disk.

As an artefact, the DVD is ambiguous in its ideological implications. Although it holds out the promise of individualised film

consumption – contrasting with the corporate disciplines that govern a film's exhibition at the cinema – we would be unwise to regard it as affirming the user's sovereign power. Klinger points out that the contemporary DVD collector, far from untrammelled in his or her film connoisseurship, is subject to and even, in a sense, constructed by continuous marketing initiatives by the movie and audiovisual equipment industries: 'Solipsism is central to the pleasures and the paradoxes of collecting: considered a most private, even eccentric, activity, collecting is unavoidably tethered to public enterprises and discourses' (*Beyond the Multiplex*, p. 89). Yet just as we must recognise the vast commercial operations powering home consumption of DVDs, so we should not be paralysed by this awareness. The domestic viewing of films in this format brings new pleasures and knowledges, at least some of which are potentially progressive. The DVD's compressing of information allows spectators access not merely to the feature presentation itself but to an array of extra materials, which may, for example, contextualise the film in ways denied the cinema viewer, or guard against the absorption in on-screen spectacle characteristic of the multiplex by revealing how certain special effects are achieved. In addition, the DVD has made the home spectator's screen a place potentially of greater textual variety than any theatrical venue. As well as increasing the circulation of locally made lower-budget work, it helps to internationalise exhibition, extending spectatorship for films from around the world that have little or no prospect of securing theatrical release outside their own countries.

Competing evaluations have also been given of DVD consumption as a social experience. For some commentators, in fact, domestic spectatorship of films in this format scarcely counts as a *social* activity at all. The DVD is construed from this perspective as the preoccupation of a privatised viewer, someone who has become detached from the interpersonal bonds of cinemagoing and now takes a solipsistic pleasure not only in disks themselves but in the expensive audiovisual hardware that plays them at optimum level. But while this portrait has a certain truth, it is also unsustainable as a generalisation about DVD spectatorship: the technology supports a much broader range of social forms than just elitist, stereotypically male connoisseurship. Domestic DVD watching may be occasion not only for fetishising the completeness of a collection or the definition of an image but for fostering the solidarity of couples, families, friends, even larger communal networks. It need not, then, erase that sense of social collectivity which is historically represented by the crowd gathered at a cinema. Indeed, we may again want to challenge a simplistic politics of exhibition spaces and argue that engaged home spectatorship of a film on DVD with family or friends is richer in collective life than, say, a mid-afternoon multiplex showing in which the few spectators present sit isolated from one another across the auditorium.

It is important, finally, not to overstate a sense of separation between home and cinema as loci of film reception. A specialised audience may well be recruited by each of these venues: on the one hand, the older or disabled spectator who is attracted by home consumption; on the other, the teenagers who affirm a sense of freedom more readily in the multiplex than in front of the domestic screen. For the most part, however, film-consuming subjects are likely, as occasion demands, to move fluidly between spaces rather than be confined to one or the other. Home has not replaced cinema but co-exists with it in a complex economy of film reception. This example reminds us there is no unilinear history of exhibition sites. Instead, modes of film spectatorship are repeated across the nineteenth, twentieth and twenty-first centuries, albeit recurring in different technological guises and with different social, psychological and economic implications. As hinted above, the privatised reception today of films on such surfaces as mobile phone screen, PC monitor or home theatre system recapitulates the ethos of the pre-theatrical Kinetoscope; while some current exhibition practices are oddly congruent with that earlier, carnivalesque period in which films sat alongside other forms of the spectacular.

STOP and THINK

- Consider what happens when you watch at home a film you have already seen at the cinema. What difference does it make to relocate your spectatorship of *Titanic*, say, from the multiplex to a domestic TV screen (or another piece of domestic media apparatus)? Are you still viewing the same film, as proponents of a notion of textual continuity regardless of variations in exhibition format would argue; or should we actually speak of a new text? Are any differences you detect traceable to the means of exhibition itself, such as the consequences of shrinking a multiplex-scale image? Or is the process of consumption modified, too, by other circumstances of domestic spectatorship, including light (rather than the cinema's darkness), distraction (rather than a cinema-style ethos of compulsory concentration) and segmentation of the text (as against continuous viewing at the cinema)?

- When he wrote 'Leaving the Movie Theater', Barthes could only picture domestic film consumption occurring around a living-room TV set. This activity is, for him, a mechanism of ideological conservatism: 'television *doomed* us to the Family, whose household instrument it has become – what the hearth used to be, flanked by its communal kettle' (p. 346). However, compare this model of a repressive, family-dominated spectatorship with your own experiences of film consumption at home. Itemise the various modalities of domestic film-watching now and the forms of social life – or of solipsism – associated with them. Again, how does each of these reception contexts modify the film text?

- As argued above, it seems unwise to conclude that contemporary spectators express a binding preference for *either* the cinema *or* the home as a place of film consumption; many people oscillate between the two venues (each of these categories of reception space having, of course, multiple permutations). Analyse your own movements across the geography of film spectatorship: what underpins your choices of where to watch particular films?

Analysing consumption: Metro Cinema, Derby

The Metro Cinema opened near the middle of Derby in January 1981. It was, from its inception, conceived as an alternative to the city's dominant film culture (although multiplexes would not arrive in Derby until 1988, there was competition from an existing city-centre cinema given over to more popular fare). During the succeeding quarter of a century the Metro has maintained and exploited this strategic position. Its marginality with respect to mainstream exhibition practices has been manifested in several ways. Rather than having its own dedicated space, for example, the cinema occupied, until relocation early in 2007, part of the upstairs of a neo-Gothic building belonging first to the city's Central School of Art, then to the art department of the University of Derby; the visitor to the Metro in this site thus gained an impression of film as somehow connected to fine arts experiment rather than to vulgar entertainment (Figure 24). Outside the auditorium were the plain appurtenances of a cash desk, several wooden benches and a small bar, rather than the multiplex's extensive carpeting, comfortable waiting areas and large-scale refreshment counters. If a glass of wine or an ice-cream could be purchased at the Metro, a box of popcorn – cinemas' iconic food since its introduction in the United States during the 1930s – could not. Inside the auditorium itself, leg room was relatively restricted and seats lacked the indulgent softness of multiplex accommodation: although Barthes writes in 'Leaving the Movie Theater' that many cinemagoers 'slide down into their seats as if into a bed' (p. 346), seating at the Metro tended to discourage such a somnolent posture and to solicit a sober and alert uprightness.

Much of the Metro's programming throughout its existence has affiliated it with that determinedly non-mainstream, 'arts cinema' movement that began in the US and elsewhere after the First World War. Suggestively, the film shown to an invited audience after the cinema's opening was a foreign-language work, Tati's *Les Vacances de M. Hulot/M. Hulot's Holiday* (1953); the first public screening was of Derek Jarman's bracingly unconventional reworking of *The Tempest* (1979). Over subsequent years the

Figure 24   The Metro Cinema, Green Lane, Derby.

Metro has shown, with a fair measure of commercial success, such canonical European arthouse works as Buñuel and Dalí's *L'âge d'or*, Straub and Huillet's *Chronik der Anna Magdalena Bach* (1968), Beineix's *37°2 le matin/Betty Blue* (1986), Berri's *Jean de Florette* and *Manon des sources* (both 1986), Kieslowski's *Three Colours* trilogy (1993–94), the films of Almodóvar and Haneke's

Caché/Hidden (2005). The cinema's reach also extends to non-European works, with short seasons of, for example, films from Africa. At the other geographical extreme, the Metro actively supports British productions. Sometimes, as with Jane Austen adaptations or *Mrs Henderson Presents* (2005), these are more categorisable as 'heritage' than as 'arthouse' films; however, there is also space for lower-budget but more aesthetically and narratively combative British work, such as films by the East Midlands director Shane Meadows or Andrea Arnold's *Red Road* and Paul Andrew Williams's *London to Brighton* (both 2006).

What is the politics of the Metro's assertive programming of non-Hollywood materials? For assistance we might turn first to a quite acerbic reading which has been given of another regional film theatre in the East Midlands: Nottingham's Broadway Media Centre, which developed out of a long-established society of local cineastes. Jancovich et al. argue that, in varyingly implicit and explicit ways, the Broadway situates itself in the city's cinema culture by proffering an ethos of diversity, experiment and intellectual adventure in contrast to 'the supposedly undifferentiated nature of mass culture and its audiences' (*The Place of the Audience*, p. 219). Questionnaires the authors issued to Nottingham's cinemagoers disclosed that fans and critics alike of the Broadway strongly identify it 'with the values of cultural knowledge rather than the values of entertainment' (p. 222). Even an association which the cinema has built up with the crime and mystery genres does not, for Jancovich et al., truly signify a movement into the territory of 'the popular', since these genres are among those from mainstream film entertainment that have been 'taken up by legitimate culture in both its middlebrow and avant-garde manifestations' (p. 218).

Though this analysis of the Broadway's cultural politics is somewhat unforgiving, it may also be partly applicable to the Metro. Sally Griffith, one of the Metro's senior staff, is careful in a private email exchange to suggest that the relationship of her cinema to the multiplexes of Derby is one of dissimilarity rather than superiority: 'we offer such a different service and tend to have a different audience profile.' She stresses that 'different' is not synonymous with 'better' but allows that other people do make such a 'value judgement'. Though ethnographic evidence is lacking here, it is likely that a sense of cinematic hierarchy of this sort is active in Derby, with at least some potential spectators investing the Metro with connotations of 'cultural knowledge' rather than 'entertainment' and thereby reaching the conclusion that it is less of a place for them than the city's multiplexes. In this situation occasional overlaps in programming between multiplex and Metro – *March of the Penguins* (2005), say, or *Pride & Prejudice* – are perhaps only partially successful in extending the latter's demographic. Even an association with examples of popular genre film may not be sufficient to reconfigure the Metro's ethos for those cinemagoers in Derby who have inter-nalised a sense of exclusion. Where the Broadway had a festival of crime films, the Metro is aligned with the horror genre: for many years it has put on successful Halloween triple bills, featuring such works as *Exorcist 2: The Heretic* (1977) and *The Evil Dead* (1981). However, the nature of the Metro as a venue still limits the conces-sion to the popular which these events seem to promise: a film like *Friday the 13th* (1980) becomes, after all, a somewhat different film from its multiplex version when viewed in a relatively austere auditorium within a university fine arts building.

Nevertheless, not all of the charges which Jancovich et al. make against the Broadway would stick against the Metro (despite congruencies between the two institutions). More so than its Nottingham equivalent, the Metro is positioned as not only an arthouse venue equipped to satisfy more rarefied film tastes but as what Sally Griffith calls 'a "community" resource'. It is a regis-tered charity and organises many screenings aimed at reaching such vulnerable or disadvantaged spectators as adults with complex needs, young people with hearing difficulties and chil-dren with autism; in addition, some screenings are scheduled at times convenient for parents to attend with babies (further evidence of the reversible rather than linear history of film exhibi-tion, since this echoes a ploy used by nickelodeon proprietors to attract young mothers). As part of its appeal to people across a broad spectrum of social need, the Metro also addresses Derby's multiracial population, for example by discreet showings of Indian films for Asian women who might feel uncomfortable at other film exhibition sites in the city. All of these examples recall an earlier optimism that cinemas may constitute an alternative, progressive public sphere. At times, the Metro counters hegemonic values still more directly, as with its programmes of gay and lesbian film or its cooperation with activist organisations like Greenpeace, Amnesty International and the Stop the War Coalition. But while this staggering set of activities embeds the Metro in its locality in ways much deeper than can be emulated by Derby's multiplexes, it is not without risks. What looks from one perspective like the cinema's lively pluralism could seem from another to be an over-ambitious, even incoherent attempt to reach all interest groups, with events ranging from an evening with *Miss Potter* (2006) to a showing of *An Inconvenient Truth* (2006) introduced by a local environmentalist, and from *The Simpsons Movie* (2007) to a silent classic accompanied by live piano.

At the time of writing, the Metro is in its final year of existence in current form. It has moved from the city-centre site it has occupied since 1981 to accommodation within a lecture theatre on the campus of the University of Derby. Time will tell what effects this relocation – amounting to a still deeper enfolding of the cinema within university space – has upon the Metro's demographic. The move is only temporary, however: the Metro has already merged with the local Q Arts organisation to produce a new body called QUAD, which is due in the spring of 2008 to take up occupancy of a purpose-built arts centre near Derby's market square. Besides galleries and workshops, this building will house not one cinema auditorium but three – the first having 230 seats, the second 128 (reproducing the capacity of the Metro in its original venue) and the smallest sixty. To a still greater extent than in the old Metro building, there will be the perception of close relationships between film and fine arts as expressive forms.

The QUAD project looks to be adding, on a smaller scale, to the recent series of arts-led renewals of inner cities in Britain (consider, for example, Tate Liverpool or the BALTIC Centre for Contemporary Art at Gateshead). Cultural geographers, arts practitioners and others have sometimes asked hard questions about the politics of such venues. Do they tend to appeal primarily to a largely white, middle-class elite, thereby inhibiting access by poorer or non-white city-dwellers whose local taxes partly fund the projects? Does some of the difficulty and radicalism of art – including cinematic art – leach away in its repositioning as part of a fashionable, consumer experience? Inevitably, these questions will also hang over the QUAD building, even if grounds for optimism are supplied by the Metro's exemplary record of activism in the community. One further complication is that the three new auditoria will form part of a more extensively rearranged cinema economy in Derby. Shortly to join two existing, out-of-town multiplexes is a new city-centre multi-screen cinema, within a stone's throw of QUAD. Again, the effects of this augmentation and transformation of film exhibition sites are impossible to calculate at present. We may, however, conclude by using these imminent changes to Derby's cinemagoing to reiterate two points that have been central to this chapter's account of exhibition more generally. First, we witness again the loops and discontinuities in exhibition history: once more there is to be significant city-centre film consumption, something which would have been thought unlikely as the ring-road multiplex began to dominate. Second, the ideology of spaces of consumption can never be settled in advance but will always be up for grabs: just as the current Metro has the complex politics sketched above, so it is likely that the new QUAD building will support a variety of cinemagoing politics, from conservative connoisseurship to more unruly, radical engagement.

Selected reading

Acland, Charles R., *Screen Traffic: Movies, Multiplexes, and Global Culture* (Durham, NC and London: Duke University Press, 2003).
Vividly written, comprehensive study of the impact upon cultures of cinemagoing of post-1980 shifts in production, distribution and exhibition; keeps a keen eye on the politics of attendance at the contemporary multiplex.

Breakwell, Ian and Paul Hammond (eds), *Seeing in the Dark: A Compendium of Cinemagoing* (London: Serpent's Tail, 1990).
Engaging compilation of memories of the 'collective rite' of cinema attendance; by turns nostalgic, lyrical, comic, political and erotic.

Gomery, Douglas, *Shared Pleasures: A History of Movie Presentation in the*

United States (London: BFI, 1992).

Densely researched account of film exhibition in the US from Kinetoscope parlours to home video; industry-centred but an indispensable resource for study, too, of changing cultures of spectatorship.

Hansen, Miriam, *Babel and Babylon: Spectatorship in American Silent Film* (Cambridge, MA and London: Harvard University Press, 1991).

Important, detailed study of one culture of film reception – though open to challenge for its narrative of a fall into conformist spectatorship with the coming of sound film.

Jancovich, Mark and Lucy Faire, with Sarah Stubbings, *The Place of the Audience: Cultural Geographies of Film Consumption* (London: BFI, 2003).

Fascinating, meticulously detailed account of changing spaces of film reception in Nottingham; questionable for its lack of interest in films themselves but a major contribution to audience studies.

Klinger, Barbara, *Beyond the Multiplex: Cinema, New Technologies, and the Home* (Berkeley, Los Angeles and London: University of California Press, 2006).

Timely survey of what, in the US and many other nations, is now the major space of film consumption. Avoids both morbidly pessimistic and uncritically celebratory assessments of this development.

Kuhn, Annette, *An Everyday Magic: Cinema and Cultural Memory* (London and New York: I. B. Tauris, 2002).

Wonderfully rich, often moving exploration of British cinemagoing in the 1930s, articulating ethnographic and cultural geographic approaches with the textual sensitivity repressed in Jancovich et al.

Stokes, Melvyn and Richard Maltby (eds), *Hollywood Abroad: Audiences and Cultural Exchange* (London: BFI, 2004).

Lively, globetrotting essays on how Hollywood's product has been absorbed and negotiated in sites ranging from a Southampton picture palace to Australian suburbia and central African mining towns.

Stokes, Melvyn and Richard Maltby (eds), *Hollywood Spectatorship: Changing Perceptions of Cinema Audiences* (London: BFI, 2001).

Inconsistent in quality but containing stimulating reflections on mainly American contexts of film spectatorship that extend from raucous nickelodeons to lavishly equipped home cinema systems.

Waller, Gregory A. (ed.), *Moviegoing in America: A Sourcebook in the History of Film Exhibition* (Malden, MA and Oxford: Blackwell, 2002).

Absorbing collection of contemporaneous writings on US film exhibition by journalists, architects, management scientists and others; also includes valuable current overviews of the subject.

Useful websites

www.cinema-theatre.org.uk/home.htm.

Home page of the UK-based Cinema Theatre Organisation; besides rich material on the histories of British cinemas, includes links to sources on sites of film consumption worldwide (click on, for example, 'American Picture Palaces', 'Cinema in the Netherlands' and 'Cinema Tour').

www.screenonline.org.uk/film/cinemas/sect6.html.

The BFI's helpful overview of changing contexts of film exhibition in Britain from the end of the nineteenth century.

www.ipsos-na.com/news/client/act_dsp_pdf.cfm?name =mr050614-4tables.pdf&id=2712.

Detailed results of survey undertaken in 2005 into film consumption habits in the US, indicating an American preference now for home spectatorship.

Conclusion: film studies in the digital age

The landscape of present-day film studies is more variegated than at some moments in the past. Where a theoretical orthodoxy once prevailed – that amalgam of semiotics, psychoanalysis, Marxism and textual study that David Bordwell mischievously terms 'SLAB theory' after the initials of Saussure, Lacan, Althusser and Barthes – there is now use of multiple conceptual frameworks. Though some conservative film scholars have interpreted the cracks in Althusserian Marxism or Lacanian psychoanalysis as an invitation to do away with hard theoretical work altogether, it is better to agree with Bordwell and Carroll that the present phase of the discipline witnesses not so much 'the end of film theory' as 'the end of Theory' ('Introduction', *Post-Theory: Reconstructing Film Studies*, eds David Bordwell and Noël Carroll (Madison: University of Wisconsin Press, 1996), p. xiii). In the same volume, Carroll speaks up for 'piecemeal' rather than systematic theorising, and evokes film theory not as a set of canonical propositions but as 'a field of activity' ('Prospects for Film Theory: A Personal Assessment', pp. 39–40). Temporary, adjustable conceptual structures of this sort may lack the Parisian glamour that attached to unified film theory during the 1970s and 1980s; however, they promise to enable finer-grained, more case-sensitive work than has sometimes been produced in this discipline.

The editors of another manifesto for a reconfigured film studies propose that research be concentrated in five key areas. These topics for exploration are: film's sensory as well as meaning-bearing aspects; cinema's character as a 'mass' phenomenon; its capacity to constitute an 'alternative public sphere'; film history, especially in the light of debates about the status of historical narratives; and the dissolution of film in an increasingly crowded and heterogeneous mediascape (*Reinventing Film Studies*, eds Christine Gledhill and Linda Williams (London: Arnold, 2000), p. 1). We will come in a moment to Gledhill and Williams's fifth area of research. Here, though, we might briefly argue that valuable work on film will prove more diverse even than allowed for by this multi-faceted programme. Two examples can be given of additional lines of inquiry. First, although we have not had space to consider philosophically oriented work on cinema, writers from both Anglo-American and Continental intellectual traditions continue to be interested not only in identifying topics of mutual concern to film and philosophical study – matters of aesthetics, knowledge, being and so on – but in evaluating film as a distinctive way of *doing* philosophy. Second, much detailed research remains to be carried out into certain stylistic and formal problems. Take the Dalle Vacche and Price collection of essays on colour in film (listed in Chapter 1's 'Selected reading'). While this is a welcome volume, the technical, aesthetic and historical complexities of cinematic colour still await the kind of magisterial treatment that will do for the discipline what John Gage's trilogy – *Colour and Culture*, *Colour and Meaning* and *Colour in Art* – has achieved for fine arts study.

Rather than indicating the diversity of future research projects, however, we might return to the fifth item on Gledhill and Williams's agenda and briefly outline some of the questions posed to film studies and its established paradigms by the digital revolution. The growth of digital media requires the discipline not only to rethink questions of film production and consumption but also to revisit the fundamental issue of film's relationship to 'the real'.

For photography's enthusiasts and detractors alike in the nineteenth century, the magic of this new medium consisted in the fact that the operation of light upon chemical emulsion left an imprint, or indexical trace, of whatever had passed in front of the camera lens. While cinema itself has been a playground of illusionists from the pioneering Frenchman Georges Méliès to generations of Hollywood special effects designers, its roots in photography mean that it, too, has traditionally carried with it the promise – or, according to taste, the taint – of the real. In a memorable phrase, David Thomson writes of films 'scooping up the momentary appearance of things, like a blood sample at a crime' (*The Whole Equation: A History of Hollywood* (London: Little, Brown, 2005), p. 100). As Chapter 1 notes, a belief that film is defined as a medium by these transcriptions of reality itself underpins the theoretical writing of André Bazin, Siegfried Kracauer and others. Such faith in film's indexical power is unlikely wholly to disappear even as increasing numbers of images are computer-generated rather than photographically produced. At the same time, however, more and more people will lose the habit of viewing cinematic images as material evidences of the real. Film studies will need to explore the resulting 'structures of feeling' (to borrow a term from the cultural theorist Raymond Williams).

Filmmakers themselves have responded to digitisation in very diverse ways. Some who are especially wedded to the tactility of filmmaking – to sensuous encounters with celluloid – react with horror to the coming of odourless, non-touchable digital video. The Polish director Andrzej Wajda deplores the sheer facility of digital production: 'video is a technique that offers no resistance … This means you work without tension, without the familiar atmosphere of being on the edge, constantly at risk' (*Double Vision: My Life in Film* (New York: Holt, 1989), pp. 43–4). For other figures, however, like Mike Figgis and Robert Rodriguez, digital video is indispensable in supporting a filmmaking that is characterised by speed, spontaneity, lightness of touch and ease of revision. Rodriguez, in particular, constructs a linear narrative of technological progress to rationalise his movement away from celluloid: 'any filmmaker who compares film and digital on-set will suddenly look at their film camera like it's a lead brick or an old vinyl LP record' (Brian McKernan, *Digital Cinema: The Revolution in Cinematography, Postproduction, and Distribution*, pp. 125–6).

Despite their shared technological commitment, Rodriguez and Figgis generate very different kinds of work: compare Figgis's split-screen narrative experiment, *Timecode* (2000) with the lustrous images and noir nostalgia of Rodriguez's *Sin City*. These divergent results remind us that there is no such thing as a uniform digital aesthetic. Digitisation enables a broad formal and stylistic repertoire, from the rough-grained 'found footage' of *The Blair Witch Project* to the seamless CGI (computer-generated imagery) of *Sky Captain and the World of Tomorrow* (2004), or from the webcam look of the British horror *My Little Eye* (2002) to the prodigious experiments in framing and layering images carried out by the British filmmaker Peter Greenaway. While for many other directors digitisation is a revolution almost exclusively at the production level, Greenaway's innovations demand a reformatting of exhibition too. Take his project, *The Tulse Luper Suitcases*, which comprises not only three feature films (2003–4) suitable for conventional cinema showing but also the post-theatrical outputs of a website, a television series, books and no fewer than ninety-two DVDs. Though not giving up absolutely on 'the concept of screening in cinemas', Greenaway speaks fervently of his desire to generate materials that solicit the interactivity and capacity for repeated, non-linear reception associated more with domestic forms of digital exhibition. 'We must', he says, 'concentrate on the CD-ROM' (http://petergreenaway.co.uk: accessed 25 February 2007).

Greenaway argues that the digital revolution finally frees film to become the 'all-embracing medium' hoped for by some early twentieth-century visionaries. But if he abandons celluloid in a spirit of aesthetic utopianism, other filmmakers do so with quite different motivations. Holly Willis writes of the 'rejuvenation of activist media' enabled by quicker, less expensive processes of shooting and editing on digital videotape (*New Digital Cinema: Reinventing the Moving Image*, p. 96). Many documentary makers have embraced the new technology in insurrectionary mode, launching guerrilla-style strikes against the versions of public events proposed by mainstream information channels. While some of these films derive more from conspiracy theory than systematic political critique – the home-made 9/11 documentary, *Loose Change* (2006) perhaps being a case in point – they still extend and enliven film's public sphere. Such increased enfranchisement can also, with caution, be seen at a global level. The emergence of relatively cheap digital movie cameras and desktop editing programs, coupled with distribution routes based around DVDs and downloads, potentially gives a voice not only to marginal groups inside Western nations already boasting cinema industries but to countries historically subordinate within the world filmmaking system.

Besides taking account of changes in production, film studies needs to respond to digitisation by developing new models of the spectator. For the moment, few transformations of spectatorship are noticeable in the public spaces of cinemagoing. The costs of installing digital projection equipment currently deter exhibitors from adopting the technology with the alacrity that studios, hoping to replace multiple, expensive prints with digital delivery at the click of a mouse, would like; even when cinemas have switched over to digital projection, however, audiences are still subject as before to uniform, inexorably unfolding spectacle. Yet in non-theatrical situations, digital spectatorship seems much more mobile and liberatory. The DVD viewer, for example, may skip between segmented chapters of a film, introducing discontinuity and even reversibility into a previously rigid narrative structure; she can also transit back and forth between the film itself and a bank of other images. This freedom of manoeuvre leads Anne Friedberg to argue that 'the viewer becomes a *montagiste*, editing at will with the punch of a fingertip, "zipping", "zapping" and "muting"' ('The End of Cinema: Multimedia and Technological Change', *Reinventing Film Studies*, p. 447). The tone here may be a little too celebratory, however. More soberly, Victor Burgin juxtaposes such rapid spectatorial switching between images with an early form of radical viewer activity. If zapping recalls French Surrealist efforts to disrupt narrative sequence in film by dropping in and out of a series of cinemas – a practice mentioned above in Chapter 4 – it does so without the Surrealists' psychological excitation and political programme; as Burgin writes: 'The decomposition of narrative films, once subversive, is now normal' (*The Remembered Film* (London: Reaktion, 2004), p. 9). Even so, it would be unwise to rule out in advance potentially progressive effects of contemporary multimedia spectatorship. The digital technology itself is ideologically neutral and may precipitate liberation as well as boredom or a consumer mentality.

Alain J.-J. Cohen has written about a particular type of viewer he calls the 'hyper-spectator'. Studios and film libraries alike will, he presumes, expand their recent initiative of making films available for computer downloading (something the BFI, for example, started doing in 2006). In theory at least, the hyper-spectator seated at a PC will be able to navigate a vast archive of films, her actual, partial knowledge of the medium's past prosthetically enhanced by 'memory (or hyper-memory) of the whole history of cinema' ('Virtual Hollywood and the Genealogy of its Hyper-Spectator', *Hollywood Spectatorship: Changing Perceptions of Cinema Audiences*, eds Melvyn Stokes and Richard Maltby (London: BFI, 2001), p. 159). While this is a seductive prospect, we should be careful not to give it an uncritical endorsement. One major problem is the privilege, the conspicuous consumption even, bound up with the figure of the hyper-spectator. Even if costs of both computers and access to digital delivery continue to fall, it will still be some time before all film viewers have an equal capacity to 'hyper-spectate'.

Film studies should, more generally, be vigilant in the face of celebratory, even utopian accounts of film production and consumption in the digital age. A suitably cautious note is struck by Holly Willis at the end of her largely positive report on digital developments. She points out that while filmmakers and viewers alike have the chance in the contemporary media-system to be the manipulators of new technology, they also face the prospect of being the manipulated: 'as we experience new forms of digital media, we are also being configured by new forms of digital media; and as much as we enjoy the power and freedom they offer, it behooves us to be cognisant of the systems of power and control that they allow over us as well' (*New Digital Cinema*, p. 97). Just as the ideologically unmarked material of celluloid supported a vast range of political positions and purposes over the course of the twentieth century, so twenty-first-century digital video will be multiple rather than singular in its political effects. Despite the type of euphoric manifesto that always accompanies any technological breakthrough, digitisation's progressiveness cannot be assumed in advance. If this is a technology that facilitates such things as nimbler, sassier documentaries, it is also one appropriated by Hollywood for the production of ever more lavish and overpowering spectacle.

Selected reading

Elsaesser, Thomas and Kay Hoffmann (eds), *Cinema Futures: Cain, Abel or Cable?: The Screen Arts in the Digital Age* (Amsterdam: Amsterdam University Press, 1998).
Pleasingly wide-ranging, soberly argued assessments by a mix of scholars and practitioners of digitisation's effects upon film (and television).
Hanson, Matt, *The End of Celluloid: Film Futures in the Digital Age* (Mies and Hove: RotoVision SA, 2004).
Well-illustrated, attractively designed companion to digital video's recent incursions into filmmaking; written spiritedly, if at times uncritically.
McKernan, Brian, *Digital Cinema: The Revolution in Cinematography, Postproduction, and Distribution* (New York: McGraw-Hill, 2005).
A handy, accessible source of technical information that also includes interviews with such pioneers of digital filmmaking as George Lucas and Robert Rodriguez.
Murray, Janet H., *Hamlet on the Holodeck: The Future of Narrative in Cyberspace* (New York: The Free Press, 1997).
Engaging, richly suggestive account of the proliferation into other media of videogaming's narrative processes and immersive worlds; not exclusively movie-oriented but with much of interest for film students.
Shaw, Jeffrey and Peter Weibel (eds), *Future Cinema: The Cinematic Imaginary after Film* (Boston: MIT Press, 2003).
Compendious explorations of post-celluloid filmmaking, including assessment of its continuities with earlier marginal practices within cinema.
Willis, Holly, *New Digital Cinema: Reinventing the Moving Image* (London: Wallflower, 2005).
An excellent introduction to its subject: economical, accessible, well-informed and with a sharp argumentative edge.

Useful websites

www.theasc.com/magazine/sep02/exploring/index.html.
American Cinematographer magazine's detailed interview with George Lucas on the promise of digital technology; best read in dialogue with the manifestos below for a more guerrilla-style digitisation.
www.iranchamber.com/cinema/articles/digital_revolution_future_cinema.php.
Address on 'The Digital Revolution and The Future Cinema' by the

Iranian filmmaker Samira Makhmalbaf; her largely optimistic text includes the claim that digital technology is 'the death of Hollywood production and not the death of cinema'.

www.geocities.com/rrparkhurst/timelight.html.

Underground meditations on the impact of digital technology upon film production and consumption; eclectic, even patchy, but alert to the technology's politically radical exploitations.

Further reading

Books listed here are supplementary to those already cited in each chapter's 'Selected reading'.

Reference

Cook, Pam (ed.), *The Cinema Book*, 3rd ed. (London: BFI, 2007).
  Enlarged, updated edition of a well-established guide to film studies: more internationalist than its precursors, and also responsive to the discipline's increasing interest in film consumption.

Hayward, Susan, *Cinema Studies: The Key Concepts*, 3rd ed. (London and New York: Routledge, 2006).
  Valuable dictionary-style text, albeit stronger on the high theoretical paradigms of the 1970s and after than on more recent cultural studies approaches to film.

Hill, John and Pamela Church Gibson (eds), *The Oxford Guide to Film Studies* (Oxford: Oxford University Press, 1998).
  Compendious volume, with entries on most technical and theoretical aspects of film, and a pleasingly substantial section on non-American cinemas.

Nowell-Smith, Geoffrey (ed.), *The Oxford History of World Cinema* (Oxford: Oxford University Press, 1996).
  An impressive and stimulating feat of global scholarship, which would now benefit from an updated edition.

Thomson, David, *The New Biographical Dictionary of Film*, 4th ed. (London: Little, Brown, 2003).
  Fulfils its reference function by filmographies of countless directors, stars, etc., but even more notable for its eloquent, provocative assessments.

Film theory and criticism

Bordwell, David and Noël Carroll (eds), *Post-Theory: Reconstructing Film Studies* (Madison: University of Wisconsin Press, 1996).

Major collection of essays proposing ways beyond what the editors regarded as the discipline's conceptual blockage; historically valuable as a scourging corrective to 'Grand Theory', more dubious if used as an invitation to dispense altogether with theoretical reflection on film.

Brakhage, Stan, *Essential Brakhage: Selected Writings on Filmmaking* (Kingston, NY: McPherson, 2001).

Indispensable meditations by this American filmmaker, theorising fifty years of his formally rich, determinedly non-commercial work.

Braudy, Leo and Marshall Cohen (eds), *Film Theory and Criticism: Introductory Readings*, 6th ed. (New York: Oxford University Press, 2004).

At over 900 pages, a very generous sampling of film writings from across the twentieth century; best read alongside an overview such as Stam's *Film Theory: An Introduction*.

Bresson, Robert, *Notes on the Cinematographer* (Los Angeles: Green Integer, 1997).

Reissue of fragmentary, suggestive reflections on film's aesthetic distinctiveness by one of France's major post-war directors.

Deleuze, Gilles, *Cinema I: The Movement-Image* (London: Continuum, 2005).

Originally published in French in 1983, and a provocative, demanding exploration by one of twentieth-century France's major philosophers of the distinctiveness of cinematic perception; the many directors cited comprise a familiar auteurist class from Europe, Japan and the United States.

Deleuze, Gilles, *Cinema 2: The Time-Image* (London: Continuum, 2005).

A companion volume to *Cinema 1* that considers the complexities of cinematic treatment of such topics as time and memory. Again, dense, absorbing, sometimes unconvincing (and with the French intellectual's characteristic weakness for Jerry Lewis).

Hollows, Joanne, Peter Hutchings and Mark Jancovich (eds), *The Film Studies Reader* (London: Arnold, 2000).

Not as hefty as Braudy and Cohen but still an expansive, rewarding collection, with especially strong selections from historically-minded approaches to film.

Metz, Christian, *Film Language: A Semiotics of the Cinema* (New York: Oxford University Press, 1974).

High water-mark of attempts to read the production of meaning in film in the light of theories of the sign derived from linguistics.

Metz, Christian, *The Imaginary Signifier: Psychoanalysis and Cinema* (Bloomington: Indiana University Press, 1982).

Historically important volume, marking Metz's 'turn' from a systematic semiotics to an approach to cinematic signification underpinned by psychoanalysis; like *Film Language*, needs reading with awareness of subsequent conceptual developments.

Miller, Toby and Robert Stam (eds), *A Companion to Film Theory* (Malden, MA and Oxford: Blackwell, 1999).

Covers the field of current film theory thoroughly and, on the whole, with clarity.

Miller, Toby and Robert Stam (eds), *Film and Theory: An Anthology* (Malden, MA and Oxford: Blackwell, 2000).

Rival in size and scope to the Braudy/Cohen doorstop; less introductory than the other Miller/Stam collection but with many vivid selections and an attractively global and contemporary emphasis.

Stam, Robert, *Film Theory: An Introduction* (Malden, MA and Oxford: Blackwell, 2000).

Highly recommended; a thorough overview of film studies from its beginnings, written with zest and an argumentative edge.

Turner, Graeme (ed.), *The Film Cultures Reader* (London and New York: Routledge, 2002).

Lively sampling of critical and theoretical voices, organised by categories of 'understanding film', 'technologies', 'industries', 'meanings and pleasures', 'identities' and 'audiences and consumption'.

Film history

Abel, Richard (ed.), *Encyclopedia of Early Film* (London and New York: Routledge, 2004).

Comprehensive, readily searchable volume on film from the 1890s to the 1910s; sensitive to questions of exhibition and consumption as well as to innovations in the technology of production.

Armes, Roy, *African Filmmaking: North and South of the Sahara* (Edinburgh: Edinburgh University Press, 2006).

Good, lucid attempt to place a range of African cinemas within diverse historical and aesthetic contexts.

Cherchi Usai, Paolo, *Silent Cinema: An Introduction* (London: BFI, 2000).

Does the scholarly things promised by the title, but also pursues aesthetic, ethical and theoretical questions relevant to all cinema.

Diawara, Manthia, *African Cinema: Politics and Culture* (Bloomington: Indiana University Press, 1992).
Vivid account of African filmmaking from the colonial era onwards; helpfully supplemented by Armes's newer study.

Eleftheriotis, Dimitris and Gary Needham (eds), *Asian Cinemas: A Reader and Guide* (Edinburgh: Edinburgh University Press, 2006).
Very chunky volume, exploring developments in Asian cinemas ranging from the Turkish to the Taiwanese. Also asks pointed questions about the applicability to these cinematic cultures of theoretical models deriving from the West.

Elsaesser, Thomas (ed.), *Early Cinema: Space, Frame, Narrative* (London: BFI, 1990).
Substantial set of essays, historically important in redirecting focus towards this era of cinema. A useful counterpart to Abel's and Cherchi Usai's volumes.

Enticknap, Leo, *Moving Image Technology: From Zoetrope to Digital* (London: Wallflower, 2005).
Starts unpromisingly with a sideswipe at 'Freudian claptrap' but settles into a wonderfully well-informed, accessibly written account of evolving technologies of film production and exhibition.

Ezra, Elizabeth (ed.), *European Cinema* (New York: Oxford University Press, 2004).
Valuable essays on shifts in European filmmaking from the beginnings of production to the present.

Fowler, Catherine (ed.), *The European Cinema Reader* (London and New York: Routledge, 2002).
A good companion for Ezra's volume; helpfully includes key manifestos from across twentieth-century European filmmaking, besides contemporary scholarship on a range of national cinemas.

Galt, Rosalind, *The New European Cinema: Redrawing the Map* (New York: Columbia University Press, 2006).
A study that, given its post-1990 and 'post-national' orientations, enters productively into dialogue with the Ezra and Fowler collections.

Grainge, Paul, Mark Jancovich and Sharon Monteith, *Film Histories: An Introduction and Reader* (Edinburgh: Edinburgh University Press, 2007).
Invaluable collection, interpreting its remit generously and suggesting new priorities for film studies by exploring not only aesthetic evolution but the histories of exhibition, marketing and consumption.

King, John, *Magical Reels: A History of Cinema in Latin America*, 2nd ed. (London and New York: Verso, 2000).

The subject's standard work in English; wide-ranging, and combining political urgency with sensitivity to film style. Needs a postscript now discussing the prominence of Latin American filmmakers in a transnational cinema economy.

Mannoni, Laurent, *The Great Art of Light and Shadow: Archaeology of the Cinema* (Exeter: University of Exeter Press, 2000).

A mighty scholarly achievement, placing the cinematic apparatus in a densely recovered history of optical experiment beginning as early as the thirteenth century.

Moran, Albert and Errol Veith, *Historical Dictionary of Australian and New Zealand Cinema* (Lanham, MD: Scarecrow Press, 2005).

Valuable resource that assembles detailed chronologies and alphabetised inventories of these two cinemas (treated here as related but distinct).

Ross, Steven J. Ross (ed.), *Movies and American Society* (Malden, MA and Oxford: Blackwell, 2002).

An engaging, enlightening way into study of American films in their historical contexts, bringing together contemporary documents and recent essays. Extends chronologically from the earliest US production to current 'global' Hollywood.

Staiger, Janet, *Interpreting Film: Studies in the Historical Reception of American Cinema* (Princeton: Princeton University Press, 1992).

Fascinating in itself – discussing the reception of US films from *Birth of a Nation* to Woody Allen's *Zelig* – but also pioneering in its arguments that an adequate film history must reckon with the effect of different cultures of spectatorship.

Thompson, Kristin and David Bordwell, *Film History: An Introduction*, 2nd ed. (New York: McGraw-Hill, 2003).

Like the authors' *Film Art*, this is scholarly, articulate and sumptuously illustrated.

Print journals

Camera Obscura.

Important, long-established journal of feminist film studies, published triannually by Duke University Press. The issue dated December 2004 is devoted to Todd Haynes, including *Far From Heaven* (discussed above in Chapter 8).

Cineaste.

US quarterly, founded in 1967. Risks populism in its dislike of 'academic jargon' and 'obtuse Marxist terminology' but maintains an impressive thematic range, such as the neglected topic of 'acting in the cinema' (Vol. XXXI: 4).

Film Criticism.

US-based triannual, publishing since 1976; besides a broad range of single topics, devotes special issues to such subjects as 'complex narratives' (Spring 2006).

Film and History: An Interdisciplinary Journal of Film and Television Studies.

Published biannually by the US-based Historians Film Committee; American – or more broadly Anglophone – in emphasis but salutary in its insistence on history in film discussion.

Film Quarterly.

Lively, internationally minded journal, published by University of California Press; includes good longer pieces, but especially valuable for its comprehensive reviews of new books in the field.

Framework: The Journal of Cinema and Media.

Relaunched in 1999 after an earlier life from 1971–92, this journal appears biannually and includes articles of global range and theoretical ambition.

KINEMA: A Journal for Film and Audiovisual Media.

Published biannually from the University of Waterloo, Canada. Articles are eclectic in coverage, if sometimes variable in quality. The archive of earlier issues is available free online at www.uwaterloo.ca.

New Cinemas: Journal of Contemporary Film.

British-based triannual publication, originating in 2002; exemplary in its internationalist outlook.

Screen.

British academic quarterly, published under its present title since 1969. Played a key role in the 1970s in developing and disseminating screen theory but subsequently hospitable to other orientations in the discipline.

Sight and Sound.

The British Film Institute's monthly publication, containing intelligent longer articles as well as thorough reviews of cinema and DVD releases. Glossy, topical, frequently internationalist in outlook.

Velvet Light Trap.

Excellent biannual, collectively edited by film and TV studies postgraduates at the Universities of Wisconsin and Texas. Each edition is themed, with issues in 2006, for example, including authorship (Spring) and narrative (Fall).

Online resources

Reference

www.bfi.org.uk.

Home page of the British Film Institute; a major portal to archives, educational materials and sources of film news.

www.close-upfilm.com.

Less intellectually challenging than some other film sites but offering a substantial archive of features, reviews and interviews.

http://fii.chadwyck.co.uk/home.

Site of Film Index International; globally and historically comprehensive in its indexing and cross-referencing of film titles. Access is by ATHENS password.

www.filmsite.org.

Marked in places by film buff excitability – 'Scariest Movie Moments' – but including resources such as a glossary of film terms and useful, if American-centred historical summaries and timelines.

www.imdb.com.

Despite its commercial trappings, an invaluable mine of information, enabling the rapid tracking of details that could range from the date and Swedish title of Bergman's first film to the names of minor actors in *Scary Movie 4*.

Film history

http://earlycinema.com.

Well-maintained site on cinema's inaugural decade from 1895–1905; especially helpful is the A–Z guide.

www.mediasalles.it/ybkcent/ybk95_hi.htm.

Useful starting point for research into European cinema, with brief but informative histories of film production and exhibition in many countries.

www.moderntimes.com.

Nicely maintained resource on classical Hollywood; especially enjoyable for the lustrous film images it houses alongside some informative text.

www.screenonline.org.uk.

Rich archive of materials on British film and television from the late nineteenth century to the present.

www.victorian-cinema.net.

Attractive and scholarly site on key developments and personnel in cinema's earliest history; international in outlook.

http://widescreenmuseum.com.

Fascinating, wittily designed resource, including material not only on varieties of widescreen experiment but on other aspects of early cinema such as colour processing and the introduction of sound.

Online journals

Bright Lights Film Journal.

Self-styled 'popular-academic hybrid of movie analysis, history, and commentary', published quarterly from Portland, Oregon. Lively, politically engaged and available free at www.brightlightsfilm.com.

Film-Philosophy.

Occasionally self-regarding in its presentation as a 'salon-journal' but packed with sophisticated responses to film from a range of philosophical positions. Founded in 1996; available free at www.film-philosophy.com.

Images: A Journal of Film and Popular Culture.

Attractively designed journal, offering serious, accessible articles and reviews on a broad range of film and television topics. Published quarterly from the US and available free at www.imagesjournal.com.

JUMP CUT: A Review of Contemporary Media.

Published online following a printed history from 1974–2001; covers film in accessible, lively fashion from a leftist and feminist standpoint. Available free at www.ejumpcut.org.

Kinoeye: New Perspectives on European Film.

Published from the UK since 2001, and refreshing in its detailed concern with European film cultures – particularly those of Eastern

Europe – that may lack fashionable 'world cinema' status. Available free at www.kinoeye.org.

Scope

Published triannually from the University of Nottingham; includes thorough book reviews and good essays on all aspects of film studies. Available free at www.scope.nottingham.ac.uk.

Screening the Past.

E-journal active since 1997, based at La Trobe University, Melbourne. Publishes historically-minded work on film, television, photography and multimedia forms.

Available free at www.latrobe.edu.au/screeningthepast/.

Senses of Cinema.

Australian quarterly especially attentive to its own national cinema, but containing articles written with brio on topics of international range. Available free online at www.sensesofcinema.com (though donations are welcomed).

The Film Journal.

American quarterly, with particular interests in contemporary global cinema. Available free online at www.thefilmjournal.com (though donations are welcomed).

Index

Note: film titles appear here under the names of their directors; page numbers in *italic* refer to illustrations.